MY HOMEWORK

A Self-Study English Grammar Practice Book

SALEH AL-SHALABY

Copyright © 2019 by Saleh Al-Shalaby.

ISBN-13:   9781645504528

All rights reserved. No part of this book may be reproduced or transmitted in any form or by any means, electronic or mechanical, including photocopying, recording, or by any information storage and retrieval system, without permission in writing from the copyright owner.

Any people depicted in stock imagery provided by Thinkstock are models, and such images are being used for illustrative purposes only.
Certain stock imagery © Thinkstock.

To my late parents, May Allah Bless them in Paradise.
To my wife, sons and daughters who encouraged me a lot.
To my brothers, sister and all family members who buoyed me a lot.
To my colleagues, friends and students everywhere.

ACKNOWLEDGEMENTS

I would like to express my appreciation to all my teaching staff members who taught me throughout my learning process. Besides, I thank my professors at the Faculty of Languages, AL-Alsun, Ain Shams University, Egypt who supported me a lot. I'm also grateful to Mr. Sam Christian, the famous Canadian author, who reviewed the book thoroughly and methodically. The teaching staff at Saudi Aramco Training Centers and the Saudi Arabian Drilling Academy also allowed me to quote their remarks and assisted in the editing, proofreading stage. Special thanks to my son Ahmad Saleh Al-Shalaby who designed the cover.

RECOMMENDATION

I have recently reviewed the above book which was forwarded to me by its author Mr. Saleh Al-Shalaby. I was impressed by the book and the content. I wish Mr. Al-Shalaby all the best and good luck to you, too, with this publication which I am sure will find a great number of readers.

KINDEST REGARDS

SAM CHRISTIAN
AUTHOR OF A NUMBER OF BOOKS
TORONTO-ONTARIO-CANADA

There are many books written for the learning of English grammar but this book is different in many ways. It is different because all the activities are created by keeping in view, the needs of independent learner. These activities are supported with examples which ensure learner's clear understanding. They are supported with a variety of exercises.

This book is equally beneficial for learners of any age and level of English. It can be used as a home study tool. It will give learner a chance to comprehend thoroughly.

This is the brain child of Mr. Al-Shalaby who has put in a lot of effort and time to compile a very handy resource for self-study. He has touched upon every aspect of English grammar in a very comprehensive way. Answer key at the end makes it user friendly and a quick source of learning.

I hope that you will find this book very useful, engaging and fun. Enjoy using this book in your class or individually at home.

Malik Muhammad Farooq
ELT Consultant
British Council

My HomeworK **Table of Contents**

SECTION	DESCRIPTION	FROM PAGE TO PAGE	
Section 01	Singular & Plural Nouns	01	27
Section 02	Singular & Plural Nouns	28	36
Section 03	Pronouns & Demonstrative Adjectives	37	59
Section 04	Prepositions of Place & Time	60	81
Section 05	Auxiliary Verbs	82	111
Section 06	The Simple Present Tense	112	133
Section 07	The Gerund	134	138
Section 08	The Present Progressive (Continuous) Tense	139	164
Section 09	The Past Progressive (Continuous) Tense	165	181
Section 10	The Present Perfect Tense	182	198
Section 11	The Present Perfect Progressive (Continuous) Tense	199	203
Section 12	The Simple Past Tense	204	234
Section 13	The Past Perfect Tense	235	248
Section 14	The Present Perfect Progressive (Continuous) Tense	249	251
Section 15	The Future Time	252	271
Section 16	Modals; (Modal Auxiliaries)	272	299
Section 17	Imperatives, Suggestions & Preferences	300	306
Section 18	Active & Passive Voice	307	341
Section 19	Conditionals; If & Unless	342	361
Section 20	Wish Clauses	362	366
Section 21	Connecting Ideas	367	419
Section 22	Reported Speech	420	450
Section 23	Comparative & Superlative Adjectives	451	472
Section 24	Punctuation	473	486
Section 25	Relative Pronouns	487	498

SECTION 1 — Indefinite Articles

A and *An*

A is an indefinite article that is used before a singular noun that starts with a *consonant sound*.

An is an indefinite article that is used before a singular noun that starts with a *vowel*.

NOTE 01
When the singular noun starts with the letter *u*, and it sounds like *y*, we use *a* before it.

Examples:

> I read <u>a unit</u> in the new book.
> Mr Blake is <u>a union</u> member.

NOTE 02
When the singular noun starts with a silent *h*, we use *an* before it.

Examples:

      an hour   **an h**onest person

> I spent <u>an hour</u> swimming.
> Miss Helen is <u>an honest</u> young woman.

> *Exercise One*

Write **a** or **an** before the word.

1. ____ bottle
2. ____ queen
3. ____ lamp
4. ____ hat
5. ____ apple
6. ____ pen
7. ____ fan

8. _____ kite
9. _____ egg
10. _____ word
11. _____ rat
12. _____ cat
13. _____ nose
14. _____ yard
15. _____ icon
16. _____ door
17. _____ tree
18. _____ jar
19. _____ zebra
20. _____ orange
21. _____ gun
22. _____ van
23. _____ man
24. _____ umbrella
25. _____ house

My Homework

➢ **Exercise Two**

Complete the sentences. Use an article, **a** or **an**.

1. I am _____ student.
2. My brother is _____ engineer.
3. Paris is _____ European city.
4. Mary is _____ old woman.
5. A villa is _____ building.
6. Africa is _____ large continent.
7. Malaysia is _____ country in South-East Asia.
8. Ahmad is _____ active student.
9. _____ camera is used for taking photos.
10. There is _____ umbrella on that table.
11. Tuka has _____ urgent call.
12. Batool is _____ pharmacist.
13. Helen needs _____ orange.
14. There is _____ ice cream on the table.
15. Jane is _____ Filipino student.
16. This is _____ ugly place.
17. We can wait for _____ hour.

18. My grandfather is _____ honest person.
19. Are you _____ employee here?
20. Sam is _____ Canadian teacher.

My Homework

> ### Exercise Three

Complete the sentences. Use an article, **a** or **an**.

1. Alaska is _____ American state.
2. My son is _____ expert in IT.
3. Oman is _____ Gulf country.
4. Football is _____ popular sport.
5. Ronaldo is _____ talented player.
6. Lilly is _____ Indian air hostess.
7. The Great Pyramid in Egypt is _____ ancient building.
8. The Eiffel Tower is _____ steel building.
9. There is _____ bank about two kilometres from here.
10. Is Kris reading _____ exciting story?
11. That is _____ beautiful flower.
12. Jane Austen is _____ well-known novelist.
13. Is there _____ elevator in this building?
14. Does Anna want to be _____ actress?
15. Is there _____ round table in your kitchen?
16. Did Kevin carry _____ white umbrella this morning?
17. Abdullah is eating _____ sandwich.
18. This is _____ expensive car.
19. We watched _____ interesting match.
20. Do you have _____ camera?
21. Does Lee have _____ Austrian pal?
22. My sister is reading _____ Korean newspaper.
23. My brother supports _____ Irish football team.
24. My uncle has _____ modern car.
25. This is _____ easy exercise.

My Homework

> *Exercise Four*

✤ Complete the sentences. Use an article, **a** or **an**.

1. This is _____ useful book.
2. Donald is _____ very tall man.
3. Pablo wants to buy _____ Italian car.
4. There's _____ apartment building near our villa.
5. Does Sally have _____ new dress?
6. Our neighbour has _____ unpleasant dog.
7. My elder sister bought _____ litre of apple juice.
8. Have you ever seen _____ hippo?
9. Has Adam ever chased _____ dog?
10. Mike has _____ yellow car.
11. Anita is _____ hard-working nurse.
12. Annie is _____ Australian businesswoman.
13. Boody is _____ university student.
14. Picasso is _____ artist.
15. Has your father ever seen _____ kangaroo?
16. Kim drank _____ cup of tea.
17. My brother is _____ postman.
18. I would like to buy _____ pair of shoes.
19. Mathew is _____ handsome man.
20. _____ sparrow has two wings.
21. _____ opera is a musical play.
22. _____ tree has a lot of leaves.
23. My father is _____ pilot.
24. My mother is _____ good cook.
25. _____ iron is used to iron clothes.

🙰🙰🙰 *My Homework* 🙰🙰🙰

A, An and Some

Some is used before a plural count noun or a non-count noun.

Examples:
- Liza has some new **books**.
- The little boy asked for some **food**.

Exercise Five

Complete the sentences with **a**, **an**, or **some**.

1. We need _____ water.
2. There are _____ books on the shelf.
3. I drank _____ bottle of milk.
4. We met _____ tourists in New Jersey.
5. I bought _____ computer.
6. Paul is riding _____ camel.
7. Did you buy _____ expensive mobile phone?
8. My father usually drinks _____ cup of coffee in the morning.
9. There is _____ orange on the table.
10. There is _____ orange juice in the glass.
11. There is _____ apple in the basket.
12. There are _____ apple trees on our farm.
13. There is _____ office next to the workshop.
14. There are _____ office buildings near my house.
15. There are _____ horses in the barn.
16. I can see _____ owls in the tree.
17. I can see _____ lark in the tree.
18. I can hear _____ birds singing.
19. I can hear _____ sparrow singing.
20. My sister is reading _____ English play by Bernard Shaw.
21. Donald has _____ old farmhouse.
22. London is _____ beautiful city.
23. Ted needs _____ uniform.
24. There is _____ gas in the tank.
25. There is _____ gas station near the farm.

My Homework

➢ *Exercise Six*

♣ Complete the sentences with **a**, **an**, or **some**.

1. I need _____ pen and _____ paper to write a letter.
2. In the zoo, we saw _____ lion and _____ tiger.
3. My uncle planted _____ palm tree and _____ apricot trees.
4. I saw _____ snake and _____ mouse in the garden.
5. Lara has _____ ball and _____ racket.
6. Anna is going to buy _____ newspaper and _____ books.
7. Marwa has read _____ stories and _____ play.
8. I have _____ pencil, _____ eraser, and _____ paper.
9. Lilly drinks _____ juice while eating.
10. I can see _____ pigeon, _____ lark, and _____ geese.
11. Mary wants _____ cup of tea.
12. There are _____ books, _____ pens, and _____ dictionary on the desk.
13. Kevin is watching _____ American movie.
14. Tina has got _____ milk, _____ butter, and _____ cheese.
15. Keith needs _____ money to buy _____ meal.
16. My brother has _____ stamps and _____ coins.
17. I need _____ shirt and _____ hats.
18. There are _____ geese and _____ duck in the pool.
19. I met _____ French scientist in Paris.
20. Piers is eating _____ Chinese food.
21. I need _____ table and _____ chairs.
22. I want _____ notebook, _____ sharpener, and _____ clips.
23. There is _____ white fridge in the kitchen.
24. My mother made _____ cake and _____ biscuits.
25. Saleh wrote _____ poem and _____ essay.

ಐಐಐ*My Homework*ಐಐಐ

The Definite Article

The

The is used to refer to somebody/something that has already been mentioned or is easily understood.

In addition, *the* is used before

	Examples
the names of seas	the Red Sea
the names of rivers	the Nile
the names of oceans	the Atlantic Ocean
the names of peninsulas	the Arabian Peninsula
the names of canals	the Suez Canal
the names of tunnels	the Channel Tunnel
the names of gulfs	the Gulf of Mexico
the names of landmarks	the Statue of Liberty
the names of museums	the Wax Museum, the Louvre
the names of islands	the Bahamas
the names of isles	the British Isles
the names of mountains	the Alps
nationalities	the English
when there is only one	the moon
numbers	the first part of the story
dates	the third of May

the names of sport events	the World Cup, the Olympic Games
The **is also used when we refer to**	the fire department the army the police the rich the piano the dolphin
The ___, the ___.	The more you read, the more you know.
the names of universities	the British University in Egypt

	the bank
	the post office
	the police station
	the hospital
	the doctor
	the optician
	the dentist
	the city
	the country = the countryside
	the sky
	the sun
	the stars
	the ground
	the floor
	the sea
	the beach
	the movies
	the theatre
	the radio
	the telephone
	the Arabs

the ____ of ____	the life of Dickens
the names of countries and states	the United Kingdom
	the United Arab Emirates
	the United States
	the Republic of Ireland
	the Sultanate of Oman
	the Netherlands
	the Philippines

↓ **Examples:**

- Jane will study **the** history of ancient Egypt next semester.
- This is **the** teacher's dictionary.
- We have a new house near **the** beach.
- **The** police arrested some shoplifters last night.
- I usually watch **the** news before going to bed.
- Jana is driving to **the** city.
- My grandparents live in **the** country.
- **The** computer is a great invention.

> *Exercise Seven*

↓ Complete the sentences. Use an article **a**, **an**, or **the**.

1. We are going to do _____ homework.
2. We have _____ large farm.
3. This is _____ difficult exercise about articles.
4. I met _____ owner of my house.
5. **Helen**: Where's Ellen?
   Henry: She's on _____ farm.
6. There are many beautiful cities located on _____ Red Sea.
7. We visited _____ Great Pyramid last winter.
8. Our beach house is just three miles from _____ ocean.
9. We have to help _____ poor.
10. I am reading _____ English novel.
11. _____ smartphone is useful.

12. I put some oil in _____ engine of my car.
13. We left _____ house at noon.
14. My books are on _____ table.
15. Sarah is reading _____ useful report.
16. The child wants _____ slice of cake.
17. We are going to have _____ oral test.
18. Helen passed _____ final test.
19. I saw _____ ewe and a ram on the farm.
20. We met _____ American teacher who teaches us math.

➢ **Exercise Eight**

✚ Complete the sentences. Use an article: **a**, **an**, or **the**.

1. I opened _____ door of _____ old house you told me about.
2. Peter has _____ new car. _____ car is grey.
3. Andrew has _____ old bus. _____ bus is very slow.
4. I saw _____ elephant and _____ wolf in _____ zoo.
5. There is _____ sparrow and _____ owl in the tree.
6. We bought _____ kilo of sugar and _____ ounce of butter.
7. There is _____ nice picture on _____ wall.
8. There is _____ chair and _____ sofa in _____ sitting room.
9. I gave Ali ____ smartphone. ____ smartphone is new.
10. _____ helicopter is _____ aircraft without wings that has large blades.
11. We are having _____ fun day on _____ beach.
12. ____ house is ____ building.
13. ____ camera is ____ instrument.
14. ____ bus is ____ vehicle.
15. ____ saw is ____ tool.
16. ____ ant is ____ insect.
17. ____ hammer is ____ tool.
18. ____ fox is ____ animal.
19. ____ owl is ____ bird.
20. ____ elephant is ____ large animal.
21. ____ phone is ____ a communication device.
22. I eat ____ sandwich every morning.
23. Sue drinks ____ cup of coffee at breakfast.
24. Excuse me. I have ____ important meeting.
25. ____ ewe is ____ female sheep.

A, An, The, Some, and Any

> *Any* is used with non-count or plural nouns in negative statements and questions.

Examples:

- **Sebastian**: Is there **any** water in the well?
  Walid: Yes, there is a lot.
- **Mike** doesn't have **any** money.

> *Exercise Nine*

Choose the correct answer from **a**, **b**, **c**, or **d**.

1. Linda bought _____ new camera.

a.	an	b.	some
c.	any	d.	a

2. _____ Mississippi is a major river in North America.

a.	An	b.	The
c.	Any	d.	A

3. We listened to the man who was speaking in _____ Hyde Park.

a.	an	b.	the
c.	any	d.	no article

4. I need _____ money to buy a meal.

a.	an	b.	some
c.	any	d.	a

5. After getting married, Faisal moved to live in _____ city.

a.	an	b.	some
c.	any	d.	the

6. _____ money that I found in the kitchen belongs to my mother.

a.	An	b.	Some
c.	Any	d.	The

7. When I visited Luxor, I met _____ Turkish tourists there.

a.	an	b.	some
c.	any	d.	a

8. Tourists usually enjoy the natural scenery in _____ Bahamas.

a.	an	b.	the
c.	any	d.	a

9. Dubai is a famous city on _____ Arabian Gulf.

a.	an	b.	some
c.	any	d.	the

10. I don't need _____ more food. I'm full.

a.	an	b.	some
c.	any	d.	a

11. _____ Chinese are very active and creative.

a.	The	b.	Some
c.	Any	d.	A

12. I met my friends near _____ national park.

a.	an	b.	some
c.	any	d.	the

13. _____ 2004 Olympic Games was held in Athens.

a.	An	b.	Some
c.	Any	d.	The

14. The Sphinx is _____ ancient monument.

a.	an	b.	some
c.	any	d.	the

15. **Ronald**: Would you like _____ glass of juice?
    Kim: No, thanks. I'll have a cup of coffee.

a.	an	b.	some
c.	a	d.	the

16. There are _____ books on the table.

a.	an	b.	some
c.	any	d.	the

17. _____ Indian Ocean is a very useful waterway.

a.	An	b.	Some
c.	Any	d.	The

18. Did you buy _____ food at the supermarket?

a.	an	b.	a
c.	any	d.	the

19. Lilly went to _____ post office to send a letter to her friend.

a.	an	b.	some
c.	any	d.	the

20. The government is building _____ university near our house.

a.	an	b.	some
c.	any	d.	a

21. I hope to spend some time hiking in _____ Himalayas.

a.	an	b.	a
c.	any	d.	the

22. After finishing my high school, I will join _____ Japanese University.

a.	an	b.	some
c.	any	d.	the

23. They carried the old woman to a nearby hospital in _____ ambulance.

a.	an	b.	some
c.	a	d.	the

24. When Ahmad visited China, he took many pictures of _____ Great Wall of China.

a.	an	b.	some
c.	any	d.	the

25. There isn't _____ water in the well. The camels drank it all.

a.	an	b.	some
c.	any	d.	the

➢ **Exercise Ten**

✦ Choose the correct answer from **a**, **b**, **c**, or **d**.

1. Bahrain is a small kingdom in _____ Arabian Peninsula.

a.	an	b.	some
c.	any	d.	the

2. My parents are having their lunch in _____ garden.

a.	an	b.	some
c.	any	d.	the

3. Look! _____ moon is shining brightly tonight.

a.	An	b.	Some
c.	Any	d.	The

4. I don't want _____ books. I have got too many.

a.	an	b.	some
c.	any	d.	the

5. Alexandria is a beautiful city located on _____ Mediterranean Sea.

a.	an	b.	some
c.	any	d.	the

6. Look! Jeff is eating _____ apple.

a.	an	b.	some
c.	any	d.	a

7. I am going to _____ park to meet my friends there.

a.	an	b.	some
c.	any	d.	the

8. After you read the book, take it back to _____ library.

a.	an	b.	some
c.	any	d.	the

9. You can find a lot of information about this topic on _____ Internet.

a.	an	b.	some
c.	any	d.	the

10. I want _____ more soup, please.

a.	an	b.	some
c.	any	d.	the

11. _____ Suez Canal connects the Red Sea with the Mediterranean Sea.

a.	An	b.	Some
c.	Any	d.	The

12. I need _____ loaf of bread, please.

a.	an	b.	some
c.	a	d.	the

13. We are going to visit _____ Tower of London next week.

a.	an	b.	some
c.	any	d.	the

14. **Steven**: Do you have _____ money?
    Lisa: No, I don't.

a.	an	b.	a
c.	any	d.	the

15. My brother has a lot of homework. He needs _____ help.

a.	an	b.	some
c.	any	d.	the

16. I took some photographs near _____ Statue of Liberty.

a.	an	b.	some
c.	any	d.	the

17. I am going to start my new course on _____ second of July.

a.	an	b.	some
c.	any	d.	the

18. There are _____ nice photos in the album.

a.	an	b.	some
c.	any	d.	the

19. _____ Thames flows through London.

a.	an	b.	some
c.	any	d.	the

20. John hasn't been to _____ theatre for a long time.

a.	an	b.	some
c.	any	d.	the

21. Mary is in _____ living room.

a.	an	b.	some
c.	a	d.	the

22. Last month, I read an article about _____ life and works of Rousseau.

a.	an	b.	some
c.	any	d.	the

23. When we were in London, we visited _____ Wax Museum.

a.	an	b.	some
c.	any	d.	the

24. My parents usually have a walk in _____ afternoon.

a.	the	b.	some
c.	any	d.	an

25. _____ piano is an important musical instrument.

a.	An	b.	The
c.	Any	d.	Some

🙠🙠🙠 *My Homework* 🙢🙢🙢

➤ Exercise Eleven

✤ Choose the correct answer from **a**, **b**, **c**, or **d**.

1. The carpenter repaired _____ door of our villa.

a.	an	b.	some
c.	any	d.	the

2. France won _____ World Cup in 1998.

a.	an	b.	some
c.	any	d.	the

3. _____ Harvard University is famous all over the world.

a.	No article	b.	Some
c.	Any	d.	The

4. _____ police arrested three gangsters near my house.

a.	An	b.	Some
c.	Any	d.	The

5. My cousin studies engineering in _____ university in New Zealand.

a.	an	b.	some
c.	the	d.	a

6. My elder brother wants to join _____ army.

a.	the	b.	some
c.	any	d.	a

7. I asked _____ policeman to guide me to my hotel.

a.	an	b.	some
c.	any	d.	a

8. We met _____ foreigner in the street.

a.	an	b.	some
c.	any	d.	a

9. I would like to go to _____ bank to cash a check.

a.	an	b.	some
c.	any	d.	the

10. The players were happy because _____ queen honoured them.

a.	a	b.	some
c.	any	d.	the

11. _____ students are absent today.

a.	A	b.	Some
c.	Any	d.	An

12. _____ dolphin is a mammal that mostly eats fish and squid.

a.	An	b.	Some
c.	Any	d.	The

13. _____ foreigner that we met was lost.

a.	A	b.	Some
c.	Any	d.	The

14. _____ earth revolves on its axis.

a.	A	b.	Some
c.	Any	d.	The

15. The sun is _____ useful star.

a.	an	b.	a
c.	any	d.	the

16. Football is _____ interesting sport.

a.	an	b.	some
c.	any	d.	a

17. Sharm el-Sheikh is a beautiful resort on _____ Red Sea.

a.	a	b.	some
c.	any	d.	the

18. I am very thirsty. I need _____ water.

a.	an	b.	some
c.	any	d.	a

19. Sydney is _____ Australian city.

a.	an	b.	some
c.	any	d.	a

20. Jane and Albert first met on a cruise on _____ Nile.

a.	an	b.	some
c.	any	d.	the

21. _____ dentist advised me to brush my teeth daily.

a.	An	b.	Some
c.	Any	d.	The

22. Abraham studied _____ unit in his English book.

a.	an	b.	some
c.	any	d.	a

23. Adrian dropped a glass on _____ floor. It broke into pieces.

a.	an	b.	some
c.	any	d.	the

24. Diana is reading _____ article about tourism in Spain.

a.	an	b.	a
c.	any	d.	the

25. _____ Mona Lisa is one of the most famous portraits in the world.

a.	An	b.	Some
c.	Any	d.	The

✤✤✤ *My Homework* ✤✤✤

➢ *Exercise Twelve*

✦ Choose the correct answer from **a**, **b**, **c**, or **d**.

1. My grandmother likes to listen to _____ radio.

a.	an	b.	a
c.	any	d.	the

2. There isn't _____ juice in the glass.

a.	an	b.	a
c.	any	d.	the

3. Adam is planning to visit _____ UK next July.

a.	an	b.	a
c.	any	d.	the

4. _____ Reading is my favorite hobby.

a.	No article	b.	Some
c.	Any	d.	The

5. _____ telephone is an important invention.

a.	An	b.	No article
c.	Any	d.	The

6. When Louis saw the robbers, he called _____ police.

a.	an	b.	some
c.	any	d.	the

7. _____ gold is very expensive these days.

a.	An	b.	No article
c.	Any	d.	The

8. _____ Swimming is my favourite sport.

a.	An	b.	Some
c.	The	d.	No article

9. I took a taxi to _____ train station because I was late.

a.	an	b.	some
c.	any	d.	the

10. I don't have _____ French books.

a.	an	b.	no article
c.	any	d.	the

11. _____ money doesn't usually bring happiness.

a.	An	b.	No article
c.	Any	d.	The

12. My brother speaks _____ Italian very well.

a.	an	b.	some
c.	no article	d.	the

13. Leila taught herself to play _____ guitar.

a.	an	b.	some
c.	any	d.	the

14. I met my classmates in front of _____ post office.

a.	an	b.	some
c.	any	d.	the

15. Mr Muhammad is _____ honest man. All his friends trust him.

a.	an	b.	some
c.	a	d.	the

16. _____ English are used to drinking tea in the afternoon.

a.	An	b.	Some
c.	Any	d.	The

17. We are going to have a party on _____ Monday.

a.	an	b.	no article
c.	any	d.	the

18. Don't forget to invite _____ Shalabys to your wedding party.

a.	an	b.	some
c.	any	d.	the

19. Sam likes watching news reports on _____ TV.

a.	an	b.	no article
c.	any	d.	some

20. My mother is flying to _____ Melbourne next week.

a.	an	b.	a
c.	no article	d.	the

21. _____ sun gives us light and heat.

a.	An	b.	Some
c.	Any	d.	The

22. My aunt travelled to California in _____ January.

a.	an	b.	no article
c.	a	d.	the

23. We should do our best to help _____ poor.

a.	an	b.	some
c.	any	d.	the

24. The child was angry because his toy fell on _____ floor.

a.	an	b.	some
c.	any	d.	the

25. Pollution is _____ universal problem.

a.	an	b.	some
c.	a	d.	the

🎀🎀🎀 *My Homework* 🎀🎀🎀

> **Exercise Thirteen**

✦ Choose the correct answer from **a**, **b**, **c**, or **d**.

1. Ibrahim often spends the weekend in _____ country.

a.	an	b.	some
c.	any	d.	the

2. My father is usually busy during _____ day. You can call him at night.

a.	an	b.	some
c.	any	d.	the

3. Nancy likes playing _____ handball.

a.	an	b.	no article
c.	a	d.	the

4. Doris would like to visit _____ Philippines soon.

a.	an	b.	some
c.	any	d.	the

5. _____ stars look bright at night.

a.	An	b.	A
c.	Any	d.	The

6. Millions of tourists visit _____ United States every year.

a.	an	b.	no article
c.	any	d.	the

7. _____ French are known for their nice dressing styles.

a.	An	b.	Some
c.	No article	d.	The

8. _____ French and Spanish are easy to learn.

a.	An	b.	Some
c.	No article	d.	The

9. Osaka is a fantastic city in _____ Japan.

a.	an	b.	some
c.	no article	d.	the

10. A ram is _____ male sheep.

a.	an	b.	some
c.	any	d.	a

11. _____ unit is a part of a book.

a.	A	b.	Some
c.	Any	d.	The

12. _____ union is a group of people.

a.	An	b.	Some
c.	Any	d.	A

13. _____ airplane is a flying vehicle with wings.

a.	An	b.	Some
c.	Any	d.	No article

14. An apple is _____ round fruit with shiny skin.

a.	an	b.	some
c.	any	d.	a

15. _____ oasis is an area in the desert where there is water and where plants grow.

a.	An	b.	Some
c.	Any	d.	The

16. My sister is _____ optician, but my brother is a pilot.

a.	an	b.	some
c.	any	d.	the

17. _____ Hudson River flows from the Adirondack Mountains to New York.

a.	An	b.	Some
c.	Any	d.	The

18. My aunt is _____ teacher.

a.	an	b.	a
c.	any	d.	the

19. Sally will study _____ history of Egypt next semester.

a.	an	b.	some
c.	any	d.	the

20. There is _____ old sofa in the garden.

a.	an	b.	some
c.	any	d.	the

21. Omar will attend _____ Sunday meeting.

a.	an	b.	some
c.	any	d.	the

22. I have to leave now. I have _____ meeting with my manager.

a.	an	b.	some
c.	any	d.	a

23. I often watch _____ TV in the evening.

a.	an	b.	some
c.	no article	d.	any

24. _____ football is a popular sport.

a.	An	b.	No article
c.	Any	d.	The

25. Mr Oliver teaches us _____ geometry.

a.	an	b.	no article
c.	Any	d.	the

🌿🌿🌿 My Homework 🌿🌿🌿

➢ **Exercise Fourteen**

✦ Correct the mistake in each sentence. Follow the example.

➢ Den is engineer.

✓ Den is an engineer.

1. Ronny is farmer.

🌿 ___ ___ ___ ___ ___ ___ ___ ___ ___

2. Suzanna has new dress.

🌿 ___ ___ ___ ___ ___ ___ ___ ___ ___

3. Margret and Madonna are a friends.

🌿 ___ ___ ___ ___ ___ ___ ___ ___ ___

4. My brother is good driver.

🌿 ___ ___ ___ ___ ___ ___ ___ ___ ___

5. I have a two ears.

🌿 ___ ___ ___ ___ ___ ___ ___ ___ ___

6. They got new computer.

🌿 ___ ___ ___ ___ ___ ___ ___ ___ ___

7. My aunt owns old house.

🌿 ___ ___ ___ ___ ___ ___ ___ ___ ___

8. My uncle has a white cars.

🌿 ___ ___ ___ ___ ___ ___ ___ ___ ___

9. This is beautiful rose.

🌿 ___ ___ ___ ___ ___ ___ ___ ___ ___

10. These shoes are a new.
✎ ____ ____ ____ ____ ____ ____ ____ ____ ____

11. I have English book.
✎ ____ ____ ____ ____ ____ ____ ____ ____ ____

12. Messi is famous player.
✎ ____ ____ ____ ____ ____ ____ ____ ____ ____

13. Huda is a active doctor.
✎ ____ ____ ____ ____ ____ ____ ____ ____ ____

14. Nepal is Asian country.
✎ ____ ____ ____ ____ ____ ____ ____ ____ ____

15. Egypt and Algeria are an African countries.
✎ ____ ____ ____ ____ ____ ____ ____ ____ ____

16. Abdul-Rahman is a energetic student.
✎ ____ ____ ____ ____ ____ ____ ____ ____ ____

17. horse is a powerful animal.
✎ ____ ____ ____ ____ ____ ____ ____ ____ ____

18. An America is a large country.
✎ ____ ____ ____ ____ ____ ____ ____ ____ ____

19. Germany is advanced country.
✎ ____ ____ ____ ____ ____ ____ ____ ____ ____

20. This is easy test.
✎ ____ ____ ____ ____ ____ ____ ____ ____ ____

21. The next test will be on the Sunday.
✎ ____ ____ ____ ____ ____ ____ ____ ____ ____

22. Shakespeare was born in the 1564.
✎ ____ ____ ____ ____ ____ ____ ____ ____ ____

23. Could you give me a boxes of matches?
✎ ____ ____ ____ ____ ____ ____ ____ ____ ____

24. Is there no body who can solve this problem?
✎ ____ ____ ____ ____ ____ ____ ____ ____ ____

25. There isn't some water in the glass. It's empty.
✎ ____ ____ ____ ____ ____ ____ ____ ____ ____

✎✎✎ My Homework ✎✎✎

Somebody, Someone, Something, Somewhere

Everybody, Everyone, Everything, Everywhere

Anybody, Anyone, Anything, Anywhere

Somebody (also *someone*) is used to refer to a person who is not known or not mentioned by name.

Something is used to refer to a thing that is not known or not named.

Somewhere (also *someplace*) is used to refer to a place that you do not know or name exactly.

Everybody (also *everyone*) means every person, all people.

Everything means each thing, all things.

Everywhere (also *everyplace*) means in or to every place.

Nobody (also *no one*) means no person.

Nothing means not anything, no thing.

Nowhere means not anywhere, (in or to) no place.

Anybody (also *anyone*) means any person. It is usually used in questions or negative statements.

Anything means one thing (of any kind).
It is usually used in questions or negative statements.

> *Anywhere* (also *anyplace*) means in, at or to any place. It is usually used in questions or negative statements.

➤ Exercise Fifteen
✦ Choose the correct answer from a, b, c, or d.

1. Listen! _____ is calling.

a.	Someone	b.	Anyone
c.	Something	d.	Anything

2. Sandy is very hungry. She wants to eat _____.

a.	someone	b.	something
c.	anyone	d.	anything

3. Look! _____ is coming towards us.

a.	Anyone	b.	Someone
c.	Somewhere	d.	Anything

4. Listen to me. I have _____ to tell you about.

a.	anything	b.	anyone
c.	something	d.	someone

5. I didn't call _____ yesterday. I was very busy.

a.	someone	b.	something
c.	anyone	d.	anything

6. Harry didn't buy _____ last week.

a.	anyone	b.	anything
c.	something	d.	someone

7. I got to my school at 3:30 p.m. I didn't see _____ there.

a.	anyone	b.	no one
c.	no body	d.	someone

8. I gave my sister _____ on her birthday.

a.	someone	b.	anyone
c.	something	d.	anything

9. Allen is going to meet _____ in the evening.

a.	someone	b.	anyone
c.	something	d.	anything

10. **Lewis**: Did you buy _____ at the mall?
    Sam: Yes, I bought a pair of socks.

a.	someone	b.	anyone
c.	something	d.	anything

11. My wife didn't know _____ at the party.

a.	someone	b.	anyone
c.	something	d.	anywhere

12. You can't find these nice goods _____ else.

a.	someone	b.	anyone
c.	something	d.	anywhere

13. Switch the TV off, please. There isn't _____ exciting in the news.

a.	someone	b.	anyone
c.	something	d.	anything

14. I am sure that _____ will enjoy the comic show.

a.	everyone	b.	anyone
c.	something	d.	anything

15. I can't find anything to eat. Chris ate _____ in the fridge.

a.	someone	b.	anyone
c.	everything	d.	anything

16. **Carl**: Did you find your dictionary?

    Tariq: I've looked _____, but I couldn't find it.

a.	anywhere	b.	everywhere
c.	everyone	d.	anything

17. I've asked all my friends to attend my birthday party, but _____ is free. They are studying for their final test.

a.	someone	b.	anyone
c.	nobody	d.	anything

18. When my teacher blamed me for coming late, I had _____ to say.

a.	someone	b.	anyone
c.	nothing	d.	anything

19. Keith is going to buy _____ from the stationery shop.

a.	someone	b.	anyone
c.	something	d.	anything

20. The tourists got bored because there was _____ interesting to go to.

a.	somewhere	b.	anyone
c.	someplace	d.	nowhere

21. I know _____ about wild animals. I have to read about them.

a.	nothing	b.	anyone
c.	something	d.	anything

22. Jasmine didn't meet _____ at the club yesterday.

a.	someone	b.	anybody
c.	somebody	d.	anything

23. This math problem is too difficult. _____ can work it out.

a.	Nobody	b.	Anyone
c.	Something	d.	Anything

24. Alice didn't say _____ about the report.

a.	nothing	b.	anyone
c.	something	d.	anything

25. Samar doesn't have _____ in her backpack. It's empty.

a.	someone	b.	anyone
c.	something	d.	anything

🙰🙰🙰 *My Homework* 🙰🙰🙰

➤ Exercise Sixteen

✦ Correct the mistakes in each of the following sentences. Follow the example.
➤ I am very hungry. I want somewhere to eat.
✓ I am very hungry. I want **something** to eat.

1. I looked for my mobile phone everything, but I couldn't find it.
   🖎 _____

2. The police questioned anyone who saw the car accident.
   🖎 _____

3. I am angry because anyone visited me when I was sick.
   🖎 _____

4. Anybody has left their sunglasses in the library.
   🖎 _____

5. Layan didn't tell the news to somebody.
   🖎 _____

6. Omar logged on to the Internet and chatted with anyone.
   🖎 _____ .

7. There's anything wrong with my computer. It doesn't work.
   🖎 _____

8. There isn't nothing wrong with the plane. It's going to take off soon.
   🖎 _____ .

9. I know anywhere we can go to spend the weekend.
   🖎 _____

10. Anyone called and left a message for you, Dad.
    🖎 _____

11. Alex went to the market, but he didn't buy something.
    🖎 _____

12. Logan doesn't want to talk to nobody at all.
    🖎 _____

13. Erin said anything about her new plans.

    ✍ _____

14. Kim will tell anybody about his project. It is secret.

    ✍ _____

15. I am very busy this week. I can't meet no one.

    ✍ _____

16. Don't tell someone about our secrets.

    ✍ _____

17. The cottage is empty. Anybody lives there.

    ✍ _____

18. Sarah is lonely. She has anyone to talk to.

    ✍ _____

19. There is anything important on TV tonight. I prefer having a walk.

    ✍ _____

20. My grandmother has a bad memory. She can't remember something.

    ✍ _____

21. Lina doesn't know nothing about computer programming.

    ✍ _____

22. My grandparents live anywhere in Ontario.

    ✍ _____

23. Karim is looking for his shoes. He can't find them somewhere.

    ✍ _____

24. We don't like this village. There is anywhere to go to.

    ✍ _____

25. **Jerica**: What are you doing here?
    Elisa: I am waiting for anyone.

    ✍ _____

🙰🙰🙰 *My Homework* 🙵🙵🙵

SECTION 2 — Singular and Plural Nouns

We usually add -s to change the noun into the plural form.

Examples:

singular	plural	singular	plural
a knob	knobs	a head	heads
an employee	employees	a computer	computers
a track	tracks	an owl	owls
a home	homes	a forest	forests

We add -es to change the noun into the plural form if it ends in -s /-ss /-sh /-ch /-x /-o.

Examples:

singular	plural	singular	plural
a gas	gases	a class	classes
a crash	crashes	a watch	watches
a fox	foxes	a tomato	tomatoes
a tax	taxes	a bus	buses

We double the final -z and add an -es to change the noun into the plural form.

Examples:

singular	plural	singular	plural
a quiz	quizzes	a fez	fezzes

Some nouns that end in -o just take -s.

Examples:

singular	plural	singular	plural
a radio	radios	a piano	pianos
a kilo	kilos	a studio	studios

Some nouns that end in *-o* can take *-s* or *-es* in the plural.

Examples:

singular	plural [1]	plural [1]
a mango	mango**s**	mango**es**
a tornado	tornado**s**	tornado**es**

We change the final *-y* into *-i* and add *-es* if the *-y* is preceded by a consonant.

Examples:

singular	plural	singular	plural
a city	cit**ies**	**an** enemy	enem**ies**
a family	famil**ies**	**a** party	part**ies**
a study	stud**ies**	**a** hobby	hobb**ies**
a try	tr**ies**	**a** ferry	ferr**ies**

If the final *-y* is preceded by a vowel, we just add *-s*.

Examples:

singular	plural	singular	plural
a way	way**s**	**a** boy	boy**s**
a day	day**s**	**a** toy	toy**s**
a tray	tray**s**	**a** guy	guy**s**
a play	play**s**	**a** journey	journey**s**
a donkey	donkey**s**	**a** monkey	monkey**s**

We change some nouns that end in *-f* or *-fe* into *-ves*.

Examples:

singular	plural	singular	plural
a wife	wi**ves**	**a** knife	kni**ves**
a life	li**ves**	**a** shelf	shel**ves**

Some nouns that end in -f just take a final -s.

✤ Examples:

singular	plural	singular	plural
a roof	roof**s**	a cliff	cliff**s**
a belief	beliefs	a chief	chief**s**

Some nouns have the same singular and plural form.

✤ Examples:

singular	plural	singular	plural
a deer	deer	a fish	fish
a sheep	sheep	a means	means

Some nouns have irregular plural forms.

✤ Examples:

singular	plural	singular	plural
a man	men	a woman	women
a child	children	an ox	oxen
a mouse	mice	a louse	lice
a foot	feet	a goose	geese
a tooth	teeth		

Some nouns keep their foreign plural forms.

✤ Examples:

singular	plural	singular	plural
an oasis	oases	a medium	media
a datum	data	a syllabus	syllabi/syllabuses

✎✎✎ My Homework ✎✎✎

> *Exercise One*

✦ Fill in the missing word.

	SINGULAR	PLURAL
1.	One boy	Two _____
2.	One _____	Two tries
3.	One family	Two _____
4.	One _____	Two wives
5.	One mile	Two _____
6.	One _____	Two boxes
7.	One door	Two _____
8.	One _____	Two oxen
9.	One mouse	Two _____
10.	One _____	Two women
11.	One cat	Two _____
12.	One _____	Two bushes
13.	One roof	Two _____
14.	One _____	Two geese
15.	One half	Two _____
16.	One _____	Two feet
17.	One calf	Two _____
18.	One _____	Two teeth
19.	One belief	Two _____
20.	One _____	Two ladies
21.	One businessman	Two _____
22.	One _____	Two shelves
23.	One fax	Two _____
24.	One _____	Two lice
25.	One kite	Two _____
26.	One _____	Two babies
27.	One story	Two _____
28.	One _____	Two mirrors
29.	One branch	Two _____

➢ **Exercise Two**
✦ Change the singular sentences into plural sentences.
✦ Follow the example:
➢ My sister is a teacher.
✓ My sisters are teachers.
1. A fox is an animal.
🐭 ____ ____ ____ ____ ____ ____ ____ ____ ____
2. A fly is an insect.
🐭 ____ ____ ____ ____ ____ ____ ____ ____ ____
3. A car is a vehicle.
🐭 ____ ____ ____ ____ ____ ____ ____ ____ ____
4. A goose is a bird.
🐭 ____ ____ ____ ____ ____ ____ ____ ____ ____
5. A hammer is a tool.
🐭 ____ ____ ____ ____ ____ ____ ____ ____ ____
6. A bank is a building.
🐭 ____ ____ ____ ____ ____ ____ ____ ____ ____
7. A banana is a fruit.
🐭 ____ ____ ____ ____ ____ ____ ____ ____ ____
8. A carrot is a vegetable.
🐭 ____ ____ ____ ____ ____ ____ ____ ____ ____
9. A mobile phone is a device.
🐭 ____ ____ ____ ____ ____ ____ ____ ____ ____
10. A fridge is a home appliance.
🐭 ____ ____ ____ ____ ____ ____ ____ ____ ____

🐭🐭🐭 *My Homework* 🐭🐭🐭

➢ **Exercise Three**
✦ Change the singular sentences into plural ones.
✦ Follow the example:
➢ Madrid is a nice city.
➢ Madrid and Rome ____ ____ ____ ____ _____ ____ ____ _
✓ Madrid and Rome are nice cities.
1. France is a European country.
🐭 France and Germany ____ ____ ____ ____ ____ ____ ____
2. Jane is a teacher.
🐭 Jane and Lina ____ ____ _____ ____ ____ ____ ____
3. Ross is a pilot.
🐭 Ross and Edwin ____ ____ ____ ____ ____ ____ ____

4. Mohamed Salah is a famous player.
→ Mohamed Salah and Ronaldo _____ _____ _____ _____ _____
5. Egypt is an Arab country.
→ Egypt and Saudi Arabia _____ _____ _____ _____ _____ _____
6. Lamar is a kind woman.
→ Lamar and Jasmine _____ _____ _____ _____ _____ _____ _____
7. Asia is a large continent.
→ Asia and Africa _____ _____ _____ _____ _____ _____ _____
8. The Nile is a long river.
→ The Nile and the Mississippi _____ _____ _____ _____ _____ _____
9. Manchester City is a famous football team.
→ Manchester City and Manchester United _____ _____ _____ _____ _____ _____ _____ _____ _____ _____ _____

❧❧❧ My Homework ❧❧❧

➢ **Exercise Four**

✦ Choose the correct answer from a, b, c, or d.

1. My sister Batool is _____.

a.	doctor	b.	doctor's
c.	a doctor	d.	doctors

2. John and his wife are _____.

a.	teacher's	b.	teacher
c.	teacher	d.	teachers

3. Ralf and his brother are _____.

a.	policeman's	b.	policemen
c.	a policeman	d.	policeman

4. My grandfather has two _____ on his farm.

a.	oxen's	b.	ox's
c.	ox	d.	oxen

5. I always clean my _____ before I go to bed.

a.	tooth's	b.	teeth
c.	teeth's	d.	a tooth

6. There are a lot of _____ in this old house.

a.	mice	b.	mouse
c.	a mouse	d.	mice's

7. The police arrested three _____ last night.

a.	spies'	b.	spy's
c.	spy	d.	spies

8. My _____ dislike swimming.

a.	child	b.	children's
c.	child's	d.	children

9. Mr Arnold keeps a lot of _____ on his farm.

a.	a sheep	b.	sheep
c.	sheep's	d.	sheeps

10. My aunt has some _____ on her own farm.

a.	goose	b.	goose's
c.	a goose	d.	geese

11. There are seven Portuguese _____ in our class.

a.	students	b.	a student
c.	student	d.	students'

12. I can see two _____ in the picture.

a.	man	b.	man's
c.	men	d.	men's

13. My brother has two _____. They are made in Japan.

a.	watches	b.	watches'
c.	a watch	d.	watch

14. There are two _____ on the table.

a.	a box	b.	boxes'
c.	boxes	d.	box

15. Brian and Scott are my _____.

a.	cousins'	b.	cousin
c.	cousins	d.	a cousin

16. I have one aunt and five _____.

a.	uncle	b.	an uncle
c.	uncle's	d.	uncles

17. There are a lot of _____ in this cupboard.

a.	shelf	b.	a shelf
c.	shelves	d.	shelves'

18. We visited a lot of _____ in the desert.

a.	an oasis	b.	oasis
c.	oases	d.	oasis's

19. Harry's _____ are kind and helpful.

a.	parent	b.	parents
c.	parents'	d.	parent's

20. Ruth ate two _____ and an orange.

a.	apples	b.	apple's
c.	apple	d.	an apple

21. There were a lot of _____ in the market.

a.	woman	b.	woman's
c.	a woman	d.	women

22. Many _____ trust their husbands.

a.	a wife	b.	wives
c.	wife	d.	wives'

23. Jane has three _____ of bread.

a.	loafs	b.	a loaf
c.	loaves	d.	loaf

24. The boys chased some _____ in the jungle.

a.	foxes	b.	foxes'
c.	fox	d.	a fox

25. My _____ Robert is very close to me.

a.	friend's	b.	friends
c.	friend	d.	a friend

My Homework

> ### Exercise Five
Correct the mistake in each sentence. Follow the example.
> I can see three bird in the tree.
✓ I can see three **birds** in the tree.

1. My mother cooked two chicken.
   _____

2. I met four man in the park.
   _____

3. These woman are my aunts.
   _____

4. These person are my relatives.
   _____

5. I drank two glass of milk. They were without sugar.
   _____

6. George sent me three fax.
   _____

7. The secretary typed many letter and gave them to her boss.
   _____
   _____

8. The mechanic fixed two machine and checked them.
   _____

9. Helen visited many city in Asia. However, she liked Tokyo the most.
   _____
   _____

10. The farmer bought three camel. They are brown.
    _____

11. My parents are engineer. They work in a steel factory.
    _____
    _____

12. There is one dining tables in the hall.
    _____
    _____

13. The player of my team are skilled. They rarely lose games.
   ✎ ____ ____ ____ ____ ____ ____ ____ ____ ____
   ____ ____ ____ ____ ____ ____ ____ ____ ____

14. Mobile phone are important. They help us a lot.
   ✎ ____ ____ ____ ____ ____ ____ ____ ____ ____

15. My mother has ten goose. She feeds them every morning.
   ✎ ____ ____ ____ ____ ____ ____ ____ ____ ____
   ____ ____ ____ ____ ____ ____ ____ ____ ____

16. There are many oasis in this desert. We stay in them when it is hot.
   ✎ ____ ____ ____ ____ ____ ____ ____ ____ ____
   ____ ____ ____ ____ ____ ____ ____ ____ ____

17. The teacher thanked his student for their efforts. They are active.
   ✎ ____ ____ ____ ____ ____ ____ ____ ____ ____
   ____ ____ ____ ____ ____ ____ ____ ____ ____

18. After the accident, Jane's foot were broken. The doctor advised her not to walk on them for a week.
   ✎ ____ ____ ____ ____ ____ ____ ____ ____ ____
   ____ ____ ____ ____ ____ ____ ____ ____ ____

19. There are many way to achieve success.
   ✎ ____ ____ ____ ____ ____ ____ ____ ____ ____

20. Mammal feed their kids on milk.
   ✎ ____ ____ ____ ____ ____ ____ ____ ____ ____

21. I used hammer to fix the table.
   ✎ ____ ____ ____ ____ ____ ____ ____ ____ ____

22. She met three classmate in the library.
   ✎ ____ ____ ____ ____ ____ ____ ____ ____ ____

23. Many girl attended the party.
   ✎ ____ ____ ____ ____ ____ ____ ____ ____ ____

24. This large tree has thousands of green leaf.
   ✎ ____ ____ ____ ____ ____ ____ ____ ____ ____

25. There are many dictionaries on those shelf.
   ✎ ____ ____ ____ ____ ____ ____ ____ ____ ____

✿✿✿ My Homework ✿✿✿

SECTION 3

PRONOUNS

Subject Pronoun	Object Pronoun	Possessive Adjective	Possessive Pronoun	Reflexive Pronoun
I	me	my	mine	myself
He	him	his	his	himself
She	her	her	hers	herself
It	it	its	-	itself
You	you	your	yours	yourself
They	them	their	theirs	themselves
We	us	our	ours	ourselves

> *Exercise One*

✦ Fill in the spaces with the correct pronoun.
Use one of these pronouns: *I, he, she*, or *it*.

1. _____ is a policeman.
2. _____ is a policewoman.
3. _____ am from London.
4. _____ is my sister.
5. _____ is my brother.
6. _____ is a new car.
7. _____ is a small cat.
8. _____ is my father.
9. _____ is my aunt.
10. _____ is my uncle.
11. _____ is my grandfather.
12. _____ is my grandmother.
13. _____ am seventeen years old.
14. _____ is a big city.
15. _____ is a tall tree.
16. _____ is a black dog.
17. _____ is a businessman.
18. _____ is a yellow cow.

19. _____ am Canadian.
20. _____ is an easy exercise.
21. _____ is an apple.
22. _____ is my cousin Ahmad.
23. _____ am interested in swimming.
24. _____ is fifteen to five.
25. _____ is a nice day.

☙❧❧ *My Homework* ☙❧❧

➤ *Exercise Two*
✤ Fill in the spaces with the correct pronoun.
   Use one of these pronouns: *I, he, she, it,* or *you.*
1. _____ are a good teacher.
2. _____ is a polite girl.
3. _____ is an active boy.
4. _____ is a white cat.
5. _____ is my friend Sarah.
6. _____ is my brother Jessie.
7. _____ is a red apple.
8. _____ is a large office.
9. _____ is an old woman.
10. _____ are late.
11. _____ is my sister Tuka.
12. _____ is my aunt.
13. _____ is my friend Julia.
14. _____ is a big city.
15. _____ is a large animal.
16. _____ is my passport.
17. _____ are active students.
18. _____ are my classmates.
19. _____ are from England.
20. _____ am fifteen years old.
21. _____ are my friend.
22. This is my aunt. _____ is a famous dentist.
23. My teacher is a woman. _____ is very kind.
24. Dale's teacher is a man. _____ is very active.
25. This is my father. _____ is a police officer.

☙❧❧ *My Homework* ☙❧❧

➢ **Exercise Three**
✦ Fill in the spaces with the correct pronoun.
  Use one of these pronouns: *I, he, she, it,* or *you.*
1. This is my new car. _____ is made in Korea.
2. _____ is my new mobile phone.
3. Wake up, Osama. _____ is seven thirty now.
4. Ellen is an active student. _____ works hard.
5. Henry is helpful. _____ helps his friends.
6. _____ is hot today.
7. _____ are British.
8. _____ is a beautiful girl.
9. _____ is my old car.
10. _____ is my English/French dictionary.
11. _____ are from Australia.
12. _____ is a young man.
13. _____ is a fast car.
14. _____ is an old bus.
15. _____ are my best friend.
16. _____ are late.
17. _____ am on time.
18. _____ is an accurate watch.
19. _____ is an interesting game.
20. _____ is a new stadium.

🌺🌺🌺 *My Homework* 🌺🌺🌺

➢ **Exercise Four**
✦ Fill in the spaces with the correct pronoun.
  Look at the words in brackets. Follow the example.
➢ Example: _____ often goes to school by bus. (Eve)
✓ She often goes to school by bus.
1. _____ is reading a short story.   (Alfred)
2. _____ is fond of swimming.   (Cecily)
3. _____ is drinking some milk.   (My cat)
4. _____ is blue.   (The sky)
5. _____ are my friends.   (Gary and Eric)
6. _____ are on the table.   (The books)
7. _____ are friends.   (Sally and Sandra)
8. _____ is black.   (My car)
9. _____ are teachers.   (My aunts)
10. _____ is sleeping.   (Jane)

11. _____ is new. (My mobile phone)
12. _____ are playing chess. (My friend and I)
13. _____ are on the farm. (The yellow cows)
14. _____ is in the barn. (The camel)
15. _____ is Australian. (Annie)
16. _____ is watering the flowers. (My little sister)
17. _____ are doing their homework. (My brothers)
18. _____ is helping her mother. (My sister Batool)
19. _____ is watching a football match. (Mr Majid)
20. _____ are watching TV. (Ali and his friend)
21. _____ is feeding her baby. (Mrs Nora)
22. _____ is flying his kite. (Ibrahim)
23. _____ is very big. (My school)
24. _____ are on the bus. (Many people)
25. _____ are late for their school. (Maya and Oliver)

✎✎✎ My Homework ✎✎✎

➢ **Exercise Five**

✚ Choose the correct answer from a, b, c, or d.

1. _____ am in the library.

a.	He	b.	We
c.	I	d.	You

2. _____ are at home.

a.	He	b.	You
c.	She	d.	I

3. _____ is my aunt.

a.	We	b.	She
c.	I	d.	You

4. _____ is Mr Abdul-Rahman Saleh.

a.	You	b.	We
c.	I	d.	He

5. _____ is Mrs Sarah Adams.

a.	You	b.	We
c.	I	d.	She

6. _____ are nice girls.

a.	They	b.	He
c.	She	d.	It

7. _____ is a naughty boy.

a.	I	b.	You
c.	They	d.	He

8. Manchester and Leeds are British cities. _____ are always busy.

a.	We	b.	It
c.	They	d.	You

9. _____ are older than me.

a.	He	b.	We
c.	I	d.	You

10. _____ is a good teacher.

a.	You	b.	I
c.	They	d.	He

11. _____ are a beautiful woman.

a.	She	b.	We
c.	I	d.	You

12. _____ helps her mother.

a.	You	b.	I
c.	We	d.	She

13. _____ visits his father.

a.	I	b.	He
c.	We	d.	They

14. My name is Ahmad. _____ live in Cairo.

a.	He	b.	She
c.	I	d.	It

15. The nurse's name is Lina. _____ is from Nepal.

a.	They	b.	We
c.	I	d.	She

16. Athens is an ancient city. _____ is the capital of Greece.

a.	I	b.	He
c.	We	d.	It

17. Lee and Yuan are from China. _____ are new students.

a.	She	b.	I
c.	They	d.	He

18. Miriam is from Tanta. _____ is a teacher of English.

a.	You	b.	I
c.	They	d.	She

19. Pierre is from France. _____ is a businessman.

a.	He	b.	We
c.	I	d.	You

20. _____ am a new student.

a.	We	b.	They
c.	It	d.	She

21. My brother and I work in a bank. _____ live in the same house.

a.	They	b.	We
c.	I	d.	You

22. _____ meet our friends every day.

a.	I	b.	We
c.	It	d.	She

23. _____ walk to their school five times a week.

a.	They	b.	She
c.	He	d.	It

24. Yomna likes swimming. _____ goes to the beach weekly.

a.	I	b.	She
c.	We	d.	They

25. Adam likes reading. _____ reads a short story every night.

a.	We	b.	You
c.	You	d.	He

Subject and Object Pronouns

> *Exercise Six*

✤ Choose the correct answer from a, b, c, or d.

1. My name is Emma. My teachers help _____ a lot.

a.	him	b.	her
c.	them	d.	me

2. This is my new laptop. I bought _____ last night.

a.	me	b.	him
c.	you	d.	it

3. My friend and I live together. _____ share the same room.

a.	He	b.	We
c.	I	d.	You

4. My uncle is a pilot. _____ flies planes around the world.

a.	He	b.	We
c.	I	d.	You

5. **Tony**: Could you tell me _____ brother's name, please?
   Toby: Sure. My brother's name is Samuel.

a.	his	b.	its
c.	your	d.	their

6. My aunt is on the farm. _____ went there an hour ago.

a.	She	b.	He
c.	I	d.	It

7. My grandparents are very old. I visit _____ from time to time.

a.	us	b.	me
c.	them	d.	it

8. My parents are visiting Tokyo. _____ are staying there for a week.

a.	They	b.	I
c.	She	d.	He

9. William had a car accident. I am going to visit _____ soon.

a.	me	b.	us
c.	him	d.	her

10. Sophia is flying to Michigan. _____ has a meeting there.

a.	We	b.	I
c.	You	d.	She

11. Salah is a famous player. _____ plays for Liverpool.

a.	They	b.	He
c.	It	d.	You

12. Miranda lives in the country. _____ has a farmhouse there.

a.	We	b.	I
c.	You	d.	She

13. I am busy now. You can call _____ later.

a.	her	b.	me
c.	you	d.	him

14. Ms Elizabeth is a famous writer. Do you know _____?

a.	her	b.	it
c.	him	d.	you

15. **Lexi:** Could _____ spell your family name, please?
    Erin: Sure. A-L-B-R-I-G-H-T.

a.	you	b.	yours
c.	your	d.	yourself

16. Please give _____ this book. I need it.

a.	him	b.	me
c.	I	d.	my

17. Adrian is a doctor. _____ works in a famous hospital.

a.	I	b.	He
c.	It	d.	You

18. My car is new. _____ is dark blue.

a.	He	b.	They
c.	It	d.	She

19. Kim and Shang are my friends. _____ are from China.

a.	He	b.	They
c.	She	d.	I

20. George and I like swimming. _____ swim at the club.

a.	Our	b.	Ours
c.	We	d.	Us

21. Olivia is my sister. I visit _____ now and then.

a.	her	b.	hers
c.	it	d.	she

22. I can't drink this tea. _____ is too hot.

a.	She	b.	He
c.	I	d.	It

23. _____ are my friend Scott.

a.	He	b.	She
c.	It	d.	You

24. My friend Alan is lazy. I usually ask _____ to study hard.

a.	himself	b.	he
c.	him	d.	his

25. Can you help _____, sir?

a.	he	b.	me
c.	I	d.	you

☙☙☙ My Homework ☙☙☙

➢ Exercise Seven
✦ Choose the correct answer from a, b, c, or d.

1. This is my room. I usually clean it _____.

a.	myself	b.	itself
c.	yourself	d.	herself

2. Look at the cats! They are cleaning _____.

a.	myself	b.	itself
c.	themselves	d.	herself

3. This is Ahmad's laptop. He can fix it _____.

a.	myself	b.	himself
c.	yourself	d.	herself

4. The cat is washing _____.

a.	myself	b.	itself
c.	yourself	d.	herself

5. This is Jane's new dress. She sewed it _____.

a.	myself	b.	itself
c.	yourself	d.	herself

6. We usually clean our father's car _____.

a.	themselves	b.	ourselves
c.	yourselves	d.	itself

7. The electrician can fix these appliances _____.

a.	himself	b.	itself
c.	themselves	d.	myself

8. The teacher said to the naughty student, 'Behave _____.'

a.	myself	b.	itself
c.	yourself	d.	herself

9. Hi, Neil! Hi, John! Please come in and make _____ at home.

a.	yourself	b.	yourselves
c.	themselves	d.	ourselves

10. Hi, Sally! Please come in and make _____ at home.

a.	yourself	b.	yourselves
c.	themselves	d.	ourselves

11. Kevin and his brother have their own business. They work for _____.

a.	yourself	b.	yourselves
c.	themselves	d.	ourselves

12. Don't worry. The computers will shut down by _____.

a.	himself	b.	herself
c.	themselves	d.	itself

13. My brothers enjoyed _____ on the farm last weekend.

a.	himself	b.	themselves
c.	yourselves	d.	ourselves

14. Please try this cake. I made it _____.

a.	itself	b.	herself
c.	myself	d.	yourself

15. Some of my friends blame _____ for failing the final test.

a.	yourself	b.	yourselves
c.	themselves	d.	ourselves

16. Dina and Leila have to cook for _____ as their mother is sick.

a.	themselves	b.	itself
c.	myself	d.	himself

17. Oliver was hungry, so he bought _____ a sandwich.

a.	myself	b.	itself
c.	himself	d.	herself

18. My elder sister made lunch all by _____ at home.

a.	myself	b.	itself
c.	himself	d.	herself

19. While the baby girl was crawling in the garden, she hurt _____.

a.	myself	b.	yourself
c.	himself	d.	herself

20. The teacher asked his students to push _____ to work harder.

a.	yourself	b.	yourselves
c.	themselves	d.	ourselves

21. The babies were happy to see _____ in the mirror.

a.	yourself	b.	yourselves
c.	themselves	d.	ourselves

22. Don't worry, sir. We will fix the car for you _____.

a.	yourself	b.	yourselves
c.	themselves	d.	ourselves

23. Our new manager prefers to reply to all the emails _____.

a.	yourself	b.	yourselves
c.	themselves	d.	himself

24. You and your classmate must submit this assignment _____.

a.	yourself	b.	yourselves
c.	themselves	d.	ourselves

25. It's thrilling for me to meet the Prime Minister _____.

a.	ourselves	b.	itself
c.	himself	d.	yourself

✄✄✄ My Homework ✄✄✄

Subject and Object Pronouns
Possessive Adjectives
Reflexive Pronouns

➢ **Exercise Eight**

✦ Choose the correct answer from a, b, c, or d.

1. I have a camera. _____ camera is digital.

a.	Its	b.	My
c.	Mine	d.	Me

2. Nora has a dress. _____ dress is beautiful.

a.	Hers	b.	She
c.	Her	d.	Herself

3. You have a mobile phone. _____ mobile phone has two cameras.

a.	Yourself	b.	Yours
c.	Your	d.	You

4. Albert has a car. _____ car is black.

a.	It	b.	His
c.	Him	d.	Its

5. You are our new classmate. This is _____ desk.

a.	yourself	b.	yours
c.	your	d.	you

6. We are brothers. _____ father is a teacher.

a.	We	b.	Our
c.	Ourselves	d.	Ours

7. They have a farm. _____ farm is very large.

a.	They	b.	Their
c.	Theirs	d.	Them

8. This house has two gates. _____ gates are brown.

a.	Its	b.	Itself
c.	It	d.	They

9. This is my watch. It is _____.

a.	its	b.	my
c.	mine	d.	me

10. This is Abdul-Rahman's iPod. It is _____.

a.	he	b.	his
c.	him	d.	its

11. This is Fatima's dictionary. It is _____.

a.	she	b.	her
c.	herself	d.	hers

12. These are my shoes. They are _____.

a.	myself	b.	my
c.	mine	d.	me

13. These are your jeans. They are _____.

a.	you	b.	your
c.	yourself	d.	yours

14. This is our new flat. We painted it _____.

a.	we	b.	our
c.	ourselves	d.	ours

15. This is my uncle's house. It is _____.

a.	he	b.	his
c.	him	d.	its

16. This is Amelia's washing machine. _____ uses it daily.

a.	Her	b.	She
c.	Herself	d.	Hers

17. Mr Simon is a teacher. _____ works in a high school.

a.	He	b.	His
c.	Him	d.	Its

18. My sisters are active. _____ do a lot of work.

a.	They	b.	Theirs
c.	Theirs	d.	Them

19. My father is a policeman. _____ often spends the night on duty.

a.	He	b.	His
c.	Him	d.	Its

20. My mother is a housewife. _____ cares for our family.

a.	She	b.	Her
c.	Herself	d.	Hers

21. My name is Marwa. _____ live in Cairo.

a.	She	b.	I
c.	He	d.	It

22. My sister's name is Tuka. _____ lives in Canada.

a.	She	b.	Her
c.	Herself	d.	Hers

23. Dina and Leila are friends. _____ like diving.

a.	They	b.	Theirs
c.	Themselves	d.	Them

24. I changed the flat tire _____.

a.	yourself	b.	themselves
c.	himself	d.	myself

25. Ortega fixed his van _____.

a.	yourself	b.	ourselves
c.	himself	d.	myself

🐾🐾🐾 My Homework

> Exercise Nine

Choose the correct answer from a, b, c, or d.

1. Our grandmother usually tells _____ nice stories.

a.	us	b.	we
c.	ourselves	d.	our

2. This is your mobile phone. Please take _____.

a.	him	b.	you
c.	it	d.	me

3. I'm sorry. I can't recognize _____.

a.	your	b.	yourself
c.	I	d.	you

4. My car doesn't work well. Please check _____.

a.	him	b.	me
c.	it	d.	her

5. Those children are noisy. Please ask _____ to be quiet.

a.	them	b.	they
c.	theirs	d.	their

6. This is my sister Bato. I love _____ very much.

a.	her	b.	hers
c.	it	d.	she

7. This is my book. Put _____ on the shelf, please.

a.	you	b.	her
c.	it	d.	me

8. _____ is sunny today.

a.	They	b.	We
c.	It	d.	I

9. These are my new glasses. I bought _____ yesterday.

a.	it	b.	themselves
c.	them	d.	they

10. My brother is a web designer. _____ lives in Nebraska.

a.	Him	b.	Himself
c.	His	d.	He

11. My sister cleaned the villa _____.

a.	she	b.	her
c.	herself	d.	hers

12. You should arrange the furniture in this room _____.

a.	you	b.	your
c.	yourself	d.	yours

13. We cooked this nice meal _____.

a.	we	b.	our
c.	ourselves	d.	ours

14. The workmen cleaned the garden of the villa _____.

a.	they	b.	theirs
c.	themselves	d.	them

15. **Olivia:** Are these your glasses?
    Ross: Yes, they are _____.

a.	I	b.	my
c.	mine	d.	me

16. Neil has a large van. He drives _____ daily.

a.	itself	b.	its
c.	her	d.	it

17. _____ are having their breakfast.

a.	They	b.	Theirs
c.	Themselves	d.	Them

18. _____ are my friend.

a.	He	b.	She
c.	I	d.	You

19. Kim and Lee are _____ true friends.

a.	I	b.	my
c.	mine	d.	me

20. Our teacher is kind to _____.

a.	we	b.	our
c.	ourselves	d.	us

21. My car is new, but _____ is old.

A.	you	b.	your
C.	yourself	d.	yours

22. James and Allen like _____ school.

A.	they	b.	their
C.	themselves	d.	them

23. _____ house is near the National Park.

a.	I	b.	My
c.	Mine	d.	Me

24. This car doesn't work. _____ engine is defective.

a.	It	b.	Itself
c.	Its	d.	It's

25. Maria likes _____ history class.

a.	she	b.	her
c.	herself	d.	hers

> *Exercise Ten*

✦ Choose the correct answer from a, b, c, or d.

1. I want to sit between him and _____.

a.	you	b.	your
c.	yourself	d.	yours

2. We are pleased that our aunt will spend a week with _____.

a.	we	b.	our
c.	us	d.	ours

3. Abdullah came to visit _____ last night.

a.	I	b.	my
c.	mine	d.	me

4. Our teacher is speaking. Listen to _____ carefully.

a.	he	b.	his
c.	him	d.	himself

5. It was my brother who went with _____.

a.	my	b.	I
c.	me	d.	mine

6. Our teacher taught _____ a new grammar lesson.

a.	we	b.	our
c.	us	d.	ours

7. _____ work in a bank.

a.	He	b.	She
c.	They	d.	It

8. I usually feed the cats _____.

a.	itself	b.	myself
c.	themselves	d.	yourself

9. Ronald fixed the car _____. Nobody helped him.

a.	herself	b.	myself
c.	themselves	d.	himself

10. Mr Edgar read the announcement _____.

a.	herself	b.	himself
c.	themselves	d.	yourself

11. My father bought a television. _____ is new.

a.	He	b.	It
c.	I	d.	She

12. This is our teacher's dictionary. It is _____.

a.	she	b.	her
c.	herself	d.	hers

13. Greg broke _____ camera. He will buy a new one.

a.	he	b.	his
c.	him	d.	himself

14. Andrew goes to his school by taxi. _____ is very far.

a.	He	b.	It
c.	I	d.	She

15. Can I help _____, sir?

a.	you	b.	your
c.	yourself	d.	yours

16. The girl is looking at _____ in the mirror.

a.	she	b.	her
c.	herself	d.	hers

17. This jacket does not suit me. _____ is too long.

a.	It	b.	He
c.	you	d.	She

18. The nurse is helping _____ patients.

a.	she	b.	her
c.	herself	d.	hers

19. Mr Jeff is visiting _____ uncle in Atlanta.

a.	he	b.	his
c.	him	d.	himself

20. This is _____ new office.

a.	we	b.	our
c.	ourselves	d.	us

21. My aunt is a great woman. She does her best to please _____ family.

a.	she	b.	her
c.	herself	d.	hers

22. Saleh sold _____ old car.

a.	he	b.	his
c.	him	d.	himself

23. Nada and her sister visited _____ parents in Amsterdam.

a.	hers	b.	their
c.	she	d.	herself

24. This is my laptop. It is _____.

a.	my	b.	I
c.	me	d.	mine

25. **Kim**: Is this your phone?
    Ted: No, it's _____.

a.	you	b.	your
c.	yourself	d.	yours

🙰🙰🙰 *My Homework* 🙰🙰🙰

Possessive Nouns

NOTE 01:
We add an apostrophe (') before the *s* if the noun is singular.
Examples:
- My father's car
- Alan's house.

NOTE 02:
We add an apostrophe (') after the *s* if the noun is plural.
Example:
- My parents' plan

NOTE 03:
We add an apostrophe (') before the *s* if the noun is irregular plural.
Example:
- My children's room

NOTE 04:
We can add an (') after the original *s* or add an apostrophe + *s* if the person's name ends in an *s*.
Example:
- Dickens' novels or Dickens's novels

 My Homework

> ### Exercise Eleven
↓ Choose the correct answer from a, b, c, or d.

1. This is _____ notebook. It is his.

a.	Adam'	b.	Adam
c.	Adams	d.	Adam's

2. This is _____ apartment. It is hers.

a.	Olivia's	b.	Olivias
c.	Olivia	d.	Olivia'

3. This is my _____ country house. He bought it last year.

a.	uncles'	b.	uncle
c.	an uncle	d.	uncle's

4. This is my _____ private room. It is theirs.

a.	brothers'	b.	a brother
c.	brother	d.	brother's

5. Steven is my _____ husband. He married her last week.

a.	sisters'	b.	sister
c.	sister's	d.	a sister

6. I broke my _____ vase. She wasn't angry.

a.	aunt's	b.	an aunt
c.	aunt	d.	aunts

7. _____ son is a pilot. He flies all types of planes.

a.	Kevin	b.	Kevins
c.	Kevin's	d.	Kevins'

8. **Nancy:** Whose mobile phone is this?
    Nora: It is _____.

a.	Lauras	b.	Laura
c.	Lauras'	d.	Laura's

9. I went into the _____ office as I had a meeting with him.

a.	manger	b.	manger's
c.	mangers	d.	mangers'

✿✿✿ *My Homework* ✿✿✿

➢ Exercise Twelve

✦ Find the mistake in each of the following sentences and correct it.

1. This is not me book. It's yours.
   ✎ _____

2. These are not you shoes. They are Ashraf's.
   ✎ _____

3. Please call Mr Sam and thank his.
   ✎ _____

4. Him doesn't like water sports.
   ✎ _____

5. This is not Sara's camera. It's me.
   ✎ _____

6. Emma didn't go to school. Her is at home.
   ✎ _____

7. This is Jacob's shirt. It's him.
   ✎ _____

8. Me write a report every day.
   ✎ _____

9. I meet Carol and Linda every day. Their are my friends.
   ✎ _____

10. It's mine old bike.
    ✎ _____

11. Us study English daily.
    ✎ _____

12. Them always drive safely.
✎ _____ _____ _____ _____ _____ _____ _____ _____ _____ _____.
13. Her doesn't speak English well.
✎ _____ _____ _____ _____ _____ _____ _____ _____ _____ _____.
14. Baker is doing he homework.
✎ _____ _____ _____ _____ _____ _____ _____ _____ _____ _____.
15. His doesn't live alone.
✎ _____ _____ _____ _____ _____ _____ _____ _____ _____ _____.
16. Paul can express him in French very well.
✎ _____ _____ _____ _____ _____ _____ _____ _____ _____ _____.
17. Ted and Charles took them grandmother to the park.
✎ _____ _____ _____ _____ _____ _____ _____ _____ _____ _____.
18. Harry invited him friends to a party.
✎ _____ _____ _____ _____ _____ _____ _____ _____ _____ _____.
19. I usually clean my office mine.
✎ _____ _____ _____ _____ _____ _____ _____ _____ _____ _____.
20. Your have to do your homework yourself.
✎ _____ _____ _____ _____ _____ _____ _____ _____ _____ _____.

🌺🌺🌺 *My Homework* 🌺🌺🌺

> ### *Exercise Thirteen*
✦ Complete the sentences. Use *it, it's,* or *its*.
1. _____ a large tree.
2. This is a black wolf. _____ cry is scary.
3. This is a large elephant. _____ is grey.
4. This is a yellow ox. _____ has two large horns.
5. _____ cold today.
6. _____ is very cold in Russia in winter.
7. _____ is sunny today.
8. _____ is my old car.
9. _____ our new villa.
10. This shirt is very nice. _____ colors are wonderful.
11. **Alan:** Who's knocking?
    Ben: _____ me.
12. _____ my first day at school.
13. The cat is crying because _____ is very hungry.
14. I have a new mobile phone. _____ made in Japan.
15. _____ is the last sentence.

🌺🌺🌺 *My Homework* 🌺🌺🌺

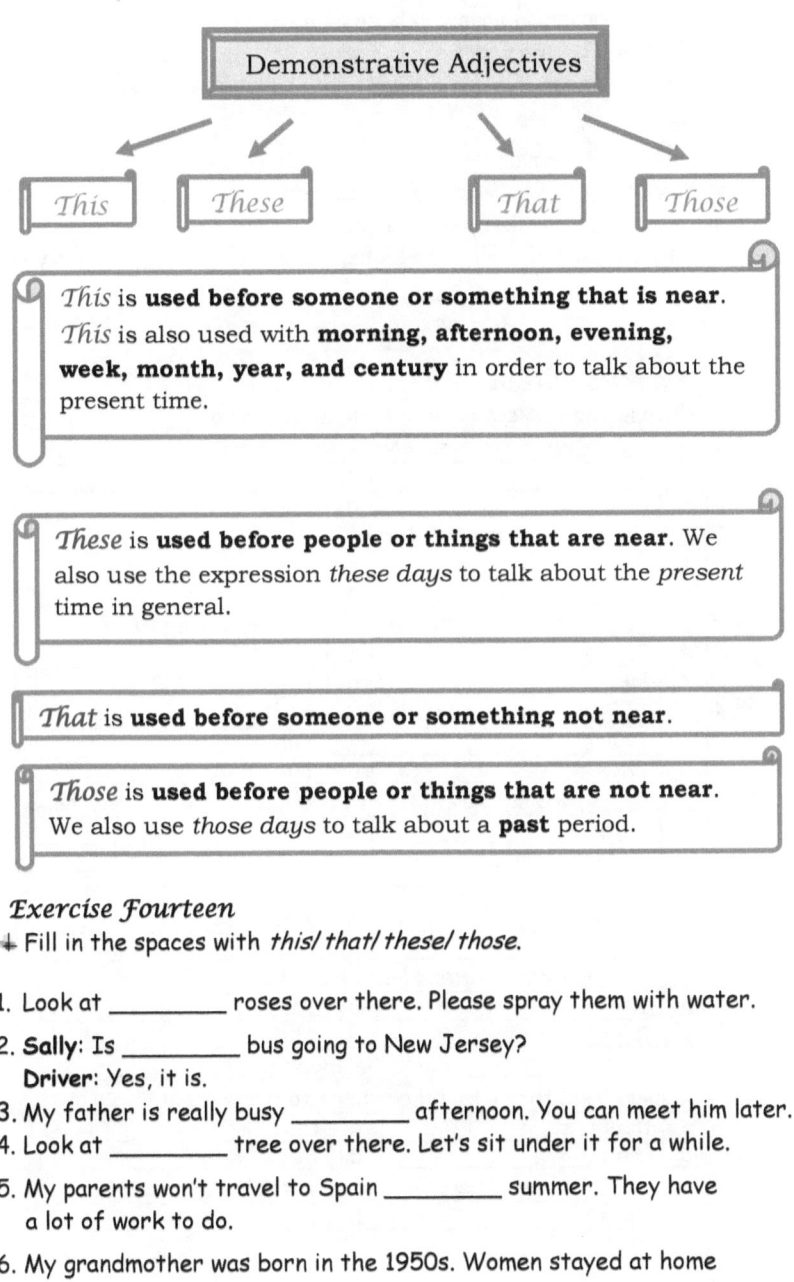

This is **used before someone or something that is near**. *This* is also used with **morning, afternoon, evening, week, month, year, and century** in order to talk about the present time.

These is **used before people or things that are near**. We also use the expression *these days* to talk about the *present* time in general.

That is **used before someone or something not near**.

Those is **used before people or things that are not near**. We also use *those days* to talk about a **past** period.

Exercise Fourteen
Fill in the spaces with *this/ that/ these/ those*.

1. Look at _____ roses over there. Please spray them with water.
2. **Sally**: Is _____ bus going to New Jersey?
   Driver: Yes, it is.
3. My father is really busy _____ afternoon. You can meet him later.
4. Look at _____ tree over there. Let's sit under it for a while.
5. My parents won't travel to Spain _____ summer. They have a lot of work to do.
6. My grandmother was born in the 1950s. Women stayed at home in _____ days.

7. Isabel: How long have you been living in _____ country?
   Freddy: For ten years.
8. I haven't seen Sue for a long time. She never comes to see me _____ days.
9. Ali: Do you remember when we went to Luxor?
   David: _____ was a good vacation.
10. Edwin: Do you like your new job?
    Jessi: Sure. Salaries are higher here than _____ in my country.

My Homework

> ## Exercise Fifteen
✦ Choose the correct answer from a, b, c, or d.
1. _____ are my shirts. Please wash them.

a.	That	b.	This
c.	It	d.	These

2. _____ is not my tea. It's yours. It is with milk.

a.	This	b.	These
c.	They	d.	Those

3. _____ is my new teacher. I'd love you to meet her.

a.	These	b.	This
c.	He	d.	Those

4. _____ is my car. I parked it over there.

a.	These	b.	This
c.	Those	d.	That

5. _____ are my parents. They are having a walk over there.

a.	That	b.	This
c.	These	d.	Those

6. _____ smartphone doesn't work. Please fix it for me.

a.	These	b.	This
c.	It	d.	Those

7. _____ are my pants. Please iron them.

a.	That	b.	This
c.	It	d.	These

8. Sophie: Do _____ books belong to you?
   Cooper: Yes, they are. I'll go there to bring them.

a.	these	b.	that
c.	those	d.	this

9. _____ is my camera. Would you repair it, please?

a.	Those	b.	This
c.	She	d.	These

10. _____ is my new bike. I bought it yesterday.

a.	These	b.	This
c.	They	d.	Those

11. _____ is Andrew's house. He renovated it last year.

a.	Those	b.	This
c.	They	d.	These

12. _____ are my glasses. I can't see without them.

a.	That	b.	This
c.	It	d.	These

13. _____ glass over there is empty.

a.	That	b.	This
c.	It	d.	These

14. _____ computer doesn't work well.

a.	They	b.	This
c.	It	d.	These

15. _____ is a beautiful tree. We are sitting under it right now.

a.	Those	b.	This
c.	That	d.	These

16. _____ is my farm. I bought it yesterday.

a.	These	b.	This
c.	They	d.	Those

17. The manager is really busy _____ afternoon.

a.	these	b.	this
c.	an	d.	those

18. My friends are going to visit me _____ morning.

a.	these	b.	this
c.	they	d.	those

19. _____ new teacher is really helpful. We all respect her.

a.	These	b.	This
c.	They	d.	Those

20. _____ man we met yesterday was silly.

a.	These	b.	This
c.	That	d.	Those

My Homework

➢ **Exercise Sixteen**

✦ Change the following sentences from singular to plural. Follow the example.

➢ This is an active player.
✓ These are active players.

1. This is my brother.
   ✎ _____ _____ _____ _____ _____ _____ _____ _____ _____

2. That is a tall tree.
✍ _____ _____ _____ _____ _____ _____ _____ _____ _____

3. This man is English.
✍ _____ _____ _____ _____ _____ _____ _____ _____ _____

4. That woman is from China.
✍ _____ _____ _____ _____ _____ _____ _____ _____ _____

5. That boy has a toy.
✍ _____ _____ _____ _____ _____ _____ _____ _____ _____

6. This teacher works hard.
✍ _____ _____ _____ _____ _____ _____ _____ _____ _____

7. That train doesn't go to Madrid.
✍ _____ _____ _____ _____ _____ _____ _____ _____ _____

8. This is my aunt.
✍ _____ _____ _____ _____ _____ _____ _____ _____ _____

9. This train is fast.
✍ _____ _____ _____ _____ _____ _____ _____ _____ _____

10. This child is six years old.
✍ _____ _____ _____ _____ _____ _____ _____ _____ _____

11. That is my new shirt.
✍ _____ _____ _____ _____ _____ _____ _____ _____ _____

12. This beach is wonderful.
✍ _____ _____ _____ _____ _____ _____ _____ _____ _____

13. That plane is full of passengers.
✍ _____ _____ _____ _____ _____ _____ _____ _____ _____

14. That truck driver got a fine.
✍ _____ _____ _____ _____ _____ _____ _____ _____ _____

15. This is my future plan.
✍ _____ _____ _____ _____ _____ _____ _____ _____ _____

🖎🖎🖎 My Homework 🖎🖎🖎

➢ **Exercise Seventeen**
✚ Correct the mistake in each of the following sentences. Follow the example.
➢ That books are expensive.
✓ Those books are expensive.

1. This are my sisters. I love them.
✍ _____ _____ _____ _____ _____ _____ _____ _____ _____

2. Those is a fantastic car. I bought it yesterday.
✍ _____ _____ _____ _____ _____ _____ _____ _____ _____

3. That are your new classmates. I met them last Monday.
✎ ____ ____ ____ ____ ____ ____ ____ ____ ____

4. Fix these engine, please. It doesn't work well.
✎ ____ ____ ____ ____ ____ ____ ____ ____ ____

5. Please check this patients before you leave and give him his drugs.
✎ ____ ____ ____ ____ ____ ____ ____ ____ ____

6. Take these pill before you go to bed. They are good for you.
✎ ____ ____ ____ ____ ____ ____ ____ ____ ____

7. Give me that dictionaries. I need them now.
✎ ____ ____ ____ ____ ____ ____ ____ ____ ____

8. Send me this emails. I want to read them soon.
✎ ____ ____ ____ ____ ____ ____ ____ ____ ____

9. Answer this questions, please. They are easy.
✎ ____ ____ ____ ____ ____ ____ ____ ____ ____

10. Ann: Is these my soup?
    Ralf: Yes, it's yours.
✎ ____ ____ ____ ____ ____ ____ ____ ____ ____

11. Diana: Do you know these teacher?
    Jack: Yes, of course. She's my math teacher.
✎ ____ ____ ____ ____ ____ ____ ____ ____ ____

12. Shall I choose this car or those one?
✎ ____ ____ ____ ____ ____ ____ ____ ____ ____

13. Hi, Donald. These is my new friend Khalid.
✎ ____ ____ ____ ____ ____ ____ ____ ____ ____

14. These is my food. I prepared it myself.
✎ ____ ____ ____ ____ ____ ____ ____ ____ ____

15. This are my pants. Please wash them.
✎ ____ ____ ____ ____ ____ ____ ____ ____ ____

16. This are Lilly's gifts. Please give them to her.
✎ ____ ____ ____ ____ ____ ____ ____ ____ ____

17. This are Helen's documents. Don't copy them.
✎ ____ ____ ____ ____ ____ ____ ____ ____ ____

18. That are Ahmad's kids. They are smart.
✎ ____ ____ ____ ____ ____ ____ ____ ____ ____

19. Please clean this rooms as quickly as you can.
✎ ____ ____ ____ ____ ____ ____ ____ ____ ____

20. That are my mother's hens. She feeds them now and then.
✎ ____ ____ ____ ____ ____ ____ ____ ____ ____

✎✎✎ My Homework ✎✎✎

SECTION 4

Prepositions of Place

Write (In), (At) and (On) at the beginning of the table.

Prep.	Use	Example
In		in the house
		in hospital
		in bed
		in jail
		in the garden
		in the park
		in prison
		in England
		in Cairo
		in Australia
		in the United States
		at the handball game
		at the meeting
		at the party
		at the airport
		at the station
		at home
		at work

At		at the seashore
		at the movies
		at the cinema
		at the theatre
		at Jane's house
		at a concert
		at a conference
		at school
		at college
		at a hotel
		at the door
		at a restaurant
		at my office
		on the farm
		on the table
		on the floor
		on the wall
		on the river
		on the sea
		on the right
		on the left
		on the bus
		on the plane

On		on the train	
		on the metro	
		on the underground	
		on the tube	
		on the subway	
		on foot	
		on a bicycle	
		on my bike	
		on my motorbike	
		on the Internet	
		on my computer	
		on the laptop	
		on TV	
		on the television	
		on the radio	
		on the stage	
		on the telephone	
		on the phone	
		on the back (of the paper)	
		on the front (of the train)	
In front of	↓ in a position that is further forward than another person or thing, but not very far away	in front of my house	
		in front of the bank	
		in front of me	

Behind	✦ in, at, or to the back of someone or something	behind the mosque behind the post office behind you
Under	✦ in, to, or through a position that is below or beneath something	under the table under the sofa under the dictionary
Above	✦ at or to a higher place of something or somebody	above my head
Next to	✦ in or into a position right beside somebody or something; beside	next to me next to my office
Between	✦ in or into the space that separates two points, objects, people, etc.	between Ali and Ola between the bank and the cinema
Near	✦ a short distance away, close to	near my house
Far from	✦ a long distance away	far from the city
To	✦ in the direction of something ✦ towards something	to school to work
Over	✦ higher than but not touching somebody or something ✦ above somebody or something	over the bookcase
Towards Toward	✦ in the direction of somebody or something	towards the airport towards his mother

Across	↟ from one side to the other side	across the field
Into	↟ to a position or inside in something	into the house
After	↟ one follows the other	The dog ran after the child.
Along	↟ in a line ↟ from one point to another	Jane is jogging along the beach.
Among	↟ in a group	among the trees
Around	↟ in a circular way	around the building
Below	↟ at or to a lower level or position than somebody or something	below the surface of the water
Beside	↟ next to or at the side of somebody or something	beside the river
By	↟ near somebody or something	by the coast
Close to	↟ near, not far away	near the bank
Down	↟ from a high or higher point on something to a lower one	down the mountain
From	↟ used to show where somebody or something starts	from London
Inside	↟ on or to the inner part of something or somebody ↟ within something or somebody	inside the house
Off	↟ down or away from a place or at a distance in space	off the grass off the roof

Onto	⬇ used with verbs to express movement on or to a particular place or	onto the terrace
Opposite	⬇ on the other side of a particular area from somebody or something	opposite my house
Out of	⬇ away from the side of a place or a thing	out of the room
Outside	⬇ away from or in a particular place	outside the bank
Past	⬇ on or the other side of somebody or something	past the building
Through	⬇ from one end or side of something or somebody to the other	through the crowd
Up	⬇ to or in a higher position somewhere	up the hill

> *Exercise One*

⬇ Choose the correct answer from a, b, c, or d.

1. Dan is _____ his room. He's lying on a sofa.

A.	in	B.	on
C.	across	D.	under

2. The motorist asked about the nearest bridge _____ the river.

a.	in	b.	between
c.	across	d.	under

3. Kris flew _____ Italy. He spent three weeks there.

a.	across	b.	under
c.	to	d.	on

4. My father didn't go to his office today. He is _____ home.

a.	in	b.	on
c.	across	d.	at

5. A lot of people were walking _____ the bridge.

a.	on	b.	over
c.	under	d.	between

6. I took a limousine _____ the post office. I wanted to post a letter there.

a.	in	b.	on
c.	across	d.	to

7. The plane was flying _____ the clouds.

a.	above	b.	out
c.	between	d.	of

8. The subway passed _____ the tunnel.

a.	between	b.	on
c.	through	d.	over

9. Last week, we spent a very nice time _____ the farm.

a.	in	b.	on
c.	across	d.	under

10. Ibrahim lives _____ Sadat Street.

a.	in	b.	on
c.	at	d.	outside

11. The children came _____ the house after they finished playing.

a.	into	b.	on
c.	between	d.	under

12. I just cross the street to school. It is _____ from my house.

a.	in	b.	on
c.	across	d.	under

13. Olivia doesn't walks to her office as it is _____ from her house.

a.	over	b.	far
c.	across	d.	under

14. During the play, there were about forty actors and actresses _____ stage in one scene.

a.	in	b.	on
c.	across	d.	over

15. The child hid _____ the bed. His mother looked for him everywhere.

a.	in	b.	on
c.	between	d.	under

16. A lot of children spend much time _____ the Internet.

a.	in	b.	on
c.	across	d.	under

17. Planes aren't allowed to fly _____ this military area.

a.	far	b.	between
c.	over	d.	under

18. Julia is my neighbour. Her apartment is _____ mine.

a.	in	b.	on
c.	next to	d.	far from

19. There are a lot of trees _____ the River Nile. It's a nice view.

a.	on	b.	above
c.	over	d.	between

20. The student put his books _____ the table.

a.	over	b.	on
c.	across	d.	between

My Homework

Exercise Two
Choose the correct answer from a, b, c, or d.

1. Leila's sister told me she was _____ work.
a.	in	b.	on
c.	at	d.	under

2. Come _____ the kitchen. I will teach you how to cook.
a.	into	b.	on
c.	across	d.	under

3. Karim usually goes to school _____ his bicycle.
a.	into	b.	on
c.	between	d.	at

4. Sarah is sitting _____ Doha and Soha. She is in the middle.
a.	into	b.	by
c.	between	d.	at

5. When I called Tuka, she was _____ school.
a.	at	b.	on
c.	between	d.	under

6. Max is standing in front of the bank. It is _____ him.
a.	in	b.	behind
c.	through	d.	under

7. Arthur watched a nice movie _____ TV last night.
a.	in	b.	on
c.	across	d.	under

8. Henry is driving _____ the airport. His plane is going to take off in three hours.
a.	towards	b.	between
c.	above	d.	under

9. Boody lives _____ 4 Muhammad Reda Street, Maadi, Cairo.
a.	in	b.	on
c.	over	d.	at

10. I take a taxi to my school as it is _____ my house.
a.	above	b.	between
c.	far from	d.	in front of

11. There's a bus stop _____ our apartment building.
a.	over	b.	between
c.	in front of	d.	above

12. Keith is keen on listening to the news _____ the radio.
a.	in	b.	on
c.	at	d.	out

13. Be careful when you stand up. The light is _____ your head.
a.	above	b.	between
c.	in	d.	under

14. I first met my fiancée _____ the plane to New York.
a.	in	b.	on
c.	across	d.	under

15. My father usually keeps his wallet _____ the drawer of his desk.

a.	in	b.	between
c.	across	d.	over

16. This is my new friend Kim. I met him _____ the park a week ago.

a.	in	b.	on
c.	between	d.	over

17. Linda arrived _____ her office on time.

a.	in	b.	at
c.	for	d.	since

18. My grandmother is lying _____ her bed. She is very tired.

a.	over	b.	on
c.	above	d.	between

19. There are many nice drawings _____ the wall of Leila's room.

a.	at	b.	on
c.	between	d.	under

20. I read a good report about wars _____ the paper.

a.	in	b.	on
c.	across	d.	under

☙☙☙ My Homework ❧❧❧

> ## Exercise Three

✤ Choose the correct answer from a, b, c, or d.

1. I met my friend Muhammad _____ my way to school.

a.	in	b.	on
c.	about	d.	from

2. Adnan arrived _____ Toronto last night.

a.	in	b.	at
c.	for	d.	since

3. My sisters are going _____ the train station now.

a.	above	b.	to
c.	over	d.	under

4. Children mustn't go _____ the road alone.

a.	between	b.	across
c.	under	d.	in

5. The climbers went _____ the mountain and spent the night there.

a.	up	b.	at
c.	over	d.	between

6. My grandfather has never been _____ New Zealand.

a.	in	b.	at
c.	for	d.	to

7. Our new house is _____ the shopping mall.

a.	over	b.	opposite
c.	from	d.	between

8. The cat is running _____ the mice.

a.	after	b.	in
c.	for	d.	outside

9. The teacher is sitting _____ his students.

a.	between	b.	above
c.	over	d.	among

10. Ahmad studied IT _____ Loughborough University.

a.	at	b.	on
c.	in	d.	to

11. The police checked the cars that parked _____ the bank.

a.	in front of	b.	over
c.	to	d.	between

12. Greg went _____ the house and climbed up the stairs.

a.	out	b.	into
c.	over	d.	between

13. Shush! My cat is sleeping _____ the table.

a.	under	b.	over
c.	between	d.	through

14. The farmer walked _____ the field to look for the lost lamb.

a.	across	b.	under
c.	between	d.	above

15. My mother asked me to lock the door _____ me.

a.	behind	b.	under
c.	between	d.	through

16. I go to school on foot because it is _____ my house.

a.	far from	b.	between
c.	next to	d.	over

17. You can walk to the bank. It is very _____.

a.	next to	b.	near
c.	beside	d.	towards

18. My father is used to going _____ his office on foot.

a.	between	b.	for
c.	to	d.	above

19. My elder sister put a blanket _____ her sleeping kid because the room was too cold.

a.	to	b.	inside
c.	off	d.	over

20. The camera had fallen down _____ the seat and the desk.

a.	between	b.	through
c.	to	d.	above

🌸🌸🌸 My Homework 🌸🌸🌸

> ## Exercise Four
> ### Choose the correct answer from a, b, c, or d.

1. When I met my friends, they were heading _____ the club.

a.	above	b.	between
c.	below	d.	towards

2. The burglars crept into the villa _____ the kitchen window.

a.	between	b.	to
c.	through	d.	over

3. Mr Robin lives in the apartment _____ mine.

a.	above	b.	through
c.	into	d.	between

4. You will find the bank _____ the post office.

a.	between	b.	after
c.	through	d.	to

5. The teacher dismissed the naughty student _____ his class.

a.	outside	b.	into
c.	inside	d.	onto

6. It is raining heavily. Let's go _____ the house.

a.	inside	b.	from
c.	between	d.	along

7. My parents have a walk _____ the park every morning.

a.	between	b.	above
c.	along	d.	below

8. The child looked _____ the window and saw his mother coming.

a.	among	b.	out of
c.	in	d.	between

9. My grandmother feels happy when she sits _____ her grandkids. They enjoy playing and running around her.

a.	onto	b.	through
c.	among	d.	over

10. There is a wooden fence _____ my grandfather's house.

a.	around	b.	between
c.	through	d.	above

11. When we were in the restaurant, my wife sat on the other side of the table. She was _____ me.

a.	between	b.	among
c.	over	d.	opposite

12. The librarian moved the dictionaries _____ the first shelf as it is stronger.

a.	between	b.	among
c.	onto	d.	off

13. Please move this rock _____ the road. It may cause serious accidents.

a.	off	b.	over
c.	between	d.	among

14. When the child saw his mother, he sat _____ her.

a.	outside	b.	among
c.	between	d.	beside

15. Emily: Has the bus _____ Toronto arrived?
    Charles: Not yet.

a.	between	b.	from
c.	among	d.	opposite

16. My uncle has a beautiful house _____ the river.

a.	among	b.	inside
c.	by	d.	between

17. As soon as James jumped into the swimming pool, he dived _____ the surface of the water.

a.	below	b.	between
c.	beside	d.	among

18. My mother usually sits _____ us.

a.	outside	b.	inside
c.	close to	d.	along

19. While the shepherd was looking after his sheep, a large rock rolled _____ the hill and hit a lot of ewes and rams.

a.	among	b.	between
c.	down	d.	up

20. Be careful. A thief is walking straight _____ us.

a.	up	b.	down
c.	past	d.	over

🌿🌿🌿 My Homework 🍃🍃🍃

> ## Exercise Five
✤ Fill in the blanks with appropriate prepositions of place.
1. I can see a young woman _____ this picture.
2. Please sit _____ that chair over there. It's vacant.
3. My cat is lying _____ the floor.
4. Jerica is driving home _____ the hospital.
5. Go on walking and you'll find the bank _____ your right hand.
6. My parents are _____ work.
7. My mother put the pot _____ the stove to cook some rice.
8. A lot of passengers were sitting _____ the bus.
9. I usually keep my clothes _____ the cupboard.
10. My father took me _____ the farm.
11. A lot of workmen are working _____ the farm.
12. We study German and Italian _____ school.
13. The actors are appearing _____ stage right now.
14. There is a beautiful picture _____ the wall.

15. We have a lot of furniture _____ our house.
16. The robbers spent ten years _____ jail.
17. I think there is somebody _____ the door.
18. I met many tourists _____ the plane.
19. Dan is sitting _____ me. I'm in front of him.
20. The students walked _____ the classroom.

🕮🕮🕮 *My Homework* 🕮🕮🕮

Prepositions of Time

PREP.	USE	EXAMPLE
In	✦ centuries ✦ years ✦ seasons ✦ months ✦ parts of the day ✦ duration	in the twentieth century in the year 1564 in 1990 in the summer in November in Ramadan in the afternoon in the week in years
At	✦ clock times ✦ parts of the day ✦ meals ✦ religious festivals and celebrations ✦ some special expressions ✦ fixed phrases	at one o'clock at night at midnight at Christmas at Easter at Eid al-Fitr at Eid al-Adha at the time at the weekend at present at the moment at noon

		at the end of the year
		at that time
		at the beginning of
		at the end of
		at the age of
		at the same time
		at sunrise
		at sunset

PREP.	USE	EXAMPLE
On	✦ days of the week ✦ parts of special days ✦ special days ✦ dates ✦ special occasions ✦ special holidays ✦ a special part of a day	on Friday on Sundays on Sunday morning on New Year's Day on March 31st on the tenth of March on Batool's birthday on the morning of November the 19th on the weekend (American) on Good Friday on Easter Sunday
Until till	✦ up to the point in time	from the morning till night

After	↳ later than something, following something in time	after the game after school
Before	↳ earlier than something	before the lecture before Easter
From ... to	↳ from (time) to (time)	from Sunday to Friday
During	↳ all through a period of time	during the summer
Ago	↳ how far something happened (in the past)	ten years ago
Between	↳ time that separates two points	between Saturday and Tuesday
By	↳ no later than a special time	by Friday
for	↳ period of time	for five days
Past	↳ time of the day	seventeen minutes PAST four (4:17 a.m./p.m.)
Since	↳ point of time	since March
To	↳ time of the day	thirteen minutes TO seven (7:47 a.m./p.m.)
Up to	↳ not more than a special time	up to five hours a day
Within	↳ during a period of time	within a week

➢ *Exercise Six*
↳ Choose the correct answer from a, b, c, or d.
1. Shakespeare was born _____ the sixteenth century.

a.	in	b.	on
c.	from	d.	at

2. I usually get up _____ half past five.
a.	in	b.	on
c.	since	d.	at

3. We got married _____ 1991.
a.	in	b.	on
c.	since	d.	at

4. We usually go to the beach _____ the summer.
a.	in	b.	on
c.	at	d.	to

5. Muslims fast _____ Ramadan.
a.	for	b.	on
c.	in	d.	at

6. Jack moved to Paris _____ July.
a.	for	b.	on
c.	in	d.	at

7. Emily often watches TV _____ the evening.
a.	in	b.	on
c.	at	d.	about

8. I usually wake up _____ seven thirty.
a.	about	b.	at
c.	on	d.	in

9. Noah arrived there _____ six o'clock.
A.	in	b.	on
c.	since	d.	at

10. Lucas always has a rest _____ noon.
a.	after	b.	in
c.	at	d.	on

11. Ruby doesn't like to go out alone _____ night.
a.	on	b.	in
c.	at	d.	to

12. We usually go to the beach _____ Saturday.
a.	in	b.	on
c.	to	d.	at

13. Boody was born _____ October 18.
a.	to	b.	at
c.	in	d.	on

14. Andrew usually goes to the library _____ the afternoon.
a.	to	b.	at
c.	in	d.	on

15. Last night, Jane woke up _____ midnight to finish a report.
a.	at	b.	to
c.	in	d.	on

16. We usually start our new school year _____ September.
a.	in	b.	on
c.	at	d.	to

17. I often visit my grandparents _____ Friday.

a.	at	b.	on
c.	to	d.	in

18. I will celebrate my birthday _____ the 19th of November.

a.	in	b.	on
c.	at	d.	for

19. The girls are going to visit their aunt _____ the weekend.

a.	in	b.	at
c.	about	d.	from

20. Ahmad was born _____ 1992.

a.	in	b.	from
c.	at	d.	on

❧❧❧ My Homework ❧❧❧

➢ **Exercise Seven**

✦ Choose the correct answer from a, b, c, or d.

1. There are extra flights to Cairo _____ the winter.

a.	on	b.	at
c.	in	d.	from

2. I am going to meet my friends _____ the evening.

a.	in	b.	on
c.	to	d.	at

3. I am going to start my new course _____ the first of May.

a.	for	b.	at
c.	on	d.	in

4. Dr Ibrahim has been living in London _____ fifteen years.

a.	in	b.	on
c.	across	d.	for

5. We waited for the dentist _____ 9:15 a.m. until 10:35 a.m.

a.	at	b.	on
c.	from	d.	under

6. Lilly started her career as a teacher _____ the 1990s.

a.	in	b.	on
c.	at	d.	between

7. My aunt visited us three weeks _____.

a.	during	b.	ago
c.	at	d.	on

8. We will go on working _____ night.

a.	in	b.	on
c.	until	d.	between

9. I am going to meet my friends _____ sunset.

a.	on	b.	in
c.	at	d.	ago

10. My relatives will gather in my grandfather's house _____ Easter.

a.	on	b.	in
c.	at	d.	ago

11. This task will have been finished _____ Friday.

a.	by	b.	in
c.	at	d.	ago

12. We go to school _____ Monday to Friday.

a.	on	b.	at
c.	for	d.	from

13. We are going to stay in our farmhouse _____ the summer.

a.	on	b.	at
c.	between	d.	during

14. Our new course will start _____ April.

a.	until	b.	between
c.	before	d.	ago

15. It may stop raining _____ midnight.

a.	between	b.	ago
c.	on	d.	after

16. We are going to have a nice party _____ our mother's birthday.

a.	in	b.	on
c.	ago	d.	at

17. It's sixteen minutes _____ five. The match is going to start at five thirty.

a.	past	b.	on
c.	at	d.	in

18. My grandfather is active. He usually works _____ ten hours a day.

a.	past	b.	on
c.	at	d.	for

19. My uncle is going to come back from Madrid _____ a week.

a.	past	b.	within
c.	at	d.	since

20. We have lived in this small apartment _____ March.

a.	between	b.	on
c.	at	d.	since

My Homework

➢ *Exercise Eight*

✦ Correct the mistakes in the following sentences.

1. The movie lasted at three in the morning.

   ➤ _____ _____ _____ _____ _____ _____ _____ _____ _____ _____

2. I have lived in Rome since five years.

   ➤ _____ _____ _____ _____ _____ _____ _____ _____ _____ _____

3. My parents travelled to Ankara in train.
✎ _____ _____ _____ _____ _____ _____ _____ _____ _____

4. Paul is busy. He is working at his computer.
✎ _____ _____ _____ _____ _____ _____ _____ _____ _____

5. You can find a lot of information in the Internet.
✎ _____ _____ _____ _____ _____ _____ _____ _____ _____

6. Charlotte is driving at the country. She'll be there in an hour.
✎ _____ _____ _____ _____ _____ _____ _____ _____ _____

7. I can see a lot of birds on the tree.
✎ _____ _____ _____ _____ _____ _____ _____ _____ _____

8. There are a lot of lovely roses on our garden.
✎ _____ _____ _____ _____ _____ _____ _____ _____ _____

9. The manager was tired, so he fell asleep on the meeting.
✎ _____ _____ _____ _____ _____ _____ _____ _____ _____

10. Before you write the email, forward it.
✎ _____ _____ _____ _____ _____ _____ _____ _____ _____

11. We go to school from Sunday in Thursday.
✎ _____ _____ _____ _____ _____ _____ _____ _____ _____

12. I always study math at 9:30 a.m. to 11:30 a.m.
✎ _____ _____ _____ _____ _____ _____ _____ _____ _____

13. I will wait on the meeting finishes.
✎ _____ _____ _____ _____ _____ _____ _____ _____ _____

14. You should review your homework after giving it to your teacher.
✎ _____ _____ _____ _____ _____ _____ _____ _____ _____

15. My grandfather spends his free time in the farm.
✎ _____ _____ _____ _____ _____ _____ _____ _____ _____

16. The children jumped under the fence of the garden.
✎ _____ _____ _____ _____ _____ _____ _____ _____ _____

17. Please put these books in the top shelf over there.
✎ _____ _____ _____ _____ _____ _____ _____ _____ _____

18. I usually keep my purse above my handbag.
✎ _____ _____ _____ _____ _____ _____ _____ _____ _____

19. My school is not far from my house. I often go there in foot.
✎ _____ _____ _____ _____ _____ _____ _____ _____ _____

20. I am going to take a shower in breakfast.
✎ _____ _____ _____ _____ _____ _____ _____ _____ _____

21. Hurry up, please. The bus is leaving on half an hour.
✎ _____ _____ _____ _____ _____ _____ _____ _____ _____

22. We don't have time. The office closes on 2:45 p.m.
🌿 ___ ___ ___ ___ ___ ___ ___ ___ ___ ___

23. I'm planning to visit my parents on Easter.
🌿 ___ ___ ___ ___ ___ ___ ___ ___ ___

24. I dislike my classmates visiting me at the week.
🌿 ___ ___ ___ ___ ___ ___ ___ ___ ___

25. Millions of birds migrate south on winter.
🌿 ___ ___ ___ ___ ___ ___ ___ ___ ___

❧❧❧ My Homework ❧❧❧

➢ *Exercise Nine*

✢ Correct the mistakes in each of the following sentences.

1. Alexander Graham Bell was born at 1847.
🌿 ___ ___ ___ ___ ___ ___ ___ ___ ___

2. They left the campsite in the sixth of October.
🌿 ___ ___ ___ ___ ___ ___ ___ ___ ___

3. In Christmas, we visit our relatives and friends.
🌿 ___ ___ ___ ___ ___ ___ ___ ___ ___

4. In Saturday mornings, I walk to my office.
🌿 ___ ___ ___ ___ ___ ___ ___ ___ ___

5. My elder sister was born on 1994.
🌿 ___ ___ ___ ___ ___ ___ ___ ___ ___

6. My brother was born in the thirteenth of March.
🌿 ___ ___ ___ ___ ___ ___ ___ ___ ___

7. My father goes at work at 6:15 a.m.
🌿 ___ ___ ___ ___ ___ ___ ___ ___ ___

8. Oliver and Jaxon live at Main Street.
🌿 ___ ___ ___ ___ ___ ___ ___ ___ ___

9. Sam travelled to Toronto on plane.
🌿 ___ ___ ___ ___ ___ ___ ___ ___ ___

10. Andrew lives on 19 King Arthur Street.
🌿 ___ ___ ___ ___ ___ ___ ___ ___ ___

11. I took the train at Tokyo an hour ago.
🌿 ___ ___ ___ ___ ___ ___ ___ ___ ___

12. My children played on the garden for a long time.
🌿 ___ ___ ___ ___ ___ ___ ___ ___ ___

13. Marwa was sitting in Tuka and Batool.
🌿 ___ ___ ___ ___ ___ ___ ___ ___ ___

14. I usually leave my office on 3:35 p.m.
🖎 _____ _____ _____ _____ _____ _____ _____ _____ _____

15. We spent much time waiting in the doctor.
🖎 _____ _____ _____ _____ _____ _____ _____ _____ _____

16. My father works up a famous drilling company in the Gulf.
🖎 _____ _____ _____ _____ _____ _____ _____ _____ _____

17. We sometimes go fishing in Saturday.
🖎 _____ _____ _____ _____ _____ _____ _____ _____ _____

18. My mother stopped working in midnight.
🖎 _____ _____ _____ _____ _____ _____ _____ _____ _____

19. My uncle is going to build a wooden fence with his house.
🖎 _____ _____ _____ _____ _____ _____ _____ _____ _____

20. The television was invented on the twentieth century.
🖎 _____ _____ _____ _____ _____ _____ _____ _____ _____

21. The employees are going to have lunch on the cafeteria.
🖎 _____ _____ _____ _____ _____ _____ _____ _____ _____

22. The conference is going to finish on ten minutes.
🖎 _____ _____ _____ _____ _____ _____ _____ _____ _____

23. We always dream of living on the countryside.
🖎 _____ _____ _____ _____ _____ _____ _____ _____ _____

24. We have been learning math for February.
🖎 _____ _____ _____ _____ _____ _____ _____ _____ _____

25. Sandra has been working on this plan since a long time.
🖎 _____ _____ _____ _____ _____ _____ _____ _____ _____

🖎🖎🖎 *My Homework* 🖎🖎🖎

SECTION 5

Auxiliary Verbs

Verb *to be* (in the present tense)

Affirmative

I	am
He, she, it	is
You, they, we	are

Negative

I	am not ('m not)
He, she, it	is not (isn't)
You, they, we	are not (aren't)

Examples:

- I am at home.
- My wife is worried.
- We are married.

> *Exercise One*

Complete the sentences. Use 'm, not, isn't, or aren't:

1. I _____ a student.
2. Mr Charles _____ a policeman.
3. I _____ from England.
4. Mrs Alice _____ a housewife.
5. We _____ Lebanese.
6. Edward and George _____ brothers.
7. Ruby and Isabella _____ sisters.
8. My father _____ an active teacher.
9. My uncles _____ very kind.
10. My mother _____ an engineer.
11. My aunts _____ helpful.

12. A lemon _____ sour.
13. My pencil _____ new.
14. My uncle's car _____ powerful.
15. This house _____ large.
16. These houses _____ very old.
17. This farm _____ very big.
18. These oranges _____ tasty.
19. Shikabala and Ikramy _____ good football players.
20. Madrid and Stockholm _____ famous European cities.

🕮🕮🕮 My Homework 🕮🕮🕮

➢ *Exercise Two*
  ✤ Complete the sentences. Use *am*, *is*, or *are*.
1. I _____ Canadian.
2. My roommate _____ friendly.
3. My friends _____ active.
4. My little sister _____ beautiful.
5. This man _____ smart.
6. These books _____ new.
7. Airplanes _____ fast.
8. Swimming _____ enjoyable.
9. Football and handball _____ team sports.
10. My old computer _____ out of order.
11. I _____ a schoolboy.
12. My sister _____ a university student.
13. We _____ in the same school.
14. My brother _____ a doctor.
15. My aunt _____ a teacher.
16. This _____ my pencil.
17. My friends _____ helpful.
18. The cat _____ hungry.
19. This iPhone _____ new.
20. Hanna _____ a doctor in a famous hospital.

🕮🕮🕮 My Homework 🕮🕮🕮

➢ *Exercise Three*
  ✤ Complete the sentences. Use *am*, *is*, or *are*.
1. The boys _____ in the park now.
2. This _____ a fast car.
3. A plane _____ faster than a train.

4. I _____ from Amman.
5. Mr Lucas _____ French.
6. The tourists _____ from Italy.
7. Korea _____ an Asian country.
8. Korea and Japan _____ Asian countries.
9. Camels _____ desert animals.
10. The lion _____ a wild animal.
11. Cats _____ domestic animals.
12. Mr Sam _____ an active teacher.
13. We _____ from Singapore.
14. Axel _____ from Australia.
15. Mr Taro and his wife _____ from Japan.
16. They _____ careful drivers.
17. These _____ my shoes.
18. The Philippines _____ an Asian country.
19. Physics _____ my favourite subject.
20. Gymnastics _____ important for us.

My Homework

> ## Exercise Four
> Choose the correct answer from a, b, c, or d.

1. I _____ a police officer.

a.	is	b.	be
c.	are	d.	am

2. Mr Jeff _____ a German engineer.

a.	is	b.	be
c.	are	d.	am

3. The men _____ in the garden.

a.	is	b.	be
c.	are	d.	am

4. The little dog _____ in its small house.

a.	is	b.	be
c.	are	d.	am

5. We _____ hungry.

a.	is	b.	be
c.	are	d.	am

6. You _____ Mr Scott.

a.	is	b.	be
c.	are	d.	am

7. Jeannette _____ in her class.

a.	is	b.	be
c.	are	d.	am

8. Thomas and Toby _____ not active.

a.	is	b.	be
c.	are	d.	am

9. Marawan _____ a good student.

a.	is	b.	be
c.	are	d.	am

10. Emma and Grace _____ good students.

a.	is	b.	be
c.	are	d.	am

11. Kim and Dalia _____ friends.

a.	is	b.	be
c.	are	d.	am

12. This _____ my father.

a.	is	b.	be
c.	are	d.	am

13. That _____ a yellow car.

a.	is	b.	be
c.	are	d.	am

14. Who _____ the best boy in this class?

a.	is	b.	be
c.	are	d.	am

15. Where _____ your books?

a.	is	b.	be
c.	are	d.	am

16. Who _____ taller? Osama or Omar?

a.	is	b.	be
c.	are	d.	am

17. Today _____ Thursday.

a.	is	b.	be
c.	are	d.	am

18. Summer _____ usually hot in many countries.

a.	is	b.	be
c.	are	d.	am

19. The sky _____ clear today.

a.	is	b.	be
c.	are	d.	am

20. Helen _____ a policewoman.

a.	is	b.	be
c.	are	d.	am

My Homework

➤ **Exercise Five**

✦ Complete the sentences. Use *am*, *is*, or *are*.

1. Daniel and I _____ pupils.

a.	is	b.	be
c.	are	d.	am

2. I _____ taller than Sam.

a.	is	b.	be
c.	are	d.	am

3. They _____ in class.

a.	is	b.	be
c.	are	d.	am

4. The clouds _____ grey.

a.	is	b.	be
c.	are	d.	am

5. The stars _____ bright.

a.	is	b.	be
c.	are	d.	am

6. It _____ ten o'clock.

a.	is	b.	be
c.	are	d.	am

7. We _____ friends.

a.	is	b.	be
c.	are	d.	am

8. This classroom _____ big.

a.	is	b.	be
c.	are	d.	am

9. The doors _____ closed.

a.	is	b.	be
c.	are	d.	am

10. This _____ the last sentence.

a.	is	b.	be
c.	are	d.	am

🙞🙞🙞 *My Homework* 🙜🙜🙜

➤ **Exercise Six**

✦ Complete the sentences. Use *am not*, *isn't*, or *aren't*.

1. I _____ late.
2. This car _____ new.
3. We _____ Japanese.
4. My father _____ a pilot.
5. They _____ at school.
6. We _____ on the farm.
7. I _____ football player.

8. My teachers _____ lazy.
9. Lolo and her sister _____ from Canada.
10. Roses _____ ugly.
11. Russia _____ hot in summer.
12. Kuwait _____ an African country.
13. Middlesbrough _____ a small English town.
14. Tokyo _____ a dirty city.
15. Makkah and Riyadh _____ African cities.
16. Lemons _____ sweet.
17. Our flat _____ big.
18. Cairo _____ a coastal city.
19. Algeria and Tunisia _____ Asian countries.
20. Swimming _____ boring.

🖎🖎🖎 *My Homework* 🖎🖎🖎

> ➢ *Exercise Seven*
> ✦ Correct the mistake in each of the following sentences.

1. I is a businessman.
🖎 ____ ____ ____ ____ ____ ____ ____ ____ ____ ____

2. Holly are a good girl.
🖎 ____ ____ ____ ____ ____ ____ ____ ____ ____ ____

3. We am firemen.
🖎 ____ ____ ____ ____ ____ ____ ____ ____ ____ ____

4. He are happy.
🖎 ____ ____ ____ ____ ____ ____ ____ ____ ____ ____

5. Stella am a doctor.
🖎 ____ ____ ____ ____ ____ ____ ____ ____ ____ ____

6. It are my smartphone.
🖎 ____ ____ ____ ____ ____ ____ ____ ____ ____ ____

7. They is pupils.
🖎 ____ ____ ____ ____ ____ ____ ____ ____ ____ ____

8. You am my teacher.
🖎 ____ ____ ____ ____ ____ ____ ____ ____ ____ ____

9. She are not my sister.
🖎 ____ ____ ____ ____ ____ ____ ____ ____ ____ ____

10. They is not at school.
🖎 ____ ____ ____ ____ ____ ____ ____ ____ ____ ____

11. He am not sad.
🖎 ____ ____ ____ ____ ____ ____ ____ ____ ____ ____

12. We is not at home.
🖎 ____ ____ ____ ____ ____ ____ ____ ____ ____ ____

13. It are not a cat.
🐭 ___ ___ ___ ___ ___ ___ ___ ___ ___

14. You am not at work.
🐭 ___ ___ ___ ___ ___ ___ ___ ___ ___

15. They am not on the farm.
🐭 ___ ___ ___ ___ ___ ___ ___ ___ ___

16. Maya am not my aunt.
🐭 ___ ___ ___ ___ ___ ___ ___ ___ ___

17. I are not lazy.
🐭 ___ ___ ___ ___ ___ ___ ___ ___ ___

18. We am not naughty.
🐭 ___ ___ ___ ___ ___ ___ ___ ___ ___

19. My computer are not slow.
🐭 ___ ___ ___ ___ ___ ___ ___ ___ ___

20. This plane are not cheap.
🐭 ___ ___ ___ ___ ___ ___ ___ ___ ___

🐭🐭🐭 *My Homework* 🐭🐭🐭

Yes/no questions with verb *to be* in the present tense

Am	I	?
Yes,	you	are.
No,	you	aren't.

Is	he, she, it	............?
Yes,	he, she, it	is.
No,	he, she, it	isn't.

Are	you	?
Yes,	I	am.
No,	I	'm not.

Yes,	we	are.
No,	we	aren't.

Are	they	?

Yes,	they	are.
No,	they	aren't.

Are	we	?

Yes,	you	are.
No,	you	aren't.

Are	we	?

Yes,	we	are.
No,	we	aren't.

♦ Examples:

➢ **Mark**: Are you American?
   Nancy: Yes, I am.

➢ **Fred**: Is your sister married?
   Tony: No, she isn't.

➢ *Exercise Eight*
   ♦ Rearrange these words to form meaningful questions.
   ♦ Follow the example.
   ➢ **Ashly**: / Diana / home / Is / at /
   ✓ **Ashly**: Is Diana at home?

   Sienna: Yes, she is.

🖎____ ____ ____ ____ ____ ____ ____ ____ ____ ____

1. / the / Are / students / late /
   No, they aren't.

🖎____ ____ ____ ____ ____ ____ ____ ____ ____ ____

2. / I / Am / mistaken /
No, you aren't.
✍ _____

3. / the / the / on / Are / farmers / farm /
Yes, they are.
✍ _____

4. / Basim / active / Is / player / an /
Yes, he is.
✍ _____

5. / happy / she / Is /
No, she isn't.
✍ _____

6. / they / Are / sad /
Yes, they are.
✍ _____

7. / hot / it / today / Is /
Yes, it is.
✍ _____

8. / Ivy / absent / Is /
No, she isn't.
✍ _____

9. / Khalid / Is / present /
Yes, he is.
✍ _____

10. / Lola / class / Is / today / in /
Yes, she is.
✍ _____

11. / France / Is / Mary / from /
Yes, she is.
✍ _____

12. / home / Are / you / at /
Yes, I am.
✍ _____

13. / in / they / Are / hurry / a /
No, they aren't.
✍ _____

14. / work / they / Are / at /
Yes, they are.

✿✿✿ My Homework ✿✿✿

➤ **Exercise Nine**

✦ Choose the correct answer from a, b, c, or d.

1. Judi: Are you a student?
➤ Jana: Yes, _____.

a.	you are	b.	I am
c.	she is	d.	are you

2. Mahmoud: Are the boys at home?
➤ Saleh: Yes, _____.

a.	they are	b.	are they
c.	aren't they	d.	they aren't

3. Alan: Is your uncle on the farm?
➤ Stephen: Yes, _____.

a.	he is	b.	my uncle
c.	is he	d.	your uncle

4. Mother: Are your sisters in the kitchen?
➤ Lilly: Yes, _____.

a.	she is	b.	are they
c.	she is	d.	they are

5. John: Am I on the right way, sir?
➤ William: No, _____.

a.	you are	b.	you aren't
c.	are you	d.	I am not

6. Lee: Are you new students?
➤ Andrew: No, _____.

a.	we aren't	b.	we are
c.	you aren't	d.	are you

7. Yazan: Is Alexis from Canada?
➤ Ibrahim: No, _____.

a.	Alexis is	b.	is he
c.	he isn't	d.	he is

8. Ali: Am I active in class, sir?
➤ Wesam: No, _____.

a.	you are	b.	you aren't
c.	I'm not	d.	are you

9. Ahmad: Are Omar and Austin absent?
➤ Tuka: No, _____.

a.	they are	b.	are they
c.	they aren't	d.	are you

10. Batool: Is Indie hungry?
➤ Abdul-Rahman: No, _____.

a.	isn't she	b.	she is
c.	she isn't	d.	Indie isn't

11. George: Are you thirsty?
➢ Lara: No, _____.

| a. | you are | b. | I'm not |
| c. | am I | d. | I am |

12. Sara: Is Alyssa from Germany?
➢ Yara: Yes, _____.

| a. | Alyssa is | b. | she isn't |
| c. | she is | d. | is she |

13. Layan: Is Zahra at home?
➢ Salma: Yes, _____.

| a. | Zahra is | b. | Zahra isn't |
| c. | she is | d. | is she |

14. Samah: Are you in the park?
➢ Yaseen: Yes, _____.

| a. | you are | b. | I am |
| c. | she is | d. | are you |

15. Maha: Are you in grade six?
➢ Juri: No, _____.

| a. | I'm not | b. | you are |
| c. | I am | d. | are you |

16. Michael: Are your brothers active students?
➢ Asaad: Yes, _____.

| a. | you are | b. | they are |
| c. | he is | d. | are you |

17. Merna: Is Ayman a good player?
➢ Lamya: Yes, _____.

| a. | he is | b. | he isn't |
| c. | my cousin is | d. | is he |

18. Manal: Are you an engineer?
➢ Kevin: Yes, _____.

| a. | you are | b. | I am |
| c. | he is | d. | are you |

19. Omar: Is your car new?
➢ David: Yes, _____.

| a. | I am | b. | it is |
| c. | it isn't | d. | is it |

20. Jade: Are these buses old?
➢ Emily: Yes, _____.

| a. | they are | b. | they aren't |
| c. | are they | d. | are you |

21. Maya: Is it hot in Dubai in summer?
➢ Hana: Yes, _____.

| a. | Dubai is | b. | it is |
| c. | it isn't | d. | is it |

22. Hafiz: Am I reading well?
➤ Sonya: Yes, _____.

a.	you are	b.	I am
c.	she is	d.	are you

23. Osama: Am I walking slowly?
➤ Seif: No, _____.

a.	you are	b.	I am
c.	she is	d.	you aren't

24. Kris: Is Shakespeare a famous poet?
➤ Christina: Yes, _____.

a.	Shakespeare is	b.	is he
c.	he is	d.	he isn't

25. Carl: Is Cairo an Arab city?
➤ Dale: Yes, _____.

a.	Cairo is	b.	is it
c.	it isn't	d.	it is

26. Hatem: Is Ronaldo a famous football player?
➤ Kareem: Yes, _____.

a.	you are	b.	I am
c.	he is	d.	are you

27. Muhammad: Is Budapest an African city?
➤ Abraham: No, _____.

a.	Budapest is	b.	it is
c.	it isn't	d.	is it

28. Nelson: Are your friends helpful?
➤ Nataly: : Yes, _____.

a.	are they	b.	they are
c.	he is	d.	they aren't

29. Madiha: Are Ahmad and Saleh present?
➤ Saker: Yes, _____.

a.	are they	b.	they are
c.	he is	d.	they aren't

30. Malik: Is Margret a self-motivated girl?
➤ Sagid: Yes, _____.

a.	she is	b.	Margret is
c.	she isn't	d.	is she

My Homework

Auxiliary Verbs — Verb *to be* (in the past tense)

Affirmative

I, he, she, it	was
You, they, we	were

Negative

I, He, she, it	was not (wasn't)
You, they, we	were not (weren't)

+ Examples:

- I was in class an hour ago.
- We were at home when you called.

Yes/no questions with verb *to be* in the past tense

Was	I, he, she, it	?
Were	you, they, we	

Wasn't	I, he, she, it	?
Weren't	you, they, we	

Affirmative Answer

Yes,	I, he, she, it	was.
	you, they, we	were.

Negative Answer

No,	I, he, she, it	wasn't.
	you, they, we	weren't.

Examples:

> **Fred**: Were you in the cinema last night?
> **Daniel**: Yes, I was.

> **Gary**: Were your parents in Athens last week?
> **Yuan**: No, they weren't.

> *Exercise Ten*

Choose the correct answer from a, b, c, or d.

1. Jessica and Linda _____ asleep in the classroom.

a.	was	b.	be
c.	weren't	d.	wasn't

2. Hardy _____ tired last night.

a.	was	b.	weren't
c.	were	d.	be

3. Howard _____ on the farm yesterday.

a.	were	b.	are
c.	weren't	d.	was

4. Michael and his family _____ at home.

a.	was	b.	isn't
c.	were	d.	wasn't

5. Three lions _____ in the cage.

a.	were	b.	is
c.	isn't	d.	wasn't

6. The baby _____ in its cradle.

a.	was	b.	weren't
c.	were	d.	be

7. My mobile phone _____ lost.

a.	were	b.	are
c.	weren't	d.	was

8. My sisters _____ at the party.

a.	was	b.	weren't
c.	wasn't	d.	is

9. Where _____ you at five thirty yesterday?

a.	were	b.	are
c.	was	d.	wasn't

10. This time last year, we _____ in Paris.

a.	was	b.	were
c.	are	d.	wasn't

11. Teacher: When were you born?
    Lama: I _____ born in 1999.

a.	weren't	b.	am
c.	were	d.	was

12. The hotel _____ near the airport.

a.	are	b.	was
c.	were	d.	weren't

13. My brother _____ at home.

a.	were	b.	are
c.	weren't	d.	wasn't

14. Harry and his wife _____ in Madrid last Monday.

a.	was	b.	weren't
c.	wasn't	d.	is

15. Who _____ that man talking to our teacher earlier?

a.	were	b.	are
c.	weren't	d.	was

16. Alan: _____ you in the park with your children?
    Paul: No, I wasn't.

a.	Wasn't	b.	Weren't
c.	Was	d.	Aren't

17. Secretary: _____ there any mistakes in my email?
    Boss: No, there weren't.

a.	Were	b.	Are
c.	Was	d.	Wasn't

18. Jeffery: _____ Alan and Dane at the seaside last Sunday?
    Theresa: Yes, they were.

a.	Was	b.	Are
c.	Were	d.	Is

19. Charles Dickens _____ an English writer.

a.	were	b.	are
c.	weren't	d.	was

20. Teacher: _____ the quiz easy?
    Donald: Sure, sir.

a.	Was	b.	Weren't
c.	Were	d.	Are

My Homework

➢ *Exercise Eleven*
✦ Complete the sentences. Use *was* or *were*.

1. Jason _____ in London last week.
2. Evans and Clark _____ at the ticket office.
3. Garcia _____ very busy.
4. My parents _____ in Melbourne yesterday.
5. My children _____ on the beach this afternoon.
6. Karin _____ in the mall an hour ago.
7. Liza and Chelsea _____ in the computer lab.
8. The students _____ in the test room.
9. We _____ in the cafeteria.
10. Tuka _____ very happy this morning.
11. There _____ a lot of patients at the clinic.
12. There _____ an accident on the road to my city.
13. That _____ a wrong answer.
14. The camels _____ thirsty.
15. We _____ very happy when we visited Frankfurt.
16. My parents _____ angry.
17. The stars _____ bright last night.
18. The weather _____ cold last week.
19. We _____ at the movies.
20. Layla _____ born in 1990.

My Homework

➢ *Exercise Twelve*
✦ Change the sentences to the past tense. Follow the example.
➢ Lewis is at school today.
✓ Lewis was at school yesterday too.
1. Julia is absent today.
✍ ____ ____ ____ ____ ____ ____ ____ ____ ____ ____ ____
2. The teachers are in their offices today.
✍ ____ ____ ____ ____ ____ ____ ____ ____ ____ ____ ____
3. The engineers are in the workshop today.
✍ ____ ____ ____ ____ ____ ____ ____ ____ ____ ____ ____
4. The farmer is in the village market today.
✍ ____ ____ ____ ____ ____ ____ ____ ____ ____ ____ ____
5. The mechanics are in their workshop today.
✍ ____ ____ ____ ____ ____ ____ ____ ____ ____ ____ ____
6. The workmen are in the factory today.
✍ ____ ____ ____ ____ ____ ____ ____ ____ ____ ____ ____

7. Alice is in Kuala Lampur today.
☙ ____ ____ ____ ____ ____ ____ ____ ____ ____

8. The students are active today.
☙ ____ ____ ____ ____ ____ ____ ____ ____ ____

9. I am in China today.
☙ ____ ____ ____ ____ ____ ____ ____ ____ ____

10. Heidi is late today.
☙ ____ ____ ____ ____ ____ ____ ____ ____ ____

11. Holly isn't at the bank today.
☙ ____ ____ ____ ____ ____ ____ ____ ____ ____

12. My parents are tired today.
☙ ____ ____ ____ ____ ____ ____ ____ ____ ____

13. Safia is lazy today.
☙ ____ ____ ____ ____ ____ ____ ____ ____ ____

14. The students are in the classroom today.
☙ ____ ____ ____ ____ ____ ____ ____ ____ ____

15. Evelyn and her sister are at the club today.
☙ ____ ____ ____ ____ ____ ____ ____ ____ ____

16. Jacob is alert today.
☙ ____ ____ ____ ____ ____ ____ ____ ____ ____

17. Boody and Ahmad are awake tonight.
☙ ____ ____ ____ ____ ____ ____ ____ ____ ____

18. Salma and Layan are lively today.
☙ ____ ____ ____ ____ ____ ____ ____ ____ ____

19. The policemen are watchful tonight.
☙ ____ ____ ____ ____ ____ ____ ____ ____ ____

20. Max is tardy today.
☙ ____ ____ ____ ____ ____ ____ ____ ____ ____

❧❧❧ My Homework ❧❧❧

> ## Exercise Thirteen
> ✦ Choose the correct answer from a, b, c, or d.

1. Was Sherif late for the meeting?
   No, he _____.

a.	was	b.	wasn't
c.	is	d.	isn't

2. Was the child naughty?
   Yes, _____.

a.	he wasn't	b.	was he
c.	he was	d.	the child was

3. Were the teachers helpful?
   Yes, _____.

a.	they were	b.	were they
c.	they weren't	d.	they are

4. Were the students in the library?
   No, _____.

a.	they weren't	b.	they were
c.	the students weren't	d.	were they

5. Were the drivers careful?
   Yes, _____.

a.	they weren't	b.	they were
c.	was he	d.	were they

6. Was the nurse helpful?
   Yes, _____.

a.	was she	b.	the nurse was
c.	she wasn't	d.	she was

7. Were you at college in Mexico?
   Yes, I _____.

a.	were	b.	am
c.	was	d.	were

8. Were the birds in the tree?
   Yes, _____.

a.	they were	b.	was he
c.	he was	d.	the child was

9. Was the road busy?
   No, it _____.

a.	was	b.	wasn't
c.	are	d.	is

10. Were you at school this morning?
    Yes, _____.

a.	we were at	b.	we were
c.	I wasn't	d.	were we

🌸🌸🌸 My Homework 🌸🌸🌸

There is / There are

Affirmative

There is	+ a singular noun
There is	+ an uncountable noun
There are	+ a plural noun

Examples:

- There is a sparrow in the tree.
- There are some hens over there.

> **Exercise Fourteen**

Complete the sentences. Use *There is, There are*.

1. _____ one student in the lab.
2. _____ two students in the library.
3. _____ many trees in the park.
4. _____ a few books on the table.
5. _____ some milk in the glass.
6. _____ some boys on the street.
7. _____ a banana on the table.
8. _____ an apple in the basket.
9. _____ some girls in the kitchen.
10. _____ some passengers on the bus.
11. _____ some tea in the cup.
12. _____ a lot of pens in my case.
13. _____ a lot of money in his wallet.
14. _____ five fingers in my hand.
15. _____ eleven players in a football team.
16. _____ many cars in the parking lot.
17. _____ much sugar in my tea.
18. _____ millions of stars in the sky.
19. _____ hundreds of TV channels these days.
20. _____ thousands of students at Helwan University.
21. _____ many wild animals in this forest.
22. _____ twelve months in a year.
23. _____ sixty seconds in a minute.

24. _____ some ice cream cones in the fridge.
25. _____ an owl in the garden.
26. _____ an accident on the road to the farm.
27. _____ a lot of factories near our city.
28. _____ a large university near the airport.
29. _____ a lot of water springs in this oasis.
30. _____ thirty sentences in this exercise.

Negative

There isn't	a / an	+ a singular noun
There isn't	any	+ an uncountable noun
There aren't	any	+ a plural noun

✦ **Examples:**
 ➢ There isn't any smoke in the room.
 ➢ There aren't any books on the desk.

➢ *Exercise Fifteen*
 ✦ Complete the sentences. Use *There isn't, There aren't.*
1. _____ an apartment for rent.
2. _____ any students in the playground.
3. _____ any juice in the jug.
4. _____ a book on the table.
5. _____ any pens on the desk.
6. _____ any boys in the pool.
7. _____ any money in my bank account.
8. _____ any water in this well.
9. _____ any people in the park.
10. _____ any oil in the pan.

✎✎✎ *My Homework* ✐✐✐

Exercise Sixteen

✦ Choose the correct answer from a, b, c, or d.

1. Is there any juice in this glass?
   Yes, _____.

a.	there is	b.	there are
c.	is there	d.	there isn't

2. Is there any milk in the bottle?
   No, _____.

a.	there is	b.	there are
c.	is there	d.	there isn't

3. Are there any clothes in your cupboard?
   No, _____.

a.	there aren't	b.	there are
c.	is there	d.	there isn't

4. Are there any cars outside?
   No, _____.

a.	there is	b.	there are
c.	there aren't	d.	there isn't

5. Is there any money in your bank account?
   Yes, _____.

a.	there is	b.	there are
c.	is there	d.	there isn't

6. Are there any pictures on the wall?
   Yes, _____.

a.	there are	b.	there is
c.	is there	d.	there isn't

7. Are there any people in the park?
   No, _____.

a.	there is	b.	there isn't
c.	is there	d.	there aren't

8. Is there a policeman near the bank?
   Yes, _____.

a.	is there	b.	there was
c.	there is	d.	there isn't

9. Are there any firemen near the building?
   Yes, _____.

a.	there is	b.	are there
c.	there are	d.	there isn't

10. Is there any food left?
    Yes, _____.

a.	there is	b.	there are
c.	is there	d.	there isn't

There was / There were

Affirmative

There was	+ a singular noun
There was	+ an uncountable noun
There were	+ a plural noun

Negative

There wasn't	+ a singular noun
There wasn't	+ an uncountable noun
There weren't	+ a plural noun

Examples:
- Last night, there was a burglar in our neighbour's house.
- Yesterday, there were many employees in the meeting.

Exercise Seventeen
Complete the sentences. Use *there was, there were*.

1. _____ an accident near the city last night.
2. Yesterday, _____ a lot of animals on the farm.
3. _____ a lot of audience in the theatre.
4. Yesterday, _____ many fans in the stadium.
5. _____ a boy at the door.
6. _____ a lot of rain last night.
7. _____ an accident on the road to the airport.
8. Yesterday, _____ ten students in the computer lab.
9. _____ two pairs of glasses on the table.
10. _____ many people at the party.

My Homework

Exercise Eighteen
Complete the sentences. Use *there wasn't, there weren't*.

1. _____ any cold water in the fridge.
2. _____ any money in my wallet.

3. _____ any teachers in the room an hour ago.
4. _____ any children in the living room.
5. When I looked out of the window, _____ any stars in the sky.
6. Last night, _____ any action movies on TV.
7. _____ an earthquake in Indonesia last year.
8. _____ any people at the museum.
9. _____ any mistakes in your homework.
10. I phoned Saleh, but _____ anybody at home.
11. _____ any oranges left on the table.
12. _____ any oil in the bottle.
13. _____ any pencils in my case.
14. _____ much fog this morning.
15. _____ any lions in the cage.
16. _____ many people on the street.
17. _____ any goats on the farm.
18. _____ much food in the fridge.
19. _____ any problems with my family.
20. _____ many customers in the mall.

🌿🌿🌿 My Homework 🍂🍂🍂

Verb *to have* (in the present tense)

Affirmative

I, you, they, we	have
He, she, it	has

Examples:
- I have a new watch.
- My sister has a digital camera.

> *Exercise Nineteen*

Complete the sentences. Use *have* or *has*.

1. I _____ an old car.
2. We _____ a new villa in Berlin.
3. My uncle _____ a big farm near Cairo.
4. My sister _____ a lot of dresses.
5. Hayley _____ a modern laptop.
6. My parents _____ a lot of money.
7. Osama and his brother _____ a lot of books.
8. He _____ a good idea.
9. Eden _____ a nice dress.
10. Jonathan _____ a new mobile phone.
11. My sister _____ a lot of pens.
12. My sisters _____ other plans.
13. My friend _____ a new house.
14. I _____ a fast motorbike.
15. Batool _____ a big pharmacy.
16. Abdul-Rahman _____ a nice shirt.
17. My aunt _____ a lot of friends.
18. She _____ a lovely smile.
19. A horse _____ a long tail.
20. I _____ two sisters and one brother.

My Homework

> *Exercise Twenty*

Complete the sentences. Use *have* or *has*.

1. An elephant _____ a long trunk.
2. Animals _____ four legs.
3. You _____ a good reason.

4. Tina _____ some troubles at work.
5. China _____ a large population.
6. This pen _____ red ink.
7. This truck _____ sixteen wheels.
8. A bike _____ two wheels.
9. We _____ a lot of sugar.
10. My friends _____ a nice party every month.
11. Simon and Amy _____ a lot of pencils.
12. Mr Harry _____ a nice tie.
13. Bella and Imogen _____ the same interests.
14. My cat _____ beautiful fur.
15. Lauren _____ new pants.
16. This sentence _____ a few words.
17. Jacob and Hunter _____ a lot of problems.
18. My classmates _____ a final test.
19. My sister _____ a grey scarf.
20. They _____ some mistakes.

🕮🕮🕮 *My Homework* 🕮🕮🕮

Verb *to have* (in the present tense)

Negative

I, you, they, we	don't	have
He, she, it	doesn't	

✤ **Examples:**
 ➢ My brothers don't have any French books.
 ➢ My mother has a headache.

➢ *Exercise Twenty-one*
 ✤ Complete the sentences. Use *don't have* or *doesn't have*.
1. Ellen _____ a new perfume bottle.
2. I _____ any money right now.
3. They _____ a large villa.
4. Ali _____ any friends.
5. Audrey _____ a private room.
6. They _____ good ideas.
7. You _____ another chance.
8. We _____ any chairs.

9. Arthur _____ enough time.
10. The students _____ their notebooks.
11. Emily and Ariana _____ new clothes.
12. Piers _____ blue jeans.
13. My father _____ a red car.
14. We _____ cereal for breakfast.
15. Cats _____ wings.

My Homework

Verb *to have* (in the past tense)

Affirmative

| Subject | had |

Negative

| Subject | didn't have |

Examples:
- I **had** a meeting with the manager yesterday.
- I **didn't have** a meeting with the manager yesterday.

> *Exercise Twenty-two*
  - Choose the correct answer from a, b, c, or d.

1. Hugo _____ a car accident yesterday.

a.	has	b.	have
c.	having	d.	had

2. Matilda did not _____ an appointment with the dentist.

a.	has	b.	have
c.	having	d.	had

3. Lara _____ a birthday party last night.

a.	has	b.	have
c.	having	d.	had

4. Madison _____ a walk with her friends an hour ago.

a.	had	b.	have
c.	having	d.	has

5. We _____ a nice day on the beach last Sunday.

a.	has	b.	have
c.	having	d.	had

6. We usually _____ a swim in the afternoon.

a.	has	b.	have
c.	having	d.	to have

7. Saker and his wife _____ a cute baby girl last month.

a.	has	b.	have
c.	having	d.	had

8. The students _____ a five-minute break every hour.

a.	has	b.	have
c.	having	d.	doesn't have

9. Our teacher _____ five classes daily.

a.	has	b.	have
c.	don't have	d.	having

10. Stella _____ a new robe.

a.	has	b.	have
c.	having	d.	don't have

11. I _____ a history class every Tuesday.

a.	has	b.	doesn't have
c.	having	d.	have

12. Scarlet _____ a nice time at the club last Sunday.

a.	has	b.	had
c.	having	d.	have

13. How many sisters do you _____?

a.	has	b.	had
c.	having	d.	have

14. Annabelle _____ a chance to improve her reading skills.

a.	has	b.	don't have
c.	having	d.	have

15. We _____ our breakfast at 8:15 a.m.

a.	to have	b.	doesn't have
c.	having	d.	have

My Homework

➢ **Exercise Twenty-three**

✤ Choose the correct answer from a, b, c, or d.

1. Violet _____ a little cat.

a.	has	b.	don't have
c.	having	d.	have

2. I _____ a color printer at home.

a.	has	b.	doesn't have
c.	having	d.	have

3. My mother _____ a lot of fashionable dresses.

a.	has	b.	don't have
c.	having	d.	have

4. Ahmad _____ a famous computer company.

a.	has	b.	don't have
c.	having	d.	have

5. Yoursa _____ a new laptop.

a.	has	b.	doesn't have
c.	had	d.	have

6. Last night, Eliza _____ a terrible cold.

a.	has	b.	doesn't have
c.	had	d.	have

7. Taylor _____ any problems.

a.	has	b.	doesn't have
c.	having	d.	have

8. My wife _____ a lot of housework yesterday.

a.	has	b.	had
c.	having	d.	have

9. The students _____ enough time to finish these exercises.

a.	has	b.	doesn't have
c.	having	d.	have

10. My sisters _____ a lot of dolls in their room.

a.	has	b.	doesn't have
c.	having	d.	have

11. Lily and I _____ a weekly meeting.

a.	has	b.	doesn't have
c.	having	d.	have

12. Our new boss _____ very good opinions.

a.	has	b.	don't have
c.	having	d.	have

13. My parents _____ a plan to visit the country in the summer.

a.	has	b.	doesn't have
c.	having	d.	have

14. Keith and his wife _____ three children.

a.	has	b.	doesn't have
c.	having	d.	have

15. Rose _____ a nice mood today.

a.	has	b.	don't have
c.	having	d.	have

✿✿✿ My Homework ✿✿✿

Verb *to do* (in the present tense)

Affirmative

I, you, they, we	do
He, she, it	does

Negative

I, you, they, we	don't	do
He, she, it	doesn't	

⁜ Examples:
- I do a lot of work daily.
- Molly does her best to succeed.
- They don't do their work on time.
- Kate doesn't do her homework well.

> *Exercise Twenty-four*

⁜ Complete the sentences. Use *do, does, don't,* or *doesn't*.

1. I _____ my homework at night.
2. They _____ do a lot of research.
3. My mother _____ the dishes herself.
4. I _____ make any troubles.
5. Abeer _____ a lot of work every day.
6. My sisters _____ a lot of housework.
7. Holly _____ the kitchen before going to bed.
8. Claire _____ the cleaning after lunch.
9. Jade _____ make any mistakes.
10. We _____ our best to pass the test.

ⓐⓐⓐ *My Homework* ⓐⓐⓐ

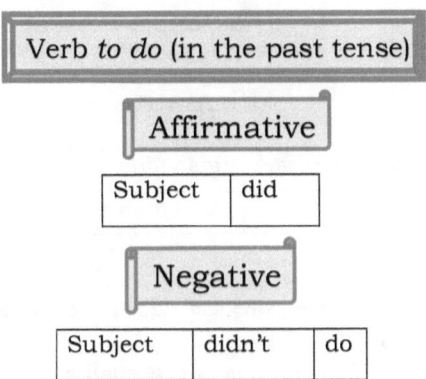

Examples:
- We did many things yesterday.
- I didn't do anything last night.

> *Exercise Twenty-five*

Complete the sentences. Use *did* or *didn't*.
1. Tyson _____ do his homework last night.
2. Leo _____ a lot of mistakes in the report.
3. We _____ do the cleaning yesterday.
4. Gareth _____ do his job well.
5. Carter _____ his work in a good way.

🌿🌿🌿 My Homework 🌿🌿🌿

SECTION 6 — The Simple Present Tense

Affirmative

I, you, they, we	*Base form (verb 1)*
He, she, it	*Base form + (s)*

Notes:
- In the third person singular, add –es to the base form if it ends in: -ss, -sh, -ch, -x or -o.
- If the base form ends in -y preceded by a consonant, drop the –y and add –ies.

It is used to express the following:
- *Repeated or usual actions and events*
- *Habits*
- *General truths*
- *Fixed arrangements*
- *Future constructions*

Examples:
- My sister takes the subway to school every day.
- My grandfather watches the news in the evening.
- Water boils at 100 °C or 212 °F.
- The plane arrives at 10:25 PM.
- After I graduate, I will move to another city.

These adverbs are commonly used with the simple present tense.

		Other phrases of time
always	*regularly*	*every week*
usually	*generally*	*once a week*
often	*frequently*	*on Mondays*
sometimes	*never*	*twice a month*
occasionally		*now and then*
rarely		*from time to time*
seldom		
scarcely		

> *Exercise One*

✦ Choose the correct answer from a, b, c, or d.

1. I usually _____ to school by bus.

a.	go	b.	going
c.	goes	d.	to go

2. My brother often _____ a taxi to his office.

a.	taking	b.	takes
c.	take	d.	to take

3. My uncle _____ for a famous American bank.

a.	work	b.	to work
c.	working	d.	works

4. We always _____ our father at the weekend.

a.	help	b.	helping
c.	helps	d.	to help

5. Freya often _____ her room herself.

a.	tidy	b.	tidying
c.	to tidy	d.	tidies

6. Antony _____ his car every morning.

a.	washing	b.	washes
c.	wash	d.	to wash

7. The earth _____ on its axis.

a.	rotates	b.	rotate
c.	to rotate	d.	rotating

8. Young mammals _____ on milk.

a.	feed	b.	feeds
c.	feeding	d.	to feed

9. My brother's car _____ on diesel.

a.	running	b.	to run
c.	run	d.	runs

10. It usually _____ in Dubai in winter.

a.	raining	b.	rain
c.	to rain	d.	rains

11. It always _____ in London in December.

a.	snow	b.	snows
c.	snowing	d.	to snow

12. My younger brother _____ his kite every afternoon.

a.	to fly	b.	fly
c.	flying	d.	flies

13. My sister _____ the flowers daily.

a.	watering	b.	waters
c.	to water	d.	water

14. My friends usually _____ me good advice.

a.	gives	b.	giving
c.	given	d.	give

15. Our teachers always _____ their best to help us.

a.	does	b.	to do
c.	do	d.	done

16. This train _____ for Paris at 10:35 a.m.

a.	leaving	b.	leave
c.	to leave	d.	leaves

17. We _____ in the dorm.

a.	to live	b.	lives
c.	live	d.	living

18. They usually _____ TV in the evening.

a.	watching	b.	watches
c.	to watch	d.	watch

19. Martin often _____ a shower in the morning.

a.	takes	b.	to take
c.	taking	d.	take

20. Adam _____ to his school every morning.

a.	walks	b.	to walk
c.	walking	d.	walk

The Simple Present Tense

Negative

I, you, they, we	do not (don't)	Base form
He, she, it	does not (doesn't)	

✦ **Examples:**
➢ I don't go to bed early.
➢ Sandra doesn't live alone.

➢ *Exercise Two*
  ✦ Change these sentences into negative.
  ✦ Follow the example.
➢ Ivan **goes** to bed early.
✓ Ivan **doesn't go** to bed early.

1. My father **works** in a bank.
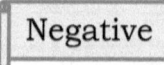_____

2. Tommy **hurries** to school.
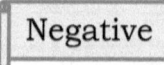_____

3. This student **relies** on his teachers.
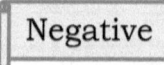_____

4. My uncle **flies** to Melbourne monthly.
✎_____ _____ _____ _____ _____ _____ _____ _____ _____

5. Our new teacher **comes** from England.
✎_____ _____ _____ _____ _____ _____ _____ _____ _____

6. My friends **like** diving.
✎_____ _____ _____ _____ _____ _____ _____ _____ _____

7. Daisy **speaks** Italian.
✎_____ _____ _____ _____ _____ _____ _____ _____ _____

8. My grandfather **reads** some newspapers in the morning.
✎_____ _____ _____ _____ _____ _____ _____ _____ _____

9. Joseph **watches** American films.
✎_____ _____ _____ _____ _____ _____ _____ _____ _____

10. You **send** your reports on time.
✎_____ _____ _____ _____ _____ _____ _____ _____ _____

11. My sisters **help** my mother in the kitchen.
✎_____ _____ _____ _____ _____ _____ _____ _____ _____

12. Freddie **lives** in New Jersey.
✎_____ _____ _____ _____ _____ _____ _____ _____ _____

13. Ahmed **fixes** laptops perfectly.
✎_____ _____ _____ _____ _____ _____ _____ _____ _____

14. Jacob **washes** his car every day.
✎_____ _____ _____ _____ _____ _____ _____ _____ _____

15. Lucy **tries** to answer the questions in class.
✎_____ _____ _____ _____ _____ _____ _____ _____ _____

16. Erin **gets up** at five thirty every morning.
✎_____ _____ _____ _____ _____ _____ _____ _____ _____

17. My sister **studies** pharmacy.
✎_____ _____ _____ _____ _____ _____ _____ _____ _____

18. My grandfather **suffers** from insomnia.
✎_____ _____ _____ _____ _____ _____ _____ _____ _____

19. Georgia **has** a weekly quiz.
✎_____ _____ _____ _____ _____ _____ _____ _____ _____

20. Aya **writes** short stories.
✎_____ _____ _____ _____ _____ _____ _____ _____ _____

✎✎✎ *My Homework* ✎✎✎

➤ Exercise Three
✦ Choose the correct answer from a, b, c, or d.

1. Andy _____ have a car.

a.	do not	b.	does not
c.	is not	d.	was not

2. My children _____ play with matches.

a.	do not	b.	does not
c.	is not	d.	was not

3. We _____ go to the beach in winter.

a.	do not	b.	does not
c.	is not	d.	was not

4. Our teacher _____ come to class late.

a.	do not	b.	does not
c.	is not	d.	was not

5. Sami _____ live with me.

a.	do not	b.	does not
c.	is not	d.	was not

6. Mathew _____ study history this semester.

a.	do not	b.	does not
c.	is not	d.	was not

7. This bus _____ run on natural gas.

a.	do not	b.	does not
c.	is not	d.	was not

8. My sisters _____ work in a hospital.

a.	do not	b.	does not
c.	is not	d.	was not

9. Dave _____ like diving.

a.	do not	b.	does not
c.	is not	d.	was not

10. The moon _____ shine during the day.

a.	do not	b.	does not
c.	is not	d.	was not

11. Ibrahim _____ leave his office early.

a.	do not	b.	does not
c.	is not	d.	was not

12. Boxing _____ appeal to me.

a.	do not	b.	does not
c.	is not	d.	was not

13. Harvey and Dylan _____ enjoy Japanese food.

a.	do not	b.	does not
c.	is not	d.	was not

14. Luke and Archie _____ study French. They study German.

a.	do not	b.	does not
c.	is not	d.	was not

15. Fatima _____ like music. She likes reading.

a.	do not	b.	does not
c.	is not	d.	was not

16. Eliot and Ryan _____ play handball.

a.	was not	b.	does not
c.	is not	d.	do not

17. Michael _____ usually go to the mall at the weekend.

a.	do not	b.	does not
c.	is not	d.	was not

18. Othman _____ get up late.

a.	do not	b.	does not
c.	is not	d.	was not

19. Aiden and his friend _____ prefer rap music.

a.	do not	b.	does not
c.	is not	d.	was not

20. Martina _____ review her lessons at night.

a.	is not	b.	was not
c.	do not	d.	does not

🕮🕮🕮 My Homework 🕮🕮🕮

➢ **Exercise Four**

✚ Rearrange these words to form meaningful sentences.

1. / football / every / We / watch / week / matches /
🕮 ___ ___ ___ ___ ___ ___ ___ ___

2. / weekend / my / meet / the / friends / I / usually / at /
🕮 ___ ___ ___ ___ ___ ___ ___ ___

3. / drinks / in / coffee / the / Camila / some / morning /
🕮 ___ ___ ___ ___ ___ ___ ___ ___

4. / speaks / well / Spanish / Ali / very / Portuguese / and /
🕮 ___ ___ ___ ___ ___ ___ ___ ___

5. / likes / and / Abdullah / swimming / rowing /
🕮 ___ ___ ___ ___ ___ ___ ___ ___

6. / reading / loves / novels / French / Saleh /
🕮 ___ ___ ___ ___ ___ ___ ___ ___

7. / medicine / Jane / Henry / study / and /
🕮 ___ ___ ___ ___ ___ ___ ___ ___

8. / eat / lunch / at / sisters / noon / often / My / their /
🕮 ___ ___ ___ ___ ___ ___ ___ ___

9. / Royce / smartphones / computers / fixes / and /
🕮 ___ ___ ___ ___ ___ ___ ___ ___

10. / build / and / Engineers / roads / bridges /
🌿 ___ ___ ___ ___ ___ ___ ___ ___ ___

11. / Doctors / nurses / people / take care of / sick / and /
🌿 ___ ___ ___ ___ ___ ___ ___ ___ ___

12. / fly / and / planes / Pilots / helicopters /
🌿 ___ ___ ___ ___ ___ ___ ___ ___ ___

13. / ask / usually / Students / class / questions / many / in /
🌿 ___ ___ ___ ___ ___ ___ ___ ___ ___

14. / farmhouse / uncles / a / have / small / My /
🌿 ___ ___ ___ ___ ___ ___ ___ ___ ___

15. / starts / at / School / the / seven thirty / morning / in /
🌿 ___ ___ ___ ___ ___ ___ ___ ___ ___

16. / replace / need / tires / of / car / I / to / the / my /
🌿 ___ ___ ___ ___ ___ ___ ___ ___ ___

17. / time / wastes / rarely / Alan / his /
🌿 ___ ___ ___ ___ ___ ___ ___ ___ ___

18. / brother / copies / My / classmates / never / from / his /
🌿 ___ ___ ___ ___ ___ ___ ___ ___ ___

19. / badly / These / play / players / sometimes /
🌿 ___ ___ ___ ___ ___ ___ ___ ___ ___

20. / don't / talk / phone / driving / I / during / on / the /
🌿 ___ ___ ___ ___ ___ ___ ___ ___ ___

🌿🌿🌿 *My Homework* 🌿🌿🌿

> *Exercise Five*
  ✢ Rearrange these words to form meaningful sentences.

1. / life / materials / use / We / our / recycled / in / daily /
🌿 ___ ___ ___ ___ ___ ___ ___ ___ ___

2. / day / twice / father / the / a / Internet / surfs / My /
🌿 ___ ___ ___ ___ ___ ___ ___ ___ ___

3. / clothes / wear / People / summer / usually / light / in /
🌿 ___ ___ ___ ___ ___ ___ ___ ___ ___

4. / speak / well / Italian / I / very / don't /
🌿 ___ ___ ___ ___ ___ ___ ___ ___ ___

5. / competition / year / takes place / a / This / once /
🌿 ___ ___ ___ ___ ___ ___ ___ ___ ___

6. / farmers / daily / tomatoes / pick / These / a lot of /
🌿 ___ ___ ___ ___ ___ ___ ___ ___ ___

7. / welcome / visitors / We / morning / many / every /
🌿 ___ ___ ___ ___ ___ ___ ___ ___ ___

8. / tourists / Millions / the / visit / Luxor / of / winter / during /
➢ _____
9. / stories / kind / attract / children / This / of / usually / young /
➢ _____
10. / best / students / class / My / their / in / do /
➢ _____

✍ My Homework ✍

➢ **Exercise Six**
  ✦ Rearrange these words to form meaningful sentences.
1. / China / company / has / Mr / in / Alaa Allam / a /
➢ _____
2. / in / her / Dublin / lives / with / aunt / My / family /
➢ _____
3. / breakfast / morning / I / the / my / in / have / early /
➢ _____
4. / to / my / club / friends / usually / the / go / I / with /
➢ _____
5. / night / on / We / rarely / watch / movies / at / TV / action /
➢ _____
6. / always / gets / My / o'clock / at / up / mother / five /
➢ _____
7. / and / eating / always / I / hands / wash / before / after / my /
➢ _____
8. / grandfather / every day / coffee / a / of / drinks / My / lot /
➢ _____
9. / cousins / go / the / beach / Saturday / My / on / to /
➢ _____
10. / English / teaches / very / Mr / Al-Nashar / well /
➢ _____
11. / sister / homework / My / evening / her / in / does / the / usually /
➢ _____
12. / many / like / looks / Ahmad / his / in / father / ways /
➢ _____
13. / seven / first / period / at / always / The / thirty / starts /
➢ _____
14. / sometimes / have / test / Monday / We / a / on /
➢ _____
15. / rarely / lunch / have / outdoors / I / my /
➢ _____

16. / new / the / job / enjoys / Kathy / mall / her / at /
🕮 _____
17. / Jane / play / John / together / often / tennis / and /
🕮 _____
18. / students / waste / time / never / their / Active /
🕮 _____
19. / always / work / 7:45 / a.m. / at / Tony / starts /
🕮 _____
20. / usually / Merhan / to / aunt / on / talks / phone / her / the /
🕮 _____

🕮🕮🕮 My Homework 🕮🕮🕮

➢ **Exercise Seven**
  ✦ Correct the mistakes in each of the following sentences.
  ✦ Follow the example.
➢ Jane often need help with homework.
🕮 Jane often <u>needs</u> help with homework.

1. My mobile phone don't work properly.
🕮 _____
2. Aya don't help her mother in the kitchen.
🕮 _____
3. Santos walk to the farm every morning.
🕮 _____
4. Hagar visit her grandmother twice a week.
🕮 _____
5. Our teacher correct our homework daily.
🕮 _____
6. Windsor and Kevin speaks Spanish very well.
🕮 _____
7. Pierre attend English classes five days a week.
🕮 _____
8. My uncle never smoke.
🕮 _____
9. Kahraba usually score a lot of goals.
🕮 _____
10. Amr always come to class on time.
🕮 _____
11. Dr Batool help many patients every day.
🕮 _____

12. Mr Yong teach us Chinese at Wuhan University.
✎ _____ _____ _____ _____ _____ _____ _____ _____ _____
13. Ronny phone his family once a day.
✎ _____ _____ _____ _____ _____ _____ _____ _____ _____
14. Catharine usually go swimming on Thursday.
✎ _____ _____ _____ _____ _____ _____ _____ _____ _____
15. My parents always travels to Beijing in summer.
✎ _____ _____ _____ _____ _____ _____ _____ _____ _____
16. Ralph often bike to school.
✎ _____ _____ _____ _____ _____ _____ _____ _____ _____
17. Mr. Bakeer always gives his students a lot of weekly assignments.
✎ _____ _____ _____ _____ _____ _____ _____ _____ _____
18. We often rides our bikes in the afternoon.
✎ _____ _____ _____ _____ _____ _____ _____ _____ _____
19. Alden sometimes watch football matches on TV.
✎ _____ _____ _____ _____ _____ _____ _____ _____ _____
20. I checks my bank account from time to time.
✎ _____ _____ _____ _____ _____ _____ _____ _____ _____

My Homework

➢ **Exercise Eight**
   ✦ Use the given words to form correct sentences.
   ✦ You may add your own words. Follow the example.

➢ / Daniel / usually / go / shopping / evening /
   ✎ *Daniel usually <u>goes</u> shopping in the evening.*

1. / Yusuf / visit / friends / weekly/
✎ _____ _____ _____ _____ _____ _____ _____ _____ _____
2. / Hagar / sometimes / listen / music / night /
✎ _____ _____ _____ _____ _____ _____ _____ _____ _____
3. / Rudi / write / email / father / every day /
✎ _____ _____ _____ _____ _____ _____ _____ _____ _____
4. / sister / drink / glass / juice / evening /
✎ _____ _____ _____ _____ _____ _____ _____ _____ _____
5. / Patrick / never / play / football / street /
✎ _____ _____ _____ _____ _____ _____ _____ _____ _____
6. / Jana / always / go / bed / early /
✎ _____ _____ _____ _____ _____ _____ _____ _____ _____
7. / Karl / study / English / grammar / school /
✎ _____ _____ _____ _____ _____ _____ _____ _____ _____

8. / Ammar / often / eat / lunch / five / o'clock /
🌿 ___ ___ ___ ___ ___ ___ ___ ___ ___ ___

9. / Rahma / go / diving / weekend / friends /
🌿 ___ ___ ___ ___ ___ ___ ___ ___ ___ ___

10. / Alvin / do / homework / evening /
🌿 ___ ___ ___ ___ ___ ___ ___ ___ ___ ___

11. / Zeinab / usually / help / mother / housework /
🌿 ___ ___ ___ ___ ___ ___ ___ ___ ___ ___

12. / father / always / read / newspaper / morning /
🌿 ___ ___ ___ ___ ___ ___ ___ ___ ___ ___

13. / uncle / always / come / office / six thirty /
🌿 ___ ___ ___ ___ ___ ___ ___ ___ ___ ___

14. / aunt / usually / start / cooking / afternoon /
🌿 ___ ___ ___ ___ ___ ___ ___ ___ ___ ___

15. / brother / often / studies / history / evening /
🌿 ___ ___ ___ ___ ___ ___ ___ ___ ___ ___

16. / Jackie / sweeps / floor / day /
🌿 ___ ___ ___ ___ ___ ___ ___ ___ ___ ___

17. / I / usually / meet / family / at / weekend /
🌿 ___ ___ ___ ___ ___ ___ ___ ___ ___ ___

18. / I / take / brothers / beach / Saturday /
🌿 ___ ___ ___ ___ ___ ___ ___ ___ ___ ___

19. / They / build / many / schools / every /
🌿 ___ ___ ___ ___ ___ ___ ___ ___ ___ ___

20. / teacher / correct / our / mistakes /
🌿 ___ ___ ___ ___ ___ ___ ___ ___ ___ ___

🌿🌿🌿 *My Homework* 🌿🌿🌿

The Simple Present Tense

Yes/No Questions

Do	I, you, they, we	Base form	?
Does	he, she, it		

Examples:

- **Rania**: Do you have an extra copy?
  Bakr: Yes, I do.

- **Rimas**: Does your father offer you help?
  Hend: Yes, he does.

- **Pears**: Does your friend visit you at the weekend?
  Leveroni: Yes, he does.

- **Salma**: Does your roommate annoy you?
  Salama: No, he doesn't.

> *Exercise Nine*

Choose the correct answer from a, b, c, or d.

1. **Ben**: Do you drive to school?
   Ted: Yes, I _____ to school.

a.	drive	b.	don't
c.	do	d.	did

2. **Mahmoud**: Do you live alone?
   Charley: No, I _____.

a.	do	b.	doesn't
c.	don't live	d.	don't

3. **Adam**: Does Sabah have a walk every day?
   James: Yes, Sabah _____ a walk every day.

a.	has	b.	was
c.	does	d.	doesn't

4. **Leona**: Does Jim watch American movies at night?
   Lorenzo: Yes, Jim _____ American movies at night.

a.	watches	b.	does not
c.	does	d.	was not

5. **Rolf**: Does Liu Xiang cook Chinese food well?
   Ronald: Yes, Liu Xiang _____ it very well.

a.	doesn't	b.	does
c.	was	d.	cooks

6. **Helen:** _____ Rawya go to school alone?
   Alexa: No, she doesn't.

a.	Do	b.	Does
c.	Is	d.	Was

7. **Sandy:** _____ you have tickets for the concert next Saturday?
   Mandy: Yes, we do.

a.	Does	b.	Were
c.	Are	d.	Do

8. **Phillip:** Do you phone your teachers now and then?
   Anton: Yes, I _____ them from time to time.

a.	do	b.	did
c.	phone	d.	phoned

9. **Saleh:** Do you work in a hospital?
   Sohair: No, I _____.

a.	didn't	b.	don't
c.	doesn't	d.	isn't

10. **Tamer:** Do you eat or drink while driving?
    Dalia: No, I _____.

a.	didn't	b.	can't
c.	don't use	d.	don't

The Simple Present Tense

Information Questions

Question word	do	I, you, they, we	Base form	?
	does	he, she, it		

> *Note:*

We use	Where ___?	to ask for information about place.

We use	When ___?	to ask for information about time.

We use	What time _?	to ask for information about time.

We use	Why ___?	to ask for information about reason.

We use	What ___?	to ask for information about something.

We use	How many ___?	to ask for information about numbers.
We use	How much ___?	to ask for information about quantity.
We use	How much ___?	to ask for information about the price of something.
We use	How old ___?	to ask for information about age.
We use	How far ___?	to ask for information about distance.
We use	How long ___?	to ask for information about a period of time.
We use	Whose ___?	to ask who something belongs to.
We use	Who ___?	to ask about the name, identity, or function of one or more people.
We use	Whom ___?	to ask about the object of a verb or preposition.

+ *Examples:*

➢ **Mark:** What time do you usually leave your school?
   Wilson: I usually leave my school at four thirty in the afternoon.

➢ **Lama:** Where does Annie live?
   Diego: She lives in Toronto.

➢ *Exercise Ten*
   + Choose the correct answer from a, b, c, or d.
1. **Andre:** _____ does the first class start?
   Greg: It starts at seven thirty.

a.	What time	b.	Who
c.	What	d.	Where

2. **Majid:** _____ does Joseph usually have his dinner?
   Hamid: He usually has his dinner at home.

a.	What time	b.	Why
c.	When	d.	Where

3. **Linda:** _____ shirts do you want?
   Suzan: I want three.
a.	How many	b.	How much
c.	How far	d.	How old

4. **Hameed:** _____ Mahmoud usually eat for lunch?
   Doha: He usually eats steak and salad.
a.	What	b.	Why
c.	When	d.	Where

5. **Lilly:** _____ does Suzanna go in the evening?
   Dolly: She goes to her office in the evening.
a.	Why	b.	What
c.	Where	d.	When

6. **Abeer:** _____ do the students have a vacation?
   Essam: They have a vacation in August.
a.	**How far**	b.	**When**
c.	**Where**	d.	**How old**

7. **Nabil:** _____ do you often come late?
   Mia: I often come late because I miss the school bus.
a.	What	b.	Why
c.	When	d.	Where

8. **Zahra:** _____ money do you have?
   Layan: I have five hundred dollars.
a.	How many	b.	How much
c.	How far	d.	How old

9. **Alexander:** _____ does Ann go to bed?
   Dennis: She goes to bed at eleven fifteen.
a.	When	b.	Who
c.	What	d.	Where

10. **Atif:** _____ does Samah do during her free time?
    Wesam: She reads classic plays.
a.	What time	b.	Who
c.	What	d.	Where

11. **Eman:** _____ do your parents travel to Johannesburg?
    Aliaà: My parents travel there in January.
a.	What time	b.	Who
c.	What	d.	Where

12. **Ross:** _____ do you usually buy your clothes?
    Ivan: I usually buy them from the city mall.
a.	What time	b.	Who
c.	What	d.	Where

13. **Ronald:** _____ do you go hunting?
    Frank: Once a week.
a.	How often	b.	Who
c.	What	d.	Where

14. **Nada:** _____ does it take you to fix this laptop?
    Nabila: It takes me three hours to fix it.
a.	How many	b.	How far
c.	How old	d.	How long
15. **Sohair:** _____ do you go to your office?
    Toto: I walk.
a.	What time	b.	Who
c.	What	d.	How
16. **Abdo:** _____ patients do you check every day?
    Bato: A lot.
a.	How old	b.	How much
c.	How many	d.	How long
17. **Lama:** _____ does it cost to paint my house?
    Sama: It costs two thousand dollars.
a.	How much	b.	How long
c.	How many	d.	How old
18. **Dina:** _____ do you usually stay in this desert camp?
    Lina: I usually spend a week there.
a.	How long	b.	How much
c.	How old	d.	How many
19. **Felix:** Where _____ Saleh come from?
    Allan: He comes from Egypt.
a.	do	b.	doing
c.	did	d.	does
20. **Mayada:** Why _____ you study Italian?
    Manal: I study it because I want to work in Rome.
a.	do	b.	doing
c.	did	d.	does
21. **Maha:** How often does Manal _____ her grandmother?
    Taha: Manal visits her daily.
a.	visits	b.	visiting
c.	to visit	d.	visit
22. **Musa:** When _____ your father usually call you up?
    Serena: He usually calls me up in the morning.
a.	doing	b.	do
c.	does	d.	did
23. **Hagar:** What do you _____ before you get into your car?
    Khalid: I check the tires before I get into my car.
a.	did	b.	to do
c.	do	d.	does
24. **Rahma:** _____ do your sons do at the weekend?
    Azzah: They go to our country house.
a.	What time	b.	Who
c.	What	d.	Where

25. **Farah**: How many cigarettes do you _____ a day?
    Zeyad: I smoke only three a day.

a.	smokes	b.	smoke
c.	smoking	d.	smoked

🌸🌸🌸 My Homework 🌸🌸🌸

➤ Exercise Eleven

✦ Rearrange these words to form meaningful questions.

➤ / do / have / dinner / you / What / your / time /
🔖 **What time do you have your dinner?**
I have my dinner at 9:30 p.m.

1. / they / What / do / study /
🔖 _____?
They study English and math.

2. / Omar / Whom / to / want / does / meet /
🔖 _____?
He wants to meet the senior teacher.

3. / leave / does / the / What / train / time /
🔖 _____?
The train leaves at five thirty in the morning.

4. / spend / grandfather / weekend / How / does / your / his /
🔖 _____?
My grandfather spends his weekend reading novels.

5. / does / cry / baby / When / your /
🔖 _____?
My baby often cries when it is hungry.

6. / Indiana / How / stay / does / Lee / long / in /
🔖 _____?
He stays there for a week.

7. / need / much / do / you / money / How /
🔖 _____?
I need ninety dollars.

8. / they / in / go / the / do / Where / evening / usually /
🔖 _____?
They usually go to the park.

9. / many / want / you / How / do / books /
🔖 _____?
I want three books.

10. / your / cost / new / How / does / much / car /
🐌 _____?
It costs forty thousand dollars.
11. / the / time / plane / does / arrive / What /
🐌 _____?
The plane arrives at 5:45 p.m.
12. / James / Which / to / car / does / want / buy /
🐌 _____?
James wants to buy the blue one.
13. / snow / your / How / it / city / does / often / in /
🐌 _____?
It rarely snows in my city.
14. / do / usually / you / What / lunch / for / eat /
🐌 _____?
I usually eat rice and green peas.
15. / class / What / does / Atif / to / go / time / Mr /
🐌 _____?
Mr Atif goes to class at ten o'clock.
16. / you / Whom / meet / at / do / club / the / usually /
🐌 _____?
I usually meet my friends Laura and Amanda there.
17. / time / start / does / the / What / game /
🐌 _____?
The game starts at six thirty.
18. / How / the / take / does / it / reach / to / station / long /
🐌 _____?
It takes half an hour to reach the station.
19. / cost / much / does / smartphone / your / How /
🐌 _____?
My smartphone costs six hundred dollars.
20. / you / Which / do / start / usually / with / food /
🐌 _____?
I usually start with the soup.

🐌🐌🐌 *My Homework* 🐌🐌🐌

➢ *Exercise Twelve*
   ✤ Complete the questions by using *is*, *are*, *does*, or *do*.
1. Barbara: What time _____ your father usually get up?
   Lucy: At five thirty.

2. Julia: What _____ your nationality?
   Saleh: I am Chinese.

3. **Ibrahim:** Where _____ your dictionary?
   Ahmadi: On that table over there.
4. **Shalaby:** How much _____ your new shirt cost?
   Paula: Sixty dollars.
5. **Alissa:** Where _____ you spend the weekend?
   Carol: In the mountains.
6. **Cameron:** _____ your father have a job now?
   Jayden: Yes. He works as a clerk in an oil company.
7. **Noah:** What _____ your favourite food?
   Anna: I like Italian pizza.
8. **Leon:** Where _____ your cat sleep?
   Leonor: It sleeps next to my bed.
9. **Gabriel:** Where _____ your sisters?
   Nikole: In the kitchen.
10. **Sameh:** What plays by Shakespeare _____ you like?
    Basmala: I like *Hamlet* and *King Lear*.

My Homework

> ## Exercise Thirteen
> 🞢 Add the adverb of frequency in brackets in its correct place. Follow the examples:
> ➤ Our teacher of English is late.   (never)
> ⋙ *Our teacher of English **is** never late.*
> ➤ Darya comes to his office on time.   (often)
> ⋙ *Darya often comes to his office.*

1. Suzan and Olfat are punctual.   (always)
   ⋙ _____

2. I visit my grandparents on Saturday.   (sometimes)
   ⋙ _____

3. Patricia laughs or smiles in class.   (rarely)
   ⋙ _____

4. I keep my mobile phone in a safe place.   (always)
   ⋙ _____

5. Karen is tardy for school.   (usually)
   ⋙ _____

6. My grandmother wakes up very early.   (always)
   ⋙ _____

7. Hamza helps his friends and classmates. (always)
⇒ ___ ___ ___ ___ ___ ___ ___ ___ ___

8. We eat dinner outdoor. (sometimes)
⇒ ___ ___ ___ ___ ___ ___ ___ ___ ___

9. Boody logs on his Facebook account. (seldom)
⇒ ___ ___ ___ ___ ___ ___ ___ ___ ___

10. My sister is keen on her young children. (always)
⇒ ___ ___ ___ ___ ___ ___ ___ ___ ___

My Homework

➢ *Exercise Fourteen*
  ✦ Complete these sentences with *do/does* or *don't/doesn't*.

1. Robert doesn't like swimming, but I _____.
2. Keith doesn't speak Italian, but his brothers _____.
3. Nora lives alone, but her sister _____.
4. My father has a modern car, but my mother _____.
5. Pierre lives in Paris, but his parents _____.
6. Taro doesn't speak Russian, but his friend Zuki _____.
7. We _____ have a new villa, but my grandparents do.
8. Henry _____ wear glasses, but his wife does.
9. Raul doesn't watch English movies, but his friends _____.
10. Linda leaves her office early, but Lena _____.

My Homework

➢ *Study this pattern:*

When		
After		
As soon as	*Simple present*	*Simple present*
Before		
By the time		
Once		
Simple present	until	*Simple present*
Simple present	till	*Simple present*

Exercise Fifteen

Choose the correct answer from a, b, c, or d.

1. As soon as our teacher enters the class, we _____ the lesson.

a.	starts	b.	staring
c.	started	d.	start

2. When I _____, I take a warm shower.

a.	waking up	b.	wakes up
c.	wake up	d.	woke

3. After Teresa finishes her work, she _____ TV.

a.	watch	b.	to watch
c.	watches	d.	watched

4. Before Dane goes to her office, she _____ her kids.

a.	feed	b.	feeds
c.	feeding	d.	fed

5. Once we _____ our homework, the teacher checks it.

a.	submit	b.	submitted
c.	submits	d.	submitting

6. As soon as Steve _____ his email inbox, he sends replies.

a.	check	b.	checking
c.	checks	d.	to check

7. We have our lunch break when it _____ 12:45 p.m.

a.	be	b.	is
c.	was	d.	to be

8. The train leaves as soon as the doors _____ locked.

a.	are	b.	were
c.	is	d.	be

9. My mother usually starts cooking when she _____ home.

a.	return	b.	returns
c.	returned	d.	returning

10. We play computer games as soon as we _____ our homework.

a.	do	b.	to do
c.	doing	d.	did

11. I take my son to the dentist when his teeth _____ him.

a.	to hurt	b.	hurting
c.	hurts	d.	hurt

12. Birds go back to their nests by the time the sun _____.

a.	sets	b.	to set
c.	set	d.	setting

13. I usually relax on the beach until the sun _____.

a.	rising	b.	rises
c.	risen	d.	rose

14. If you heat ice, it _____.

a.	melt	b.	melted
c.	melting	d.	melts

15. I don't have my lunch until my brothers _____ home from school.

a.	returning	b.	return
c.	returns	d.	returned

My Homework

➢ *Exercise Sixteen*

✦ Fill in the correct form of the verb.

1. Suzy _____ to classical music every morning.   (to listen)
2. Anas _____. He stopped a year ago.   (not smoke)
3. My sisters _____ us nice meals every day.   (to cook)
4. My daughters _____ French in Paris this year.   (to study)
5. Sosa and Mike belong to the same family. They
   _____ in the same company.   (to work)
6. Sue often _____ diving in her free time.   (to go)
7. Bara'a _____ to his office every morning.   (to drive)
8. Saleh _____ English and French.   (to speak)
9. Nathalie _____ computers and laptops.   (to fix)
10. Arnold rarely _____ us.   (to help)

My Homework

SECTION 7 — **The Gerund**

> The gerund is the noun in the form of the present participle of a verb (that ends in *-ing*).

➢ The gerund can be used as the subject of a sentence.
✦ Smoking kills.

➢ The gerund can be used as the object of a sentence.
✦ We love reading.

➢ The gerund can be used as the complement of the verb *to be*.
✦ One of my habits is having a walk in the evening.

✦ Ann's favourite hobby is fishing.

➢ The gerund is used after prepositions.
✦ My sister is good at playing chess.

✦ My brother finds pleasure in scuba-diving.

➢ The gerund can be used after phrasal verbs.
✦ My brother promised me to give up smoking.

➢ The gerund can be used after some expressions.
✦ The little girl couldn't help crying as soon as her mother left the room.

✦ Mark can't stand listening to pop music.

✦ It's no use persuading her to take part in the competition.

✦ It's no good waiting for the bus.

✦ I don't mind attending the lecture.

✦ Your new plan is worth considering.

➢ The gerund can be used as a present participle that functions as an adjective.
✦ There is a swimming pool in the park.

✦ Abdul-Rahman married a fascinating young woman.

➢ The gerund is used after the helping verb *to be* to form the continuous tenses.
- The players are training in the field right now.
- Look! Some ships are passing over there.
- I was sleeping when you called me.
- We were hunting some animals when it started to know.
- I will be flying to Lisbon this time tomorrow.
- I have been waiting for you since lunchtime.

➢ The *-ing form* is formed by adding *-ing* as in the following examples:

Base form	-ing	Base form	-ing
visit	visiting	behave	behaving
see	seeing	plan	planning
pay	paying	mix	mixing

➢ **Exercise One**
- Add *-ing* to the following verbs.

Base form	-ing	Base form	-ing
aid	____	wander	____
have	____	wave	____
build	____	come	____
drink	____	break	____
take	____	fix	____
stay	____	delay	____
jog	____	greet	____
pray	____	dry	____
wait	____	judge	____
love	____	keep	____
move	____	need	____
order	____	kneel	____
warn	____	urge	____

Base form	-ing	Base form	-ing
fill	---------------	kill	---------------
do	---------------	play	---------------
pray	---------------	cry	---------------
fly	---------------	enjoy	---------------
empty	---------------	smile	---------------
wear	---------------	swear	---------------
mount	---------------	count	---------------
develop	---------------	submit	---------------
lay	---------------	lie	---------------
die	---------------	draw	---------------
stain	---------------	rain	---------------
think	---------------	kick	---------------
stab	---------------	end	---------------
finish	---------------	freeze	---------------
sneeze	---------------	relax	---------------
squeeze	---------------	tax	---------------
race	---------------	dance	---------------
get	---------------	bet	---------------
fit	---------------	suit	---------------
weep	---------------	commit	---------------
creep	---------------	admit	---------------
bite	---------------	write	---------------
fight	---------------	win	---------------
sign	---------------	resign	---------------
decline	---------------	make	---------------
bake	---------------	land	---------------
swim	---------------	beat	---------------
clap	---------------	trap	---------------
swap	---------------	tear	---------------
fear	---------------	bring	---------------
sing	---------------	laugh	---------------

yawn	_____	read	_____
lend	_____	send	_____

Base form	-ing	Base form	-ing
explain	_____	expect	_____
train	_____	detect	_____
extend	_____	suspect	_____
speak	_____	read	_____
listen	_____	heal	_____
kneel	_____	steal	_____
curse	_____	cure	_____
knock	_____	deal	_____
rest	_____	twist	_____
insist	_____	persist	_____
observe	_____	conserve	_____
reserve	_____	complain	_____
sustain	_____	obtain	_____
repeat	_____	meet	_____
defeat	_____	feed	_____
wipe	_____	yell	_____
sleep	_____	sell	_____
tell	_____	fill	_____
smell	_____	squeeze	_____
pretend	_____	step	_____
stop	_____	slip	_____
drop	_____	flow	_____
snow	_____	grow	_____
reply	_____	violate	_____
pretend	_____	find	_____
bend	_____	inform	_____
begin	_____	start	_____
quit	_____	permit	_____

chew	_____	fry	_____
hop	_____	let	_____
wrap	_____	hunt	_____
hurt	_____	beat	_____
fax	_____	fit	_____

My Homework

SECTION 8

The Present Progressive (Continuous) Tense

✦ The *present continuous tense* expresses an event that is happening at the time of speaking.

➢ It is formed as follows:

Affirmative

I	am	
He		
She	is	
It		-ing
You		
They	are	
We		

Negative

I	am		
He			
She	is		
It		not	-ing
You			
They	are		
We			

The Keywords of the Present Progressive (Continuous)

Now	Right now	Look!
Listen!	Look out!	Be careful!
Take care!	At present	At the present time
At the moment	Watch out!	

✦ Examples:

- I **am watching** a movie at the moment.
- Hend **is walking** alone.
- We **are getting** hungry.
- Believe me. I **am not kidding**.
- Walid **isn't thinking** about the project.
- My friends **aren't taking** history classes now.

➢ Exercise One

✦ Choose the correct answer from a, b, c, or d.

1. I _____ my lessons right now.

a.	reviews	b.	was reviewing
c.	am reviewing	d.	to review

2. We _____ a new grammar lesson at the moment.

a.	are studying	b.	to study
c.	studies	d.	studying

3. Listen! Someone _____.

a.	are calling	b.	call
c.	is calling	d.	to call

4. Listen! Some children _____.

a.	shouts	b.	are shouting
c.	shout	d.	to shout

5. Look! Some birds _____ over there.

a.	flying	b.	is flying
c.	flies	d.	are flying

6. Look! An eagle _____ over there.

a.	hover	b.	hovered
c.	to hover	d.	is hovering

7. Look out! A fast car _____.

a.	is coming	b.	come
c.	came	d.	to come

8. Be careful! The bus _____ backward.

a.	are moving	b.	move
c.	to moving	d.	is moving

9. At present, the government _____ a lot of factories.

a.	build	b.	building
c.	is building	d.	built

10. These days, my uncle _____ his old villa.

a.	is renovating	b.	renovate
c.	to renovate	d.	renovating

11. I can't go out now. It _____ heavily.

a.	raining	b.	is raining
c.	rains	d.	rain

12. I can't touch the pot. The water inside _____.

a.	boil	b.	to boil
c.	is boiling	d.	are boiling

13. I can't enter my father's room because he _____.

a.	sleeps	b.	sleeping
c.	sleep	d.	is sleeping

14. The maid is busy. She _____ the house.

a.	cleaning	b.	is cleaning
c.	cleans	d.	clean

15. Now, we _____ hard because we have an important match.

a.	training	b.	trains
c.	are training	d.	to train

16. My mother is in the kitchen. She _____ our lunch.

a.	was preparing	b.	is prepared
c.	prepare	d.	is preparing

17. Look! Someone _____ to us.

a.	waving	b.	wave
c.	is waving	d.	are waving

18. Listen! Some children _____.

a.	cry	b.	is crying
c.	are crying	d.	cries

19. The farmer _____ a tree now.

a.	plants	b.	was planting
c.	to plant	d.	is planting

20. The boys _____ at the moment.

a.	are studying	b.	is studying
c.	were studying	d.	studies

21. I have to hurry. My father _____ in front of the bank.

a.	waiting	b.	to wait
c.	wait	d.	is waiting

22. The workmen _____ the walls.

a.	are painting	b.	paints
c.	to paint	d.	painting

23. Watch out! A dog _____ towards us.

a.	running	b.	is running
c.	are running	d.	run

24. Look out! A bear _____ us.

a.	was chasing	b.	chase
c.	is chasing	d.	chasing

25. Please drive carefully. It is still _____.

a.	is raining	b.	raining
c.	rains	d.	rain

➢ **Exercise Two**

🞧 Choose the correct answer from a, b, c, or d.

1. Please don't switch the lights off. We are still _____.

a.	are studying	b.	were studying
c.	study	d.	studying

2. My father is in the field. He _____ the wheat.

a.	is irrigating	b.	irrigating
c.	are irrigating	d.	to irrigate

3. My grandfather is in the garden. He _____ his favourite newspaper.

a.	reading	b.	reads
c.	to read	d.	is reading

4. Batool is at home. She _____ her lunch.

a.	is having	b.	are having
c.	having	d.	were having

5. Boody is in his room. He _____ his email.

a.	checking	b.	check
c.	to check	d.	is checking

6. Now, my friends are at the beach. They _____.

a.	are sunbathing	b.	is sunbathing
c.	to sunbathe	d.	sunbathing

7. Look out! Some rocks _____.

a.	is falling	b.	are falling
c.	falls	d.	falling

8. I _____ Ibrahim. Do you know where he is?

a.	am looking for	b.	is looking for
c.	are looking for	d.	looking for

9. Please turn on the lights. It _____ dark.

a.	is getting	b.	was getting
c.	get	d.	getting

10. Hassan: Where is your father?
    Baher: He _____ a water well in the garden.

a.	digs		digging
c.	dig	d.	is digging

11. Alan: What is your sister doing right now?
    Antony: She _____ her bed.

a.	making	b.	is making
c.	make	d.	makes

12. Let's not have a walk now. It is still _____.

a.	is snowing	b.	to snow
c.	snowing	d.	snow

13. Please stop talking. I _____ with my teacher.

a.	to concentrate	b.	is concentrating
c.	am concentrating	d.	was concentrating

14. Please keep quiet! My baby _____ to sleep.

a.	trying	b.	is trying
c.	try	d.	are trying

15. Right now Osama is in class. He _____ at his desk.

a.	sits	b.	was sitting
c.	is sitting	d.	sit

16. My father is busy. He _____ on his mobile phone.

a.	speaks	b.	is speaking
c.	speak	d.	speaking

17. My uncles are on their farm. They _____ some apricot trees.

a.	planting	b.	plants
c.	is planting	d.	are planting

18. My sister is in her room. She _____ a dress for her baby girl.

a.	sews	b.	sewing
c.	is sewing	d.	sew

19. My aunt is busy. She _____ a nice pie.

a.	is making	b.	make
c.	making	d.	to make

20. Right now, I _____ about my future job.

a.	thinking	b.	thinks
c.	to think	d.	am thinking

21. Listen. Some dogs _____ over there.

a.	barking	b.	is barking
c.	are barking	d.	barks

22. Fasten your seat belt. The plane _____.

a.	take off	b.	taking off
c.	to take off	d.	is taking off

23. We _____ a soccer match on TV right now.

a.	are watching	b.	were watching
c.	watching	d.	watches

24. The employees are really _____ hard at the moment.

a.	are working	b.	working
c.	works	d.	work

25. Cayla: This part of the play is fantastic. I _____ it.
    Amira: I couldn't agree more.

a.	enjoying	b.	to enjoy
c.	am enjoying	d.	enjoys

🌺🌺🌺 My Homework

The Present Progressive (Continuous) Yes/No Questions

| Am | I | -ing | ? |

| Yes, | you | are | -ing | . |

| Yes, | you | are. |

Example:
> Jonah: Am I playing well, sir?
> Coach: Yes, you are playing well.
> Coach: Yes, you are.

| Am | I | -ing | ? |

| No, | you | are not | -ing | . |

| No, | you | aren't. |

Example:
> Lexi: Am I driving fast, Dad?
> Father: No, you aren't driving fast.
> Father: No, you aren't.

| Is | he / she / it | -ing | ? |

| Yes, | he / she / it | is | -ing | . |

| Yes, | he / she / it | is. |

Example:
> Henrik: Is the manager calling?
> Aisha: Yes, the manager is calling.
> Aisha: Yes, he is.

| Is | he / she / it | -ing | ? |

| No, | he / she / it | isn't | -ing | . |

| No, | he / she / it | isn't. |

✚ Example:

➤ Carmen: Is it raining outside?
Craig: No, it isn't raining outside.
Craig: No, it isn't.

| Are | you | -ing | ? |

| Yes, | I | am | -ing | . |

| Yes, | I | am. |

✚ Example:

➤ Salwa: Are you fixing the car engine?
Dina: Yes, I am fixing the car engine.
Dina: Yes, I am.

| Are | you | -ing | ? |

| No, | I | am not | -ing | . |

| No, | I | 'm not. |

✚ Example:

➤ Gary: Are you flying home?
Raul: No, I am not flying home.
Raul: No, I 'm not.

| Are | they | -ing | ? |

| Yes, | they | are | -ing | . |

| Yes, | they | are. |

♦ Example:

> Seif: Are your parents having their dinner now?
> Toni: Yes, my parents are having their dinner now.
> Toni: Yes, they are.

| Are | they | -ing | ? |

| No, | they | aren't | -ing | . |

| No, | they | aren't. |

♦ Example:

> Ammar: Are your brothers sharing in the tournament?
> Daylen: No, my brothers are not sharing in the tournament.
> Daylen: No, they aren't.

| Are | we | -ing | ? |

| Yes, | you | are | -ing | . |

| Yes, | you | are. |

♦ Example:

> Madden and Lima: Are we behaving badly?
> Nour: Yes, you are behaving badly.
> Nour: Yes, you are.

| Are | we | -ing | ? |

| No, | you | are | -ing | . |

| No, | you | aren't. |

♦ Example:

> Randa and Nada: Are we running fast?
> Yasser: No, you aren't running fast.
> Yasser: No, you aren't.

| Are | we | -ing | ? |

| Yes, | we | are | -ing | . |

| | Yes, | we | are. |

✚ **Example:**
➤ Ali and Ibrahim: Are we training hard?
Maher: Yes, we are training hard.
Maher: Yes, we are.

| Are | we | -ing | ? |

| No, | we | are | -ing | . |

| | No, | we | aren't. |

✚ **Example:**
➤ Hala and Reem: Are we applying the safety rules?
Classmates: No, we aren't applying the safety rules.
Classmates: No, we aren't.

➤ *Exercise Three*
  ✚ Choose the correct answer from a, b, c, or d.
1. Omar: Is your brother swimming in the pool?
    Ahmad: Yes, he _____.

a.	is	b.	were
c.	was	d.	are

2. Garson: Are your brothers studying for the test?
    Mark: No, they _____.

a.	are	b.	aren't
c.	is	d.	were

3. Zain: Am I reading well, sir?
    Mira: Yes, _____.

a.	I am	b.	are you
c.	you are	d.	you aren't

4. Asmaà: Are you working out the math problem?
    Rania and Lama: Yes, _____.

a.	you are	b.	are you
c.	we are	d.	you aren't

5. Yassin: Are you _____ in the river?
    Mariam: Yes, I am.

a.	fishing	b.	fished
c.	fished	d.	fishes

6. Anas: Is your son working in an office at the moment?
    Ahmadi: Yes, _____.

a.	he is working	b.	he was
c.	he is	d.	he isn't

7. Karim: Are the players doing their best?
    Randal: Yes, _____.

a.	they are	b.	they aren't
c.	they are doing	d.	they weren't

8. Lina: Is the patient getting ready for the surgery?
    Nahla: Yes, _____ ready the surgery.

a.	he is	b.	he is getting
c.	he isn't	d.	is he getting

9. Lamya: Are you _____ for the dentist?
    Batool: Yes, I am.

a.	waiting	b.	wait
c.	waits	d.	waited

10. Ibrahim: _____ you travelling on business?
    Majid: Yes, I am.

a.	Am	b.	Were
c.	Is	d.	Are

11. Roy: Is it _____ at the moment?
    Gerald: No, it isn't.

a.	snow	b.	snows
c.	snowing	d.	snowed

12. Adam: _____ Lucas living in Toronto?
    Nicolas: Yes, he is.

a.	Am	b.	Were
c.	Is	d.	Are

13. Albert: Is the sun _____ outside?
    Walter: Yes, it is.

a.	shine	b.	shines
c.	to shine	d.	shining

14. Billy: Are you listening to pop music?
    Lee: Yes, _____.

a.	you are	b.	are you
c.	I am	d.	I'm not

15. Rauf: Are you _____ for the optician?
    Rahaf: Yes, I am.

a.	waiting	b.	wait
c.	waits	d.	waited

16. Charlotte: Is the child _____ on the table?
    Annie: Yes, he is.

a.	sitting	b.	sits
c.	sit	d.	to sit

17. Rumen: Are you reading a short story?
    Chloe: Yes, _____ a short story.

a.	I am	b.	I'm not
c.	I am reading	d.	You are reading

18. Maysa: Am I spelling the word correctly?
    Mia: Yes, _____.

a.	you are spelling	b.	I'm not
c.	I am spelling	d.	you are

19. Ava: Is Cooper taking a geography class this semester?
    Ann: Yes, _____.

a.	he is	b.	he is taking
c.	takes	d.	he isn't

20. Edgar: Are the students taking their test right now?
    Ralf: No, _____.

a.	they are taking	b.	they aren't
c.	they aren't taking	d.	they are

The Present (Progressive (Continuous) Wh- Questions

Question Word	am	I	-ing?
	is	he	
		she	
		it	
	are	you	
		they	
		we	

✦ **Example:**
➢ **Sahar: What are the boys doing?**
➢ **Samar: They are hunting some rabbits.**

➢ *Exercise Four*
   ✦ Choose the correct answer from a, b, c, or d.
1. Tommie: What are the students doing?
    Jacob: They _____ their homework.

a.	doing	b.	is doing
c.	were doing	d.	are doing

2. Wesson: _____ are you writing?
    Mother: I am writing an email to your father.

a.	Who	b.	When
c.	Why	d.	What

3. Mennah: ____ is Tuka sleeping?
   Marlin: Because she is very tired.

A.	Why	B.	What
C.	Who	D.	When

4. James: ____ are the boys playing?
   Judi: In the garden.

A.	Why	B.	What
C.	Where	D.	When

5. Ronald: ____ are you doing now?
   Jason: I'm watching a comic play.

A.	Why	B.	What
C.	Where	D.	When

6. Karma ____ are you going?
   Henri: I'm going to the bank.

A.	Why	B.	What
C.	Where	D.	When

7. Ethan: ____ are you calling your friend now?
   Essam: We are having an important appointment.

A.	Who	B.	When
C.	Why	D.	What

8. Mohamed: ____ isn't the student wearing his safety shoes?
   Drayton: Because he left them in the gym.

A.	Who	B.	What
C.	Why	D.	When

9. Elham: ____ are your brothers staying?
   Dillan: They are staying in a five-star hotel near the beach.

A.	Who	B.	What
C.	Why	D.	Where

10. Saeed: ____ are you staying in Athens?
    Jaber: I'm staying in Athens for three weeks.

A.	How often	B.	How long
C.	How many	D.	How much

▰▰▰ *My Homework*

> **Exercise Five**

✤ Rearrange the following words to make correct sentences.

1. / mother / tea / making / is / cup / a / of / My / me /
   ✍ ____ ____ ____ ____ ____ ____ ____ ____ ____ ____

2. / mountains / are / hiking / The / boys / the / in /
   ✍ ____ ____ ____ ____ ____ ____ ____ ____

3. / book / Ahmad / is / a / peace / reading / about /
   ✍ ____ ____ ____ ____ ____ ____ ____ ____

4. / girl / picture / is / The / very / drawing / a / nice /
_____

5. / hens / sister / now / feeding / My / is / the / right /
_____

6. / The / training / at / players / not / are / moment / the /
_____

7. / little / on / scratching / nail / My / cat / itself / is / a /
_____

8. / having / lunch / their / in / They / now / are / restaurant / a /
_____

9. / digging / hole / a / workmen / are / The / deep /
_____

10. / playing / games / computer / The / boys / are / young /
_____

11. / you / studying / or / Are / ? / Arabic / English /
_____

12. / falling / window / rain / The / is / on / the /
_____

13. / this / plane / flying / Is / Dubai / Dublin / ? / or / to /
_____

14. / raining / Is / outside / still / it / ? /
_____

15. / plane / landing / moment / is / The / at / the /
_____

16. / writing / his / email / is / brother / to / an / My / boss /
_____

17. / secretary / documents / The / filing / is / some /
_____

18. / teacher / correcting / homework / is / the / Our /
_____

19. / buffalo / lions / are / a / Two / chasing / Look! /
_____

20. / drawing / some / are / students / The / pictures /
_____

21. / laptop / is / working / his / on / Ahmad /
_____

22. / having / Osama / swim / Abdul-Rahman / are / and / a /
_____

23. / sister / Batool / her / is / lessons / My / reviewing /
_____

24. / mechanic / fixing / father's / is / my / The / van /
✎ ____ ____ ____ ____ ____ ____ ____ ____

25. / Saleh / final / are / for / the / and / test / studying / Omar /
✎ ____ ____ ____ ____ ____ ____ ____ ____ ____

✿✿✿ My Homework

> ## Exercise Six
✦ Use the given words to form meaningful sentences in the present continuous. Follow the example.

1. / baby / cry / loudly
✎ The baby is crying loudly.

2. / boy / play / game /
✎ ____ ____ ____ ____ ____ ____ ____ ____

3. / girl / read / story /
✎ ____ ____ ____ ____ ____ ____ ____ ____

4. / man / drink / coffee /
✎ ____ ____ ____ ____ ____ ____ ____ ____

5. / women / have / lunch /
✎ ____ ____ ____ ____ ____ ____ ____ ____

6. / father / not / sleep /
✎ ____ ____ ____ ____ ____ ____ ____ ____

7. / mother / cook / meal /
✎ ____ ____ ____ ____ ____ ____ ____ ____

8. / sister / study / geography /
✎ ____ ____ ____ ____ ____ ____ ____ ____

9. / brother / watch / not / match /
✎ ____ ____ ____ ____ ____ ____ ____ ____

10. / grandfather / smile /
✎ ____ ____ ____ ____ ____ ____ ____ ____

11. / grandmother / sew / dress /
✎ ____ ____ ____ ____ ____ ____ ____ ____

12. / uncle / work / farm /
✎ ____ ____ ____ ____ ____ ____ ____ ____

13. / aunt / shop / mall /
✎ ____ ____ ____ ____ ____ ____ ____ ____

14. / boys / sit / living room /
✎ ____ ____ ____ ____ ____ ____ ____ ____

15. / girls / chat / Internet /

✎_____
16. / We / ride / camels /
✎_____
17. / I / talk / teacher /
✎_____
18. / She / speak / phone /
✎_____
19. / He / build / house /
✎_____
20. / sister / look for / bag /
✎_____

✿✿✿ My Homework

➤ **Exercise Seven**
  ✤ Use the given words to form meaningful sentences in the present continuous.
  1. / dog / chase / cat /
  ✎_____
  2. / The sparrow / sing /
  ✎_____
  3. / Mike / wash / pants /
  ✎_____
  4. / They / wait / doctor /
  ✎_____
  5. / parents / go / market /
  ✎_____
  6. / teacher / wear / glasses /
  ✎_____
  7. / grandfather / paint / door /
  ✎_____
  8. / We / visit / uncle /
  ✎_____
  9. / Batool / drive / car /
  ✎_____
  10. / mother / milk / cow /
  ✎_____
  11. / sister / cook / meal /
  ✎_____
  12. / wife / prepare / breakfast /
  ✎_____

13. / Mr. Jackson / help / students /
➢ _____

14. / Mahmoud / climb / hill /
➢ _____

15. / Dawood / fix / phone /
➢ _____

16. / Anas / fly / Rome /
➢ _____

17. / friends / relax / park /
➢ _____

18. / mechanic / repair / bus /
➢ _____

19. / The sun / shine /
➢ _____

20. / Ali / leave / Cordoba /
➢ _____

➣➣➣ *My Homework*

➢ *Exercise Eight*
  ✦ Use the given words to form meaningful sentences in the present continuous.

1. / men / walk / beach /
➢ _____

2. / clerk / type / letter /
➢ _____

3. / manager / plan / project /
➢ _____

4. / classmate / write / lessons /
➢ _____

5. / classmates / do / research /
➢ _____

6. / The child / pray / room /
➢ _____

7. / children / play / with / mother /
➢ _____

8. / boss / explain / plan /
➢ _____

9. / Safia / make / cookies /
➢ _____

10. / Darien / hurry / school /
🖎_____

11. / Walid / plant / trees /
🖎_____

12. / It / snow / heavily /
🖎_____

13. / friends / swim / sea /
🖎_____

14. / Rihanna / wash / shirt /
🖎_____

15. / Ahmadi / meet / family /
🖎_____

16. / We / open / branch / Moscow /
🖎_____

17. / grandparents / stay / farm /
🖎_____

18. / Peter / water / flowers /
🖎_____

19. / Retaj / make / bed /
🖎_____

20. / Lobna / log / Internet /
🖎_____

🖎🖎🖎 My Homework

> **Exercise Ten**
  ⊹ Answer the following questions. Follow the example.
> What is Merhan doing?
✓ collect – flowers
🖎 Merhan is collecting some flowers.

1. What is Mark doing?
✓ feed – horses
🖎_____

2. What is the camel doing?
✓ eat – some – grass
🖎_____

3. What are you doing?
✓ watch – play – TV
🖎_____

4. What are the farmers doing?
✓ grow – rice
🖎_____

5. What is the policeman doing?
✓ guard - bank
✎ _____ _____ _____ _____ _____ _____ _____ _____

6. What is Samuel doing?
✓ fuel - car
✎ _____ _____ _____ _____ _____ _____ _____ _____

7. What is the teacher doing?
✓ review - grammar
✎ _____ _____ _____ _____ _____ _____ _____ _____

8. What is the nurse doing?
✓ help - patient
✎ _____ _____ _____ _____ _____ _____ _____ _____

9. What is the player doing?
✓ train - hard
✎ _____ _____ _____ _____ _____ _____ _____ _____

10. What is Hanan doing?
✓ dress - baby
✎ _____ _____ _____ _____ _____ _____ _____ _____

11. What are Mazin and Merna doing?
✓ play - toys
✎ _____ _____ _____ _____ _____ _____ _____ _____

12. What is the old man doing?
✓ jog
✎ _____ _____ _____ _____ _____ _____ _____ _____

13. What are your uncles doing?
✓ harvest - wheat
✎ _____ _____ _____ _____ _____ _____ _____ _____

14. What are the engineers doing?
✓ fix - engines
✎ _____ _____ _____ _____ _____ _____ _____ _____

15. What is Hamdi doing?
✓ draw - picture
✎ _____ _____ _____ _____ _____ _____ _____ _____

16. What is Mazin doing?
✓ take - test
✎ _____ _____ _____ _____ _____ _____ _____ _____

17. What is Tina doing?
✓ dust - room
✎ _____ _____ _____ _____ _____ _____ _____ _____

18. What is Violet doing?
✓ build - sandcastle
✎ _____ _____ _____ _____ _____ _____ _____ _____

19. What is the janitor doing?
✓ sweep - floor
✎ _____ _____ _____ _____ _____ _____ _____ _____ _____

20. What is your grandmother doing?
✓ take - nap
✎ _____ _____ _____ _____ _____ _____ _____ _____ _____

🖎🖎🖎 My Homework 🖎🖎🖎

➢ **Exercise Ten**
   ↳ Answer the following questions. Follow the example.
➢ Is Batool listening to music?
✓ No, she isn't listening to music.
✓ She is reading a short story.

1. Is Tuka watching a match on TV?
➢ help - mother - kitchen
✓ _____ _____ _____ _____ _____ _____ _____ _____ _____
✎ _____ _____ _____ _____ _____ _____ _____ _____ _____

2. Are you checking the tires of your car?
➢ fix - brakes
✓ _____ _____ _____ _____ _____ _____ _____ _____ _____
✎ _____ _____ _____ _____ _____ _____ _____ _____ _____

3. Are the boys fishing?
➢ swim
✓ _____ _____ _____ _____ _____ _____ _____ _____ _____
✎ _____ _____ _____ _____ _____ _____ _____ _____ _____

4. Are the girls playing hide and seek?
➢ study
✓ _____ _____ _____ _____ _____ _____ _____ _____ _____
✎ _____ _____ _____ _____ _____ _____ _____ _____ _____

5. Is your brother surfing the Internet?
➢ do - homework
✓ _____ _____ _____ _____ _____ _____ _____ _____ _____
✎ _____ _____ _____ _____ _____ _____ _____ _____ _____

6. Is Lama writing a report?
➢ plan - trip
✓ _____ _____ _____ _____ _____ _____ _____ _____ _____
✎ _____ _____ _____ _____ _____ _____ _____ _____ _____

7. Is Derek baking some bread?
➢ cook - rice
✓ _____ _____ _____ _____ _____ _____ _____ _____ _____
✎ _____ _____ _____ _____ _____ _____ _____ _____ _____

8. Is Poppy watching a movie?
➤ play - computer - games
✓ _____
✗ _____

9. Is Abdul-Rahman playing a soccer match?
➤ do - exercise
✓ _____
✗ _____

10. Is Ramona drawing a picture?
➤ iron - dress
✓ _____
✗ _____

11. Is Majid catching fish?
➤ have - walk
✓ _____
✗ _____

12. Are the students reviewing for their final exam?
➤ take - quiz
✓ _____
✗ _____

✍ ✍ ✍ My Homework ✍ ✍ ✍

➤ *Exercise Eleven*
   ✦ Complete the sentences with the correct form of the verbs in the simple present or present continuous tense. Follow the examples.
➤ Laura (love) action movies.
✓ *Laura loves action movies.*
➤ Pamela (fly) to Tokyo tonight.
✓ *Pamela is flying to Tokyo tonight.*

1. Salem usually (take) his kids to the country.
✗ _____

2. Suzan often (arrive) at her clinic on time.
✗ _____

3. Watch out! A wild dog (come) over there.
✗ _____

4. I (use) my mobile phone every day.
✗ _____

5. Take an umbrella with you. It (rain) heavily.
✗ _____

6. Can you see Khalid? He (walk) over there.
   ➢ _____
7. Annie (walk) to school every morning.
   ➢ _____
8. Kamila (not like) reading detective stories.
   ➢ _____
9. Yasmin still (do) her research. She hasn't finished yet.
   ➢ _____
10. Listen! Someone (shout) inside this room.
    ➢ _____
11. Look out! The car (move) downward.
    ➢ _____
12. Look! The porter (carry) a heavy bag. We should help him.
    ➢ _____
13. This postman (deliver) a lot of mail daily.
    ➢ _____
14. My sister (cook) a delicious meal at the moment.
    ➢ _____
15. Jana (check) my computer. I hope she can fix it.
    ➢ _____
16. Mustafa (drive) carefully. He never has accidents.
    ➢ _____
17. Hazim usually (think) before taking an important decision.
    ➢ _____
18. This iPad (cost) a lot of money.
    ➢ _____
19. Nelson (study) English and IT twice a week.
    ➢ _____
20. The world (consume) a lot of energy yearly.
    ➢ _____

➢➢➢ *My Homework*

Non-action Verbs

➢ **Verbs that express mental state**

realize	know
imagine	need
want	mean
believe	feel
forget	prefer
remember	recognize
suppose	doubt
think	understand

Example:
I am believing that Shakespeare is the best playwright. (X)
I believe that Shakespeare is the best playwright. (✓)

➢ **Verbs that express possession**

have	possess
own	belong

Example:
➢ Lucy is having a large farm near the river. (X)
Lucy has a large farm near the river. (✓)

➢ **Verbs that express emotional state**

love	fear	dislike
care	mind	hate
envy	like	appreciate

Example:
➢ Grace is disliking boxing. (X)
Grace dislikes boxing. (✓)

➢ **Verbs that express sense perceptions**

taste	feel
smell	see
hear	

Example:
➢ This rose is beautiful. It is smelling sweet. (X)
This rose is beautiful. It smells sweet. (✓)

➢ **Other existing verbs**

seem		consist of	
please		exist	
appear		be	
include		contain	
promise		cost	
owe		need	
agree		know	
fit		want	
sound		look = seem	
depend		matter	
see		mean	
disagree		satisfy	
doubt		wish	
lack		concern	
astonish			
weigh (= have weight)			
measure (= have length)			

✦ **Example:**
➢ The price of my new car is including taxes. (X)
The price of my new car includes taxes. (✓)

➢ *Exercise Twelve*
✦ Choose the correct answer from a, b, c, or d.

1. I _____ Mr Muhammad Ali. He is my next-door neighbor.

a.	am knowing	b.	know
c.	knowing	d.	knows

2. I _____ that my soccer team is the best.

a.	thinking	b.	am thinking
c.	think	d.	thinks

3. My grandfather _____ a large farmhouse.

a.	have	b.	has
c.	having	d.	is having

4. My grandparents _____ a chalet at the Red Sea.

a.	are having	b.	having
c.	to have	d.	have

5. My sister _____ happy. She passed her final exams.

a.	looks	b.	look
c.	is looking	d.	was looking

6. I can't lift this heavy box. It _____ more than 100 kilos.

a.	weigh	b.	is weighing
c.	weighing	d.	weighs

7. My uncle _____ a cement factory outside the city.

a.	owning	b.	is owning
c.	own	d.	owns

8. My brother _____ a large sum of money to my mother.

a.	owing	b.	is owing
c.	owe	d.	owes

9. This new laptop _____ to Mr Obaidah.

a.	belongs	b.	belong
c.	is belonging	d.	belonging

10. Sediq is a kind man. He _____ his family and friends.

a.	loving	b.	loves
c.	love	d.	is loving

11. Hatem _____ swimming to diving.

a.	is preferring	b.	prefer
c.	prefers	d.	preferring

12. I like this cake. It _____ delicious.

a.	taste	b.	is tasting
c.	tasting	d.	tastes

13. I _____ helping you when needed.

a.	am not minding	b.	don't mind
c.	was not minding	d.	isn't minding

14. My uncle's new house is expensive. It _____ a lot of money.

a.	is costing	b.	to cost
c.	costing	d.	costs

15. I am awfully sorry, madam. I _____ to hurt your feelings.

a.	wasn't meaning	b.	am not meaning
c.	hadn't been meaning	d.	didn't mean

16. I _____ that you have to review these plans once more.

a.	supposes	b.	am supposing
c.	suppose	d.	supposing

17. Adam _____ the first day he joined school.

a.	is remembering	b.	remembers
c.	remember	d.	was remembering

18. Sarah _____ to be involved in troubles with her classmates.

a.	hating	b.	is hating
c.	hate	d.	hates

19. I _____ that we visit the national museum next Saturday.

a.	agree	b.	agrees
c.	am agreeing	d.	agreeing

20. Andrew is rich as he _____ a large sum of money.

a.	possessing	b.	possesses
c.	is possessing	d.	to possess

21. We _____ Mr Hefny's strenuous efforts with his students.

a.	are appreciating	b.	appreciating
c.	appreciates	d.	appreciate

22. I _____ if our team will win the semi-final match.

a.	doubting	b.	doubt
c.	are doubting	d.	doubts

23. I hope that my father-in-law _____ my point of view.

a.	is understanding	b.	understand
c.	understands	d.	to understand

24. Sherouk _____ tired as she hasn't slept for a long time.

a.	looks	b.	is looking
c.	looking	d.	look

25. I _____ my elder brother had a better job.

a.	am wishing	b.	wishes
c.	wish	d.	to wish

🌸🌸🌸 My Homework

> **Exercise Thirteen**
  + Correct the mistake in each of the following sentences.
  + Follow the example.
> The passengers are walk in the corridor right now.
🌸 The passengers <u>are walking</u> in the corridor right now.

1. My elder sister is having a nice necklace.
🌸 _____

2. Nabila is browse the Internet at the moment.
🌸 _____

3. These new shoes are costing a lot of money.
🌸 _____

4. Listen. Our neighbor knocks on the door.
🌸 _____

5. Be careful. Some cattle cross the road.
🌸 _____

6. My grandfather is read a long poem right now.
🌸 _____

7. Look at this young man. He is jog in the park.
🌸 _____

8. Wilson learn how to dive right now.
🌸 _____

9. Hurry up. Our teacher wait for us.
🌸 _____

10. Please be quiet. My baby sleep.
➢ _____ _____ _____ _____ _____ _____ _____ _____ _____ _____

11. Don't disturb the teacher. He introduce a new lesson.
➢ _____ _____ _____ _____ _____ _____ _____ _____ _____ _____

12. Listen to my sister. She sing a beautiful song.
➢ _____ _____ _____ _____ _____ _____ _____ _____ _____ _____

13. The baby cry because it is hungry.
➢ _____ _____ _____ _____ _____ _____ _____ _____ _____ _____

14. Wait a minute. My father talk on the phone.
➢ _____ _____ _____ _____ _____ _____ _____ _____ _____ _____

15. Be careful. The metro come.
➢ _____ _____ _____ _____ _____ _____ _____ _____ _____ _____

16. Mother bake an apple cake at the moment.
➢ _____ _____ _____ _____ _____ _____ _____ _____ _____ _____

17. Mr Saleh is busy these days. He write a new book.
➢ _____ _____ _____ _____ _____ _____ _____ _____ _____ _____

18. My grandparents are in the garden. They have their lunch there.
➢ _____ _____ _____ _____ _____ _____ _____ _____ _____ _____

19. My sisters are in their room. They studying geology.
➢ _____ _____ _____ _____ _____ _____ _____ _____ _____ _____

20. I write an email to my manager right now.
➢ _____ _____ _____ _____ _____ _____ _____ _____ _____ _____

✍ ✍ ✍ My Homework ✍ ✍ ✍

SECTION 9 — The Past Progressive (Continuous) Tense

Affirmative

I	was	-ing
He		
She		
It		
You	were	
They		
We		

Negative

I	wasn't	-ing
He		
She		
It		
You	weren't	
They		
We		

When

When	Simple Past	Past Progressive

OR

Past Progressive	when	Simple Past

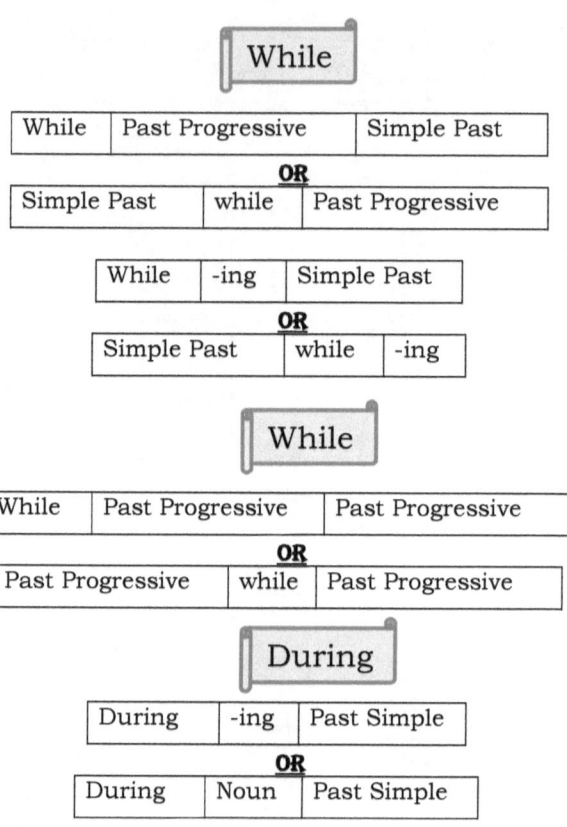

✦ Examples:

- *When* the teacher entered, the students were studying.
- We were sleeping *when* our father called us.
- *While* I was fixing some devices, my friend came.
- John phoned me *while* I was doing my homework.
- *While* walking in the garden, I found a wallet.
- I discovered many mistakes *while* reviewing the reports.
- *While* Dina was cooking, Sally was washing her clothes.
- My grandfather was having a walk *while* Amr was watering the roses.
- *While* I was using my mobile phone, it fell down and broke into pieces.
- *While* using my mobile phone, it fell down and broke into pieces.

- <u>*During*</u> using my mobile phone, it fell down and broke into pieces.
- <u>*While*</u> we were watching the game, it started to snow.
- <u>*While*</u> watching the game, it started to snow.
- <u>*During*</u> the game, it began to rain.
- Millions of people met their end <u>*during*</u> the war.
- A lot of young men were injured <u>*during*</u> the fight.

- Exercise One

  ✦ Rearrange these words to form meaningful sentences.
  ✦ Follow the example.

- / swimming / The / were / boys /
✓ The boys were swimming.

1) / was / I / sleeping /
🐌 _____

2) / and / meal / Grey / were / a / having / Ellie / nice /
🐌 _____

3) / planting / trees / Mohsen / was / some /
🐌 _____

4) / were / My / match / friends / playing / a /
🐌 _____

5) / watching / on / news / They / the / were / TV /
🐌 _____

6) / studying / new / I / plan / was / a /
🐌 _____

7) / was / the / Nora / dishes / doing /
🐌 _____

8) / student / library / The / the / walking / was / to /
🐌 _____

9) / a / building / They / house / were / new /
🐌 _____

10) / were / the / bus / We / for / waiting /
🐌 _____

➢ **Exercise Two**

✦ Rearrange these words to form meaningful sentences.

1) / father / shaving / My / was /
🖎 _____

2) / shower / a / was / brother / My / taking /
🖎 _____

3) / showering / It / heavily / was /
🖎 _____

4) / uncle / driving / was / Bloomington / My / driving / to /
🖎 _____

5) / sister / was / My / preparing / the / supper /
🖎 _____

6) / was / My / reading / reports / father / news / some /
🖎 _____

7) / blowing / fast / The / very / wind / was /
🖎 _____

8) / Gabriel / drawing / picture / was / a /
🖎 _____

9) / was / glass / juice / drinking / a / of / Hala /
🖎 _____

10) / sandwich / Fares / a / was / eating /
🖎 _____

🖎🖎🖎 *My Homework* 🖎🖎🖎

➢ **Exercise Three**

✦ Rearrange these words to form meaningful sentences.

1) / man / some / was / The / feeding / sheep /
🖎 _____

2) / were / We / home / flying /
🖎 _____

3) / going / beach / They / to / were / the /
🖎 _____

4) / praying / Hassan / were / Osama / and /
🖎 _____

5) / cleaning / office / janitor / was / my / The /
🖎 _____

6) washing / car / was / Paolo / his /
🖎 _____

7) / writing / He / emails / was / some /
🖎 _____

8) / checking / homework / our / The / teacher / was /
✎ ____ ____ ____ ____ ____ ____ ____ ____

9) / test / having / We / a / were /
✎ ____ ____ ____ ____ ____ ____

10) / speaking / phone / I / on / the / was /
✎ ____ ____ ____ ____ ____ ____ ____

My Homework

The Past Progressive (Continuous) Tense

Yes-No Questions

Was	I	
	he	
	she	
	it	-ing ...?
Were	you	
	they	
	we	

➕ Examples:

Clinton: Was it sleeting heavily?
✓ **Helena:** Yes, it was.
Alia: Were you driving safely?
✓ **Adel:** Yes, I was.

My Homework

Exercise Four
Choose the correct answer from a, b, c or d.

1) **Samir:** Were you running fast?
   ✓ Juliet: Yes, I _____.

a	was running	b	was
c	were	d	am

2) **Cary:** Were you shopping in the market?
   ✓ Charlie: No, we _____.

a	were	b	weren't shopping
c	weren't	d	aren't

3) **Tamer:** Were you driving to work?
   ✓ Garett: Yes, I _____ to work.

a	was	b	was driving
c	wasn't	d	am driving

4) **Jason:** Were the students having a break?
   ✓ Wilson: No, they _____.

a	were	b	weren't having
c	weren't	d	were having

5) **Jessica:** Were you hiking alone?
   ✓ Amany: Yes, I _____ alone.

a	wasn't	b	hiking
c	were	d	was hiking

6) **Maria:** Was Muhammad studying French?
   ✓ Nilsson: Yes, he _____.

a	was	b	studying
c	was studying	d	is studying

7) **Amir:** Were your parents flying to Cairo?
   ✓ Elizabeth: Yes, they _____ there.

a	were	b	are flying
c	were flying	d	are

8) **Tariq:** Were you chatting with your friend?
   ✓ Dina: Yes, _____.

a	I was chatting	b	I am chatting
c	I was	d	I wasn't

9) **Carver:** Was your father jogging in the park?
   ✓ Yasmina: No, he _____.

a	isn't	b	was jogging
c	couldn't	d	wasn't

10) **Nada:** Was it hailing heavily?
    ✓ Saliva: Yes, it _____.

a	is	b	was hailing
c	was	d	wasn't

11) **Tom:** Were the boys swimming in the pond?
    ✓ Tim: Yes, they _____.

a	were swimming	b	were
c	weren't	d	are

12) Anas: Was the motorist driving fast?
   ✓ Policeman: Yes, he _____ .

| a | is | b | was driving |
| c | was | d | wasn't |

13) Oscar: Was the clerk writing the reports?
   ✓ Tommy: Yes, he _____ them.

| a | were writing | b | was writing |
| c | was | d | wasn't |

14) Sherif: Were the students having a break?
   ✓ Zahra: No, they _____ .

| a | were having | b | weren't having |
| c | are | d | weren't |

15) Layan: Was Omar watching the local derby on TV?
   ✓ Salma: Yes, he _____ .

| a | is | b | was watching |
| c | was | d | wasn't watching |

16) Qassim: Were you having lunch with your family?
   ✓ Selena: Yes, I _____ .

| a | wasn't having | b | was having |
| c | was | d | wasn't |

17) Mahitab: Was Amira waiting for Saged?
   ✓ Cade: Yes, she _____ for him.

| a | was waiting | b | was |
| c | is | d | wasn't |

18) Kinsey: Were you riding your bike?
   ✓ Kenzie: No, I _____ it.

| a | is | b | was riding |
| c | wasn't | d | wasn't riding |

19) Nicole: Was Shaima'a making her bed when she found the ring?
   ✓ Iven: Yes, she _____ .

| a | wasn't making | b | was |
| c | was making | d | wasn't |

20) Eslam: Was Youssef wearing a new shirt?
   ✓ Eliza: No, he _____ .

| a | was wearing | b | wasn't |
| c | was | d | wasn't wearing |

My Homework

The Past Progressive (Continuous) Tense

Information Questions

Question Word	was	I	-ing?
		he	
		she	
		it	
	were	you	
		they	
		we	

> Exercise Five

➕ Answer the following questions. Follow the example.

> Oscar: What were you doing?
✓ Jamal: /listen / news/

🐌 I was listening to the news.

1) Principal: What were the students doing?
✓ Teacher: /read / short / stories/

🐌 ____ ____ ____ ____ ____ ____ ____ ____

2) Michael: What was Ahmad doing?
✓ Nadine: /fly / kite/

🐌 ____ ____ ____ ____ ____ ____ ____ ____

3) Max: What was Batool doing?
✓ Walter: /chat / friend / Sarah/

🐌 ____ ____ ____ ____ ____ ____ ____ ____

4) Adrian: What were your classmates doing?
✓ Maher: /surf / Internet/

🐌 ____ ____ ____ ____ ____ ____ ____ ____

5) Poppy: What was Yaseen doing?
✓ Kim: /dig / hole/

🐌 ____ ____ ____ ____ ____ ____ ____ ____

6) Connor: What were you doing?
✓ Luke: /sing / song/

🐌 ____ ____ ____ ____ ____ ____ ____ ____

7) Kareem: What were you doing?
   ✓ Hanan: /write / email/
   ➢ _____

8) Jasmine: What were you doing?
   ✓ Serena: /make / cake/
   ➢ _____

9) Molly: What were you doing?
   ✓ Joseph: /swim / sea/
   ➢ _____

10) Mary: What was the mechanic doing?
    ✓ Maggie: /repair / car/
    ➢ _____

11) Ayman: What was the farmer doing?
    ✓ Sameh: /store / crops/
    ➢ _____

12) Maha: What was your teacher doing?
    ✓ Mustafa: /check / attendance / list/
    ➢ _____

13) Rawda: What was the nurse doing?
    ✓ Raneem: /help / patient/
    ➢ _____

14) Katie: What were the policemen doing?
    ✓ Abeer: /chase / thief/
    ➢ _____

15) Chloe: What were your parents doing?
    ✓ Taro: /have / breakfast/
    ➢ _____

16) Edwin: What were your friends doing?
    ✓ Perez: /dive/
    ➢ _____

17) Marawan: What were the workmen doing?
    ✓ Susan: /paint / walls/
    ➢ _____

18) Merhan: What were you doing?
    ✓ Hamada: /watch / movie/
    ➢ _____

19) Lisa: What was the man doing?
    ✓ Salwa: /sell / goods/
    ➢ _____

20) Archie: What were the birds doing?
    ✓ Dylan: /feed / kids/
    ➢ _____

21) Harry: What was the cat doing?
   ✓ Albert: /chase /mice/
   ✍ ____ ____ ____ ____ ____ ____ ____ ____

22) Thomas: What was the maid doing?
   ✓ Thomson: /clean / floor/
   ✍ ____ ____ ____ ____ ____ ____ ____ ____

23) Muhammad: What was the gardener doing?
   ✓ Kamal: /water / flowers/
   ✍ ____ ____ ____ ____ ____ ____ ____ ____

24) Lobna: What was the guard doing?
   ✓ Leila: /watch/ crowds/
   ✍ ____ ____ ____ ____ ____ ____ ____ ____

My Homework

> *Exercise Six*
  ↓ Choose the correct answer from a, b, c, or d.

1) Nour: _____ were you running very fast?
   ✓ Ayah: Because I was late for my class.

| a. | When | b. | Why |
| c. | How | d. | Where |

2) Khalid: _____ was knocking at the door?
   ✓ Lewis: My grandmother.

| a. | When | b. | Why |
| c. | How | d. | Who |

3) Ismail: _____ were you going?
   ✓ Ibrahim: To the bank.

| a. | When | b. | Why |
| c. | How | d. | Where |

4) Jake: _____ was your mother doing?
   ✓ Jane: She was cooking a nice meal.

| a. | When | b. | Why |
| c. | How | d. | Who |

5) Policeman: _____ were you driving?
   ✓ Nader: I was driving carefully.

| a. | When | b. | Why |
| c. | How | d. | Who |

6) Teacher: _____ weren't you studying?
   ✓ Noah: I was very sick.

| a. | When | b. | Why |
| c. | How | d. | Who |

7) Jane: Why were you sleeping?
   ✓ Jana: I _____ very tired, sir.

| a. | were | b. | is |
| c. | was | d. | am |

8) Maha: Why was the baby _____?
✓ Huda: Because its diapers were wet.

a.	cry	b.	cried
c.	cries	d.	crying

➢ Exercise Seven

✦ Choose the correct answer from a, b, c, or d.

1) I _____ my lunch when the telephone rang.

a	having	b	am having
c	was having	d	were having

2) While Ali _____ a shower, his friend called.

a	is taking	b	taking
c	take	d	was taking

3) While Dalia _____ on Main Street, she saw her friend Leila.

a	walks	b	was walking
c	walking	d	is walking

4) Kathrin and her sister _____ in the garden when they found a treasure.

a	was digging	b	digging
c	are digging	d	were digging

5) While our teacher _____ the new lesson, a newcomer knocked at the door.

a	explains	b	explaining
c	explain	d	was explaining

6) As Basim was playing a football match, he _____ down and broke his toe.

a	was falling	b	fallen
c	fall	d	fell

7) While I was flying to Bucharest, they _____ me a delicious meal.

a	serve	b	served
c	serves	d	have served

8) We _____ some trees when it started to rain.

a	were planting	b	was planting
c	planting	d	are planting

9) While we were sitting in our classroom, our teacher _____.

a	come	b	coming
c	is coming	d	came

10) While Salma was doing the washing, she _____ a dish.

a	breaks	b	braking
c	broke	d	broken

11) While Ibrahim was wandering downtown, he _____ some tourists.

a	met	b	meet
c	meets	d	has met

12) As Khalid was driving home, he _____ a little cat.

a	was hitting	b	is hitting
c	hits	d	hit

13) While I was going to class, I _____ my new classmate.

a	was seeing	b	saw
c	have seen	d	seen

14) While we were watching TV, we _____ shouting in the garden.

a	heard	b	hear
c	hears	d	to hear

15) While Nour was using a knife, she _____ her finger.

a	cut	b	was cutting
c	has cut	d	to cut

16) I was reading my newspaper when the phone _____.

a	rings	b	ringing
c	rang	d	rung

17) While I was going to the park, I _____ a wallet on my way.

a	was finding	b	found
c	find	d	have found

18) While my mother was cooking, my sister _____.

a	studying	b	is studied
c	studied	d	was studying

19) As I was playing computer games, Ahmad _____ a game on TV.

a	watching	b	is watching
c	was watching	d	watched

20) While John was working on his farm, his wife _____ lunch.

a	was preparing	b	preparing
c	is preparing	d	prepares

My Homework

> ## Exercise Eight
> ↳ Choose the correct answer from a, b, c, or d.

1) While I was doing my homework, my elder brother _____.

a	sleeping	b	is sleeping
c	was sleeping	d	sleeping

2) As my parents were having a walk, I _____.

a	was jogging	b	jogs
c	jogging	d	jog

3) While we were swimming, Anas _____.

a	was fishing	b	fishing
c	fishes	d	is fishing

4) Mustafa was diving while Adham _____ on the beach.

a	playing	b	was play
c	to play	d	was playing

5) While Saleh was writing a report, Hamoudy _____ the Internet.

a	surfs	b	is surfing
c	was surfing	d	was surf

6) Adam was fixing his mobile phone when I _____ his room.

a	entered	b	was entering
c	was enter	d	enters

7) Lilly and Kate were doing their homework when I _____.

a	arrived	b	was arrive
c	have arrived	d	arrive

8) William was having his lunch when his friend _____.

a	called	b	calling
c	was call	d	has called

9) Arthur was training in the gym when he _____ his foot.

a	twisting	b	twists
c	twist	d	twisted

10) We sat silently _____ our parents were praying.

a	while	b	who
c	why	d	whom

11) While Omar _____ on the beach, he found a gold ring.

a.	walk	b.	walks
c.	walking	d.	was walking

12) While Leila _____ some clothes, her kids were playing in the garden.

a.	washing	b.	was washing
c.	wash	d.	were washing

13) While _____ in the street, I ran into one of my old friends.

a.	was walking	b.	am walking
c.	walking	d.	walked

14) While we were camping in the desert, a lion _____ to attack us.

a.	tries	b.	try
c.	tried	d.	trying

15) When Sarah came back home, her mother _____.

a.	sleeping	b.	is sleeping
c.	was sleeping	d.	sleeps

16) I _____ a lecture when my assistant called me.

a.	was giving	b.	gives
c.	give	d.	to give

17) We _____ the flat tire when it began to rain.

a.	replacing	b.	are replacing
c.	replace	d.	were replacing

18) Jane fell on the floor while _____ it.

a.	sweeps	b.	was sweeping
c.	swept	d.	sweeping

19) Martin _____ his keys while he was digging in the garden.

a.	lose	b.	come
c.	lost	d.	coming

20) My brothers were flying their kites when a sandstorm _____.

a.	blew	b.	blow
c.	blows	d.	blowing

My Homework

> ## Exercise Nine
> ✦ Fill in the gab using during or while.

1) What did you do _____ the summer?
2) Did you see any birds _____ you were hunting?
3) _____ the game was going on, I was listening to music.
4) _____ the game, Alfred hurt his left arm.
5) Our manager was reviewing his plans _____ the week.
6) _____ the winter, it rained a lot in our city.
7) _____ we were swimming, we saw a strange fish.
8) Our manager was suddenly taken ill _____ the meeting.
9) _____ I was walking in the street, I met some tourists.
10) _____ the weekend, I met a lot of friends.

My Homework

> ## Exercise Ten
> ✦ Complete the sentences with the past progressive form.

1) Adam _____ [run] because he was late for the train.
2) Mido and Boody _____ [study] at 9:30 p.m.
3) My brothers _____ [not laugh] when you fell into the hole.
4) Saleh _____ [check] his email at 3:45 a.m.
5) Tina and Lina _____ [design] a website for their company.
6) Ali _____ [take] a photo when his camera fell on the floor.
7) What _____ you [do] _____ when you cut your finger?
8) Mohamed _____ [shop] while Tuka _____ [train] in the gym.
9) _____ John [drive] _____ when the accident happened?
10) The fan _____ [fall] on the floor while we were playing chess.
11) Ibrahim _____ [exercise] with his friends all the afternoon.
12) What _____ Kim [wear] _____ at his graduation party?

13) My father was having a light meal while he _____ [hear] the news on the radio.
14) My brother _____ [paint] the wall when his friends came.
15) My sister _____ [prepare] dinner when I arrived.
16) Jack _____ [talk] on the phone when the accident happened.
17) George _____ [not stay] in a furnished apartment.
18) We _____ [not sleep] when the earthquake started.
19) The children _____ [make] much noise while I was sleeping.
20) We _____ [take] a quiz while the teacher was scoring our sheets.

My Homework

➢ **Exercise Eleven**
  ↳ Answer the following questions in complete sentences.
  ↳ Follow the example.
➢ What were you doing when I called you?
✓ I was sleeping when you called me.

1) Where were you going when I met you?
   ✎ ____ ____ ____ ____ ____ ____ ____ ____ ____ .
2) Whom you were talking to when I entered?
   ✎ ____ ____ ____ ____ ____ ____ ____ ____ ____ .
3) What was the teacher doing when I knocked?
   ✎ ____ ____ ____ ____ ____ ____ ____ ____ ____ .
4) What were the players doing when it started raining?
   ✎ ____ ____ ____ ____ ____ ____ ____ ____ ____ .
5) What was Sam doing when I came?
   ✎ ____ ____ ____ ____ ____ ____ ____ ____ ____ .
6) What were you doing when I arrived?
   ✎ ____ ____ ____ ____ ____ ____ ____ ____ ____ .
7) What were the students doing when the teacher met them?
   ✎ ____ ____ ____ ____ ____ ____ ____ ____ ____ .
8) What was Edwin doing when his boss called him?
   ✎ ____ ____ ____ ____ ____ ____ ____ ____ ____ .
9) What was the manager doing when the telephone rang?
   ✎ ____ ____ ____ ____ ____ ____ ____ ____ ____ .
10) Where was John going when he fell down a hole?
   ✎ ____ ____ ____ ____ ____ ____ ____ ____ ____ .

My Homework

Exercise Twelve

- Find the mistake in each of the following sentences and correct it.
- Follow the example.

➢ When I called my sisters, they are playing chess.
☞ When I called my sisters, they **were** playing chess.

1) A lot of planes were taking off when it begin to snow.
☞ A lot of planes were taking off when it began to snow.

2) I saw Amin a minute ago. He talk to Cimon.
☞ I saw Amin a minute ago. He was talking to Cimon.

3) I get ready to leave when my boss called for a meeting.
☞ I was getting ready to leave when my boss called for a meeting.

4) When my teacher met me in the park, I jog.
☞ When my teacher met me in the park, I was jogging.

5) Gordon change a flat tire when another car hit him.
☞ Gordon was changing a flat tire when another car hit him.

6) The workmen dig a tunnel when they discovered a water well.
☞ The workmen were digging a tunnel when they discovered a water well.

7) I was surfing the Internet when I get an urgent call.
☞ I was surfing the Internet when I got an urgent call.

8) Pedro exercise in the gym when a heavy weight fell on his feet.
☞ Pedro was exercising in the gym when a heavy weight fell on his feet.

9) Mom was preparing a light meal while my aunt make a cake.
☞ Mom was preparing a light meal while my aunt was making a cake.

10) I was reading in the library when my classmates create a PowerPoint presentation about safe driving.
☞ I was reading in the library when my classmates were creating a PowerPoint presentation about safe driving.

11) Sandra was going to the post office when she see her friend Sally.
☞ Sandra was going to the post office when she saw her friend Sally.

12) We were returning from the farm when we have a flat tire.
☞ We were returning from the farm when we had a flat tire.

13) I speak on the phone when Arnold knocked on the door.
☞ I was speaking on the phone when Arnold knocked on the door.

14) While I park my car, something scratched its hood.
☞ While I was parking my car, something scratched its hood.

15) I was waiting for the subway when a thief snatched my mobile phone.
☞ I was waiting for the subway when a thief snatched my mobile phone.

16) The doctor was examining a patient when he hear an emergency siren.
☞ The doctor was examining a patient when he heard an emergency siren.

17) My sisters were cooking while my brothers study.
☞ My sisters were cooking while my brothers were studying.

18) The shepherd lost his way while he chase a wolf.
✎ ____ ____ ____ ____ ____ ____ ____ ____ ____ ____ ____

19) We were driving to Scotland when dirty slush began to fall.
✎ ____ ____ ____ ____ ____ ____ ____ ____ ____ ____ ____

20) Ahmad was writing a report when his manager come.
✎ ____ ____ ____ ____ ____ ____ ____ ____ ____ ____ ____

✿✿✿ My Homework ✿✿✿

SECTION 10 — The Present Perfect Tense

Affirmative

I / You / They / We	have	Past Participle
He / She / It	has	

Negative

I / You / They / We	haven't	Past Participle
He / She / It	hasn't	

NOTE # 01:

> We use the Present Perfect to talk about an event or situation that began in the past and still exists until now.

NOTE # 02:

> The Present Perfect is used with since or for to talk about the duration of the action.

> We use SINCE in the <u>Present Perfect</u> before a specific time.

We use FOR *in the <u>Present Perfect</u> before a length of time.*

We use EVER *when we ask questions in the Present Perfect. It means, "In the lifetime of somebody." It appears before the past participle.*

We use EVER *when we make negative in the Present Perfect. It is mainly used **after** HAVEN'T or HASN'T.*

We use STILL *when we make negative in the Present Perfect. It is mainly used **before** HAVEN'T or HASN'T.*

We use NEVER *to express negative in the Present Perfect. It means, "from the beginning of my life up to the present*

We use JUST *in the Present Perfect. It means, "a short time ago". It appears after* HAVE *or* HAS.

We use ALREADY *in the Present Perfect. It means, "before it is expected". It appears after* HAVE *or* HAS.

We use RECENTLY *in the Present Perfect. It means, "in the last few days". It appears after* HAVE *or* HAS.

We use ALWAYS *in the Present Perfect. It means a frequent repetition of the action. It appears before* HAVE *or* HAS.

We use YET *in the Present Perfect. It means, "until now". It appears at the end of a question or a negative statement.*

We use SO FAR *in the Present Perfect. It means, "until now". It appears at the end of a question or a negative statement.*

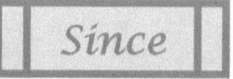 

since + (a specific time)	for + (a length of time)
2011	two years
2012	a year
November	three months
last month	a month
last week	a fortnight
Monday	a week
yesterday	a day
ten o'clock	an hour
we met	a minute
we were in Frankfurt	a long time

✦ Examples:

- I _have wrapped_ a lot of gifts since this morning.
- Salma _has_ already _started_ her English language course.
- Our manager _has_ just _got_ the offer.
- Diana _has_ never _met_ a famous soccer player.
- My teacher _has_ recently _applied_ the new teaching methods.
- Manager: _Have_ you _forwarded_ the faxes yet?

  Secretary: No, I _haven't forwarded_ them yet.
- Khalid _has been_ on duty for two nights.
- Shaima'a _hasn't_ ever _been_ abroad.
- Mackay: _Has_ Ross ever thought of changing his career?

  David: No, he _hasn't_.
- Keely still _hasn't prepared_ the meal.
- I _have read_ two chapters of the book so far.

➢ *Exercise One*
   ✤ Write the past participle of the verb.
1) I have already (finish) my lessons.   ___(finished)___
2) Sarah has (give) a lecture.   _____
3) Salma has just (lend) me some money.   _____
4) Ted has (repair) the machine.   _____
5) Lilly has (bring) her kids from school.   _____
6) The children have (go) home.   _____
7) My brothers have (succeed).   _____
8) My aunt has (be) abroad.   _____
9) The thief has (creep) into the house.   _____
10) The ship has (sail) into the sea.   _____
11) Ali has just (have) his dinner.   _____
12) I haven't (do) the homework yet.   _____
13) Sohair has just (come).   _____
14) The train hasn't (leave) yet.   _____
15) Have you (write) the email yet?   _____
16) Has James (eat) the candy alone?   _____
17) We haven't (begin) the meeting yet.   _____
18) The patient has already (feel) better.   _____
19) I have just (get) a message.   _____
20) Batool has never (fly) to Moscow.   _____

✺✺✺ *My Homework* ✺✺✺

➢ *Exercise Two*
   ✤ Write the past participle of the verb.
1) Kin has (lose) his mobile phone.   _____
2) I have never (drink) wine.   _____
3) The workman hasn't (dig) the hole yet.   _____
4) Ahmad has already (burn) the CD.   _____
5) Boody hasn't (swim) yet.   _____
6) They have just (bring) the food.   _____
7) I still haven't (fly) to Bombay.   _____
8) Ayah has (make) a nice cake.   _____
9) Miral has just (pay) the bills.   _____
10) The teacher has just (shut) the door.   _____
11) I haven't (hear) any good news yet.   _____
12) Rose has (sleep) for ten hours.   _____

13) Omar has (win) a lot of medals. _____
14) The thief has (steal) a lot of money. _____
15) Jonathan has (be) a teacher for ten years. _____
16) Hans has (grow) corn for many years. _____
17) Marawan hasn't (feed) his camels yet. _____
18) I haven't (meet) my new manager yet. _____
19) We have (know) about this case for weeks. _____
20) Anas has already (read) the newspaper. _____

🙰🙰🙰 *My Homework* 🙰🙰🙰

> ## *Exercise Three*
> - Rearrange these words to form meaningful sentences.
> - Follow the example.

> / New Jersey / lived / four / I / years / for / in / have /
> ✓ *I have lived in New Jersey for four years.*

1) / for / days / here / been / have / three / I /
🙰_____ _____ _____ _____ _____ _____ _____ _____

2) / met / were / London / haven't / since / Martin / we / in / I /
🙰_____ _____ _____ _____ _____ _____ _____ _____ _____

3) / for / known / Samah / months / have / I / seven /
🙰_____ _____ _____ _____ _____ _____ _____ _____

4) / a lot of / moved / made / the / father / he / has / money / since / city / to / My /
🙰_____ _____ _____ _____ _____ _____ _____ _____ _____

5) / years / studied / Robert / for / French / has / six /
🙰_____ _____ _____ _____ _____ _____ _____ _____

6) / me / called / month / James / since / hasn't / last /
🙰_____ _____ _____ _____ _____ _____ _____ _____

7) / as / worked / Harry / for / has / ten / teacher / years / a /
🙰_____ _____ _____ _____ _____ _____ _____ _____ _____

8) / house / years / have / this / for / I / old / twenty / owned /
🙰_____ _____ _____ _____ _____ _____ _____ _____ _____

9) / skill / was / I / young / have / learnt / since / this /
🙰_____ _____ _____ _____ _____ _____ _____ _____ _____

10) / students / since / semester / homework / done / The / started / they/ the / have / a lot of /
✎ _____ _____ _____ _____ _____ _____ _____ _____ _____ _____ _____

11) / yet / the / Farah / finished / housework / hasn't /
✎ _____ _____ _____ _____ _____ _____ _____ _____

12) / never / Chicago / sister / to / My / has / been /
✎ _____ _____ _____ _____ _____ _____ _____ _____

13) / yesterday / reviewed / vocabulary / Jane / has / a lot of / since /
✎ _____ _____ _____ _____ _____ _____ _____ _____ _____

14) / country / ever / in / lived / brother / My / hasn't / the /
✎ _____ _____ _____ _____ _____ _____ _____ _____ _____

15) / o'clock / clerk / sent / ten / emails / has / The / a lot of / since /
✎ _____ _____ _____ _____ _____ _____ _____ _____ _____ _____

The Present Perfect Yes/No Questions

Have	you	Past Participle	?

Yes,	I	have.
No,	I	haven't.

✦ Examples:
➢ **Alan:** Have you finished your task?
✦ **Paul:** Yes, I have.

➢ **Noah:** Have you reached your destination on time?
✦ **Helen:** No, I haven't.

Have	you	Past Participle	?

Yes,	we	have.
No,	we	haven't.

✦ Examples:
➢ **Teacher:** Have you written down these notes?
✦ **Students:** Yes, we have.

➢ **Teacher:** Have you submitted your writing assignment?
✦ **Students:** No, we haven't.

Have	they	Past Participle	?

Yes,	they	have.
No,	they	haven't.

✤ Examples:

➢ **James:** Have your brothers driven to the farm recently?
✤ **Nader:** Yes, they have.

➢ **Hanson:** Have your sisters stayed there for a long time?
✤ **Jason:** No, they haven't.

Has	he	Past Participle	?

Yes,	he	has.
No,	he	hasn't.

✤ Examples:

➢ **Hafis:** Has Ahmad already got married?
✤ **Tony:** Yes, he has.

➢ **Jane:** Has Albert already sent the proposal?
✤ **Serena:** No, he hasn't.

Has	she	Past Participle	?

Yes,	she	has.
No,	she	hasn't.

✤ Examples:

➢ **William:** Has your wife recently won a prize?
✤ **Stewart:** Yes, she has.

➢ **Sandra:** Has Diana got the booking confirmation yet?
✤ **Mark:** No, she hasn't.

Has	it	Past Participle	?

Yes,	it	has.
No,	it	hasn't.

➢ **Taro:** Has it rained harder than ever?
✤ **Walid:** Yes, it has.

➢ **Mona:** Has the problem become more complicated?
✤ **Michael:** No, it hasn't.

> ## Exercise Four
✤ Choose the correct answer from a, b, c, or d.

1) Mike: Has Mark hurt his feet?
✤ **Manuel:** Yes, he _____ .

| a. | has hurt | b. | has |
| c. | had | d. | have |

2) Linda: Have your friends got worried about the deal?
✤ Lara: No, they _____ .

| a. | have | b. | haven't |
| c. | hasn't | d. | hadn't |

3) Sam: Has Basma _____ a good presentation?
✤ John: Yes, she has.

| a. | gives | b. | give |
| c. | gave | d. | given |

4) Donald: Have you already read the operating instructions?
✤ Dalia: Yes, I _____ .

| a. | have | b. | haven't |
| c. | hasn't | d. | hadn't |

5) Oliver: Have you already _____ on this patient?
✤ Joshua: Not yet.

| a. | operates | b. | operate |
| c. | operated | d. | operating |

6) Doctor: Has the patient taken his medicine?
✤ Nurse: Yes, he _____ .

| a. | has taken | b. | had |
| c. | having | d. | has |

7) Pilot: Have the passengers already buckled up?
✤ Flight attendant: Yes, they _____ .

| a. | have | b. | having |
| c. | had | d. | haven't |

8) Andrew: Have you _____ a lot of fish?
✤ Samuel: No, I haven't.

| a. | caught | b. | catches |
| c. | catching | d. | catch |

9) Yara: Has Batool gone boating many times?
✤ Sara: Yes, she _____ .

| a. | has gone | b. | has |
| c. | had | d. | have |

10) Anderson: Have you finished the report?
✤ Harris: No, I _____ .

| a | haven't finished | b | have |
| c | haven't | d | didn't |

11) Thompson: Has Emily sent the faxes?
   Garcia: Yes, she _____.

a	has	b	hasn't
c	has sent	d	sent

12) Emily: Have you milked the cow _____?
   Ruby: No, I haven't.

a	yet	b	never
c	since	d	still

13) Carl: Have the street cleaners finished their task?
   Neil: Yes, they _____.

a	have finished	b	haven't
c	have	d	haven't finished

14) Omar: Have I _____ you before?
   Hagar: Yes, I have.

a	yet	b	already
c	for	d	never

15) Edwin: Have you got a salary increase this year?
   Hennery: Yes, I _____.

a	have	b	haven't
c	have got	d	haven't got

16) Leon: Has Hesham ever been to Canberra?
   Lewis: No, he _____ never been there.

a	hasn't	b	hadn't
c	has	d	haven't

17) Carmen: Have you had your lunch?
   Samar: Yes, I _____.

a	have	b	had had
c	have had	d	has had

18) Fred: Have the students started the final test?
   Farid: No, they haven't started it _____.

a	ever	b	yet
c	just	d	still

19) Mamdouh: Has Maggie got a new headscarf?
   Hossam: Yes, but she hasn't _____ it yet.

a	wore	b	wear
c	worn	d	wearing

20) Oliver: Have you received his feedback?
   Noah: Yes, I _____.

a	have received	b	haven't received
c	have	d	haven't

🌸🌸🌸 My Homework 🌸🌸🌸

The Present Perfect Wh- Questions

Question Word	have	you / they / we	Past Participle	?

Example:
➢ Alan: How much tea have you drunk today?
➢ Paul: I have drunk a lot.

Question Word	has	he / she / it	Past Participle	?

Example:
➢ Gary: How many lessons have you written so far?
➢ Paul: Five.

➢ **Exercise Five**

➢ Choose the correct answer from a, b, c, or d.

1) Dane: _____ has finished his story?
➢ Ellen: My classmate Harry.

a.	When	b.	Who
c.	Where	d.	What

2) Alfonse: _____ have you been?
➢ Majid: I have been in the mall.

a.	When	b.	Who
c.	Where	d.	What

3) Kris: _____ haven't you brought your math notebook?
➢ Dan: I forgot to put it in my school bag.

a.	When	b.	How long
c.	Where	d.	Why

4) Gordon: _____ have you been to the museum?
➢ Blake: I have been there many times.

a.	When	b.	How long
c.	Where	d.	How often

5) Ali: _____ have you eaten?
➢ Salwa: I have eaten a lot of ice cream.

a.	When	b.	How long
c.	Where	d.	What

6) Toby: _____ hasn't attended the meeting?
➢ Regan: Mr Ahmad Saleh.

a.	Who	b.	How long
c.	Where	d.	What

7) Arthur: _____ has your father visited Sidney?
➢ Jimmy: Three.

a.	How many	b.	How many times
c.	How old	d.	How far

8) David: _____ essays have you written this month?
➢ Raoul: Twenty.

a.	How far	b.	How long
c.	How many	b.	How many times

9) Eliza: _____ money have you spent so far?
➢ Talia: Six thousand dollars.

a.	How much	b.	How long
c.	How many	b.	How many times

10) Malik: _____ have you been?
➢ Pierre: I have been at home.

a.	How far	b.	How long
c.	How many	b.	Where

🌺🌺🌺 *My Homework* 🌺🌺🌺

➢ **Exercise Six**
    ✦ Choose the correct answer from a, b, c or d.

1) My grandmother hasn't fed the hens _____.

a	still	b	yet
c	since	d	for

2) We _____ in this nice hotel for three weeks.

a	have stayed	b	stays
c	to stay	d	staying

3) Kevin has _____ studied Russian.

a	ever	b	still
c	yet	d	never

4) My parents have lived in Texas _____ I was born.

a	for	b	since
c	already	d	still

5) Collin has _____ written down the notes.

a	ever	b	yet
c	already	d	still

6) The nurse has _____ injected the patient.

a	ever	b	never
c	since	d	still

7) Muhammad has worked in this company _____ twenty years.

a	ever	b	for
c	since	d	still

8) I have _____ played handball, but I'd love to.

a	ever	b	never
c	since	d	still

9) Dan hasn't eaten any food _____ three days.

a	ever	b	yet
c	since	d	for

10) Saleh hasn't _____ been to Istanbul.

a	ever	b	never
c	since	d	still

11) Axel has _____ driven a truck.

a	ever	b	never
c	since	d	still

12) The teacher has given us a lot of grammar lessons _____ the beginning of the semester.

a	ever	b	never
c	since	d	still

13) Parker has _____ lots of diet and exercise programs recently.

a	adopt	b	adopting
c	adopts	d	adopted

14) When I arrived at the airport, the plane has _____ taken off.

a	ever	b	already
c	since	d	still

15) Linda has _____ attended a seminar about T. S. Eliot.

a	ever	b	yet
c	just	d	so far

16) The farmer has cut a lot of trees _____ yesterday.

a	ever	b	never
c	since	d	still

17) I have just _____ a prize.

a	winning	b	win
c	to win	d	won

18) Andrew _____ hasn't repaired the car.

a	ever	b	never
c	yet	d	still

19) The meeting has just _____.

a	beginning	b	begin
c	began	d	begun

20) The game hasn't started _____.

a	ever	b	never
c	yet	d	still

My Homework

➢ Exercise Seven

✦ Choose the correct answer from a, b, c or d.

1) My mother has _____ done the ironing.

a	already	b	ever
c	yet	d	since

2) I have _____ received my exam results.

a	for	b	ever
c	yet	d	recently

3) Boody has already _____ married.

a	getting	b	gets
c	got	d	get

4) Tuka has _____ toxicology for six years.

a	taught	b	teaches
c	teaching	d	teach

5) This is what we have achieved _____.

a	never	b	yet
c	for	d	so far

6) Bato has already _____ the report.

a	to read	b	reading
c	reads	d	read

7) My boss is always angry. He has _____ praised me.

a	since	b	yet
c	never	d	for

8) Clark has _____ this old house for a long time.

a	owning	b	own
c	owns	d	owned

9) I have _____ Lilly for more than five years.

a	know	b	knowing
c	known	d	knows

10) The robbers _____ this bank twice since last summer.

a	has burglarized	b	burglarizes
c	burglarizing	d	have burglarized

11) We have always _____ Ross to be punctual, but in vain.

a	advise	b	advises
c	advised	d	to advise

12) The new secretary has committed a lot of mistakes _____ she joined our company.

a	for	b	already
c	recently	d	since

13) Leila has _____ visited Germany, but she hopes to.

a	never	b	always
c	just	d	recently

14) Kim and his wife have just _____ the hotel.

a	leaving	b	left
c	leaves	d	to leave

15) We're sorry, sir. The plane has just _____ .

a	takes off	b	taking off
c	take off	d	taken off

16) Our teacher has always _____ Franklin for neglecting his home assignments.

a	blames	b	blame
c	blamed	d	blaming

17) The manager has always _____ Rana to send him the emails on a daily basis.

a	told	b	tell
c	telling	d	tells

18) Sarah _____ always tried to phone you, but she couldn't.

a	has	b	having
c	have	d	to have

19) I have _____ a lot of movies since my vacation started.

a	see	b	saw
c	sees	d	seen

20) Marawan _____ hasn't returned the books to the library.

a	never	b	since
c	still	d	yet

🌸🌸🌸 My Homework 🌸🌸🌸

➢ Exercise Eight

✦ Choose the correct answer from a, b, c or d.

1) We can't begin the new lesson. Our teacher hasn't come _____ .

a	yet	b	never
c	ever	d	still

2) Salma hasn't _____ called me during my vacation in Rome.

a	never	b	yet
c	still	d	ever

3) I have _____ heard about these vacation plans.

a	yet	b	ever
c	never	d	still

4) I have _____ asked to make your bed yourself.

a	since	b	always
c	ever	d	yet

5) The doctors _____ this patient many times. However, they couldn't discover his illness.

a	have checked	b	will check
c	are checking	d	are going to check

6) Tim has _____ this nice cat for six months.

a	kept	b	keep
c	keeping	d	keeps

7) I have always _____ Hassan on my way to school.

a	meet	b	meeting
c	meets	d	met

8) David has _____ as an instructor since he graduated.

a	worked	b	been worked
c	working	d	works

9) I have always _____ Ruba to come on time.

a	asks	b	asking
c	asked	d	ask

10) My mother _____ hasn't sewed the new dresses.

a	yet	b	ever
c	still	d	never

🕮🕮🕮 *My Homework* 🕮🕮

> ## Exercise Nine
> ➕ Find the mistake in each of the following sentences and correct it. Follow the example. Some sentences may have more than one answer.
> ➤ Celia has **ever** got along with her new classmates.
> ✓ Celia has **never** got along with her new classmates.

1) I have never meet a famous movie star.
🕮_____

2) My sisters have yet cooked a delicious meal.
🕮_____

3) I can't see Eliza. Where has she go?
🕮_____

4) My cat has just drink some milk.
🕮_____

5) My brother yet hasn't come back from school.
🕮_____

6) Edward hasn't never called me.
🕮_____

7) It hasn't stopped raining since.
🕮_____

8) Malik has worked as a dentist since ten years.
🕮_____

9) Edwin hasn't visited the Philippines already 2010.
🕮_____

10) The repots haven't been forwarded just.
🕮_____

11) I have read this interesting book many time.
🕮_____

12) Sally has watched already this exciting movie.
✎_____ _____ _____ _____ _____ _____ _____ _____ _____

13) The mechanic hasn't fixed my car still.
✎_____ _____ _____ _____ _____ _____ _____ _____ _____

14) Our teacher hasn't for explained this grammar lesson.
✎_____ _____ _____ _____ _____ _____ _____ _____ _____

15) My parents haven't eaten their lunch since.
✎_____ _____ _____ _____ _____ _____ _____ _____ _____

16) The policemen have for caught a lot of wrongdoers.
✎_____ _____ _____ _____ _____ _____ _____ _____ _____

17) Sarah is happy as she has already receive a lot of presents on her birthday.
✎_____ _____ _____ _____ _____ _____ _____ _____ _____

18) Ahmad and his family recently have spent a nice time on the beach.
✎_____ _____ _____ _____ _____ _____ _____ _____ _____

19) The coach has always advise me to train hard.
✎_____ _____ _____ _____ _____ _____ _____ _____ _____

20) The student has always do a lot of mistakes in his homework.
✎_____ _____ _____ _____ _____ _____ _____ _____ _____

༜༜༜My Homework༜༜༜

Have / has been to	*Have / has gone to*
Went to a place and came back	Went to a place and is still there

✤ **Examples:**
➢ I *have been* to London International Book Fair. I saw thousands of titles there.
➢ Ibrahim *has gone* to the beach. He's going to stay there for ten hours.

➢ *Exercise Ten:*
✤ Choose the correct answer from a, b, c, or d.

1) My uncle is on holiday. He has _____ to Cyprus.

a	been	b	done
c	had	d	gone

2) I have just _____ to the farm. I brought a lot of fruits and vegetables.

a	been	b	had
c	gone	d	done

3) My brother has _____ to Paris several times.

| a | gone | b | done |
| c | had | d | been |

4) Molly isn't here right now. She has _____ to the restaurant to have her lunch.

| a | had | b | gone |
| c | been | d | done |

5) Laura: Are you going to the library?
   Mark: I have already _____ there.

| a | done | b | been |
| c | gone | d | had |

6) My friends have _____ to the zoo. They watched a lot of animals there.

| a | had | b | gone |
| c | been | d | done |

7) I have never _____ to Melbourne. However, I hope to visit it soon.

| a | done | b | been |
| c | gone | d | had |

8) My sister has _____ to the supermarket. She's still there.

| a | had | b | gone |
| c | been | d | done |

9) The optician has _____ in his clinic for ten hours.

| a | had | b | gone |
| c | been | d | done |

10) The dentist has _____ to the hospital to see his patients.

| a | had | b | gone |
| c | been | d | done |

🌸🌸🌸 *My Homework* 🌸🌸🌸

The Present Perfect Progressive (Continuous) Tense

Affirmative

| I / You / They / We | have | been | -ing | since (2006) |
| He / She / It | has | | | for (two days) / all (day) |

NOTE # 01:

We use the Present Perfect Progressive (Continuous) Tense to talk about an event that be

We use **'all'** plus a time unit; day, night, year etc. to refer to an action that was happening during this period.

✦ **Examples:**

- We couldn't sleep because this nasty dog _has been barking_ all night. (It didn't stop barking.)
- The streets are slippery and muddy. It _has been raining_ since yesterday. (It didn't stop raining.)

➢ *Exercise One*
   ✦ Choose the correct answer from a, b, c, or d.

1) It's 10:30 p.m. I _____ my Spanish lessons since 7:30 p.m.

| a | have been reviewing | b | was reviewing |
| c | am reviewing | d | review |

2) Pierre _____ physics for two years.

| a | studying | b | have been studying |
| c | have study | d | has been studying |

3) I'm sorry for not receiving your telephone call as I _____ my email box all night.

a	am checking	b	have checked
c	have check	d	have been checking

4) My uncles _____ in the garden since 8:30 a.m. They didn't take a break.

a	am working	b	has been working
c	have been working	d	have worked

5) My brothers have been watching TV _____ day.

a	for	b	since
c	every	d	all

🌸🌸🌸 *My homework* 🍂🍂🍂

➢ **Exercise Two**
  ✤ Write **for, since** or **all**.

1) Lilly has been staying in Belfast _____ seven years.
2) Ted has been browsing the Internet _____ 9:30.
3) Ernie has been studying poetry _____ he came back home.
4) We have been staying in this motel _____ two days.
5) My father has been driving _____ yesterday.
6) I have been teaching geography _____ a long time.
7) Tuka has been helping her friends _____ she graduated.
8) The plane has been flying _____ an hour.
9) I have been studying hard _____ the beginning of the course.
10) Batool has been developing her project plans _____ two months.
11) Robinson and his family have been visiting California _____ three weeks.
12) Edward and Grace have been jogging _____ this morning.
13) George has been hunting _____ five hours.
14) We have been walking on the beach _____ half an hour.
15) Keith has been learning Arabic _____ two years.
16) Donna has been checking her email _____ she woke up.
17) George has been fishing _____ a long time.
18) Andrew has been looking for his lost son _____ two days.
19) We have been rowing _____ night.
20) My elder sister has been cooking _____ day.
21) Mr. Mutlaq has been working _____ fifteen hours.
22) My grandfather has been working on his farm _____ 7:30 a.m.
23) Mr Robert has been fixing his old bus _____ hours.
24) A dusty wind has been blowing _____ I got up.
25) Harry has been learning Chinese _____ last August.

🌸🌸🌸 *My Homework* 🍂🍂🍂

Exercise Three
Rewrite the following sentences using (since) instead of (for).
1) I have been working on this report for a day.
   _____
2) Sonia has been living in Ohio for a week.
   _____
3) My parents have been staying in Saint Catharine for a year.
   _____
4) We have been studying German for a month.
   _____
5) Boody has been learning biology for three years.
   _____
6) It's ten thirty now. Kerry has been sleeping for five hours.
   _____
7) It's three o'clock now. Malik has been jogging for an hour.
   _____
8) It's eleven thirty now. It has been drizzling for five hours.
   _____

My Homework

Exercise Four
Rewrite the following sentences using (for) instead of (since).
1) We have been studying in the same school since 2016.
   _____
2) It's ten o'clock now. I have been talking on the phone since 9:15.
   _____
3) My grandparents have been living in this city since 1964.
   _____
4) My grandfather has been growing wheat since 1970.
   _____
5) Mr Saleh has been teaching English since 1987.
   _____
6) It has been snowing since yesterday.
   _____
7) Ahmad has been playing the piano since 2010.
   _____
8) Our company has been carrying out projects since 2004.
   _____

My Homework

How long ...?

How long	have	I you we they	been	-ing ...?
	has	he she it		

➤ **Exercise Five**
   ✦ Write questions to the following answers.
   ✎____ ____ ____ ____ ____ ____ ____ ____ ____
1) I have been sleeping for an hour.
   ✎____ ____ ____ ____ ____ ____ ____ ____ ____
2) My mother has been cooking since three o'clock.
   ✎____ ____ ____ ____ ____ ____ ____ ____ ____
3) Talia has been working as a pharmacist since she graduated.
   ✎____ ____ ____ ____ ____ ____ ____ ____ ____
4) Salem has been doing his assignment for an hour.
   ✎____ ____ ____ ____ ____ ____ ____ ____ ____

🙰🙰🙰 *My Homework* 🙰🙰🙰

➤ **Exercise Six**
   ✦ Rearrange these words to form meaningful sentences.
   ✦ Follow the example.
1) / o'clock / since / waiting / I / you / been / three / have / for /
   ✓ **I have been waiting for you since three o'clock.**
➤ / making / kites / paper / has / time / for / Olivia / been / a / long /
   ✎____ ____ ____ ____ ____ ____ ____ ____ ____
1) / boys / sunbathing / The / for / hours / been / two / have /
   ✎____ ____ ____ ____ ____ ____ ____ ____ ____
2) / friend / looking / job / My / has / for / for / been / a / a / year /
   ✎____ ____ ____ ____ ____ ____ ____ ____ ____
3) / have / studying/ for / plan / week / engineers / the / The / been / a / project /
   ✎____ ____ ____ ____ ____ ____ ____ ____ ____

4) / has / child / a / stamps / collecting / been / since / Pam / was / she /
🖎____ ____ ____ ____ ____ ____ ____ ____ ____ ____

> ## Exercise Seven

   ♦ Correct the mistakes in the following sentences.
   ♦ Follow the example.

> It's terribly cold. It **[snow]** all night.
✓ It <u>has been snowing</u> all night.

1) Ken is very tired. He [jog] for a long time.
🖎____ ____ ____ ____ ____ ____ ____ ____ ____

2) Yukio should rest for some time. He [work] for three hours.
🖎____ ____ ____ ____ ____ ____ ____ ____ ____

3) The doctor advised my uncle to give up smoking. He [smoke] for many years.
🖎____ ____ ____ ____ ____ ____ ____ ____ ____

4) Bob is exhausted. He [run] for two hours.
🖎____ ____ ____ ____ ____ ____ ____ ____ ____

5) Lilly is still waiting for the doctor. In fact, she [wait] for two hours.
🖎____ ____ ____ ____ ____ ____ ____ ____ ____

6) Li Jun is keen on history. He [study] history for ten years.
🖎____ ____ ____ ____ ____ ____ ____ ____ ____

🖎🖎🖎 *My Homework* 🖎🖎🖎

SECTION 12 **The Simple Past Tense**

Affirmative Form

| Subject | Base form + (-ed) (for regular verbs) |

The Simple Past Tense is used to describe an event that already took place during specific time in the past.

Examples:
- Salah _visited_ Liverpool **last year**.
- My grandfather _lived_ in Tokyo **from 1960 to 1970**.
- William _hurried_ to school because he **was** late.
- It _stopped_ raining **an hour ago**.
- Saleh _read_ an exciting short story **last night**.
- **Yesterday**, Alice _told_ us a nice story about life in the forest.
- **In the past**, people _rode_ camels and donkeys to move from one place to another.

Negative Form

| Subject | did not (didn't) | Base form |

Examples:
- I _didn't call_ Martin because I was busy.
- The plants died as you _didn't water_ them regularly.
- Jack _didn't go_ to bed early, so he is very tired.
- Rami _didn't fly_ to London this week.

🙰🙰🙰 **My Homework** 🙰🙰🙰

Simple Past Time Makers

Yesterday	
Last (week)	
(three days) ago	
in + a previous year	(in 2010)
In the past	
Once	
Once upon a time	
On + days of the week	On Monday
at the weekend	
Today	
This morning	
This evening	

Examples:
- We **did** a lot of work on the farm **yesterday**.
- **Once upon a time**, I **saw** some tigers in the forest.
- **In 1984**, the Olympic Games **took place** in Los Angles.
- **Last winter**, we **enjoyed** our vacation in Aswan.
- The train **arrived** at the station **half an hour ago**.

My Homework

Exercise One
Choose the correct answer from a, b, c, or d.

1) I _____ swimming with my friend yesterday.

a	going	b	goes
c	go	d	went

2) Sandy _____ a digital camera last week.

a	bought	b	buys
c	buying	d	to buy

3) Abdul-Rahman _____ his iPad two hours ago.

a	to fix	b	fixes
c	fixing	d	fixed

4) Mark _____ visit Florida last month.

a	doesn't	b	wasn't
c	didn't	d	don't

5) Keith and Lilly _____ married in January 2011.

a	gets	b	get
c	getting	d	got

6) Last night, Brian _____ his arm in a car accident.

a	broke	b	breaks
c	break	d	breaking

7) In 1998, France _____ the World Cup.

a	winning	b	to win
c	win	d	won

8) I _____ my friends Jessica and Ann in the morning.

a	meets	b	met
c	to meet	d	meeting

9) Dinosaurs _____ on our earth millions of years ago.

a	live	b	are living
c	lived	d	lives

10) Sally _____ the emails to the Irish company an hour ago.

a	forwarded	b	forwarding
c	forwards	d	to forward

11) Batool _____ send the fax yesterday.

a	wasn't	b	didn't
c	don't	d	isn't

12) Last year, it _____ a lot in Bridgeport.

a	rained	b	raining
c	was raining	d	rain

13) Last winter, it _____ a lot in Athens.

a	snowing	b	snowed
c	snows	d	snow

14) Once upon a time, an old man _____ to work on this farm.

a	uses	b	use
c	used	d	was using

15) My brother _____ for two hours yesterday.

a	swims	b	swam
c	swum	d	swim

16) Our teacher _____ us this lesson last Monday.

a	gives	b	giving
c	gave	d	given

17) Korea _____ a lot of cars in the 1990s.

a	was making	b	makes
c	make	d	made

18) The bus _____ on time, so we weren't late.

a	arrive	b	to arrive
c	arrived	d	arriving

19) My father _____ to his office fifteen minutes ago.

a	drives	b	drove
c	drive	d	driving

20) Robert _____ to New Jersey last night.

a	flew	b	fly
c	flying	d	flies

+ **Study these patterns.**

When		
After		
Before		
As soon as	Past Simple	Past Simple
By the time		
Because		
Since		

| Past Simple | , so | Past Simple |

| Past Simple | until (till) | Past Simple |

+ **Examples:**
> As soon as it *stopped* raining, we *resumed* our trip.
> We *waited* until the surgeon *finished* the operation.

> *Exercise Two:*
+ Correct the verb in brackets.
+ Follow the example.
> When I went home, I [have] my lunch.
✓ When I went home, I **had** my lunch.

1) When I got the letter, I [be] very happy.
🕮_____

2) As soon as I finished the report, I [give] it to my boss.
🕮_____

3) When I came to my office, I [see] some letters on my desk.
🕮_____

4) As soon as I arrived at the airport, I [check] in.
🕮_____

5) After I got into my car, I [drive] home.
🕮_____

6) After I received the letter, I [read] it.
🕮_____

7) By the time the match started, my brother [come].
🕮_____

8) As soon as the telephone rang, I [pick] it.
✎ ___ ___ ___ ___ ___ ___ ___ ___ ___

9) When the dusty storm stopped, we [leave] the house.
✎ ___ ___ ___ ___ ___ ___ ___ ___ ___

10) Before I reached the gas station, I [find] that there was no fuel.
✎ ___ ___ ___ ___ ___ ___ ___ ___ ___

11) After I saw the accident, I [report] it.
✎ ___ ___ ___ ___ ___ ___ ___ ___ ___

12) When you called me, I [reply] at once.
✎ ___ ___ ___ ___ ___ ___ ___ ___ ___

13) As soon as Mr. Salamah heard the news, he [take] a flight to Rome.
✎ ___ ___ ___ ___ ___ ___ ___ ___ ___

14) When our teacher entered the class, we [greet] him.
✎ ___ ___ ___ ___ ___ ___ ___ ___ ___

15) I was very tired, so I [sleep] for ten hours.
✎ ___ ___ ___ ___ ___ ___ ___ ___ ___

16) The bus broke down because it [run] out of oil.
✎ ___ ___ ___ ___ ___ ___ ___ ___ ___

17) Five years ago, William [buy] at a bakery downtown.
✎ ___ ___ ___ ___ ___ ___ ___ ___ ___

18) Jansen [eat] macaroni and meat for lunch an hour ago.
✎ ___ ___ ___ ___ ___ ___ ___ ___ ___

19) We [understand] yesterday's lecture clearly.
✎ ___ ___ ___ ___ ___ ___ ___ ___ ___

20) Yesterday, Jason [hit] his toe in a rock and cut it.
✎ ___ ___ ___ ___ ___ ___ ___ ___ ___

✎✎✎ My Homework ✎✎✎

➢ **Exercise Three**

✦ Choose the correct answer from a, b, c, or d.

1) After I _____ the book, I took it back to the library.

a	was read	b	reading
c	read	d	to read

2) As soon as I _____ my old friend, I ran towards him.

a	see	b	saw
c	sees	d	seen

3) The fans _____ the stadium after the match finished.

a	leaves	b	leaving
c	left	d	has left

4) We left the playground before the game _____.

a	began	b	begins
c	begun	d	beginning

5) Amelia _____ married as soon as she graduated.

a	gets	b	get
c	getting	d	got

6) After Paul got home, he _____ lunch.

a	have had	b	has
c	to have	d	had

7) We resumed our work after we _____ for some time.

a	rested	b	rest
c	rests	d	resting

8) When the child got the shot, he _____ better.

a	feel	b	to feel
c	feeling	d	felt

9) As soon as the mechanic fixed my car, he _____ it.

a	checking	b	checks
c	check	d	checked

10) By the time we _____ to the desert, we put up a large tent.

a	get	b	got
c	gets	d	have got

11) Dan cried out of joy as soon as he _____ the news of my success.

a	heard	b	hears
c	hearing	d	hear

12) After Mr. Lee entered the class, we _____ him.

a	greets	b	greet
c	greeted	d	to greet

13) Ayman _____ Lamya as soon as she graduated.

a	rewards	b	reward
c	rewarded	d	to reward

14) Before I _____ the apple, I washed it.

a	eat	b	ate
c	eaten	d	eats

15) As soon as I got up, I _____ the radio.

a	switched on	b	switches on
c	switching on	d	switch on

16) When we lived in Paris, we _____ the Louvre every week.

a	visit	b	visited
c	have visited	d	visits

17) Sam didn't catch the flight because he _____ late.

a	got up	b	has got up
c	will get up	d	is going to get up

18) Before I forwarded the email, I _____ it thoroughly.

a	checks	b	check
c	checked	d	have checked

19) The teacher _____ the student because he was honest.

a	thank	b	has thanked
c	thanking	d	thanked

20) As soon as the school day finished, the students _____ their classrooms.

a	left	b	will leave
c	are going to leave	d	leave

My Homework

➢ Exercise Four
- Change the sentences into the SIMPLE PAST.
- Follow the example.

➢ I **wash** my car **every day.**

✓ I **washed** my car **yesterday.**

1) We buy some food every day.
   _____

2) My uncle goes to his farm every day.
   _____

3) My father visits his friends every day.
   _____

4) My mother waters her flowers every day.
   _____

5) I eat a little meal before I start my work.
   _____

6) My sister watches cartoons on TV every day.
   _____

7) My brother plays baseball every day.
   _____

8) My aunt cooks a delicious meal every day.
   _____

9) My friend calls me every day.
   _____

10) My teacher helps me every day.
    _____

11) This butcher sells a lot of meat every day.
    _____

12) Abdul-Rahman rides his bike every day.
    _____

13) I fly to Manila every month.
    _____

14) Ahmad reviews his German lessons every day.
🕮 _____ _____ _____ _____ _____ _____ _____ _____ _____

15) We learn some new facts every day.
🕮 _____ _____ _____ _____ _____ _____ _____ _____ _____

16) I drive to my school every day.
🕮 _____ _____ _____ _____ _____ _____ _____ _____ _____

17) The teacher checks my homework every day.
🕮 _____ _____ _____ _____ _____ _____ _____ _____ _____

18) This doctor sees a lot of patients every day.
🕮 _____ _____ _____ _____ _____ _____ _____ _____ _____

19) The postman delivers many letters every day.
🕮 _____ _____ _____ _____ _____ _____ _____ _____ _____

20) Our professor gives us a new lecture every week.
🕮 _____ _____ _____ _____ _____ _____ _____ _____ _____

🕮🕮🕮 My Homework 🕮🕮🕮

> ## Exercise Five
> ✦ Change the sentences into the SIMPLE PAST.

1) Neil reads a short story every day.
🕮 _____ _____ _____ _____ _____ _____ _____ _____ _____

2) Edwin writes some reports every day.
🕮 _____ _____ _____ _____ _____ _____ _____ _____ _____

3) The janitors clean this class every day.
🕮 _____ _____ _____ _____ _____ _____ _____ _____ _____

4) Our principal holds a meeting with us every Monday.
🕮 _____ _____ _____ _____ _____ _____ _____ _____ _____

5) My uncle earns a lot of money every day.
🕮 _____ _____ _____ _____ _____ _____ _____ _____ _____

6) Mollie comes to her class on time every day.
🕮 _____ _____ _____ _____ _____ _____ _____ _____ _____

7) Saleh does a lot of work every day.
🕮 _____ _____ _____ _____ _____ _____ _____ _____ _____

8) Tuka prays five times every day.
🕮 _____ _____ _____ _____ _____ _____ _____ _____ _____

9) It rains in our area every month.
🕮 _____ _____ _____ _____ _____ _____ _____ _____ _____

10) My grandfather listens to the news on the radio every day.
🕮 _____ _____ _____ _____ _____ _____ _____ _____ _____

11) Sherif logs on the Internet every day.
🕮 _____ _____ _____ _____ _____ _____ _____ _____ _____

12) We swim in this pond every day.
🖎_____ _____ _____ _____ _____ _____ _____ _____ _____

13) This thief steals a lot of money every day.
🖎_____ _____ _____ _____ _____ _____ _____ _____ _____

14) We spend a nice time at the beach every day.
🖎_____ _____ _____ _____ _____ _____ _____ _____ _____

15) I listen to the birds singing every day.
🖎_____ _____ _____ _____ _____ _____ _____ _____ _____

16) Sally washes a lot of clothes every week.
🖎_____ _____ _____ _____ _____ _____ _____ _____ _____

17) My friends bring a lot of food every day.
🖎_____ _____ _____ _____ _____ _____ _____ _____ _____

18) After Reda reads the article, he comments on it.
🖎_____ _____ _____ _____ _____ _____ _____ _____ _____

19) I drink a cup of black coffee as soon as I get up.
🖎_____ _____ _____ _____ _____ _____ _____ _____ _____

20) My children build a lot of sandcastles on the beach every day.
🖎_____ _____ _____ _____ _____ _____ _____ _____ _____

🖎🖎🖎 *My Homework* 🖎🖎🖎

➢ *Exercise Six:*
✤ Change the sentences into the SIMPLE PAST.
1) Police officers catch a lot of thieves every day.
🖎_____ _____ _____ _____ _____ _____ _____ _____ _____

2) My son draws nice pictures every day.
🖎_____ _____ _____ _____ _____ _____ _____ _____ _____

3) This cat eats a lot of food every day.
🖎_____ _____ _____ _____ _____ _____ _____ _____ _____

4) A lot of snow falls on our village every day.
🖎_____ _____ _____ _____ _____ _____ _____ _____ _____

5) My little sister feeds her cat every day.
🖎_____ _____ _____ _____ _____ _____ _____ _____ _____

6) The students make some mistakes every day.
🖎_____ _____ _____ _____ _____ _____ _____ _____ _____

7) Omar takes a lot of photos every day.
🖎_____ _____ _____ _____ _____ _____ _____ _____ _____

8) Gina helps her mother every day.
🖎_____ _____ _____ _____ _____ _____ _____ _____ _____

9) Dina surfs the Internet every day.
✎_____

10) Batool does her best in class every day.
✎_____

11) Andrew exerts strenuous efforts on the farm every day.
✎_____

12) Our company produces a lot of goods every day.
✎_____

13) Roland plays chess every day.
✎_____

14) Every Saturday, Tuka takes her family to the theatre.
✎_____

15) My grandfather rides his horse every morning.
✎_____

16) My grandmother feeds her little chicks every day.
✎_____

17) My cattle drink a lot of water every day.
✎_____

18) I get an email from my boss every day.
✎_____

19) The students leave the academy at 3:05 p.m. every day.
✎_____

20) I talk to my parents every night.
✎_____

✾✾✾ My Homework ✾✾✾

➢ **_Exercise Seven_**
✚ Put these sentences in the negative form. Follow the example.
➢ We **enjoyed** the match.
✓ We **didn't enjoy** the match.

1) They drank three bottles of water.
✎_____

2) Diana helped us.
✎_____

3) My friend phoned me.
✎_____

4) The players trained well.
✎_____

5) The girls wept a lot.
✎_____

6) We hunted a wild animal.
🕬____ ____ ____ ____ ____ ____ ____ ____ ____ ____

7) The player threw the ball into the basket.
🕬____ ____ ____ ____ ____ ____ ____ ____ ____ ____

8) The referee cancelled the match.
🕬____ ____ ____ ____ ____ ____ ____ ____ ____ ____

9) The driver stopped suddenly.
🕬____ ____ ____ ____ ____ ____ ____ ____ ____ ____

10) John spoke to me.
🕬____ ____ ____ ____ ____ ____ ____ ____ ____ ____

11) Anna swept the floor.
🕬____ ____ ____ ____ ____ ____ ____ ____ ____ ____

12) The secretary spread the news.
🕬____ ____ ____ ____ ____ ____ ____ ____ ____ ____

13) I sent him a letter.
🕬____ ____ ____ ____ ____ ____ ____ ____ ____ ____

14) David ran quickly.
🕬____ ____ ____ ____ ____ ____ ____ ____ ____ ____

15) Our neighbour moved to a new house.
🕬____ ____ ____ ____ ____ ____ ____ ____ ____ ____

16) Noah read an article about drugs.
🕬____ ____ ____ ____ ____ ____ ____ ____ ____ ____

17) Harry lent me his camera.
🕬____ ____ ____ ____ ____ ____ ____ ____ ____ ____

18) Jane kept my secret.
🕬____ ____ ____ ____ ____ ____ ____ ____ ____ ____

19) We heard the news.
🕬____ ____ ____ ____ ____ ____ ____ ____ ____ ____

20) My boss found some mistakes.
🕬____ ____ ____ ____ ____ ____ ____ ____ ____ ____

🕬🕬🕬 My Homework 🕬🕬🕬

➢ *Exercise Eight*
   ✦ Put these sentences in the negative form.
1) Suzanne came alone.
🕬____ ____ ____ ____ ____ ____ ____ ____ ____ ____

2) The students chose the correct answer.
🕬____ ____ ____ ____ ____ ____ ____ ____ ____ ____

3) The game began on time.
🕬____ ____ ____ ____ ____ ____ ____ ____ ____ ____

4) Our teacher became angry.
🖎_____ _____ _____ _____ _____ _____ _____ _____ _____

5) The workmen dug a deep hole.
🖎_____ _____ _____ _____ _____ _____ _____ _____ _____

6) Dalia hurried to school.
🖎_____ _____ _____ _____ _____ _____ _____ _____ _____

7) We stayed in a good hotel.
🖎_____ _____ _____ _____ _____ _____ _____ _____ _____

8) The match lasted for ninety-five minutes.
🖎_____ _____ _____ _____ _____ _____ _____ _____ _____

9) The doctor advised Karin to quit smoking.
🖎_____ _____ _____ _____ _____ _____ _____ _____ _____

10) The child broke two glasses.
🖎_____ _____ _____ _____ _____ _____ _____ _____ _____

11) The farmers burnt a lot of hay.
🖎_____ _____ _____ _____ _____ _____ _____ _____ _____

12) Leila sang a lovely song.
🖎_____ _____ _____ _____ _____ _____ _____ _____ _____

13) Sue flew to New York last night.
🖎_____ _____ _____ _____ _____ _____ _____ _____ _____

14) Taro lent me his car for two days.
🖎_____ _____ _____ _____ _____ _____ _____ _____ _____

15) My friends went rowing last Saturday.
🖎_____ _____ _____ _____ _____ _____ _____ _____ _____

16) My father let me use his own car.
🖎_____ _____ _____ _____ _____ _____ _____ _____ _____

17) My mother set the table for lunch.
🖎_____ _____ _____ _____ _____ _____ _____ _____ _____

18) My parents had a delicious meal outdoors.
🖎_____ _____ _____ _____ _____ _____ _____ _____ _____

19) My classmates discussed the topic together.
🖎_____ _____ _____ _____ _____ _____ _____ _____ _____

20) My teacher helped me a lot.
🖎_____ _____ _____ _____ _____ _____ _____ _____ _____

🖎🖎🖎 *My Homework* 🖎🖎🖎

Exercises on the Simple Present & the Simple Past

> ### *Exercise Nine*
> Choose the correct answer from a, b, c, or d.

1) We _____ a comic play on TV last night.

a	watch	b	watches
c	have watched	d	watched

2) Miral and Yusuf _____ their lessons every night.

a	reviews	b	to review
c	review	d	reviewing

3) My mother _____ her purse yesterday.

a	loses	b	lose
c	has lost	d	lost

4) My family _____ downtown yesterday evening.

a	went	b	go
c	goes	d	Was going

5) The police _____ a lot of thieves yesterday.

a	arrests	b	arrest
c	arrested	d	to arrest

6) A cold wind _____ from the east last Friday.

a	blow	b	blew
c	blown	d	blowing

7) My sister _____ to her school every morning. She never goes by bus.

a	walks	b	walked
c	was walking	d	walk

8) Marlin _____ his office an hour ago.

a	has left	b	leaves
c	was leaving	d	left

9) My uncle usually _____ to his farm in the early morning.

a	drives	b	was driving
c	has driven	d	driven

10) Last Monday, my uncles _____ a lot of maize.

a	has harvested	b	harvest
c	harvested	d	harvests

11) Do you _____ difficult questions in class?

a	answered	b	answers
c	answer	d	to answer

12) Mark _____ a very high score in his final test.

a	getting	b	was getting
c	got	d	get

13) Walter _____ his family to the beach every weekend.

a	takes	b	has taken
c	taking	d	taken

14) Oliver usually _____ fresh juice before his breakfast.

a	drinking	b	to drink
c	has drunk	d	drinks

15) My friends _____ the zoo every month. It's their habit

a	visit	b	to visit
c	have visited	d	visits

16) My classmates always _____ good compositions.

a	writes	b	write
c	have written	d	writing

17) Hesham _____ to Frankfurt every year.

a	fly	b	flies
c	flown	d	flying

18) My family _____ to a new house in Madrid a week ago.

a	moves	b	move
c	moved	d	to move

19) Greg _____ to Dubai monthly.

a	travels	b	has travelled
c	travel	d	is travelling

20) My parents _____ in Tokyo from 2010 to 2012.

a	live	b	living
c	have lived	d	lived

21) In the past, people _____ to eat raw food.

a	used	b	have used
c	uses	d	use

22) My grandparents _____ their farmhouse a year ago.

a	sell	b	have sold
c	sold	d	were selling

23) My brother _____ to his office daily.

a	commute	b	has commuted
c	commutes	d	is commuting

24) Yesterday, I _____ my uncle's camel on the farm.

a	rides	b	ride
c	have ridden	d	rode

25) My sister _____ us a nice cake every Friday.

a	makes	b	has made
c	make	d	is making

My Homework

> Exercise Ten

Complete the sentences. Use *yesterday, last, past,* or *ago*.
1) The lesson started fifteen minutes _____.
2) In the _____, people didn't use paper money.
3) I had a nice dream _____ night.
4) _____, my friends visited me.

5) Ahmad arrived in Beijing _____ weekend.
6) My grandfather had a lot of camels and sheep in the _____.
7) My father was in the bank _____ afternoon.
8) My sisters made a nice meal half an hour _____.
9) My brother bought a small house_____ month.
10) My aunt got married _____ year.
11) My uncle bought a new van _____.
12) Mr Saleh wrote a new book two years _____.
13) Tuka completed her study about insects a month _____.
14) _____ Monday, Sara started a new English course.
15) We visited our relatives in the country _____ week.
16) My friend stopped smoking a week _____.
17) _____ Friday, we watched an exciting match.
18) The workmen painted our old house _____ Tuesday.
19) Mr Hatem earned a lot of money _____ year.
20) In the _____, Mr Atif used to smoke heavily.
21) I listened to the news twenty minutes _____.
22) _____, my family moved into a new villa downtown.
23) Leila invited her friends to dinner _____ week.
24) William flew to his home city _____ Monday.

🙤🙤🙤 *My Homework* 🙦🙦🙦

The Simple Past Tense Yes/No Questions

| Did | Subject | Base form | ? |

Examples:
- **Jessie:** Did you arrive on time?
- ✓ **Helen:** Yes, I did.
- **Martin:** Did Saleh create a Facebook group for his friends?
- ✓ **Norah:** No, he didn't.

> *Exercise Eleven*

Choose the correct answer from a, b, c, or d.
1) Muhammad: Did you have your lunch outdoors?
   ✓ Mahmoud: Yes, I _____ my lunch outdoors.

a	had	b	have had
c	have	d	did

2) Mary: Did you attend Lee's birthday party?
   ✓ Noha: Yes, I _____.

a	attended	b	have attended
c	attend	d	did

3) David: Did Serena get a prize?
✓ Aimee: Yes, she _____ it two days ago.

a	get	b	has got
c	got	d	did

4) Sean: Did Lexi see the manager?
✓ Corey: Yes, she _____ him yesterday.

a	did	b	has seen
c	saw	d	sees

5) Saker: Did the police catch the thieves?
✓ Bader: Yes, they _____ .

a	catch	b	did
c	have caught	d	caught

6) Kim: Did the police officers chase the robbers?
✓ Adrian: Yes, they _____ .

a	chased	b	chase
c	did	d	have chased

7) Lama: Did the child break the vase?
✓ Ted: No, he _____ .

a	didn't	b	did
c	doesn't	d	didn't break

8) Karin: Did the referee cancel the match?
✓ Jim: Yes, he _____ it five minutes ago.

a	cancelled	b	has cancelled
c	cancel	d	did

9) Regan: Did you come on foot?
✓ Ralf: Yes, I _____ .

a	came	b	have come
c	did	d	do

10) Mark: Did the class begin on time?
✓ Edwin: Yes, it _____ .

a	began	b	has begun
c	begin	d	did

11) Hala: _____ the plane land safely?
✓ Mahmoud: Yes, it did.

a	Does	b	Had
c	Did	d	Could

12) Sarah: Did Raul score any goals?
✓ Keith: Yes, he _____ two.

a	has scored	b	scored
c	scores	d	did

13) Sam: Did Saleh win a prize?
✓ Jane: Yes, he _____ .

a	won	b	wins
c	did	d	win

14) Jack: Did you miss the train?
   ✓ Fatima: No, I _____ .

a	missed	b	have missed
c	did	d	didn't

15) Helen: Did Alan _____ his family last night?
   ✓ Karl: Yes, he did.

a	met	b	meeting
c	meet	d	to meet

16) Sandra: Did you see your friends yesterday?
   ✓ Donald: Yes, I _____ them at school.

a	see	b	saw
c	did	d	sees

17) Fagin: Did you _____ your old car?
   ✓ Oliver: No, I didn't.

a	sold	b	to sell
c	sells	d	sell

18) Hadi: Did your teacher fly to Toronto yesterday?
   ✓ Fadi: Yes, he _____ .

a	flew	b	have flown
c	did	d	flies

19) Patrick: _____ the players train hard?
   ✓ Tamer: Yes, they did.

a	Did	b	Do
c	Can	d	Does

20) Tina: Did you _____ anything yesterday?
   ✓ Lina: No, I didn't.

a	bought	b	buys
c	buy	d	buying

21) Emma: Did the mechanic fix your old car?
   ✓ Sophie: Yes, he _____ it two days ago.

a	fixed	b	fixing
c	did	d	fix

My Homework

The Simple Past Tense Information Questions

Question Word	did	Subject	Base form	?

Example:
➢ **Eliza:** What time did the conference start?
✓ **Karl:** The conference started at 10:45 a.m.

➢ *Exercise Twelve*
  ✦ Answer the following questions.
  ✦ Follow the example.

1) Tommy: What time did the bus leave?
   ✓ Moony: It _____ half an hour ago.

a	has left	b	leaves
c	left	d	was leaving

2) Samar: Where did Andy go?
   ✓ Lamar: Andy _____ to the workshop.

a	go	b	goes
c	was going	d	went

3) Nehal: How many days did you spend in Paris?
   ✓ Nehad: I _____ five days there.

a	spent	b	had spent
c	was spending	d	have spent

4) Karma: What did you see in the zoo?
   ✓ Salma: I _____ a lot of animals there.

a	seeing	b	saw
c	see	d	have seen

5) Eliza: Why did you come late?
   ✓ Rayan: I _____ late because I didn't find a taxi.

A	have come	b	was coming
C	came	d	come

6) Hanan: What time did the lecture begin?
   ✓ Rawan: The lecture _____ ten minutes ago.

a	begun	b	begins
c	began	d	was beginning

7) Henry: Why did the team lose the match?
   ✓ Jessie: The team _____ the match because the players were lazy.

a	have lost	b	were losing
c	lose	d	lost

8) Holly: How much money did you pay?
   ✓ Lucas: I _____ ten thousand dollars.

a	to pay	b	pay
c	have paid	d	paid

9) Yoko: Why did your team win the match?
   ✓ Maryam: My team won the match because the players _____ their best.

a	to do	b	did
c	done	d	doing

10) Maia: What did Mary do yesterday?
    ✓ Eden: She tidied the room and _____ her bed.

a	has made	b	was making
c	made	d	makes

11) Tayla: _____ did the dog bark?
    ✓ Alice: Because it saw a stranger.

a	What	b	Where
c	When	d	Why

12) Anna: _____ did the plane take off?
    ✓ Brooke: It took off at half past ten.

a	Where	b	What
c	Why	d	What time

13) Amy: _____ did the team go?
    ✓ Zara: The team went to the stadium.

a	What time	b	Why
c	Where	d	When

14) Rose: _____ did you eat for breakfast?
    ✓ Poppy: I ate some jam and some cream.

a	What	b	Where
c	When	d	Why

15) Nina: _____ did your parents leave for Texas?
    ✓ Sofia: They left yesterday morning.

a	What	b	Where
c	When	d	Why

16) Sonia: _____ did you meet in the park?
    ✓ Lolo: I met some of my old friends there.

a	Who	b	How often
c	When	d	Why

17) Kate: _____ did you use to visit your grandparents?
    ✓ Maria: I used to visit them twice a week.

a	What	b	Where
c	How often	d	Why

18) Angel: _____ did you come?
    ✓ Andy: I came by bus.

a	What	b	How
c	When	d	Why

19) Ashley: _____ killed the crazy dog?
    ✓ Molly: The policemen.

a	Who	b	Where
c	When	d	Why

20) Boody: _____ children did you see?
✓ Batool: I saw four children.

a	How much	b	Where
c	How many	d	Whose

❧❧❧ My Homework ❧❧❧

➢ Exercise Thirteen
✦ Rearrange these words to form meaningful questions.
✦ Follow the example.
➢ /did / fly / you / Where/
❧ Where did you fly?
✓ I flew to Hong Kong.

1) /Lewis / What / did / win/
❧____ ____ ____ ____ ____ ____ ____ ____
✓ Lewis won a prize.

2) /Liza / Why / cry / did/
❧____ ____ ____ ____ ____ ____ ____ ____
✓ Liza cried because she saw a wild dog.

3) /arrive / did / they / When/
❧____ ____ ____ ____ ____ ____ ____ ____
✓ They arrived yesterday.

4) /Adel / How / did / drive/
❧____ ____ ____ ____ ____ ____ ____ ____
✓ Adel drove safely.

5) /did / hurry / Arthur / Why/
❧____ ____ ____ ____ ____ ____ ____ ____
✓ Arthur hurried because he was late for class.

6) /Hanna / stay / did / Where/
❧____ ____ ____ ____ ____ ____ ____ ____
✓ Hanna stayed in a five-star hotel.

7) /trees / did / you / How many / plant/
❧____ ____ ____ ____ ____ ____ ____ ____
✓ I planted seven trees.

8) /the/ break / did / What / boys/
❧____ ____ ____ ____ ____ ____ ____ ____
✓ The boys broke some glasses.

9) /give / manager / What / you / did / the/
❧____ ____ ____ ____ ____ ____ ____ ____
✓ The manager gave me three reports.

10) /car / your / How much / did / new / cost/
✎_____ _____ _____ _____ _____ _____ _____
✓ My new car cost fifty thousand dollars.
11) /What / sell / market / did / in / the / you/
✎_____ _____ _____ _____ _____ _____ _____
✓ I sold some old machines in the market.
12) / driver / did / What / hit / the/
✎_____ _____ _____ _____ _____ _____
✓ The driver hit a little cat.
13) /you / lunch / did / When / your / eat/
✎_____ _____ _____ _____ _____ _____
✓ I ate my lunch an hour ago.
14) /write / How many / the/ did/ secretary / reports /
✎_____ _____ _____ _____ _____ _____
✓ The secretary wrote four reports.
15) /way / school / you / on / meet / Who / to / did / your/
✎_____ _____ _____ _____ _____ _____ _____ _____ _____
✓ I met my new teacher on my way to school.
16) /Sara / work / today / did / to / How / come/
✎_____ _____ _____ _____ _____ _____ _____
✓ She walked.
17) /teacher / praise / your / did / Why / you/
✎_____ _____ _____ _____ _____ _____
✓ Because I got the full mark in the weekly quiz.
18) /brothers / weekend / your / do / did / at / What / the/
✎_____ _____ _____ _____ _____ _____ _____ _____
✓ They visited their grandparents in the country.
19) /break / your / Where / down / last / did / night / car/
✎_____ _____ _____ _____ _____ _____ _____ _____
✓ On the bridge near the city.
20)/Abdul-Rahman / yesterday / did / do / What/
✎_____ _____ _____ _____ _____ _____
✓ He made a model helicopter.

🙠🙠🙠 *My Homework* 🙢🙢🙢

> ### Exercise Fourteen
  ✦ Answer the following questions.
  ✦ Follow the example.
  > Did you **come** on foot?
  ✦ No, I **didn't come** on foot. I **came** by bus.
  1) Did the **train** arrive on time?
  ✎_____ _____ _____ _____ _____ _____ _____ _____

2) Did you study English?
✎_____ _____ _____ _____ _____ _____ _____ _____ _____

3) Did you drink a cup of coffee?
✎_____ _____ _____ _____ _____ _____ _____ _____ _____

4) Did you marry Sarah?
✎_____ _____ _____ _____ _____ _____ _____ _____ _____

5) Did you drop a vase?
✎_____ _____ _____ _____ _____ _____ _____ _____ _____

6) Did you buy a camera?
✎_____ _____ _____ _____ _____ _____ _____ _____ _____

7) Did you break a cup?
✎_____ _____ _____ _____ _____ _____ _____ _____ _____

8) Did you injure your knee?
✎_____ _____ _____ _____ _____ _____ _____ _____ _____

9) Did you read a novel?
✎_____ _____ _____ _____ _____ _____ _____ _____ _____

10) Did you visit the zoo?
✎_____ _____ _____ _____ _____ _____ _____ _____ _____

11) Did you bring your history book?
✎_____ _____ _____ _____ _____ _____ _____ _____ _____

12) Did you build a new villa?
✎_____ _____ _____ _____ _____ _____ _____ _____ _____

13) Did you burn some paper?
✎_____ _____ _____ _____ _____ _____ _____ _____ _____

14) Did Evans bake a cake?
✎_____ _____ _____ _____ _____ _____ _____ _____ _____

15) Did Collins behave well?
✎_____ _____ _____ _____ _____ _____ _____ _____ _____

16) Did Isabel clean the office?
✎_____ _____ _____ _____ _____ _____ _____ _____ _____

17) Did Maya attend the party?
✎_____ _____ _____ _____ _____ _____ _____ _____ _____

18) Did Rosie wash her skirt?
✎_____ _____ _____ _____ _____ _____ _____ _____ _____

19) Did you have your dinner at home?
✎_____ _____ _____ _____ _____ _____ _____ _____ _____

20) Did your brothers watch the match in the stadium?
✎_____ _____ _____ _____ _____ _____ _____ _____ _____

My Homework

➢ **_Exercise Fifteen_**
   ↳ Answer the following questions.
   ↳ Follow the example.
➢ Did you **come** on foot?
↳ No, I **didn't come** on foot. I **came** by bus.

1) Did the bus leave the station early?
🐚_____

2) Did Ahmad sell his old car?
🐚_____

3) Did Nada invite her family to the party?
🐚_____

4) Did your parents leave yesterday?
🐚_____

5) Did the tourists stay in a furnished apartment?
🐚_____

6) Did the students go to the computer lab?
🐚_____

7) Did the mechanics fix the old bus?
🐚_____

8) Did the passengers ask for coffee?
🐚_____

9) Did the driver check the brakes?
🐚_____

10) Did the teachers give the weekly quiz?
🐚_____

🐚🐚🐚 *My Homework* 🐚🐚🐚

➢ **_Exercise Sixteen_**
   ↳ Put the following verbs in the simple past then use them to complete the sentences. Follow the example.

ride	invite	feel	say	come
spend	wear	enjoy	drive	send
see	sing	find out	take	book

✓ The little baby cried when he [**saw**] the black cat.

1) Ahmad _____ three tickets for the final game.
2) Tuka _____ very well after taking the drugs.
3) Batool _____ a new way to work out the geometry exercise.

4) Abdul-Rahman _____ his time in the swimming pool.
5) Mohamed _____ to the lecture on time.
6) Carol _____ a beautiful song after class yesterday.
7) Lily _____ her uncle an email last night.
8) John _____ the weekend on his uncle's farm.
9) Ramon _____ a very nice jacket yesterday.
10) Our teacher _____ that he would explain the lesson again.
11) Nemar _____ his brothers to the club.
12) Julia _____ her friends to her birthday party.
13) Sarah _____ a camel when she was in the zoo.
14) Salma _____ to her office in the early morning.

🌺🌺🌺 *My Homework* 🌺🌺🌺

➤ *Exercise Seventeen*

✦ Find the mistake in each of the following sentences and correct it.
✦ Follow the example.

➤ Dr Ibrahim check a lot of patients last Monday.
✓ Dr Ibrahim checked a lot of patients last Monday.

1) My uncle grow ten hectares of rice last year.
✎_____
2) The teacher give us too much homework yesterday.
✎_____
3) My grandfather take the cattle to the farm an hour ago.
✎_____
4) My family spend a week in the Canary Islands last June.
✎_____
5) We fly to Hurghada last winter.
✎_____
6) Olivia read a novel for Charles Dickens last month.
✎_____
7) Susan teach biology at Harvard University last year.
✎_____
8) Lena buy a new digital camera two days ago.
✎_____
9) Osama sell his old villa last Friday.
✎_____
10) The manager send us an important email yesterday.
✎_____
11) My grandfather feed the cattle an hour ago.
✎_____
12) Yesterday, we learn how to write a business email.
✎_____

13) In the past, Bedouins dig water wells to get water.
✎_____ _____ _____ _____ _____ _____ _____ _____ _____ _____

14) Last night, I see an exciting Canadian movie.
✎_____ _____ _____ _____ _____ _____ _____ _____ _____ _____

15) Yesterday, Alfred write three reports about the new deal.
✎_____ _____ _____ _____ _____ _____ _____ _____ _____ _____

16) Charlie called the police when a burglar attack her house.
✎_____ _____ _____ _____ _____ _____ _____ _____ _____ _____

17) After we met the manager, we decide to start the new project.
✎_____ _____ _____ _____ _____ _____ _____ _____ _____ _____

18) I had my breakfast before I leave my home.
✎_____ _____ _____ _____ _____ _____ _____ _____ _____ _____

19) As soon as Batool finished her work, she go to bed.
✎_____ _____ _____ _____ _____ _____ _____ _____ _____ _____

20) Mark came late because his car break down.
✎_____ _____ _____ _____ _____ _____ _____ _____ _____ _____

✿✿✿ *My Homework*

> ### *Exercise Eighteen*
↳ Find the mistake in each of the following sentences and correct it.

1) My grandfather build this house forty years ago.
✎_____ _____ _____ _____ _____ _____ _____ _____ _____ _____

2) Michael start his new career as a pharmacist last Monday.
✎_____ _____ _____ _____ _____ _____ _____ _____ _____ _____

3) My uncle become a colonel last May.
✎_____ _____ _____ _____ _____ _____ _____ _____ _____ _____

4) We catch a lot of fish yesterday.
✎_____ _____ _____ _____ _____ _____ _____ _____ _____ _____

5) Basel and Osama drank some fruit juice before they have their lunch.
✎_____ _____ _____ _____ _____ _____ _____ _____ _____ _____

6) As soon as the policeman arrested the shoplifter, he take him to the police station.
✎_____ _____ _____ _____ _____ _____ _____ _____ _____ _____
_____ _____ _____ _____ _____ _____ _____ _____ _____ _____

7) The thief crept into the house and steal a lot of money.
✎_____ _____ _____ _____ _____ _____ _____ _____ _____ _____

8) Linda fell off her horse and hurt her knees.
✎_____ _____ _____ _____ _____ _____ _____ _____ _____ _____

9) My sister drew a nice picture before she do her homework.
✎_____ _____ _____ _____ _____ _____ _____ _____ _____ _____

10) My uncle buy a new villa in the country last June.
✎_____ _____ _____ _____ _____ _____ _____ _____ _____ _____

11) Yesterday, my sister graduate from Harvard University.
✎ ____ ____ ____ ____ ____ ____ ____ ____ ____ ____ ____

12) My mother keep a lot of food in the fridge last week.
✎ ____ ____ ____ ____ ____ ____ ____ ____ ____ ____ ____

13) Last night, Salah lead his team to win the final game.
✎ ____ ____ ____ ____ ____ ____ ____ ____ ____ ____ ____

14) My family watch a comic play for Bernard Shaw last weekend.
✎ ____ ____ ____ ____ ____ ____ ____ ____ ____ ____ ____

15) When we visit the Louvre, we be impressed by the monuments.
✎ ____ ____ ____ ____ ____ ____ ____ ____ ____ ____ ____

16) The carpenter make a lot of chairs and stools last week.
✎ ____ ____ ____ ____ ____ ____ ____ ____ ____ ____ ____

17) The sun shine brightly yesterday.
✎ ____ ____ ____ ____ ____ ____ ____ ____ ____ ____ ____

18) My friend show me the photos of her wedding last Friday.
✎ ____ ____ ____ ____ ____ ____ ____ ____ ____ ____ ____

19) It was very hot, so Mike switch the air conditioner on.
✎ ____ ____ ____ ____ ____ ____ ____ ____ ____ ____ ____

20) We were very happy because our team win the final game.
✎ ____ ____ ____ ____ ____ ____ ____ ____ ____ ____ ____

✎✎✎ *My Homework*

Used to

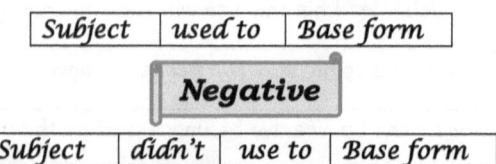

| Subject | used to | Base form |

Negative

| Subject | didn't | use to | Base form |

It expresses a habit that happened in the past.

Examples:

➢ Tamara **used to be** very active in class.
➢ Jasmine **didn't use to suffer** from serious mental problems.

➢ *Exercise Nineteen*
   ↳ Choose the correct answer from a, b, c, or d.

1) My father _____ to smoke heavily when he was young.

| a | was using | b | used |
| c | has used | d | use |

2) Rose used to _____ tricks on her classmates.

| a | playing | b | plays |
| c | play | d | played |

3) John's father used _____ shoes for a living.

| a | mended | b | to mend |
| c | mend | d | mending |

4) Ellen didn't _____ to leave her books at home.

| a | used | b | has used |
| c | was using | d | use |

5) My brother _____ drink his coffee black.

| a | is used to | b | was used to |
| c | used to | d | used |

6) My grandparents used _____ healthy food.

| a | eat | b | ate |
| c | eats | d | to eat |

7) Our primary school teacher used to _____ us a lot.

| a | helps | b | help |
| c | helped | d | helping |

8) My family didn't _____ to live in the country.

| a. | used | b. | using |
| c. | uses | d. | use |

9) I used to _____ cartoon films when I was a child.

a.	watching	b.	watch
c.	watched	d.	watches

10) Mrs Nada: Who used _____ her mother in the kitchen?
　Jamila: Tuqa and Batool.

a.	helping	b.	helps
c.	to help	d.	helped

11) Khalil: Did your grandparents _____ to travel on camels?
　Walid: Yes, they did.

a.	used	b.	using
c.	uses	d.	use

12) Jeannette used to _____ in a small house when she was a child.

a.	lives	b.	lived
c.	living	d.	live

13) Nathalie: Did your friends use _____ to the beach at the weekend?
　Laura: No, they didn't.

a.	go	b.	went
c.	to go	d.	going

14) Jean didn't used to _____ school.

a.	hate	b.	hating
c.	hates	d.	hated

15) My family didn't use to _____ the weekend outdoors.

a.	spent	b.	spending
c.	spend	d.	spends

16) Henry didn't use to play computer games when he was a child, but now he _____.

a.	did	b.	doing
c.	do	d.	does

17) My aunt used to have a small apartment, but now she _____ a large villa.

a.	had	b.	didn't have
c.	has	d.	had had

18) When Ali was in Italy, he used to watch Napoli's matches in the stadium, but now he _____ them on TV.

a.	watches	b.	watched
c.	watch	d.	doesn't watch

19) My grandmother used to _____ delicious meals for us.

a.	cooking	b.	cooks
c.	cooked	d.	cook

20) Ann didn't use to _____ the reading competitions.

a.	took part in	b.	takes part in
c.	take part in	d.	taking part in

21) When Yazan was in England, he used to _____ on the right-hand side of the road.

a.	driving	b.	drive
c.	drove	d.	drives

22) Mobile phones used to be very expensive, now their prices ____ reasonable.

a.	were	b.	had been
c.	are	d.	be

23) When Saleh was a child, he used to ____ a school three kilometres away.

a.	went	b.	goes
c.	going	d.	go

24) In the past, Bedouins used to travel on camels. However, these days they ____ modern means of transportation.

a.	used	b.	use
c.	uses	d.	using

25) My neighbour used to have an old car, now he ____ a modern one.

a.	own	b.	is owning
c.	owned	d.	owns

ꙮꙮꙮ My Homework ꙮꙮꙮ

(Be) Used to

Affirmative

I	am	used to	-ing
He / She / It	is	accustomed to	or
You / They / We	are		Noun

Negative

I	am		used to	-ing
He / She / It	is	not	accustomed to	or
You / They / We	are			Noun

It expresses a habit that still happens in the present time.

✦ **Examples:**
➤ I <u>**am used to helping**</u> my grandfather on the farm.
➤ We <u>**are used to attending**</u> German classes in the evening.

➢ Exercise Twenty

✦ Choose the correct answer from a, b, c, or d.

1) My father is accustomed to _____ his coffee without sugar.

a	drinks	b	drink
c	drank	d	drinking

2) I am not used to _____ my seat belt while driving.

a	wore	b	wearing
c	wear	d	wears

3) My brothers are used to _____ their summer vacation in Spain.

a	spend	b	spent
c	spending	d	spends

4) I am accustomed to _____ to the country at the weekend.

a	gone	b	go
c	goes	d	going

5) Diana is used to _____ very early to prepare her kids for school.

a	getting up	b	gets up
c	got up	d	get up

6) At first, it was difficult for Ahmad to speak Chinese all the time but he _____ to it now on a large scale.

a	used	b	is used
c	uses	d	was used

7) My grandfather is too old. He isn't used to _____ smartphones.

a	uses	b	using
c	use	d	used

8) Mark isn't used to _____ junk food.

a	eating	b	eat
c	ate	d	eats

9) My aunt is accustomed to _____ carefully. She sticks to the traffic rules very well.

a	drive	b	drives
c	drove	d	dricing

10) My sisters are used to _____ my mother do the housework.

a	helps	b	help
c	helping	d	helped

11) Boody is accustomed to _____ to school every morning.

a	cycle	b	cycling
c	cycles	d	cycled

12) Hamada is_____ to jogging in the afternoon.

A	used	b	uses
C	using	d	use

13) I _____ the cold weather in Russia.

a	am not used to	b	won't use to
c	don't use to	d	haven't used to

14) Our new teacher is used to _____ us weekly.

a	test	b	tested
c	to test	d	testing

15) Wilson isn't accustomed to _____ alone.

a	live	b	living
c	lived	d	lives

My Homework

SECTION 13 — The Past Perfect Tense

Affirmative

| Subject | had | Past Participle |

➢ The ancient Egyptians **had built** the Pyramids in Giza.

Negative

| Subject | hadn't | Past Participle |

➢ The players **hadn't trained** well before they played the match.

➢ *Note # 01:*

> We use the Past Perfect to express a completed action or event before something in the past.

➢ *Note # 02:*

> In order to sequence two successive actions that happened in the past, we use the Past Perfect for the first one and the past Simple for the second one.

We may use the past perfect with these conjunctions:

After

After	1st Subject	had + P.P.	,	2nd Subject	Past Simple

- After the mechanic had fixed the engine, he checked it.

Or

After	-ing	,	2nd Subject	Past Simple

- After scoring the test sheets, I put them in the drawer.

Or

1st Subject	Past Simple	after	2nd Subject	had + P.P.

- I got to the airport after the plane had taken off.

Or

1st Subject	Past Simple	after	-ing

- The farmers had a rest after harvesting the wheat.

****

As soon as

As soon as	1st Subject	had + P.P.	,	2nd Subject	Past Simple

- As soon as I had finished the reports, I reviewed them.

Or

1st Subject	Past Simple	as soon as	2nd Subject	had + P.P.

- The manager called for a meeting as soon as the project had finished.

****

Before

Before	1st Subject	Past Simple	,	2nd Subject	had + P.P.

- Before we flew to Cairo, we had booked a full package tour.

Or

1st Subject	had + P.P.	before	2nd Subject	Past Simple

- The play had started before we arrived at the theatre.

Or

1st Subject	had + P.P.	before	-ing

- My grandfather had fed the cattle before leaving the farm.

****

By the time

By the time	1st Subject	Past Simple	,	2nd Subject	had + P.P.

➢ By the time we got to the working site, the workmen had left.

Or

1st Subject	had + P.P.	by the time	2nd Subject	Past Simple

➢ Two robbers had broken into our house by the time we got home.

When

1st Subject	had + P.P.	when	2nd subject	Past Simple

➢ I hadn't recognized Helen when I saw her. She aged a lot.

Or

When	1st Subject	Past Simple	,	2nd Subject	had + P.P.

➢ When Mr Salem retired, he had run the factory for over thirty years.

****

Until

1st Subject	had + P.P.	until	2nd Subject	Past Simple

➢ We had waited in the stadium until the match had finished.

****

Because

1st Subject	Past Simple	because	2nd Subject	had + P.P.

➢ We thanked our teacher because he had helped us a lot.

****

So

1st Subject	had + P.P.	, so	2nd Subject	Past Simple

➢ We had worked for a long time, so we were very tired.

****

No sooner ... than

1st Subject	had	no sooner	P. P	than	2nd. Subject	Past Simple

➢ I had no sooner felt the pain than I went to a nearby hospital.

****

Or

No sooner	had	1st Subject	P. P	than	2nd. Subject	Past Simple

➢ No sooner had the farmers harvested the crops than they stored them.

****

Hardly ... when

1st Subject	had	hardly	P. P	when	2nd Subject	Past Simple

➢ I had hardly reached the location when I heard my name.

Hardly	had	1st Subject	P. P	when	2nd Subject	Past Simple

➢ Hardly had we finished the meeting when we went to our offices.

****

Scarcely ... when

1st Subject	had	scarcely	P. P	when	2nd Subject	Past Simple

➢ The secretary had scarcely reviewed the documents when she gave them to her manager.

Or

Scarcely	had	1st Subject	P. P	when	2nd Subject	Past Simple

➢ Scarcely had Tuka read the novel when she took it back to the library.

****

If (type 3)

If	1st Subject	had	P. P	,	2nd Subject	would have could have	P.P

➢ If I had done my best, I would have passed my final exams.

Or

1st Subject	would have could have	P. P	if	2nd Subject	had	P.P

➢ We would have gone to the park if the weather had been fine.

****

Exercise One

➕ Correct the verb in brackets. Follow the example.
➢ The meeting had already finished when Daniel [come].
✓ The meeting had already finished when Daniel came.

1) Batool [celebrate] her seventeenth birthday before she joined Helwan University.

   ✎ _____

   _____

2) Marawan [eat] his lunch before he left the house.

   ✎ _____

   _____

3) When Leila opened her purse, she found out that someone [steal] all her money.
✎ _____

4) Abdul-Rahman had known his friend Abdullah for a year before they [join] the army.
✎ _____

5) My mother was happy to know that my sister [cook] a delicious meal.
✎ _____

6) My grandfather [stay] on the farm for a long time before it started to snow.
✎ _____

7) Brazil won the World Cup because its players [exert] strenuous efforts.
✎ _____

8) Muhammad [move] to a new apartment after he had sold his old one.
✎ _____

9) Tuka [review] the email as soon as he had received it.
✎ _____

10) I hardly [have] my dinner when I fell asleep.
✎ _____

11) Lobna scarcely [leave] the house when it started to snow.
✎ _____

12) If Ahmad [get] a marketing plan, he would have carried it out.
✎ _____

13) As soon as Kim had moved to live in Indiana, he [buy] a large house.
✎ _____

14) The laundry [be] wet because the spin dryer had been out of order.
✎ _____

15) My little sister [eat] all the pie that my mother had made.
✎ _____

16) As soon as the bell [ring], all the students rushed into their classroom.
✎ _____

17) After the plane had landed, we [leave] to the arrival hall.
✎ _____

18) Before we [go] to the desert, we had prepared a lot of stuff.
✎ _____

19) After they had built the house, they [decorate] it.
✎ _____

20) The teacher didn't speak to Katie until she [apologize].
✎ _____

❦❦❦ My Homework ❦❦❦

Yes-no Questions in the Past Perfect Tense

| Had | Subject | P.P. ...? |

| Yes, | Subject pronoun | had. |

| No, | Subject pronoun | hadn't. |

✦ Examples:
➢ **Amy:** Had you met Frank before you left the office?
✓ **Bella:** Yes, I had.
➢ **Rose:** Had you done the housework already?
✓ **Eve:** No, I hadn't.

➢ *Exercise Two*
✦ Choose the correct answer from a, b, c, or d.
1) Harry: Had you sent the faxes before leaving your office?
✓ Lydia: Yes, I _____ .

| a | had | b | had sent |
| c | have | d | did |

2) Aisha: Had the teachers checked the seating numbers?
✓ Heidi: Yes, they _____ them.

a	had checked	b	have
c	have checked	d	had

3) Marcos: Had the technician _____ the fridge?
✓ Thomas: Yes, he had.

a	fixing	b	to fix
c	fixed	d	fixes

4) Jacob: Had you _____ the dictionary back to the library after using it?
✓ William: Yes, I had.

a	taken	b	taking
c	took	d	taken

5) Isabel: Had the technicians _____ the plane before taking off?
✓ Max: Yes, they had.

a	check	b	checking
c	checked	d	checks

6) Brooke: Had the players _____ well before the match?
✓ Bella: Yes, they had.

a	training	b	trains
c	to train	d	trained

7) Mason: Had the dentist sterilized his tools before using them?
✓ Harrison: Yes, he _____ them.

a	sterilized	b	sterilize
c	had sterilized	d	sterilizes

8) Riley: Had Ahmad learnt Japanese before travelling to Japan?
✓ Logan: No, he _____.

a	had	b	had learnt
c	hadn't learnt	d	hadn't

9) Freddie: Had the coach _____ a good plan for the final match?
✓ Tim: No, he hadn't.

a	putting	b	put
c	puts	d	to put

10) Isaac: Had your brothers _____ to the beach?
✓ Hardy: Yes, they had.

a	going	b	go
c	gone	d	went

My Homework

Wh- Questions in the Past Perfect Tense

| Wh- Word | had | Subject | P.P. ...? |

> **Jake:** When had the rocket exploded?
✓ **Tom:** It had exploded before reaching its destination.

> ## Exercise Three
  ✚ Choose the correct answer from a, b, c, or d.

1) **Harvey:** _____ had you done before you planted the trees?
✓ **Jenson:** I had prepared the soil very well.

a	Where	b	What
c	Why	d	When

2) **Adam:** What had the doctors _____ with the patient?
✓ **Tyler:** They had saved his life.

a	did	b	do
c	done	d	doing

3) **Adam:** _____ had your grandparents spent the weekend?
✓ **Felix:** They had spent it in the mountains.

a	Where	b	What
c	Why	d	When

4) **Evan:** _____ had Albert done to make his teacher angry?
✓ **Aiden:** He had said an offensive word.

a	Where	b	What
c	Why	d	How

5) **Ramos:** How much had the man _____ before the police arrested him?
✓ **Austin:** A lot.

a	drinks	b	drank
c	drunk	d	drink

✿✿✿ My Homework ✿✿✿

> ## Exercise Four
  ✚ Rearrange these words to form meaningful sentences.
  ✚ Follow the example.

> / fixed / old / before / it / I / I / my / sold / had / car /
✓ I had fixed my old car before I sold it.

1) / his / some / for / finished / rested / After / task / Saleh / he / had / time /

✎ ____ ____ ____ ____ ____ ____ ____ ____ ____ ____
____ ____ ____ ____ ____ ____ ____ ____

2) / referee / after / checked / The / the / the / pitch / had / started / match / he / soccer /

✍_____

3) / driver / driving / bus / fixed / after / the / on / it / had /he / went / the /

✍_____

4) / the / clerk / leave / reports / he / office / his / The / didn't / revised / until / had /

✍_____

5) / farm / fed / took / he / it / horse / John / to / As soon as / had / the / the / back /

✍_____

6) / mother / before / nice / had / a / cooked / cleaned / house / the / my / meal / she /

✍_____

7) / swimming / It / stopped / when / hardly / drizzling / we / had / went /

✍_____

8) / police / Jack / he / crime / The / arrested / committed / a / had / because /

✍_____

9) / took / parking / fixed / After / it / car / he / the / the / my / to / mechanic / area / had /

✍_____

10) / leave / building / the / the / fire / extinguished / until / firemen / didn't / had / they / the /

✍_____

11) / before / arrived / theatre / begun / I / at / play / The / the / had /

✍_____

12) / driving / go / because / we / on / snowed / last / didn't / night / a lot / had / it /

_____

13) / family / dinner / already / when / came / had / I / My / home / had /

_____

14) / angry / because / left / teacher / books / home / my / The / at / I / was / had / very /

_____

15) / found / email / I / my / lot / checked / out / mail / that / received / had / a / When / I / of / inbox / I /

_____

16) / had / father / gone / called / when / him / hardly / out / friend / My / his /

_____

17) / arrived / relatives / finished / cooking / scarcely / My / had / our / mother / when /

_____

18) / because / company / hadn't / Ahmad's / The / cancelled / he / it / flight / confirmed / airline /

_____

19) / uncle / for / to / in / My / moving / years / ten / stayed / Chicago / New Jersey / had / before /

_____

20) / getting / driver's / to / car / new / I / license / my / after / decided / buy / a / I /

_____

My Homework

> *Exercise Five*
- Rearrange these words to form meaningful sentences.

1) / would / John / have / final / he / If / studied / exam / passed / had / well / his /
   _____

2) / boxer / won / have / final / he / If / hard / the / would / round / had / trained / the /
   _____

3) / started / got / classroom / into / The / my / I / had / by the time / lesson /
   _____

4) / Maya / got / airport / passport / forgotten / to / the / had / When / she / she / discovered / her / that /
   _____

5) / mother / happy / cleaned / the / My / I / had / was / garden / because /
   _____

6) / player / share / final / the / The / didn't / broken / had / in / match / foot / because / his / he /
   _____

7) / whole / was / Lacey / college / had / amazed / won / prize / the / first / The / because /
   _____

8) / Eliza / time / she / had / Unless / the / wouldn't / have / applied / in / got / job / for / it /
   _____

9) / didn't / children / homework / their / The / watch / they / had / until / finished / TV /
   _____

10) / sister / get / until / My / didn't / she / had / married / graduated /
    _____

11) / friend / Jane / recognize / a lot / changed / she / because / didn't / her / old / had /

12) / lived / countries / by the time / had / turned / different / five / I / I / nineteen / in /

13) / before / Australia / been / parents / hadn't / My / to /

14) / brother / visited / North Pole / My / the / had / never / elder /

15) / reach / wrong / our / we / had / shepherd / us / couldn't / because / destination / the / given / directions /

16) / hadn't / months / trees / dry / rained / because / it / for / became / A lot of /

17) / pay / my / home / wallet / left / had / I / I / couldn't / for / purchases / so / at / the /

18) / sad / because / mobile / had / was / very / she / lost / phone / Salma / her /

19) / Osama / after / passed / returned / years / fifteen / home / abroad / had / he /

20) / lesson / we / had / times / until / didn't / it / grammar / the / We / practiced / many / understand /

My Homework

> ## Exercise Six:
> ✦ Choose the correct answer from a, b, c or d.

1) After _____ the portrait, the painter took it to the gallery.

a	had painted	b	painted
c	painting	d	have painted

2) As soon as I had fixed the laptop, I _____ on the Internet.

a	was logging	b	logged
c	have logged	d	log

3) Dr Marwa had hardly arrived at her clinic when she _____ a lot of patients waiting for her.

a	found	b	was finding
c	finds	d	has found

4) Before Safa worked in our company, she _____ for a long time.

a	trains	b	has trained
c	is training	d	had trained

5) I had scarcely written the report when my boss _____ me.

a	phoned	b	phones
c	was phoning	d	has phoned

6) Saleh hadn't seen a leaning tower before _____ the Leaning Tower of Pisa in Italy.

a	visited	b	had visited
c	has visited	d	visiting

7) My car was covered with a lot of snow because it _____ a lot during the night.

a	snowing	b	has snowing
c	had snowed	d	snows

8) The train had left the station before I _____.

a	came	b	coming
c	have come	d	come

9) By the time Mona got into her class, the teacher _____ the new lesson.

a	had explained	b	explaining
c	has explained	d	explains

10) I had exercised well before I _____ in the final match.

a	shares	b	has shared
c	sharing	d	shared

11) Ali and Omar _____ to the movie because they had already seen it.

a	don't go	b	didn't go
c	hasn't gone	d	haven't gone

12) I was late for the meeting. It had already begun by the time I _____ there.

a	getting	b	have got
c	get	d	got

13) If Sarah _____ early, she would have missed her flight.

| a | didn't get up | b | hasn't got up |
| c | hadn't got up | d | doesn't get up |

14) Martina had finished her higher studies before _____ married.

| a | had got | b | got |
| c | getting | d | has got |

15) My wife had read the newspaper before she _____ cooking.

| a | starts | b | starting |
| c | has started | d | started |

16) Sam _____ his comment about the book until he had read it.

| a | hasn't written | b | can't write |
| c | doesn't write | d | didn't write |

17) The farmer _____ home after he had planted the trees.

| a | returns | b | has returned |
| c | returned | d | has to return |

18) Lee had lived in Korea before _____ to Canada.

| a | leaving | b | had left |
| c | leave | d | left |

19) My father _____ the bill before he left the restaurant.

| a | had paid | b | pays |
| c | paying | d | pay |

20) My parents couldn't enter the theatre because they _____ the tickets at home.

| a | had left | b | leaves |
| c | leave | d | leaving |

21) My mother could recognize our old neighbour as soon as she _____ her.

| a | seen | b | had seen |
| c | sees | d | see |

22) I didn't have my dinner until I _____ my homework.

| a | done | b | doing |
| c | had done | d | have done |

23) Mark phoned the police because he _____ his laptop.

| a | losing | b | loses |
| c | lose | d | had lost |

24) Gareth had run for a long distance, so he _____ pain in his legs.

| a | felling | b | feels |
| c | feel | d | felt |

25) Kevin had got excellent results because he _____ hard.

| a | had studied | b | study |
| c | studies | d | has studied |

SECTION 14 — The Past Perfect Progressive (Continuous)

Affirmative

| Subject | had | been | -ing |

> The woman is tired because she **had been working** on the farm for a long time.

> *Note:*

We use the Past Perfect Continuous to show that something started in the past and continued up until another time in the past. 'For five minutes' and 'for two weeks' are both durations which can be used with the Past Perfect Continuous. Notice that this is related to the Present Perfect Continuous; however, the duration does not continue until now, it stops before something else in the past.*

* englishpage.com

Negative

| Subject | hadn't | been | -ing |

> The players hadn't been waiting for a long time before their coach arrived.

> *Exercise One*
- Rearrange these words to form meaningful sentences.
- Follow the example.

> / muddy / streets / raining / It / became / the / been / time / for / had / a / heavily / long / so /

✓ It had been raining heavily for a long time, so the streets became muddy.

1) / parents / exhausted / for / jogging / because / long / they / been / a / had / time / My / were /

_____

2) / sweated / because / hour / been / had / Mark / running / an / a lot / for / had / he /

_____

3) / family / living / born / sister / Nairobi / been / My / in / had / since / was / my / younger

_____

4) / Nelson / fired / got / he / his / working / before / fifteen / had / years / job / from / been / for /

_____

5) / rest / had / some / working / eight / for / We / get / been / hours / had to / we / so /

_____

6) / perfect / ten / Layan's / it / studying / had / French / been / for / years / she / because / is /

_____

7) / younger / sleeping / before / I / up / him / twelve / had / My / been / for / brother / hours / woke /

_____

8) / children / so / been / for / swimming / hours / The / they / tired / very / were / had / two /

_____

9) / grandparents / us / since / month / My / staying / with / had / the / been / previous /

✎ _____

10) / writing / new / for / book / I / had / been / years / my / two /

✎ _____

✿✿✿ My Homework ✿✿✿

SECTION 15 — Future Time

The Simple Future Tense with *Will*

Affirmative

Subject	will	Base form

Example:
- Somebody is knocking. I **will open** the door.

Negative

Subject	will not	Base form

OR

Subject	won't	Base form

The Future Simple Tense is used to express events or actions that will take place in a specific time in the future.

Examples:
- I **will not go** to school tomorrow morning.
- If I get up late, I **won't catch** the school bus.

Yes/No Questions with *Will* ___ ?

Will	Subject	Base form ......?

OR

Won't	Subject	Base form ......?

Examples:
- **Abdullah:** **Will** you **visit me** tomorrow?
- ✓ **Mohsen:** Yes, I will.

- **Judi:** **Won't** you **buy** this mobile phone?
- ✓ **Rana:** No, I won't.

Information Questions with *Will* ___?

Question Word	will	Subject	base form?

✦ Examples:

➤ **Yasser**: When will the new course start?
✓ **Saher**: It will start next Monday.

➤ **Sarah**: What will you do after lunch?
✓ **Marawa**: I will have a walk around the park.

➤ *Note # 01:*

> We use the Future Simple to express an action or event that takes place at a specific time in the future.

➤ *Note # 02:*

> **'Will'** expresses a voluntary action or a promise. It also expresses a spontaneous decision, an assumption or a future event that cannot be changed.

✦ Examples:
- I ***will make*** you a delicious lunch.   (***A voluntary action***)
- I ***will buy*** you a lovely present.   (***A promise***)

The Future Simple Tense with *Be going to*

Affirmative

I	am		
He - She - It	is	*going to*	*base form.*
You - They - We	are		

✦ Examples:
- I ***am going to spend*** the weekend in the mountains.
- My brother ***is going to get*** married next March.
- We ***are going to finish*** our course in July.
- My friends ***are going to visit*** the Congress Library.
- Batool ***is going travel*** to the country to visit her uncle.
- Abdul-Rahman ***is going to paint*** his bike tomorrow.

Negative

I	am			
He - She - It	is	not	going to	base form.
You - They - We	are			

Examples:
- I **am not going to sell** my old car.
- My sister **is not going to study** medicine.
- The players **are not going to train** in the afternoon.

Yes/No Questions with Be going to ___?

Am	I		
Is	he - she - it	going to	base form . . . ?
Are	you - they - we		

Examples:
- **Sally:** Am I going to attend the meeting?
- ✓ **Huda:** Yes, you are.

- **Maha:** Is Hala going to stay in a five-star hotel?
- ✓ **Manal:** No, she isn't.

- **Omar:** Are you going to come to the party?
- ✓ **Salma:** Yes, I am.

- **Keith:** Are your parents going to travel by ship?
- ✓ **Nada:** No, they aren't.

Information Questions with Be going to ___?

Question Word	am	I		
	is	he - she - it	going to	base form...?
	are	you - they - we		

Examples:
- **Tuka:** When are you going to make me a birthday cake?
- ✓ **Mom:** I'm going to make it soon.

- **Saleh:** What is Majid going to buy?
- ✓ **Mahmoud:** He's going to buy a lovely present.

> *'Be going to'* expresses a plan. It also expresses a logical conclusion or a previously planned/prepared future action.

↓ Examples:

- I **am going to stay** in Madrid for a month.   (**A plan**)
- Ali **is going to get married** in November.   (**A plan**)
- We **are going to spend** the night studying for the final test.
   (**A plan**)

> We can use *will* or *be going to* express a prediction.

↓ Examples:

- It **is going to snow** at night.   (**Prediction**)
- It **will snow** at night.   (**Prediction**)

✓ <u>**We may use the future tense with these conjunctions:**</u>

After

After	1st Subject	Present Simple	,	2nd Subject	Future Simple

➤ **After** I **finish** my shift, I **will see** the doctor.

Or

1st Subject	Future Simple	after	2nd Subject	Present Simple

➤ My uncle **will visit** Canada **after** he **gets** his PhD.

As soon as

As soon as	1st Subject	Present Simple	,	2nd Subject	Future Simple

➤ **As soon as** I **go** home, I **will have** my lunch.

Or

1st Subject	Future Simple	as soon as	2nd Subject	Present Simple

➤ I **will call** you **as soon as** I **finish** my task.

Before

Before	1st Subject	Present Simple	,	2nd Subject	Future Simple

➤ **Before** I **buy** this mobile phone, I **will check** it.

Or

1st Subject	Future Simple	before	2nd Subject	Present Simple

➤ I **will fly** to Heathrow **before** I **finish** my exams.

By the time

| By the time | 1st Subject | Present Simple | , | 2nd Subject | Future Simple |

➢ **By the time I complete** the courses, **I will start** my new career.

Or

| 1st Subject | Future Simple | by the time | 2nd Subject | Present Simple |

➢ **I will phone** Celia **by the time I get** to the station.

When

| When | 1st. Subject | Present Simple | , | 2nd. Subject | Future Simple |

➢ **When** my car **breaks down, I will take** it to a nearby workshop.

Or

| 1st. Subject | Future Simple | when | 2nd. Subject | Present Simple |

➢ Keith **will visit** Paris **when** he **takes** his annual vacation.

If

| If | 1st. Subject | Present Simple | , | 2nd. Subject | Future Simple |

➢ **If** you **take** your medicine on time, you **will feel** better.

Or

| 1st. Subject | Future Simple | if | 2nd. Subject | Present Simple |

➢ You **will recover if** you **follow** the doctor's advice.

Unless

| Unless | 1st. Subject | Present Simple | , | 2nd. Subject | Future Simple |

➢ **Unless** you **train** hard, you **will lose** the game.

Or

| 1st. Subject | Future Simple | unless | 2nd. Subject | Present Simple |

➢ Jane **will fail** the final test if she **neglects** her work.

Until

| 1st. Subject | Future Simple | until | 2nd. Subject | Present Simple |

➢ We **will wait until** the dentist **arrives**.

✦ **More examples:**

➢ After I **write** the letter, I **will post** it.
➢ We **will go** to bed **when** it **is** midnight.

➤ The waiter **will wait** until we **finish** our meal.
➤ **If** you **solve** this problem, **I will reward** you.

Using the Present Progressive (Continuous) to express Future Time

✓ We may use the present progressive (continuous) to express future time if we want to express a definite intention or a planned event:

Affirmative

I	am	
He - She - It	is	-ing
You - they - We	are	

✦ **Examples:**

1) I **am meeting** my new roommate on Friday.
2) My father **is flying** to Paris next Monday.
3) We **are moving** to a new house soon.
4) **Nada:** Are you free tomorrow morning?
   Harris: No. I **am taking** my family to the beach.
5) **Henry:** What are you going to do this evening?
   Hend: I **am meeting** my fiancé.

Negative

I	am not	
He - She - It	isn't	-ing
You - they - We	aren't	

✦ **Example:**

I'm **not going** to the farm tomorrow.

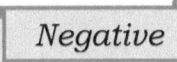

Using the Simple Present to express Future Simple

✓ We may use the present simple to express future time if we want to express an event on a scheduled time:

I - You - They - We	base form
He - She - It	base form + (-s)

Example:

1) The movie **starts** at 11:35 a.m.
2) The bank **opens** at eight thirty tomorrow.
3) The plane to New Delhi **leaves** 10:15 a.m.
4) My train **arrives** at 2:45 p.m.
5) The clothes **shops** open at eight.

🙰🙰🙰 *My Homework* 🙵🙵🙵

The Future Progressive (Continuous) Tense

It expresses activities that will be in progress during specific time in the future.

Affirmative

| Subject | will be | + -ing |

Example:

➤ Tomorrow at this time, I **will be watching** a soccer match between Brazil and France.

Negative

| Subject | will not be | + -ing |

Example:

➤ At this time next year, I **will not be studying** chemistry.

Yes/No Questions with Future Progressive (Continuous)

| Will | Subject | be + -ing? |

Example:

➤ **Anas: Will** you be **visiting your grandparents** at this time tomorrow?
✓ Mary: Yes, I will.

Information Questions with Future Progressive (Continuous)

| Question Word | will | Subject | be + -ing? |

Example:

➤ **Dan:** Where will you be waiting for me when I arrive there?
✓ **Tim:** I will be waiting for you in front of the bank.

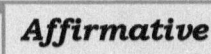
My Homework

➢ *Exercise One*
  ✦ Match the sentences. Then, write out each one.

1.	When I meet my friends,	A.	we will have a walk.
2.	Before Sara comes,	B.	until Mr. Omar comes.
3.	If you come early,		
4.	I won't leave the class,	C.	I will meet him.
5.	As soon as Ali arrives,	D.	I will welcome them.
6.	When the rain stops,	E.	I have a shower.
7.	After I wake up,	F.	you'll see the

1) When I meet my friends, I will welcome them.
2) _____
3) _____
4) _____
5) _____
6) _____
7) _____

🙜🙜🙜 *My Homework* 🙜🙜🙜

➢ *Exercise Two*
  ✦ Change these sentences from Present Simple into Future Simple.
  ✦ Follow the example.

  ➢ I usually go fishing on Fridays.   [Next Friday]
  ✓ Next Friday, I am going to go fishing.

  1) My parents always spend the weekend in the country.
                                                    [Next weekend]
  🙜 ___ ___ ___ ___ ___ ___ ___ ___ ___ ___ ___
     ___ ___ ___ ___ ___ ___ ___ ___ ___ ___ ___

  2) Sometimes, Tuka helps her mother in the kitchen.
                                                    [This afternoon]
  🙜 ___ ___ ___ ___ ___ ___ ___ ___ ___ ___ ___
     ___ ___ ___ ___ ___ ___ ___ ___ ___ ___ ___

  3) I often have my lunch in a famous restaurant downtown.
                                                    [This evening]
  🙜 ___ ___ ___ ___ ___ ___ ___ ___ ___ ___
     ___ ___ ___ ___ ___ ___ ___ ___ ___ ___

4) The secretary usually checks her email in the morning.
[in an hour]

➢ _____ ____ ____ ____ ____ ____ ____ ____ ____ ____
____ ____ ____ ____ ____ ____ ____ ____ ____ ____

5) Our teacher usually gives us remedial classes. [Next week]

➢ _____ ____ ____ ____ ____ ____ ____ ____ ____ ____
____ ____ ____ ____ ____ ____ ____ ____ ____ ____

🌸🌸🌸 My Homework 🌸🌸🌸

> ## Exercise Three
> ✤ Choose the correct answer from a, b, c or d.

1) What time are we going _____ lunch today?

a	to have	b	have
c	having	d	will have

2) Professor Malik _____ us Egyptology next semester.

a	has taught	b	taught
c	teaching	d	will be teaching

3) I _____ to Florida tonight.

a	fly	b	have flown
c	to fly	d	am going to fly

4) Gina _____ when she reaches the age of sixty.

a	will retire	b	has retired
c	retired	d	retire

5) This time tomorrow, Sam _____ on the beach.

a	relaxing	b	relax
c	was relaxing	d	will be relaxing

6) Sandra _____ her office after she sends the emails.

a	left	b	is going to leave
c	has left	d	had left

7) The students are going to review well before they _____ their final test.

a	will take	b	are going to take
c	take	d	are taking

8) Hopefully tomorrow, the farmers _____ more trees around the farm.

a	planted	b	plant
c	will be planting	d	have planted

9) Basma _____ her job soon.

a	was going to change	b	is going to change
c	changing	d	change

10) My mother _____ while my father is gardening.

a	has cooked	b	had cooked
c	to cook	d	will be cooking

11) My brothers _____ to the mountains in three days.

a	have gone	b	were going to go
c	went	d	are going to go

12) My uncle _____ a vacation in Pretoria next winter.

a	was going to take	b	is going to take
c	going to take	d	has taken

13) The manager _____ the meeting in half an hour.

a	start	b	has started
c	started	d	will start

14) Don't visit me tonight. I _____ for my final exam.

a	will be reviewing	b	have reviewed
c	reviewed	d	reviewing

15) Jane _____ to college tomorrow morning.

a	has gone	b	is going to go
c	went	d	was going to go

16) My grandfather _____ me tonight.

a	has called	b	is going to call
c	calling	d	was going to call

17) Before I start my work tomorrow, I _____ a light meal.

a	had	b	am going to have
c	is going to have	d	had had

18) We will have a final revision before we _____ our grammar course.

a	can finish	b	finish
c	are having	d	will finish

19) At this time next month, this old car _____ for more maintenance.

a	will be asking	b	is asking
c	asks	d	has asked

20) Salma will make the bed before she _____.

a	leaving	b	left
c	leaves	d	leave

My Homework

> ### Exercise Four
> Choose the correct answer from a, b, c or d.
>
> 1) Abdul-Rahman is going to start his own business before _____ his current job.
>
> | a | quitting | b | will quit |
> |---|---|---|---|
> | c | quits | d | is going to quit |
>
> 2) After Lee gets married, he _____ to live in the country.
>
> | a | will move | b | was going to move |
> |---|---|---|---|
> | c | has moved | d | is moving |

3) After Keith _____ from his operation, he is going to have a long vacation.

a	recovers	b	will recover
c	recover	d	is going to recover

4) Tomorrow at this time, we _____ to Copenhagen to spend our vacation there.

a	have flown	b	flew
c	fly	d	will be flying

5) Ibrahim is going to fix the machine after _____ it.

a	checking	b	checks
c	will check	d	has checked

6) As soon as the sun rises, we _____ to the farm.

a	will go	b	have gone
c	going	d	goes

7) I will pay you back as soon as I _____ my salary.

a	am going to get	b	get
c	got	d	will get

8) By the time we get to the conference hall, the meeting _____.

a	will begin	b	going to begin
c	begin	d	began

9) Next year at this time, my family _____ a new house in the country.

a	will be building	b	building
c	to build	d	had built

10) The weather reports say that it _____ all week.

a	will be snowing	b	snowed
c	snowing	d	have snowed

11) By the time our guests _____, we will move to the dining room.

a	arrives	b	arrived
c	will arrive	d	arrive

12) I won't have my breakfast until my mother _____.

a	is going to come	b	came
c	will have logged	d	comes

13) We will wait until the dentist _____ his tools.

a	sterilized	b	will sterilize
c	sterilizes	d	sterilize

14) If it rains heavily, the referee _____ the final match.

a	has postponed	b	postpone
c	will postpone	d	postponed

15) Marawan will not leave Canada until he _____.

a	will graduate	b	is going to graduate
c	graduates	d	graduated

16) Sally: Are you going to be in the dormitory tonight?
✓ Kerry: No, I _____ in the park.

a	jog	b	will be jogging
c	have jogged	d	jogging

17) When I _____ my teacher, I will greet him.

a	see	b	will see
c	saw	d	seen

18) I won't visit my family in Madrid _____ there is a vacant seat on Monday flight.

a	if	b	after
c	unless	d	before

19) _____ I finish my work early, I will drop by Lama.

a	If	b	Until
c	Yet	d	But

20) Next Thursday, my parents _____ to Sydney.

a	drove	b	have driven
c	will be driving	d	have been driving

🌺🌺🌺 *My Homework* 🌺🌺🌺

> ### *Exercise Five*
> 🌺 Rearrange these words to form meaningful sentences.
> 🌺 Follow the example.

> ➤ / visit / are / Louvre / week/ to / We /the / next / going /
> ✓ We are going to visit the Louvre next week.
> ➤ / be / Rome / morning / I'll / in / tomorrow /
> ✓ I'll be in Rome tomorrow morning.

1) / time / isn't / be / on / going / tomorrow / Samar / to /
🌺 ___ ___ ___ ___ ___ ___ ___ ___ ___

2) grandmother / tomorrow / waiting / I / be / for / my / airport / at / time / the / this / will / at /
🌺 ___ ___ ___ ___ ___ ___ ___ ___ ___
___ ___ ___ ___ ___

3) / afternoon / you / this / I'll / later / phone/
🌺 ___ ___ ___ ___ ___ ___ ___

4) / the / think / win / Who / do / will / you / game /
🌺 ___ ___ ___ ___ ___ ___ ___ ___

5) / will / tonight / brother / using / laptop / My / my / be /
🌺 ___ ___ ___ ___ ___ ___ ___ ___ ___

6) / send/ e-mail / Leila / going / me/ is/ to / an /
🌺 ___ ___ ___ ___ ___ ___ ___ ___

7) / fly / London / January / to / I'm / to / going / next /
🌺 ___ ___ ___ ___ ___ ___ ___ ___

8) / teacher / students / Will / his / the / help /
🌺 ___ ___ ___ ___ ___ ___

9) / will / move / house / Sam / new / week / next / probably / a / to /
✎____ ____ ____ ____ ____ ____ ____ ____ ____ ____
____ ____ ____ ____ ____ ____ ____ ____ ____

10) / possibly / It/ morning / will / cold / be / tomorrow / very /
✎____ ____ ____ ____ ____ ____ ____ ____ ____

11) / start / lesson / morning / a / We / going / tomorrow / aren't / to / new /
✎____ ____ ____ ____ ____ ____ ____ ____ ____ ____
____ ____ ____ ____ ____ ____ ____ ____

12) / parents / spend / Dubai/ vacation / My / aren't / their / to / going / in /
✎____ ____ ____ ____ ____ ____ ____ ____ ____ ____
____ ____ ____ ____ ____ ____ ____ ____

13) / train / Tokyo / sisters/ to / to/ My / travel / by / going /are /
✎____ ____ ____ ____ ____ ____ ____ ____ ____ ____
____ ____ ____ ____ ____ ____ ____ ____

14) / Friday / laptop / next/ you / your / Will / me / lend /
✎____ ____ ____ ____ ____ ____ ____ ____ ____

15) / are / start / Wasim / soon / to / a / Ted / business / and / going / new /
✎____ ____ ____ ____ ____ ____ ____ ____ ____ ____
____ ____ ____ ____ ____ ____ ____ ____

16)/ and / course / days / to / Batool / ten / finish / in / Tuka / going / their /are /
✎____ ____ ____ ____ ____ ____ ____ ____ ____ ____
____ ____ ____ ____ ____ ____ ____ ____

17) / to / villa / country/ is / the / build / a /going / Wesam / new / in /
✎____ ____ ____ ____ ____ ____ ____ ____ ____ ____
____ ____ ____ ____ ____ ____ ____ ____

18)/ to / host / is / 2030 / finals / country / World / ? /the / travel / Cup / going / Which /
✎____ ____ ____ ____ ____ ____ ____ ____ ____ ____
____ ____ ____ ____ ____ ____ ____ ____

19)/ time / we / begin / to/ are / the / What / going / lecture /
✎____ ____ ____ ____ ____ ____ ____ ____ ____
____ ____ ____ ____ ____ ____ ____ ____

20) / going / as / replace / manager / Who / Mr / is / to / Anderson / a /
✎____ ____ ____ ____ ____ ____ ____ ____ ____ ____
____ ____ ____ ____ ____ ____ ____ ____

✎✎✎My Homework✎✎✎

Exercise Six

Rearrange these words to form meaningful sentences.

1) / start / is / course / morning / going / tomorrow / Carmen / to / a

2) / graduates / as soon as / will / job / he / for / Sam / look / new / a /

3) / plane / time / Will / on / arrive / the /

4) / tonight / it / rain / Is / to / going /

5) / visit / are / We / New Zealand / going / to / this / summer /

6) / tomorrow / time / Asmaà / home / be / This / flying / will /

7) / asks / swimming / can / if / Robinson / he / go / us / with /

8) / Anita / house / her / to / old / Is / sell / going /

9) / meeting / place / will / at / take / 7:35 pm / The /

10) / visit / on / grandparents / weekend / to / her / Rosalina / Is / going / the /

11) / planes / London / going / Are / to / change / in / we /

12) / fix / machine / to / the / fax / going / Lilly / Is /

13) / conference / weather / cancelled / be / The / bad / will / because of /

14) / Ahmad / tomorrow / party / Is / be / going / the / at / to / birthday / be /

15) / kids / take / Martha / is / her / going / party / to / not / the / to /
🕮ــ

16) / we / electric / 2030 / use / in / cars / Will /
🕮ــ

17) / party / uncle / going / Are/ invite / to / you / our / to / the /
🕮ــ

18) / outdoors/ a / have / going / My / dinner / are / parents / to / nice /
🕮ــ

19) / morning / sightseeing / will / We / go / Egypt / tomorrow / in /
🕮ــ

20) / umbrella / will / my / me / be / heavily / Give / as / raining / it /
🕮ــ

🙞🙞🙞 *My Homework* 🙜🙜🙜

➤ **_Exercise Seven_**
   ✦ Use the given words to ask a meaningful question.
   ✦ Use (be going to). Follow the example.
   ➤ / start / level / we / When / to / are / the / going / new /
   ✓ When are we going to start the new level?

   1) / the / see / going / you / optician / **When** / to / are /
   🕮ــ

   2) / lunch / cook / mother / **What**/ going / is / for / to /
   🕮ــ

   3) / camp / you / tomorrow / **Where** / to / are / going /
   🕮ــ

   4) / stay / Madrid / long / going / are / you / **How** / to / in /
   🕮ــ

   5) / books / many / is / to / **How** / Ahmad / going / buy /
   🕮ــ

6) / there / we / **Who** / going / meet / are / to /
✍ _____

7) / leave / **Why** / are / to / early / going / you /
✍ _____

8) / choose / one / to / you / are / **Which** / going /
✍ _____

9) / referee / postpone / **Why** / is / to / match / the / the / going /
✍ _____

▰▰▰ *My Homework* ▰▰▰

➢ *Exercise Eight*
   ✦ Put the verb in brackets in the correct form.
   ✦ Follow the example.
      ➢ If Ayman [get up] early, he will catch the school bus.
      ✓ If Ayman gets up early, he will catch the school bus.
      ✍ _____

   1) When our teacher [enter], we will greet her.
   ✍ _____

   2) As soon as my father [retire], he is going to start his own business.
   ✍ _____

   3) John has a headache. He [see] his doctor tonight.
   ✍ _____

   4) My laptop doesn't work properly. I [take] it to a technician.
   ✍ _____

   5) My grandparents [be] home soon.
   ✍ _____

   6) Before I go to the farm tomorrow, I [have] breakfast with my family.
   ✍ _____

7) As soon as the movie [start], I will leave the cinema.
🙰____ ____ ____ ____ ____ ____ ____ ____ ____

8) After my mother [finish] cooking, she will read a newspaper.
🙰____ ____ ____ ____ ____ ____ ____ ____ ____
____ ____ ____ ____ ____ ____ ____ ____ ____

9) If I have enough money, I [join] Indiana University.
🙰____ ____ ____ ____ ____ ____ ____ ____ ____
____ ____ ____ ____ ____ ____ ____ ____ ____

10) The meeting will begin as soon as the manager [arrive].
🙰____ ____ ____ ____ ____ ____ ____ ____ ____
____ ____ ____ ____ ____ ____ ____ ____ ____

🙰🙰🙰 *My Homework* 🙰🙰🙰

➢ *Exercise Nine*

✦ Form sentences in the future simple using [will] or [won't].
✦ Follow the example.
  ➢ Watch – TV
  ✓ I will watch TV with my family tonight.
  1) study – math
  🙰____ ____ ____ ____ ____ ____ ____ ____ ____

  2) visit – aunt
  🙰____ ____ ____ ____ ____ ____ ____ ____ ____

  3) go – hunting
  🙰____ ____ ____ ____ ____ ____ ____ ____ ____

  4) buy – apartment
  🙰____ ____ ____ ____ ____ ____ ____ ____ ____

  5) check – tires – car
  🙰____ ____ ____ ____ ____ ____ ____ ____ ____

  6) eat – outdoors
  🙰____ ____ ____ ____ ____ ____ ____ ____ ____

  7) apply – job
  🙰____ ____ ____ ____ ____ ____ ____ ____ ____

  8) fly – home
  🙰____ ____ ____ ____ ____ ____ ____ ____ ____

  9) call – family
  🙰____ ____ ____ ____ ____ ____ ____ ____ ____

  10) exercise – gym
  🙰____ ____ ____ ____ ____ ____ ____ ____ ____

  11) take – family – market
  🙰____ ____ ____ ____ ____ ____ ____ ____ ____

12) leave – London
🙠 ___ ___ ___ ___ ___ ___ ___ ___ ___

13) grow – wheat
🙠 ___ ___ ___ ___ ___ ___ ___ ___ ___

14) fix – leak
🙠 ___ ___ ___ ___ ___ ___ ___ ___ ___

15) repair – car
🙠 ___ ___ ___ ___ ___ ___ ___ ___ ___

16) get – reward
🙠 ___ ___ ___ ___ ___ ___ ___ ___ ___

17) forward – emails
🙠 ___ ___ ___ ___ ___ ___ ___ ___ ___

18) start – course
🙠 ___ ___ ___ ___ ___ ___ ___ ___ ___

19) send – reports
🙠 ___ ___ ___ ___ ___ ___ ___ ___ ___

20) change – battery
🙠 ___ ___ ___ ___ ___ ___ ___ ___ ___

🙠🙠🙠 *My Homework* 🙠🙠🙠

> ## Exercise Ten
✦ Complete the sentences with [be going to]. Follow the example.

> **Daniel:** Why did you buy this wood?
✓ / make / table /
✓ **Mark:** I am going to make a table.

1) **Lilly:** Why did you buy this ticket?
✓ / watch / match /
Sam: ___ ___ ___ ___ ___ ___ ___ ___ ___ _

2) **Boody:** What is your vacation plan?
✓ / visit / Egypt /
Karl: ___ ___ ___ ___ ___ ___ ___ ___ _

3) **Ted**: Why did you bring this rice?
✓ / prepare / meal /
Sara: ___ ___ ___ ___ ___ ___ ___ ___ ___ _

4) **Nora:** Why did you join London University?
✓ / study / medicine /
Suzan: ___ ___ ___ ___ ___ ___ ___ ___ ___ _

5) **Keith:** What are you going to do on the weekend?
✓ / go / swimming /
Tony: ____ ____ ____ ____ ____ ____ ____ ____ ____ ____ _

🖎🖎🖎 *My Homework* 🖎🖎🖎

SECTION 16 — Modals (Modal Auxiliaries)

Modal auxiliaries are verbs that are used before another verb in order to express possibility, permission, intention, etc.

The modal auxiliaries are *can, could, will, would, may, might, shall, should, ought to, must, dare, have to, needn't, used to,* etc.

Modal auxiliaries are followed by the basic form of other verbs. They never take *-s, -ed,* or *-ing*.

Affirmative

Subject		Base form
	will	
	would	
	shall	
	should	
	may	
	might	
	ought to	
	must	
	have to	
	has to	
	had to	
	dare	
	used to	

* **"Used to"** shares some of the features of modal verbs. It was introduced in Section 12 in detail.

Examples:

- I can **swim**.
- You should come on time.

Negative

Subject	will / would / shall / should / may / might / ought to / must	not	Base form

Examples:

- I can't **dive**.
- Omar can't drive a truck?

Yes/No Questions

Will / Would / Shall / Should / May / Might / Must	Subject	Base form...?

Example:
- **James**: Will you solve this problem?
- ✓ Oscar: Yes, I will.

Can

Can expresses ability in the present or future.

Example:
- I **can solve** this problem.
- I **can't ride** a horse.

Yes/No Questions with *Can* ___?

Can	Subject	Base form......?
Can't	Subject	Base form......?

Example:
- ➢ *Can* you *lift* this box?
  - ✓ Yes, I can.
  - ✓ No, I can't.

Example:
- ➢ *Can't* you *use* a rifle?
  - ✓ Yes, I can.
  - ✓ No, I can't.

Information Questions with *Can*

Question Word	can	Subject	Base form......?

Example:
- ➢ Where *can* I *buy* stamps?
  - ✓ You can buy stamps at the post office.

My Homework

Could

Could expresses ability in the past.

Examples:
- ➢ I *could catch* the train to Delhi yesterday.
- ➢ I *couldn't answer* yesterday's quiz.

Yes/No Questions with *Could* ___?

Could	Subject	Base form......?
Couldn't	Subject	Base form......?

Examples:
- ➢ *Could* you *fix* Abdul-Rahman's laptop?
  - ✓ Yes, I could.
  - ✓ No, I couldn't.

- **Couldn't** you **switch** the machine on?
  - ✓ Yes, I could.
  - ✓ No, I couldn't.

Information Questions with "Could"

Question Word	could	Subject	Base form......?

Example:
- Why **couldn't** you **swim**?
  - ✓ We couldn't swim because the waves were high.

My Homework

"Be able to" in the present

> "Be able to" expresses ability in the past, present, or future.

I	am			
He – She – It	is	not	able to	Base form.
You – They – We	are			

Examples:

- I **am able to answer** the test.
- Donald **is able to speak** English well.
- We **are able to answer** the quiz.

"Be able to" in the past

I – He – She – It	was	able to	Base form.
You – They – We	were		

Examples:
- I **was able to find** an apartment.
- My parents **were able to find** a flight to Paris.

"Be able to" in the future

| Subject | will be | able to | Base form. |

Example:
- I **will be able to find** a solution to this problem.

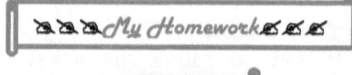

Will

"Will" talks about or predicts the future.

"Will" is used to show that somebody is willing to do something.

Examples:
- Man **will live** on the moon.
- I **will answer** the phone.

Yes-No Questions with "Will ...?"

| Will | Subject | Base form...? |
| Won't | Subject | Base form...? |

Example:
- **Will** you **visit** Carlos in hospital?
  - ✓ Yes, I will.
  - ✓ No, I won't.

- **Won't** you **attend** my birthday party?
  - ✓ Yes, I will.
  - ✓ No, I won't.

Information Questions with "Will"

| Question Word | will | Subject | Base form......? |

Examples:
- Where **will** you **spend** the weekend?
  ✓ I will spend in on my uncle's farm.

My Homework

Would

"Would" is used to express the past of "will" when reporting what somebody has said or thought.

"Would" is used to express the result of an event you imagine.

Examples:
- Marwa **asked** if I **would visit** her.
- I **would be** happy **if** I **passed** the final test.

Yes-No Questions with "Would ...?"

| Would | Subject | Base form......? |

Examples:

- **Would** you **like** to have fruit juice?
  ✓ Yes, I would.
  ✓ No, I wouldn't.

My Homework

Information Questions with "Would"

| Question Word | would | Subject | Base form......? |

✦ Examples:
- What **would** you **like to have** for lunch?
  - ✓ I would like to have fried chicken, please.

SHALL

"Shall" talks about or predicts the future.

"Shall" is used to show that the speaker is willing to do something. It is used with "I" and "We" only.

| I | shall | Base form......? |
| We | shall | Base form......? |

✦ Examples:
- I **shall be** late for class tomorrow.
- I hope we **shall win** the game.

"Shall I ...?"

"Shall I ...?" is used to offer to do something.

| Shall | I | Base form......? |

✦ Example:
- **Shall I open** the door for you, sir?

"Shall we ...?"

"Shall we ...?" is used to suggest doing something.

| Shall | we | Base form......? |

✦ Example:
- **Shall** we **go** swimming after class?
- **Shall** we **play** a basketball match?

🪶🪶🪶*My Homework*🍂🍂🍂

Should & Ought to

"Should and ought to" are both used to give advice.

| Subject | should | Base form....... |

✦ Examples:

- Students **should study** hard.
- Students **ought to come** to class on time.

Yes-No Questions with "Should ...?"

| Should | Subject | Base form......? |

✦ Examples:
- **Should** I be there before lunch?
  - ✓ Yes, you should.
  - ✓ No, you shouldn't.

🪶🪶🪶*My Homework*🍂🍂🍂

Information Questions with "Should"

| Question Word | should | Subject | Base form......? |

✦ Examples:

- What **should** I **do** to learn new vocabulary?
  ✓ You should study it daily.

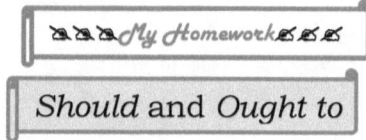

Should and Ought to

"Should and ought to" are both used to express expectation.

| Subject | should | Base form....... |
| Subject | ought to | Base form....... |

✦ Examples

- I have to be in class before 10:15 a.m. My teacher **should be** there by then.
- I have to be in the airport at 5:25 p.m. The plane **ought to be** there by then.

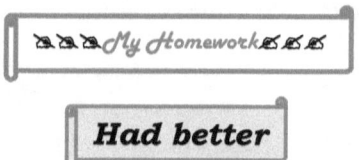

Had better

Affirmative

Had better gives a stronger meaning than that of should and ought to.

| Subject | had better | Base form........ |

Negative

| Subject | had better not | Base form... |

✦ Examples:

- You **had better** study harder or you'll fail.
- You **had better not** waste your time.

Yes-No Questions with "Had better"

| Hadn't | Subject | better | Base form......? |

Example:
- **Hadn't** you **better wake up** earlier?
  ✓ Certainly, sir.

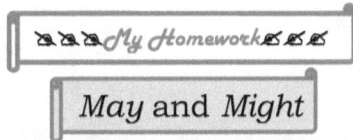

May and Might

May and *Might* are used to express possibility in the present or future. They have the same meaning.

| Subject | may | Base form........ |

OR

| Subject | might | Base form........ |

Examples:
- It **may be hot** tomorrow. I am **not sure**.
- It **might be humid** this afternoon. I am **not sure**.

Yes/No Questions with "May"

| May | Subject | Base form......? |

Example:
- **May** I **help** you, sir?
  ✓ Yes, please. Get me the menu.
  ✓ No, thank you.

Information Questions with "May"

| Question Word | may | Subject | Base form......? |

Example:
- What **may** happen if it rains during the match?
  ✓ The referee may cancel the match.

Maybe

"Maybe" is used to express possibility in the present or future. It has the same meaning of *"Perhaps"*.

Maybe	Subject	will + Base form
OR		
Maybe	Subject	am/is/are

Examples:

➢ **Maybe** it **will snow** tomorrow.
➢ Maybe our manager is sick. = Our manager may be sick.

My Homework

Permission

May / Could / Can	I	Base form . . . ?

This form is used to ask for permission to do something.

Examples:

➢ **May** I **leave** early today, sir?
➢ **Could** I **use** your dictionary, please?
➢ **Can** I **help** you, madam?

My Homework

This form is used to ask someone to do something for you.

+ **Examples:**

- **Could** you **post** this letter for me, please?
- **Would** you **help** me understand this problem, sir?
- **Will** you **wrap** this present for me, madam?
- **Can** you **fix** my car, please?

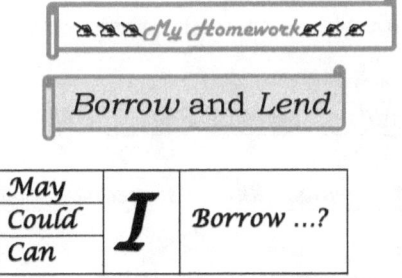

Borrow and Lend

This form is used to borrow something from someone.

+ **Examples:**

- **May** I **borrow** your telephone, sir?
- **Could** I **borrow** this book for a week, please?
- **Can** I **borrow** your pencil?

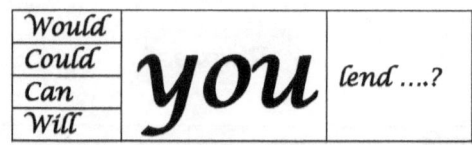

This form is used to ask someone to lend another something.

✤ Examples:
- **Could** you **lend** me your camera, please?
- **Would** you **lend** me this newspaper, sir?
- **Will** you **lend** me your telephone charger, madam?
- **Can** you **lend** me your laptop, please?

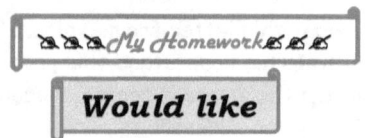

Would like

Would like is used to express desires that people haven't got yet.

Subject	would like	Base form

OR

Subject	would like	someone	Base form

✤ Examples:
- I **would like to buy** a new digital camera.
- I **would like** my brother **to study** math.
- I **would like** Ibrahim **to come** on time.
- I **would like** you **to review** well before the exam.

Yes/No Questions with "*Would like*"

Would	you	like	Base form ... ?

✤ Examples:
- **Would** you **like to have** a drink, sir?
- ✓ Yes, please. Get me apple juice.
- ✓ No, thank you.

Information Questions with "Would like"

| Question Word | would | you | like | Base form . . . ? |

Examples:
- Where **would** you **like to spend** your free time?
- ✓ In the mountains.
- What **would** you **like to eat**, sir?
- ✓ Macaroni and soup, please.

| Subject | would like | noun |

Example:
- I **would like** a cup of coffee, please?

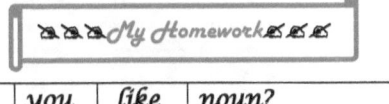

| Would | you | like | noun? |

Example:
- **Would** you **like** some more sugar, sir?
- ✓ Yes, please.

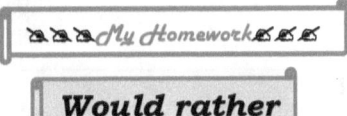

Would rather

Would rather is used to express preference or choices.

| Subject | would rather | Base form |

OR

| Subject | would rather | Base form | than | Base form |

Negative

| Subject | would rather not | Base form . . . |

Examples:
- I **would rather go** fishing.
- I **would rather go** swimming **than play** computer games.
- My father **would rather not take** a taxi.

Yes/No Questions with "Would rather"

| Would | subject | rather | Base form...? |

Examples:

➢ **Would** she **rather eat** outdoors?
  ✓ I think so.
➢ **Would** you **like to have** a walk?
  ✓ Thanks, but I would rather go to the gym.
  ✓ No, thinks.

My Homework

Expressing Necessity

"Have to", "Have got to", "Must"

They all express necessity in the present or future.

"Have to"

I		
You	have to	
They		
We		Base form
He		
She	has to	
It		

Examples:

➢ I **have to get** a visa before I travel to Canada.
➢ My sister **has to pass** a test to get the job.
➢ I **have to wear** my seat belt.
➢ My friend **has to look for** a new job.
➢ Students have to come to their class on time.
➢ Sally has to do her homework on a daily basis.
➢ My parents have to go on a diet.
➢ Mike has to improve his listening skills.
➢ Kevin has to speak English in class.

Lack of necessity

We use **"Not have to"** or **"Needn't"** to say that something is not necessary.

"Not have to"

I			
You	don't		
They		have to	Base form
We			
He			
She	doesn't		
It			

Examples:
- I **don't have to study** tonight. The teacher cancelled the test.
- My father **doesn't have to look for** another job. His company has promoted him.

"Needn't"

Subject	needn't	Base form

Examples:
- We **needn't hurry**. We are not late.
- You **needn't drive** fast. It's is still early.

🙢🙢🙢 *My Homework* 🙠🙠🙠

Yes-no Questions with "Have to"

Do	I / you / they / we	have to	Base form...?
Does	he / she / it		

Examples:
- **Driver:** Do I have to pay a fine if I run a red light?
  ✓ Policeman: Certainly.
- **Helen:** Does Leila have to pass this test?
  ✓ Teacher: Surely.

"Have got to"

I / You / They / We	have got to	Base form
He / She / It	has got to	

Examples:
- I **have got to change** the flat tire before driving to my office.
- Sara **has got to get** a driver's license before buying a new car.

ᴓᴓᴓ My Homework ᴓᴓᴓ

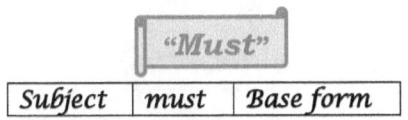

| Subject | must | Base form |

"Must" is used to say that it is obligatory to do something.

♦ Examples:
- Car drivers **must stop** when the traffic lights are red.
- I **must call** my parents in Harvard. I haven't called them for long time.

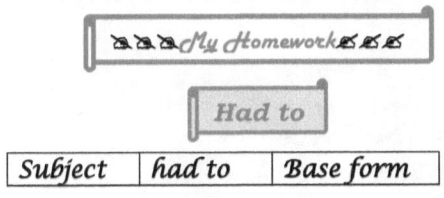

| Subject | had to | Base form |

"Had to" is used to express necessity in the past.

♦ Examples:
- I **had to** go to the bank because I wanted to cash a check.
- Yesterday, I **had to take** a taxi because I missed the school bus.

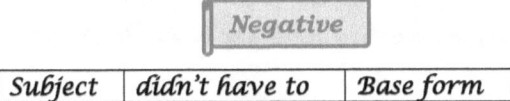

| Subject | didn't have to | Base form |

♦ Example:
- I **didn't have to revise** last night because the exam was postponed.

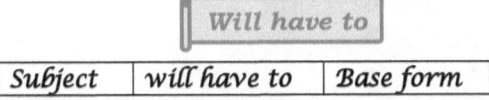

| Subject | will have to | Base form |

"Will have to" is used to express necessity in the future.

♦ Examples:
- I **will have to read** the instructions manual to operate the machine.
- Andrew **will have to book** the flight two months in advance.

| Subject | mustn't | Base form |

"Mustn't" is used to express prohibition.

Examples:
- You **mustn't run** the red lights.
- Students **mustn't use** their mobile phones in class.

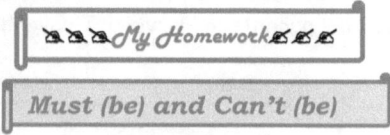

"Must (be)" is used to say that we are sure that something is true.

| Subject | must be | adjective |

OR

| Subject | must be | Base form + -ing |

Examples:
- John has a very expensive car. He **must be** wealthy.
- My father has been working for a long time. He **must be** very tired.
- Mark isn't in his office. He **must be having** his breakfast.

"Can't (be)" is used to say that something is impossible.

| Subject | can't be | adjective |

Examples:
- My parents have just had their lunch. They **can't be** hungry.
- Jack fails a lot of tests. He **can't be** a hard-working student.

Must (have been) and Can't (have been)

For the past, we use **"Must (have been)"** and **Can't (have been)**

Subject	must have (been)	adjective

Examples:
- Mark ate a large meal. He **must have been** very hungry.
- Messi played a very good match. He **must have trained** hard.

Subject	can't have (been)	adjective

Examples:
- Mark couldn't answer well. He **can't have done** his best.
- Tony lost the final boxing round. He **can't have trained** well.

My Homework

> **Exercise One**

Choose the correct answer from a, b, c or d.

1) People _____ drink water to keep alive.

a	may	b	must
c	might	d	don't have to

2) Salah played a very good match. He _____ score three goals.

a	is able to	b	was able to
c	might	d	may

3) Tomorrow is my day off. I _____ get up early.

a	won't have to	b	mustn't
c	didn't have to	d	don't have to

4) The students _____ be tired after all that work.

a	are	b	were
c	must	d	have

5) There's a very good play on show. You _____ go and see it.

a	should	b	shall
c	might not	d	will

6) Dina spilled some coffee on her dress. She _____ change it.

a	may	b	must
c	might	d	don't have to

7) The new course _____ start next week. I am not sure.

a	may	b	must
c	will	d	doesn't have to

8) Truck drivers _____ drive on the left lane of the road. It's against the traffic rules.

a	may not	b	mustn't
c	might	d	don't have to

9) My family _____ be away for the weekend, but I'm not sure.

a	shall	b	must
c	will	d	may

10) It _____ be Jane. Jane is much fatter.

a	mustn't	b	won't
c	can't	d	shouldn't

11) There's a no-parking sign. You _____ park your car here.

a	may not	b	mustn't
c	might not	d	don't have to

12) When Omar was five, he _____ swim.

a	may	b	must
c	could	d	will

13) Linda's voice was clear. I _____ hear what she was saying.

a	may	b	will
c	could	d	can

14) Lilly lost her mobile phone. She _____ be sad.

a	may	b	must
c	might	d	doesn't have to

15) The manager didn't answer my call. He _____ busy.

a	may be	b	can't have been
c	might be	d	must have been

16) Paul: ____ we go fishing?
    Mack: No, let's have a walk.

a	Shall	b	May
c	Might	d	Do

17) Alan ____ steal things from his friends. He is rich and honest.

a	should	b	may
c	can	d	can't

18) Dalia has a terrible headache. She ____ see the doctor.

a	doesn't have to	b	didn't have to
c	has to	d	may not

19) Andrew ____ go to the mountains tomorrow. It's possible.

a	can	b	might
c	must	d	will

20) Kim didn't pass the final test. He ____ well.

a	won't study	b	may have studied
c	can't have studied	d	mustn't study

✿✿✿My Homework✿✿✿

> ## Exercise Two
> ⁜ Choose the correct answer from a, b, c, or d.

1) **Sandy:** _____ you like to start another game?
   Shady: No, thanks. I have to start my homework now.

a	May	b	Might
c	Would	d	Could

2) Last night, we _____ our work before leaving the office.

a	must finish	b	might finish
c	may finish	d	must have finished

3) You _____ smoke inside a hospital. It is prohibited.

a	may not	b	mustn't
c	might not	d	don't have to

4) Cherry: _____ I speak to Ahmad, please?
   Boody: I am sorry. He isn't at home now.

a	Can't	b	Must
c	Could	d	Should

5) My passport is about to expire. I _____ renew it as soon as possible.

a	may	b	must
c	might	d	don't have to

6) Maya _____ be from Canada. She can speak neither English nor French.

a	will	b	must
c	might	d	can't

7) Waitress: _____ you like some more coffee?
   Mr Shalaby: Yes, please.

a	Would	b	Could
c	May	d	Shall

8) Car drivers _____ fasten their seatbelts before moving forward. Driving without wearing them is against the law.

a	must	b	may
c	might	d	may not

9) Abdul-Rahman: _____ I open the door for you, madam?
   Mrs Winston: Yes, please.

a	May	b	Must
c	Must	d	Should

10) You _____ drive your car without a driver's license.

a	shouldn't	b	mustn't
c	needn't	d	don't have to

11) Receptionist: _____ you spell your first name, please?
    Ahmad: It's A-H-M-A-D.

a	May	b	Must
c	Could	d	Shall

12) I _____ come to class late today. My teacher will be angry.

a	needn't	b	mustn't
c	should	d	don't have to

13) Engineers and workmen _____ wear helmets while they are in the workshop.

a	has to	b	must
c	might	d	don't have to

14) Donald: _____ the students be allowed to go to the lab tomorrow?
Ronald: Certainly, sir.

a	Shall	b	May
c	Will	d	Might

15) Ibrahim watches a lot of football matches every week. He _____ be interested in football.

a	can't	b	must
c	might	d	doesn't have to

16) Each student _____ work hard before the final exam.

a	may	b	has to
c	might	d	doesn't have to

17) My children _____ be at school now. It's already ten o'clock in the morning.

a	needn't	b	must
c	can't	d	don't have to

18) Waiter: Would you like me _____ you the menu, sir?
Mr Ali: Yes, please.

a	bringing	b	bring
c	brought	d	to bring

19) That _____ be Mary. They said she has black hair, not blond hair.

a	might	b	can't
c	doesn't have to	d	may

20) I _____ come to the game, but I may be late.

a	will	b	won't
c	don't have to	d	needn't

🙠🙠🙠 *My Homework* 🙠🙠🙠

➢ **Exercise Three**

    ✦ Choose the correct answer from a, b, c or d.

1) Children _____ watch TV too much. It shows a lot of violence.

a	needn't	b	can't
c	shouldn't	d	don't have to

2) Shahla _____ answer the test very well because she studied hard.

a	wasn't able to	b	might not be able to
c	was able to	d	couldn't

3) Lobna got a high score in the weekly quiz. She _____ be happy.

a	may	b	must
c	might	d	can't

4) Kim: I'd like _____ this letter, please.
   Clerk: Wait a minute, please.

a	post	b	posting
c	posts	d	to post

5) Lara _____ clean her teeth daily if she wants to be healthy.

a	may	b	must
c	needn't	d	doesn't have to

6) Jessica _____ do the washing yesterday. It was her turn.

a	has to	b	must
c	had to	d	didn't have to

7) Last night, some boy scouts _____ reach an island in the middle of the sea and spend two nights there.

a	can	b	must
c	could	d	will

8) The players of our team _____ train hard before the next match.

a	have to	b	may
c	might	d	shouldn't

9) John had a serious car accident last night. He _____ carefully.

a	may have driven	b	must have driven
c	might have driven	d	didn't have to drive

10) Ann _____ in the kitchen. I am not sure.

a	will be	b	might be
c	is	d	doesn't have to be

11) The manager couldn't come to his office because he _____ work late last night.

a	has to	b	must
c	had to	d	should

12) I _____ speak Chinese. I hope to learn it soon.

a	may not	b	mustn't
c	might not	d	can't

13) Aseel: _____ I use your dictionary, please?
    Nehal: Certainly.

a	May	b	Must
c	Will	d	Would

14) I _____ rather study English than start a new job.

a	will	b	could
c	would	d	should

15) Harry _____ buy any extra food. We have got a lot at home.

a	mustn't	b	has to
c	might not	d	needn't

16) Motorists _____ drive when they feel drowsy. It's dangerous.

a	might not	b	may not
c	don't have to	d	mustn't

17) Ibrahim _____ play chess. Therefore, he is going to learn it.

a	mustn't	b	can't
c	doesn't have to	d	not able to

18) All drivers _____ exceed the speed limit. It is against the law.

a	don't have to	b	shouldn't
c	might not	d	mustn't

19) You _____ respect your parents and treat them kindly.

a	might	b	may
c	must	d	don't have to

20) Children _____ carry any sharp objects. They are dangerous.

a	mustn't	b	may not
c	don't have to	d	might not

🕮🕮🕮 *My Homework* 🕮🕮🕮

> ### Exercise Four
> ✤ Choose the correct answer from a, b, c or d.

1) Yesterday, my father _____ start his car. Its battery was dead.

a	couldn't	b	would
c	didn't have to	d	could

2) You _____ wash your hands before and after eating. It's a healthy habit.

a	may not	b	don't have to
c	shouldn't	d	should

3) Boody is excellent at algebra. He _____ work out very difficult problems.

a	can't	b	might
c	may not	d	can

4) My brother got a job in a famous company because he _____ speak four languages.

a	can't	b	can
c	may not	d	might

5) Cherry's teeth hurt her a lot. She _____ better see a dentist.

a	will	b	had
c	must	d	has

6) Receptionist: _____ I help you, sir?
Mr Ismail: Yes, I'd like to book a single room for a week.

a	Will	b	Ought to
c	May	d	Would

7) My father _____ speak three foreign languages. He masters them very well.

a	don't have to	b	might
c	can	d	can't

8) My younger brother _____ drive a car. He is still young.

a	must	b	might
c	can't	d	can

9) Your room is very dirty. You _____ clean it.

a	don't have to	b	must
c	may	d	might

10) Ten years ago, Leila _____ speak French fluently. Now, she's forgotten a lot.

a	may	b	could
c	can	d	should

11) Perhaps, it _____ snow tonight.

a	must	b	might
c	will	d	may

12) When I lived in London, I _____ always go to Hyde Park.

a	shall	b	will
c	could	d	may

13) This soup is delicious. You _____ try some.

a	don't have to	b	may not
c	must	d	ought to

14) Monkeys _____ climb trees easily. It's a fact.

a	can	b	may
c	aren't able to	d	don't have to

15) Donald doesn't have any money, so he _____ borrow some.

a	must	b	doesn't have to
c	might	d	may not

16) You are carrying a lot of books. I _____ open the door for you.

a	am going to	b	will
c	ought to	d	could

17) Dina: _____ we have our lunch outdoors?
   Lina: That's a great idea.

a	Would	b	Must
c	Shall	d	Will

18) You _____ borrow this dictionary. It's not allowed.

A	shouldn't	b	don't have to
C	can't	d	may not

19) There are a lot of clouds. It _____ rain today.

a	may	b	don't have to
c	must	d	can't

20) Batool _____ talk to her manager about having extra days in her vacation. She is getting ready to her wedding party.

a	has do	b	doesn't have to
c	might	d	may

Exercise Five

Choose the correct answer from a, b, c, or d.

1) Ahmad will _____ a software program that helps drivers avoid accidents.

a	inventing	b	invents
c	invent	d	invented

2) I called the plumber to fix the water leak. I _____ do it myself.

a	couldn't	b	could
c	may not	d	might not

3) Yesterday, we _____ take the quiz again because the computers stopped working suddenly.

a	had to	b	didn't have to
c	should	d	may

4) Tuka: Do you like to spend the weekend in the mountains?
Saleh: No, I _____ rather not.

a	do	b	could
c	might	d	would

5) I'll prepare the lunch myself. You _____ relax and wait for it.

a	had to	b	could
c	shall	d	should

6) The students _____ read *Antony and Cleopatra*. It's an optional reading task for extra credit.

a	shall not	b	have to
c	don't have to	d	mustn't

7) Mrs Sohair: Could I please _____ some more tea?
Waiter: Certainly, madam.

a	having	b	has
c	have	d	had

8) I think children _____ go to bed early. Staying up late is not preferable for them.

a	ought to	b	will
c	don't have to	d	shall

9) My mother has a big smile on her face. She _____ be happy.

a	might	b	mustn't
c	must	d	may

10) Hala _____ do her homework last night because she was sick.

a	won't	b	may not
c	can't	d	couldn't

11) You _____ see the play. It's very exciting.

a	might	b	needn't
c	must	d	don't have to

12) I _____ work out all the exercises correctly. I made no mistakes.

a	must	b	can
c	could	d	may

13) I _____ call my parents. It's their wedding anniversary.

a	might	b	have to
c	won't	d	may

14) Nada: I lost my wallet an hour ago.
   Jane: You _____ cancel all your credit cards.

a	will	b	don't have to
c	'd better	d	shall

15) My grandfather is yawning. He _____ be tired.

a	may	b	will
c	must	d	should

16) Miriam is absent for her first time. She _____ be ill.

a	may	b	will
c	must	d	should

17) You _____ buy the tickets for the final game in advance. Thousands of fans are keen on attending.

a	might	b	will
c	have to	d	may

18) Let's meet for dinner tomorrow. We _____ discuss our business plans.

a	can	b	must
c	are able to	d	shall

19) Dan didn't feel very well last week. He _____ do any work.

a	needn't	b	couldn't
c	mustn't	d	may not

20) I _____ answer the previous questions easily. No one helped me.

a	can	b	shall
c	would	d	could

≈≈≈ My Homework ≈≈≈

SECTION 17 — Imperative Sentences

We use imperative sentences to give instructions, commands or make polite requests.

Affirmative Imperative

We use the infinitive without "to" to make the imperative.

Base form.

Examples:
- Stop.
- Go on.

Base form	Adjective

Examples:
- Be polite.
- Stay safe.

Base form	Adverb

Examples:
- Drive safely.
- Come early.

Base form	Object

Examples:
- Make the bed.
- Shut the door.

Base form	Complement

Examples:
- Stay in bed.
- Go to your class.

Negative Imperative

Don't	Base form.

Examples:
- Don't enter.
- Don't sit down.

Don't	Base form	Adjective

✦ Examples:
- Don't be noisy.
- Don't be rude.

Don't	Base form	Adverb

✦ Examples:
- Don't speak loudly.
- Don't behave impolitely.

Don't	Base form	Object

✦ Examples:
- Don't switch the lights on.
- Don't waste your time.

Don't	Base form	Complement

✦ Examples:
- Don't sit in the front.
- Don't stay in the class after the period finishes.

> We can use "please" in the beginning or at the end of the imperative sentence.

Please	Base form	Object

✦ Examples:
- Please answer the phone.
- Please write this report.

Base form	Object	please

✦ Example:
- Open the window, please.

🌿🌿🌿 My Homework 🌿🌿🌿

> ## Exercise One
> ✦ Choose the correct answer from a, b, c, or d.

1) _____ this letter, please.

a	Sends	b	To send
c	Sending	d	Send

2) _____ attention to me.

a	Paying	b	Pays
c	Pay	d	To pay

3) _____ your medicine on time, please.

a	Took	b	Taking
c	Take	d	Taken

4) _____ your hands before you eat.

a	Wash	b	Washed
c	Washing	d	To wash

5) _____ in pencil, please.

a	Written	b	Wrote
c	To write	d	Write

6) Please _____ your mobile phones silent.

a	to make	b	made
c	make	d	makes

7) _____ make noise in class, please.

a	Can't	b	Didn't
c	Doesn't	d	Don't

8) Please _____ the oil level in your car regularly.

a	checking	b	check
c	checks	d	to check

9) Don't _____ drive fast, please.

a	drove	b	drives
c	driven	d	drive

10) Don't _____ in this lake. Its water is polluted.

a	swum	b	swimming
c	swam	d	swim

🙢🙢🙢 *My Homework* 🙠🙠🙠

> ## Exercise Two
> ✦ Make the following instructions negative. Follow the example.
> ➢ Take your car to the garage.
>   ✓ Don't take your car to the garage.

1) Bring your little brother from school.

🙢_____ _____ _____ _____ _____ _____ _____ _____ _____

2) Fix your laptop yourself.

🙢_____ _____ _____ _____ _____ _____ _____ _____ _____

3) Call your brother tonight.

🙢_____ _____ _____ _____ _____ _____ _____ _____ _____

4) Buy some bread for your family.
   ✎_____ _____ _____ _____ _____ _____ _____ _____ _____

5) Stay at home for the whole week.
   ✎_____ _____ _____ _____ _____ _____ _____ _____ _____

6) Clean this office yourself.
   ✎_____ _____ _____ _____ _____ _____ _____ _____ _____

7) Give the lecture on time.
   ✎_____ _____ _____ _____ _____ _____ _____ _____ _____

8) Leave your room before 12:45 p.m.
   ✎_____ _____ _____ _____ _____ _____ _____ _____ _____

9) Carry out this task tomorrow.
   ✎_____ _____ _____ _____ _____ _____ _____ _____ _____

10) Train hard before the final boxing round.
    ✎_____ _____ _____ _____ _____ _____ _____ _____ _____

🙨🙨🙨 **My Homework** 🙤🙤🙤

➢ *Exercise Three:*
   ✤ Rearrange these words to make meaningful sentences.
1) / my / daily / car / please / Wash / .
   ✎_____ _____ _____ _____ _____ _____ _____ _____ _____

2) / coffee / black / too / drink / Don't / much /
   ✎_____ _____ _____ _____ _____ _____ _____ _____ _____

3) / animals / zoo / touch / Don't / the / the / in /
   ✎_____ _____ _____ _____ _____ _____ _____ _____ _____

4) / tires / car / Please/ of / check / my / the /
   ✎_____ _____ _____ _____ _____ _____ _____ _____ _____

5) / noise / Don't / class / in / make /
   ✎_____ _____ _____ _____ _____ _____ _____ _____ _____

6) / seat belt / wear / drive / before / Please / your / you /
   ✎_____ _____ _____ _____ _____ _____ _____ _____ _____

7) / play / tools / Don't / with / sharp /
   ✎_____ _____ _____ _____ _____ _____ _____ _____ _____

8) / car / Warm up / start / driving / your / you / before
   ✎_____ _____ _____ _____ _____ _____ _____ _____ _____

9) / during / use / mobile phone / your / Don't / driving /
   ✎_____ _____ _____ _____ _____ _____ _____ _____ _____

10) / poor / money / Please / man / this / some / give /
    ✎_____ _____ _____ _____ _____ _____ _____ _____ _____

🙨🙨🙨 **My Homework** 🙤🙤🙤

Making Suggestions

Let's . . .   **Why don't we . . . ?**   **Shall we . . . ?**

We use these forms to make suggestions.

| Let's | Base form. |

✦ Examples:
- **Omar:** Let's have a walk.
- **Faisal:** That's a good idea.

- **Bandar:** Let's go swimming.
- **Lama:** I'm sorry. I can't. I'm busy.

| Why don't we | Base form . . . ? |

✦ Examples:
- **Bato:** Why don't we play computer games?
- **Taqwa:** I'd love to.

| Shall we | Base form . . . ? |

✦ Example:
- **Ibrahim:** Shall we go fishing?
- **Mahmoud:** That's a great idea.

My Homework

> ### Exercise four
> ✦ Choose the correct answer from a, b, c or d.

1) **Martin:** _____ don't we order some coffee?
   ✓ **Taylor:** I'd rather have some juice.

a	Which	b	What
c	Who	d	Why

2) **Steven:** _____ we play a tennis match?
   ✓ **Adams:** I'm sorry. I'm tired.

a	Would	b	Will
c	Shall	d	Must

3) **Harry:** _____ read a short story.
   ✓ **Susan:** Fantastic idea.

a	Let	b	To let
c	Let's	d	letting

4) **Amelia**: Why _____ we watch a comic movie?
✓ **Suhaila**: I'm bored with comic movies.

a	*don't*	b	*can't*
c	*didn't*	d	*couldn't*

5) **Joseph**: Why don't you _____ a nap?
✓ **Jonathan**: That's a splendid idea. I think I will.

a	*take*	b	*took*
c	*takes*	d	*taking*

6) **Ted**: Why don't we _____ chess?
✓ **Harry**: I couldn't agree more.

a	*playing*	b	*plays*
c	*play*	d	*to play*

7) **Sara**: Shall we _____ to pop music?
✓ **Lara**: I am not keen on pop music.

a	*listen*	b	*listens*
c	*listening*	d	*listened*

8) **Kin**: Let's _____ a walk?
✓ **Layan**: Great idea.

a	*have*	b	*having*
c	*to have*	d	*had*

My Homework

Stating Preferences

Prefer | **Like ... better than** | **Would rather**

We use these forms to express preferences.

Subject	prefer	Noun	to	Noun

Examples:
> I prefer tennis to basketball.
> Marwa prefers rice to macaroni.

Subject	prefer	-ing	to	-ing

Examples:
> I prefer rowing to diving.
> Ahmad prefers hunting to mountain climbing.

| Subject | like | Noun | better than | Noun |

Examples:
- I like football better than handball.
- Boody likes poetry better than novels.

| Subject | like | -ing | better than | -ing |

Examples:
- I like cycling better jogging.
- Saleh likes reading better than watching TV.

| Subject | would rather | base form | than | base form |

Examples:
- I would rather study English than start a new career.
- Hala would rather walk on the beach than swim.

> **Exercise Five**

Choose the correct answer from a, b, c, or d.

1) Muhammad likes fruit juice _____ black coffee.

a	to	b	better than
c	rather than	d	than

2) Dalia prefers beef _____ fried chicken.

a	to	b	better than
c	rather than	d	than

3) Tamer would rather stay at home _____ go shopping.

a	to	b	better than
c	rather than	d	than

4) Nora prefers _____ to Ping-Pong.

a	have boated	b	boated
c	boat	d	boating

5) My sister would rather _____ her postgraduate studies than get married.

a	to complete	b	complete
c	completes	d	completed

SECTION 18 — Active and Passive Voice

Active

"Active" means that we know the doer of the action.

Subject	Verb	Object

Examples:
- Mary usually **helps** this poor man.
- We **are fixing** the laptop.

Passive

"Passive" means that it is not important to mention the doer of the action.

Object	Verb to be	Past Participle (verb 3)

Examples:

- This poor man **is** usually **helped** (by Mary).
- The laptop **is being fixed** (by us).

My Homework

The Different Forms of Passive

Present Simple Passive (Affirmative)		
I	am	Past Participle (Verb 3)
He - She - It	is	
You - They - We	are	

Examples:
- The workmen **clean** the class every day.
- ✓ The class **is cleaned** (by the workmen) every day.

- The farmers **plant** some trees every year.
- ✓ Some trees **are planted** by the farmer every year.

Present Simple Passive (Negative)		
I	am not	Past Participle (verb 3)
He - She - It	is not	
You - They - We	are not	

Example:
- My uncle **does not grow** vegetables.
- ✓ Vegetables **are not grown** by . . .

Present Simple Passive (Questions)		
Am	I	Past Participle (Verb 3)
Is	he - she - it	
Are	you - they - we	

Example:
- **Alan:** Does Mr Shalaby teach history?
- ✓ **Susan:** Is history taught by Mr Shalaby?

My Homework

Past Simple Passive (Affirmative)		
I - He - She - It	was	Past Participle
You - They - We	were	(Verb 3)

- ➢ *Note:*
- ➢ *We can use (got) instead of was or were.*
- **Examples:**
- The doctor **checked** the patient.
- ✓ The patient **was checked** (by the doctor).
- The policemen **arrested** the thieves.
- ✓ The thieves **got arrested** by the policemen.

Past Simple Passive (Affirmative)		
I - He - She - It	was not	Past Participle
You - They - We	were not	(Verb 3)

- **Example:**
- The dentist **did not pull out** my tooth.
- ✓ My tooth **was not pulled out** by the dentist.

Past Simple Passive (Questions)		
Was	I - he - she - it	Past Participle
Were	you - they - we	(Verb 3)

- **Example:**
- **Did** The farmer **plant** the palm trees?
- ✓ **Were** the palm trees **planted** by farmer?

🌿🌿🌿 *My Homework* 🍃🍃🍃

Present Progressive Passive (Affirmative)			
I	am	being	Past Participle (Verb 3)
-He – She - It	is		
You – They - We	are		

✦ **Example:**
✦ The woman *is feeding* the hens.
✓ The hens *are being fed* by . . .

Present Progressive Passive (Negative)			
I	am	not being	Past Participle (Verb 3)
-He – She - It	is		
You – They - We	are		

✦ **Examples:**
✦ The maid *is not cleaning* my room.
✓ My room *is not being cleaned* by maid.

✦ My daughter *is not reviewing* the plans.
✓ The plans *are not being reviewed* by my daughter.

Present Progressive (Questions)			
Am	I	being	Past Participle (Verb 3)
Is	he – she - it		
Are	you – we - they		

✦ **Examples:**
✦ *Is* the mechanic *fixing* my car?
✓ Is my *car being fixed* by the mechanic?

🙢🙢🙢 *My Homework* 🙠🙠🙠

Past Progressive Passive (Affirmative)			
I - He - She - It	was	being	Past Participle (Verb 3)
You - They - We	were		

+ **Example:**
+ The women ***were preparing*** some meals.
✓ Some meals ***were being prepared*** by ...

Past Progressive Passive (Negative)			
I - He - She - It	was	not being	Past Participle (Verb 3)
You - They - We	were		

+ **Examples:**
+ My son ***was not playing*** the guitar.
✓ The guitar ***was not being played*** by my son.
+ The girls ***were not reading*** the poems.
✓ The poems ***were not being read*** by the girls.

Past Progressive Passive (Questions)			
Was	I - he - she - it	being	Past Participle (Verb 3)
Were	you - they - we		

+ **Example:**
+ ***Was*** the carpenter ***making*** a round table?
✓ Was a round table ***was being made*** by the carpenter?

Passive with 'Going to' (Affirmative)			
I	am	going to be	Past Participle (Verb 3)
He - She - It	is		
You - They - We	are		

+ **Examples:**
+ The maid ***is going to clean*** the villa.
✓ The villa ***is going to be cleaned*** by the maid.
+ The government ***is going to build*** new schools.
✓ New schools ***are going to be built*** by the government.

Passive with 'Going to' (Negative)			
I	am		Past Participle (Verb 3)
He – She – It	is	not going to be	
You – They – We	are		

✦ **Example:**
✦ Boody ***is not going to receive*** this email.
✓ This email ***is not going to be received*** by Boody.

Passive with 'Going to' (Affirmative)			
Am	I		Past Participle (Verb 3)
Is	he – she – it	going to be	
Are	you – they – we		

✦ **Example:**
✦ ***Is*** the manager ***going to discuss*** the new plans?
✓ ***Are*** new plans ***going to be discussed*** by the manager?

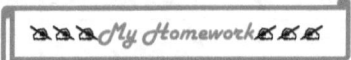

Future Simple Passive (Affirmative)		
Object	will be	Past Participle (Verb 3)

✦ **Examples:**
✦ I ***will sell*** the farm.
✓ The farm ***will be sold*** by me.

✦ The students ***will do*** the homework on time.
✓ The homework ***will be done*** by the students.

Future Simple Passive (Negative)		
	will not be	Past Participle (Verb 3)

✦ **Examples:**
✦ I ***will not send*** the package.
✓ The package ***will not be sent*** by me.

✦ The janitors ***will not carry*** the tables.
✓ The tables ***will not be carried*** by the janitors.

Future Simple Passive (Questions)			
Will	Object	be	Past Participle (Verb 3)

✦ Example:
- **Will** the technician **fix** the machine?
- ✓ Will the machine **be fixed** by the technician?

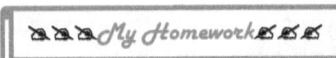

Present Perfect Passive (Affirmative)		
I - You - They - We	have been	Past Participle
He - She - It	has been	(Verb 3)

✦ Examples:
- My father **has paid** the telephone bill.
- ✓ The telephone bill **has been paid** by ....

- The teacher **has explained** the lessons.
- ✓ The lessons **have been explained** by ....

Present Perfect Passive (Negative)		
I - You - They - We	haven't been	Past Participle
He - She - It	hasn't been	(Verb 3)

✦ Examples:
- The secretary **hasn't booked** the tickets yet.
- ✓ The tickets **haven't been booked** by secretary yet.

- The painter **hasn't painted** the wall.
- ✓ The wall **hasn't been painted** by the painter yet.

Present Perfect Passive (Questions)			
Have	I - You - They - We	been	Past Participle
Has	He - She - It	been	(Verb 3)

✦ Example:
- **Has** Maha **watered** the flowers?
- ✓ **Have** the flowers **been watered** by Maha?

Past Perfect Passive (Affirmative)		
Object	had been	Past Participle (Verb 3)

Examples:
- The little boy **had broken** some glasses.
✓ Some glasses **had been broken** the little boy.

- The ancient Egyptians **had built** the pyramids.
✓ The pyramids **had been built** by . . .

Past Perfect Passive (Negative)		
Object	hadn't been	Past Participle (Verb 3)

Example:
- The plumber **had not fixed** the leak.
✓ The leak **hadn't been fixed** by the plumber.

Past Perfect Passive (Questions)			
Had	Object	been	Past Participle (Verb 3)

Example:
- **Had** the players **followed** the trainer's plan?
✓ Had the trainer's plan **been followed** by the players?

Passive with Modals (Affirmative)

Object	can / could / will / would / may / might / shall / should / must / ought to / have to / has to / had to / will have to	be	Past Participle (Verb 3)

Examples:

- I **can solve** these problems.
- ✓ These problems **can be solved** by . . .
- The students **could answer** the quiz easily.
- ✓ The quiz **could be answered** by . . .

- We **will fix** the machine.
- ✓ The machine **will be fixed** by . . .

- They **would renew** the contract.
- ✓ The contract **would be renewed** by . . .
- The teacher **may test** us today.
- ✓ We **may be tested** by . . .

- Andrew **might awake** the children.
- ✓ The children **might be awaken** by . . .

- They **should clean** the class daily.
- ✓ The class **should be cleaned** by . . .

- We **must respect** the traffic lights.
- ✓ The traffic lights **must be respected** by . . .

✘ She **ought to be** write the reports.
✓ The reports **ought to be written** by . . .

✘ They **have to issue** a visa.
✓ A visa **has to be issued** by . . .

✘ She **has to be** pay the fines.
✓ The fines **have to be paid** by . . .

✘ The driver **had to change** the flat tire.
✓ The flat tire **had to be changed** by . . .

✘ The driver **will have to renew** his driver's license.
✓ The driver's license **will have to be renewed** by . . .

Passive with Modals (Negative)

Object			
	can		
	could		
	will		
	would		
	may	not be	Past Participle
	might		(Verb 3)
	shall		
	should		
	must		

Object			
	oughtn't to		
	don't have to		
	doesn't have to	be	Past Participle
	didn't have to		(Verb 3)
	won't have to		

✦ **Examples:**
✘ I **can't control** this machine.
✓ This machine **can't be controlled** by me.

- My team **couldn't win** the match.
✓ The match **couldn't be won** by my team.

- We **will not adopt** this plan.
✓ This plan **won't be adopted** by us.

- They **wouldn't expand** the road.
✓ The road **wouldn't be expanded** by them.

- The manager **may not sign** the new contract.
✓ The new contract **may not be signed** by the manager.

- Mathew **might not buy** this farm.
✓ This farm **might not be bought** by Mathew.

- They **should not break** the appointment.
✓ The appointment **shouldn't be broken** by them.

- We **mustn't drink** polluted water.
✓ Polluted water **mustn't be drunk** by us.

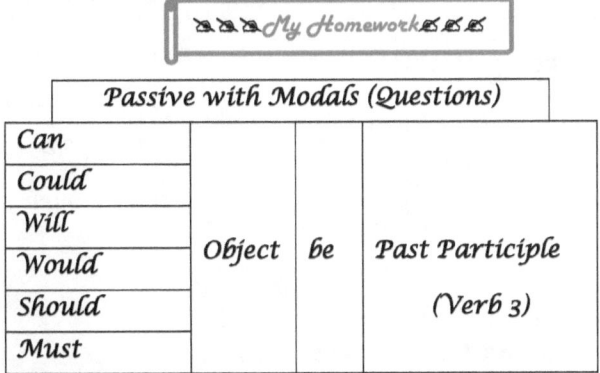

Passive with Modals (Questions)

Can			
Could			
Will	Object	be	Past Participle
Would			(Verb 3)
Should			
Must			

- **Examples:**
- **Could** you **enrol** me in the next course?
✓ **Could** I **be enrolled** in the next course?

- **Will** you **visit** the museum?
✓ **Will** the museum **be visited** by you?

- **Should** all the staff **see** the presentation?
✓ **Should** the presentation **be seen** by all the staff?

Object	could		Past Participle
	may		
	might	have been	(verb 3)
	should		
	must		
	ought to		

The Past Passive Form with Modals (Affirmative)

✦ Examples:
- The gardener **should have fixed** the water hose.
- ✓ The water hose **should have been fixed** by gardener.

- The shepherd **ought to have fed** the sheep.
- ✓ The sheep **ought to have been fed** by shepherd.

Object	could			Past Participle
	may			
	might			
	should	not	have been	(verb 3)
	must			
	ought to			

The Past Passive Form with Modals (Negative)

✦ Example:
- They **mustn't have ignored** the rules.
- ✓ The rules **mustn't have been ignored** by them.

Exercise one
- Change the following sentences from active to passive.
- Follow the example.
> The teachers _reward_ some students every term.
✓ Some students <u>are rewarded</u> _____ _____ _____ _____ _____ _____ __

1) Kevin surfs the Internet every morning.
📖_____ _____ _____ _____ _____ _____ _____ _____ _____ _____

2) Mr Shalaby teaches these classes.
📖_____ _____ _____ _____ _____ _____ _____ _____ _____ _____

3) The Egyptians grow a lot of wheat.
📖_____ _____ _____ _____ _____ _____ _____ _____ _____ _____

4) These farmers plant many trees yearly.
📖_____ _____ _____ _____ _____ _____ _____ _____ _____ _____

5) Batool will finish her shift on time.
📖_____ _____ _____ _____ _____ _____ _____ _____ _____ _____

6) Last year, our government exported a lot of products.
📖_____ _____ _____ _____ _____ _____ _____ _____ _____ _____

7) Tuka prescribed some drugs for me.
📖_____ _____ _____ _____ _____ _____ _____ _____ _____ _____

8) The government built a lot of steel factories.
📖_____ _____ _____ _____ _____ _____ _____ _____ _____ _____

9) Charles Dickens wrote great novels.
📖_____ _____ _____ _____ _____ _____ _____ _____ _____ _____

10) Ahmad completed the project a week ago.
📖_____ _____ _____ _____ _____ _____ _____ _____ _____ _____

11) A naughty student annoyed the teacher.
📖_____ _____ _____ _____ _____ _____ _____ _____ _____ _____

12) The company is going to ship the goods to New York.
📖_____ _____ _____ _____ _____ _____ _____ _____ _____ _____

13) The secretary will review the schedule.
📖_____ _____ _____ _____ _____ _____ _____ _____ _____ _____

14) The technician will fix the fridge.
📖_____ _____ _____ _____ _____ _____ _____ _____ _____ _____

15) The manager has issued a memo.
📖_____ _____ _____ _____ _____ _____ _____ _____ _____ _____

16) The police searched the building carefully.
📖_____ _____ _____ _____ _____ _____ _____ _____ _____ _____

17) The referee is going to postpone the basketball match.
📖_____ _____ _____ _____ _____ _____ _____ _____ _____ _____

18) The cinema will show a new American movie.
📖_____ _____ _____ _____ _____ _____ _____ _____ _____ _____

19) The porter should lock the door.
🌿_____ _____ _____ _____ _____ _____ _____ _____ _____

20) The clerk has to forward the reports.
🌿_____ _____ _____ _____ _____ _____ _____ _____ _____

🌿🌿🌿 My Homework 🌿🌿🌿

➢ **Exercise Two**
  ✦ Change the following sentences from active to passive.
1) The guards should watch the bank cautiously.
🌿_____ _____ _____ _____ _____ _____ _____ _____ _____

2) The teacher told us to be ready for the final test.
🌿_____ _____ _____ _____ _____ _____ _____ _____ _____

3) Picasso painted a lot of fantastic portraits.
🌿_____ _____ _____ _____ _____ _____ _____ _____ _____

4) The university is going to offer a lot of scholarships.
🌿_____ _____ _____ _____ _____ _____ _____ _____ _____

5) The robbers attacked the bank last night.
🌿_____ _____ _____ _____ _____ _____ _____ _____ _____

6) The rain filled the streets with a lot of water.
🌿_____ _____ _____ _____ _____ _____ _____ _____ _____

7) This company has trained the employees to use modern devices.
🌿_____ _____ _____ _____ _____ _____ _____ _____ _____

8) The government is going to open a new museum downtown.
🌿_____ _____ _____ _____ _____ _____ _____ _____ _____

9) You must spray the flowers with water daily.
🌿_____ _____ _____ _____ _____ _____ _____ _____ _____

10) You have to take your kids to the park weekly.
🌿_____ _____ _____ _____ _____ _____ _____ _____ _____

11) The bad weather delayed the flight.
🌿_____ _____ _____ _____ _____ _____ _____ _____ _____

12) You have to update the software of these computers.
🌿_____ _____ _____ _____ _____ _____ _____ _____ _____

13) The bus driver must replace the punctured tire.
🌿_____ _____ _____ _____ _____ _____ _____ _____ _____

14) The farmers have to harvest the wheat.
🌿_____ _____ _____ _____ _____ _____ _____ _____ _____

15) The government has to extend more ring roads around the city.
🌿_____ _____ _____ _____ _____ _____ _____ _____ _____

16) You have to find a practical solution to this problem.
🌿_____ _____ _____ _____ _____ _____ _____ _____ _____

17) Did you invite your friends to your birthday party?
➢ _____
18) Did the floods damage the village?
➢ _____
19) Will you attend the next meeting?
➢ _____
20) Did Shakespeare write *Hamlet*?
➢ _____

✿✿✿ My Homework ✿✿✿

➢ **Exercise Three**
✦ Change the following sentences from active to passive.
1) Are you going to import more goods?
➢ _____
2) Could the employees sign the requests?
➢ _____
3) The engineers didn't maintain the devices.
➢ _____
4) My boss didn't approve the marketing plan.
➢ _____
5) A thief grabbed Leila's mobile phone.
➢ _____
6) The school awarded Mr Saleh some rewards.
➢ _____
7) The students achieved very good results.
➢ _____
8) The workmen are going to dig a deep hole.
➢ _____
9) The doctor is going to check many patients.
➢ _____
10) The teachers welcomed the new students.
➢ _____
11) The maid is going to do the washing-up soon.
➢ _____
12) Millions of people visit the Statue of Liberty every year.
➢ _____
13) The earthquake destroyed a lot of buildings.
➢ _____
14) The thick fog can cause many road accidents.
➢ _____

15) The school has to give the final tests on time.
   ✎___ ___ ___ ___ ___ ___ ___ ___ ___

16) Lobna is reading a French newspaper.
   ✎___ ___ ___ ___ ___ ___ ___ ___ ___

17) The company hired a lot of IT engineers.
   ✎___ ___ ___ ___ ___ ___ ___ ___ ___

18) Jack is going to mail the letters.
   ✎___ ___ ___ ___ ___ ___ ___ ___ ___

19) My wife has cooked a delicious meal.
   ✎___ ___ ___ ___ ___ ___ ___ ___ ___

20) The school has organized a student trip to the country.
   ✎___ ___ ___ ___ ___ ___ ___ ___ ___

✿✿✿ My Homework ✿✿✿

➢ **_Exercise Four_**
✚ Change the following sentences from active to passive.

1) My sister is going to return the book to the library.
   ✎___ ___ ___ ___ ___ ___ ___ ___ ___

2) My son is going to develop an electric device.
   ✎___ ___ ___ ___ ___ ___ ___ ___ ___

3) Kevin has to empty the dustbin.
   ✎___ ___ ___ ___ ___ ___ ___ ___ ___

4) Someone is going to polish my old car.
   ✎___ ___ ___ ___ ___ ___ ___ ___ ___

5) Someone has turned the lights on.
   ✎___ ___ ___ ___ ___ ___ ___ ___ ___

6) Has Omar written the reports?
   ✎___ ___ ___ ___ ___ ___ ___ ___ ___

7) Did the postman deliver the letters?
   ✎___ ___ ___ ___ ___ ___ ___ ___ ___

8) Can the mechanic discover the mechanical problem of the engine?
   ✎___ ___ ___ ___ ___ ___ ___ ___ ___

9) Will someone adjust the clock?
   ✎___ ___ ___ ___ ___ ___ ___ ___ ___

10) The news of your marriage pleased us.
   ✎___ ___ ___ ___ ___ ___ ___ ___ ___

11) The result of the match excited the fans.
   ✎___ ___ ___ ___ ___ ___ ___ ___ ___

12) Has Omar written the reports?
   ✎___ ___ ___ ___ ___ ___ ___ ___ ___

13) The government is going to delete some taxes.
✍_____ _____ _____ _____ _____ _____ _____ _____ _____

14) We are going to defeat the other team.
✍_____ _____ _____ _____ _____ _____ _____ _____ _____

15) Lazy students make a lot of mistakes.
✍_____ _____ _____ _____ _____ _____ _____ _____ _____

16) The flight attendants offered us excellent services.
✍_____ _____ _____ _____ _____ _____ _____ _____ _____

17) Did the teacher explain these lessons?
✍_____ _____ _____ _____ _____ _____ _____ _____ _____

18) Did the police catch the thieves?
✍_____ _____ _____ _____ _____ _____ _____ _____ _____

19) Have the teachers already corrected the exam sheets?
✍_____ _____ _____ _____ _____ _____ _____ _____ _____

20) Did the teacher announce the date of the final exam?
✍_____ _____ _____ _____ _____ _____ _____ _____ _____

✿✿✿ My Homework ✿✿✿

➢ **Exercise Five**
✦ Change the following sentences from active to passive.

1) Does Lee practice sport?
✍_____ _____ _____ _____ _____ _____ _____ _____ _____

2) Did the hospital call you?
✍_____ _____ _____ _____ _____ _____ _____ _____ _____

3) The family will discuss the vacation plans.
✍_____ _____ _____ _____ _____ _____ _____ _____ _____

4) The ambulance carried my grandmother to a nearby hospital.
✍_____ _____ _____ _____ _____ _____ _____ _____ _____

5) You should have taken your medicine on time.
✍_____ _____ _____ _____ _____ _____ _____ _____ _____

6) You must have consulted your manager.
✍_____ _____ _____ _____ _____ _____ _____ _____ _____

7) You ought to have studied the project very well.
✍_____ _____ _____ _____ _____ _____ _____ _____ _____

8) He shouldn't have told her that secret.
✍_____ _____ _____ _____ _____ _____ _____ _____ _____

9) The secretary should have arranged a meeting.
✍_____ _____ _____ _____ _____ _____ _____ _____ _____

10) The clerk must have sent the faxes.
✍_____ _____ _____ _____ _____ _____ _____ _____ _____

11) You should have invited all your friends to the party.
🖎_____ _____ _____ _____ _____ _____ _____ _____ _____ _____

12) Should we tell the manager about the new deal?
🖎_____ _____ _____ _____ _____ _____ _____ _____ _____ _____

13) Jane didn't lose her books.
🖎_____ _____ _____ _____ _____ _____ _____ _____ _____ _____

14) The school should divide this large class in half.
🖎_____ _____ _____ _____ _____ _____ _____ _____ _____ _____

15) The farmers have to use fresh seeds.
🖎_____ _____ _____ _____ _____ _____ _____ _____ _____ _____

16) We can see a lovely view from the balcony.
🖎_____ _____ _____ _____ _____ _____ _____ _____ _____ _____

17) The students left their books in the computer lab.
🖎_____ _____ _____ _____ _____ _____ _____ _____ _____ _____

18) Some students couldn't understand the grammar lesson.
🖎_____ _____ _____ _____ _____ _____ _____ _____ _____ _____

19) The mice have eaten some cheese.
🖎_____ _____ _____ _____ _____ _____ _____ _____ _____ _____

20) The cats have drunk a lot of milk.
🖎_____ _____ _____ _____ _____ _____ _____ _____ _____ _____

🖎🖎🖎 *My Homework* 🖎🖎🖎

➢ *Exercise Six*
✣ Complete the sentences with be, being, or been.
1) The mirror should _____ cleaned.
2) These clothes have to _____ dried.
3) The bill has _____ paid.
4) The match is _____ played at the moment.
5) The farm is _____ supplied with water.
6) My shirts had _____ dried and ironed.
7) The cupboard has _____ polished.
8) Could you lend me your car as mine is _____ fixed?
9) The students' books have already _____ collected.
10) A lot of new roads will _____ extended around my city.
11) The exam results are going to _____ announced soon.
12) Has this naughty girl ever _____ blamed for her bad behaviour?
13) Has the car _____ fuelled yet?
14) Thousands of seats have _____ booked by the fans.
15) The trip is going to _____ cancelled because of bad weather.
16) The students are _____ tested right now.

17) My camera is _____ fixed at the moment.
18) These problems can't _____ understood easily.
19) The manager may _____ convinced by our plan.
20) The final exam will _____ cancelled.

My Homework

➢ **Exercise Seven**

✦ Choose the correct answer from a, b, c or d.

1) Your work should have been _____ on time.

a	do	b	doing
c	did	d	done

2) David's father is _____ to be stingy.

a	knew	b	known
c	knowing	d	know

3) The match _____ attended by of a lot of fans yesterday.

a	was	b	has been
c	is	d	is being

4) Four people _____ by this nasty dog.

a	bitten	b	bite
c	were bitten	d	bit

5) The devices _____ by the electrician two days ago.

a	will be checked	b	were checked
c	are checked	d	have been checked

6) My car _____ when I asked to borrow yours.

a	has been fixed	b	is fixing
c	was being fixed	d	was fixing

7) I can't travel abroad these days because my passport _____.

a	is being renewed	b	has been renewed
c	was being renewed	d	is going to renew

8) The final test material _____ by our teacher.

a	reviewed	b	is reviewing
c	reviews	d	is going to be reviewed

9) A comic play _____ on TV last night.

a	is shown	b	will be shown
c	has been shown	d	was shown

10) My father's wallet was lost _____.

a	tomorrow	b	last Monday
c	next week	d	in two days

11) The swimmers _____ by the guards that the waves were very high.

a	were warned	b	are being warning
c	will be warned	d	are warned

12) My neighbour's car _____ last Friday.

a	stolen	b	is stolen
c	stole	d	was stolen

13) Our house _____ by my grandfather fifty years ago.

a	will be built	b	is going to be built
c	was built	d	was building

14) We are going to take a nap until our lunch _____.

a	is prepared	b	will be prepared
c	was prepared	d	is going to be prepared

15) The patient was _____ to give up smoking as soon as possible.

a	tell	b	told
c	to tell	d	tells

16) The employees _____ about the new vacation rules of the company.

a	were informed	b	informs
c	informing	d	to inform

17) Batool _____ by her teachers because of her efforts at school.

a	was rewarded	b	rewarded
c	rewards	d	was rewarding

18) Boody _____ by his teachers every day.

a	is encouraged	b	encourages
c	is encouraging	d	was encouraging

19) Our villa has _____ broken in last night.

a	being	b	to be
c	be	d	been

20) A lot of presents _____ by Ahmad on his birthday.

a	were received	b	received
c	receives	d	receiving

ᴥᴥᴥ *My Homework* ᴥᴥᴥ

> ## *Exercise Eight*
+ Choose the correct answer from a, b, c, or d.

1) The exam sheets of paper _____ by our teachers tomorrow.

a	are correcting correct	b	are going to be corrected
c	will be correcting	d	will correct

2) Vegetables _____ before eating them.

a	should wash	b	should be wash
c	should be washing	d	should be washed

3) A new canal _____ to carry water to the farm.

a	is being dug	b	digging
c	is digging	d	dug

4) Some tourists _____ on the road to the country last week.

a	were lost	b	are lost
c	lost	d	losing

5) This grass is _____ by the farmers every day.

a	to cut	b	cutting
c	cuts	d	cut

6) The new website of our company _____ by Ahmad Saleh.

a	was designed	b	was designed
c	designs	d	design

7) My new car _____ last year.

a	will be produced	b	is going to be produced
c	was produced	d	is produced

8) The accidents _____ by the policeman.

a	were reported	b	reports
c	reported	d	were reporting

9) My parents _____ to my cousin's engagement party.

a	invites	b	to invite
c	invited	d	were invited

10) This laptop _____ as soon as possible.

a	maintaining	b	should be maintained
c	will be maintain	d	should maintain

11) These newspapers _____ by somebody yesterday.

a	must be forgetting	b	must forget
c	must be forgotten	d	must have been forgotten

12) A new book _____ by Mr Shalaby now.

a	was being written	b	is writing
c	was writing	d	is being written

13) The robber _____ by the police force.

a	has shot	b	has been shot
c	shot	d	has been shooting

14) A lot of sheep _____ by the wolves. Only three survived.

a	will be eaten	b	are being eaten
c	had been eaten	d	are going to be eaten

15) The software of your computer should _____ updated.

a	to be	b	being
c	be	d	been

16) The new lesson _____ by the students last Monday.

a	should be	b	should have been studied
c	should study	d	should be studying

17) This bus _____ tomorrow morning.

a	was repaired	b	will be repaired
c	repairing	d	will be repairing

18) In Egypt, winter wheat _____ in late July and early August.

a	is harvesting	b	harvesting
c	is harvested	d	harvests

19) A lot of food has already _____ bought by my parents.

A	to be	a	being
C	been	d	be

20) The new company _____ by my uncle.

a	run	b	to run
c	is run	d	running

Exercise Nine
Choose the correct answer from a, b, c, or d.

1) The test results _____ by the teachers.

a	have announced	b	have to be announced
c	have to announce	d	have been announcing

2) Is English _____ all over the world?

a	spoken	b	speaking
c	speaks	d	spoke

3) _____ the patients going to be examined by the doctors?

a	Will	b	Is
c	Were	d	Are

4) The juice has been _____ by someone.

a	drank	b	drinking
c	drunk	d	drinks

5) The stolen cars were _____ by the policemen.

a	finding	b	find
c	finds	d	found

6) A lot of emails were _____ by Ms Lara.

a	sending	b	send
c	sent	d	to send

7) Chocolate _____ by most children.

a	is preferred	b	prefer
c	prefers	d	preferred

8) The ball _____ by a tall player into the basket.

a	was thrown	b	was throwing
c	threw	d	thrown

9) Last month, a lot of palm trees _____ planted on our farm.

a	have been	b	to be
c	are	d	were

10) My sister _____ a new job as a supervisor in a tourist company.

a	was offered	b	offering
c	offer	d	to offer

11) The teacher _____ a lot of questions by the students.

a	was asking	b	to ask
c	was asked	d	ask

12) The telephone _____ by Alexander Graham Bell many years ago.

a	was inventing	b	invented
c	was invented	d	invents

13) The new teacher was _____ to his students by the senior teacher.

a	introduced	b	introduces
c	introducing	d	introduce

14) The bus driver was not seriously _____ in the accident.

a	hurting	b	hurts
c	to hurt	d	hurt

15) Papyrus _____ in ancient Egypt thousands of years ago.

a	was using	b	was used
c	used	d	using

16) My grammar skills _____ since I started this course.

a	was developed	b	will be developed
c	is developed	d	have been developed

17) Some clothes got _____ after washing them.

a	shrink	b	shrinking
c	shrinks	d	shrunk

18) The destroyed houses are going _____ soon.

a	to rebuild	b	rebuilds
c	be rebuild	d	to be rebuilt

19) This bottle of medicine should be _____ before use.

a	shaken	b	shaking
c	shook	d	shakes

20) This fine cloth _____ in China.

a	wove	b	weaves
c	is woven	d	is weaving

🐝🐝🐝 My Homework 🐝🐝🐝

> ### Exercise Ten

Choose the correct answer from a, b, c, or d.

1) A lot of gas is _____ to Europe every year.

a	exports	b	exported
c	export	d	exporting

2) It is _____ that a lot of fans will attend the final match.

a	predicting	b	predicted
c	predict	d	predicts

3) The police found out that the treasure was_____ in an old hut.

a	hidden	b	hides
c	hide	d	hid

4) My parents _____ twenty years ago.

a	get married	b	got marrying
c	got married	d	getting married

5) The librarian told me that the book _____ to the library three days ago.

a	should be returned	b	should have been returned
c	should return	d	should have been returning

6) Jane _____ her salary yesterday.

a	was paid	b	to pay
c	paying	d	pay

7) The news of my marriage _____ everywhere.

a	spreading	b	have spread
c	to spread	d	has been spread

8) This project needs another four months _____ carried out.

a	to be	b	been
c	be	d	being

9) Seventy sentences on passive voice _____ correctly.

a	are answering	b	answer
c	were answered	d	were answering

10) *Oliver Twist* was written _____ Charles Dickens.

a	in	b	of
c	with	d	by

11) Mona Lisa was _____ by Leonardo da Vinci.

a	painting	b	painted
c	paints	d	paint

12) My little sister _____ by a spider.

a	was scared	b	scaring
c	scared	d	scares

13) The house is being cleaned _____.

a	an hour ago	b	right now
c	yesterday	d	last Friday

14) These mobile phones _____ in Korea last month.

a	will be made	b	are made
c	were made	d	are being made

15) A new marketing plan has been adopted _____.

a	recently	b	yesterday
c	yet	d	two days ago

16) These computers are maintained and updated _____.

a	yearly	b	three years ago
c	last year	d	in 2013

17) The new project hasn't been approved _____.

a	yet	b	lately
c	recently	d	still

18) A lot of difficult math problems _____ by Abdo yesterday.

a	were solved	b	will be solved
c	are solved	d	have been solved

19) These grammar exercises _____ by Nancy.

a	will be doing	b	will do
c	were done	d	will be done

20) William Shakespeare's *King Lear* was performed at the National Theatre in Cairo _____.

| a | now | b | at the moment |
| c | next year | d | three months ago |

➤ Exercise Eleven
✦ Choose the correct answer from a, b, c, or d.

1) This novel _____ into many languages in the last five years.

| a | was translated | b | has been translated |
| c | were translated | d | will be translated |

2) The conflagration _____ by an electric fault.

| a | was causing | b | caused |
| c | causing | d | was caused |

3) The criminals _____ by the police officers an hour ago.

| a | were chased | b | chased |
| c | chases | d | are chased |

4) A lot of loans _____ to many clients by the bank.

| a | given | b | was given |
| c | were given | d | are giving |

5) A lot of goods _____ by our company this year.

| a | going to export | b | are going to be exported |
| c | are exporting | d | are going to export |

6) This large fish _____ by my mother.

| a | will grill | b | will be grilling |
| c | will be grilled | d | grilled |

7) The report _____ by all employees.

| a | will be read | b | reading |
| c | will read | d | will be reading |

8) My father's keys _____ in his office.

| a | were left | b | leaving |
| c | left | d | to leave |

9) We _____ one third of the world's monuments when we visit Luxor.

| a | shown | b | will be shown |
| c | will shown | d | showing |

10) The new infrastructure projects _____ next July.

| a | have been finished | b | were finished |
| c | are finished | d | will be finished |

11) Fine clothes _____ in that factory.

| a | are made | b | make |
| c | makes | d | made |

12) Abdul-Rahman _____ at chess.

a	can't be beat	b	can beaten
c	to beat	d	can't be beaten

13) Ted _____ a nice present by his parents.

a	promising	b	was promised
c	was promising	d	promise

14) These reports _____ by our manager before taking his decision.

a	looking into	b	should be looked into
c	should look into	d	look into

15) Sandy's dress _____ for tomorrow's party.

a	ought to wash	b	ought to be washing
c	washing	d	ought to be washed

16) The newspapers _____ to my grandfather every morning.

a	reading	b	are read
c	are reading	d	reads

17) A nice meal _____ by my grandmother.

a	is preparing	b	is going to be prepared
c	is prepare	d	is going to prepare

18) Our village _____ by a heavy flood last night.

a	is submerged	b	is going to be submerged
c	will be submerged	d	was submerged

19) Smoking mustn't _____ permitted in public places.

a	being	b	been
c	be	d	to be

20) These sentences _____ by my teacher.

a	corrects	b	corrected
c	will be correcting	d	will be corrected

🌸🌸🌸 *My Homework* 🌸🌸🌸

> ## *Exercise Twelve*

✦ Correct the mistake in each of the following sentences.

1) The children were give some food by their mother.
   🌸_____

2) This American movie was producing in 1999.
   🌸_____

3) This bad tooth has to removed to get rid of the pain.
   🌸_____

4) My old bus is going to be sell next Friday.
   🌸_____

5) The new computers are going be installed soon.
   🌸_____

6) This old villa must demolished at once.
   ✎_____

7) The class was painting by the students.
   ✎_____

8) This room has to redecorated by you.
   ✎_____

9) My laptop has to be check by the technician.
   ✎_____

10) When the television invented in the 1950s?
    ✎_____

11) Was the child punishing by his parents?
    ✎_____

12) Will the questions reviewed by the teachers?
    ✎_____

13) A lot of products are import by our country every year.
    ✎_____

14) Yesterday's accident was cause by the slippery road.
    ✎_____

15) These nice photos were take by my friend.
    ✎_____

✿✿✿ My Homework ✿✿✿

➢ *Exercise Thirteen*
✦ Decide whether these sentences are active or passive.
✦ Follow the example.
✦ **Example:**
➢ The match was delayed for half an hour.

| ACTIVE | PASSIVE | ✓ |

1) The teacher discovered a lot of mistakes.

| ACTIVE | PASSIVE | |

2) The bus was polished by Annie.

| ACTIVE | PASSIVE | |

3) The team must arrive at the stadium on time.

| ACTIVE | PASSIVE | |

4) The road must be expanded by the government.

| ACTIVE | PASSIVE | |

5) The hostess welcomed us warmly.

| ACTIVE | PASSIVE | |

6) The river has been polluted badly.
| ACTIVE | | PASSIVE | |

7) They may invite Sarah to the party.
| ACTIVE | | PASSIVE | |

8) They might blame you.
| ACTIVE | | PASSIVE | |

9) The building was destroyed in a short time.
| ACTIVE | | PASSIVE | |

10) The policeman warned the fast driver.
| ACTIVE | | PASSIVE | |

11) The reckless driver was given a fine.
| ACTIVE | | PASSIVE | |

12) It rained a lot yesterday.
| ACTIVE | | PASSIVE | |

13) The roof was covered with a lot of snow.
| ACTIVE | | PASSIVE | |

14) We paid the plumber a lot of money.
| ACTIVE | | PASSIVE | |

15) The president gave the winning team gold medals.
| ACTIVE | | PASSIVE | |

16) The swimmers recued the drowning lady.
| ACTIVE | | PASSIVE | |

17) The court found George guilty of murder.
| ACTIVE | | PASSIVE | |

18) The teacher blamed the tardy students.
| ACTIVE | | PASSIVE | |

19) This newspaper is issued every day.
| ACTIVE | | PASSIVE | |

20) The children were given a lot of toys.
| ACTIVE | | PASSIVE | |

21) The attendants were requested to leave the meeting.
| ACTIVE | | PASSIVE | |

22) The manager discussed the developing plans in detail.
| ACTIVE | | PASSIVE | |

23) The students thanked their teacher for his efforts.
| ACTIVE | | PASSIVE | |

24) A lot of noise disturbed the students.

ACTIVE		PASSIVE	

25) The sheep were attacked by some wolves.

ACTIVE		PASSIVE	

✿✿✿ My Homework ✿✿✿

> ### Exercise Fourteen
- Decide whether these sentences are active or passive.

1) This rocket will be launched tomorrow morning.

ACTIVE		PASSIVE	

2) The election campaign is going to start next Friday.

ACTIVE		PASSIVE	

3) My wife started a new course in HR.

ACTIVE		PASSIVE	

4) The camel race was postponed until further notice.

ACTIVE		PASSIVE	

5) This bag is made of genuine leather.

ACTIVE		PASSIVE	

6) Geologists excavate for natural resources.

ACTIVE		PASSIVE	

7) My colleagues celebrated my birthday.

ACTIVE		PASSIVE	

8) Bees produce lot of honey.

ACTIVE		PASSIVE	

9) Gulf countries export oil and natural gas.

ACTIVE		PASSIVE	

10) Alan had a terrible car accident last night.

ACTIVE		PASSIVE	

11) These emails have to be sent as quickly as possible.

ACTIVE		PASSIVE	

12) You have to replace the damaged tires of your car.

ACTIVE		PASSIVE	

13) You must be aware of the bad effects of gambling.

ACTIVE		PASSIVE	

14) This portrait was painted by a famous artist.

ACTIVE		PASSIVE	

15) The government must pave the way to foreign investment.

ACTIVE		PASSIVE	

16) The Modern Art Museum was visited by millions of people.

ACTIVE		PASSIVE	

17) Bicycles were introduced in the late 19th century in Europe.

ACTIVE		PASSIVE	

18) You should air this room from time to time.

ACTIVE		PASSIVE	

19) The criminals were accused of killing the guard.

ACTIVE		PASSIVE	

20) Our company developed a new system for ATM operations.

ACTIVE		PASSIVE	

21) This restaurant serves a lot of famous international dishes.

ACTIVE		PASSIVE	

22) The children were allowed to play in the garden.

ACTIVE		PASSIVE	

23) The police discovered the crime by chance.

ACTIVE		PASSIVE	

24) Our teacher usually tells us fantastic historical adventures.

ACTIVE		PASSIVE	

25) The spy was sentenced to death for betraying his own country.

ACTIVE		PASSIVE	

🙢🙢🙢 *My Homework* 🙠🙠🙠

> ## *Exercise Fifteen*

- Change the sentences from passive to active.
- Follow the example.
> The burglar was caught by two policemen.
✓ Two policemen caught the burglar.

1) The field is going to be tilled by the farmers.

🙢____ ____ ____ ____ ____ ____ ____ ____ ____ ____

2) My bad teeth were pulled out by the dentist.

🙢____ ____ ____ ____ ____ ____ ____ ____ ____ ____

3) The old building will be demolished by the government.

🙢____ ____ ____ ____ ____ ____ ____ ____ ____ ____

4) The four tires of my car are going to be changed by Kim.

🙢____ ____ ____ ____ ____ ____ ____ ____ ____ ____

5) These instructions must be read and carried out by you.
✍_____

6) The insects will be killed by this insecticide.
✍_____

7) The glasses were broken by Neil.
✍_____

8) The engine was fixed by three mechanics.
✍_____

9) The boy was being chased by the dogs.
✍_____

10) We were blamed by our math teacher.
✍_____

11) Three goals were scored by Salah.
✍_____

12) The test is being answered by all the students.
✍_____

13) The website is going to be updated by Ahmad.
✍_____

14) The information you need will be sent by the secretary.
✍_____

15) The crime will be investigated by the police.
✍_____

16) The kitchen is going to be cleaned by Mark.
✍_____

17) The trees are going to be planted by Ralf.
✍_____

18) My new camera was bought by Helen.
✍_____

19) The tickets are going to be booked by Sue.
✍_____

20) The new course is going to be postponed by the students.
✍_____

✍✍✍ My Homework ✍✍✍

➢ **_Exercise Sixteen_**
➕ Correct the mistake in each of the following sentences.
1) The sheep are usually feed by the shepherd three times a day.
   ✍_____ _____ _____ _____ _____ _____ _____ _____ _____ _____
2) The new building will designed by skilled engineers.
   ✍_____ _____ _____ _____ _____ _____ _____ _____ _____ _____
3) The mirror was braking by the child.
   ✍_____ _____ _____ _____ _____ _____ _____ _____ _____ _____
4) This car is making in Japan.
   ✍_____ _____ _____ _____ _____ _____ _____ _____ _____ _____
5) Yesterday, two mobile phones were steal by a shoplifter.
   ✍_____ _____ _____ _____ _____ _____ _____ _____ _____ _____
6) Our dinner will be serve on time.
   ✍_____ _____ _____ _____ _____ _____ _____ _____ _____ _____
7) Our graduation party will organized by the school principal.
   ✍_____ _____ _____ _____ _____ _____ _____ _____ _____ _____
8) The bill was bring by the waitress.
   ✍_____ _____ _____ _____ _____ _____ _____ _____ _____ _____
9) Our new students are teach Italian and Spanish.
   ✍_____ _____ _____ _____ _____ _____ _____ _____ _____ _____
10) The mail hasn't been deliver yet.
    ✍_____ _____ _____ _____ _____ _____ _____ _____ _____ _____

❧❧❧*My Homework*❧❧❧

➢ **_Exercise Sixteen_**
➕ Correct the mistake in each of the following sentences.
1) We were convince by his point of view.
   ✍_____ _____ _____ _____ _____ _____ _____ _____ _____ _____
2) They will be ask to change their plans.
   ✍_____ _____ _____ _____ _____ _____ _____ _____ _____ _____
3) Your parents have to supported by you.
   ✍_____ _____ _____ _____ _____ _____ _____ _____ _____ _____
4) The old bus has to be take to the workshop.
   ✍_____ _____ _____ _____ _____ _____ _____ _____ _____ _____
5) These sentences have to be write by the students.
   ✍_____ _____ _____ _____ _____ _____ _____ _____ _____ _____
6) These sentences have to be write by the students.
   ✍_____ _____ _____ _____ _____ _____ _____ _____ _____ _____

7) The new Smart Boards have already be installed.
🙠_____ _____ _____ _____ _____ _____ _____ _____ _____ _____

8) The Internet service has to be develop in this country.
🙠_____ _____ _____ _____ _____ _____ _____ _____ _____ _____

9) I couldn't start my car as its battery is dead.
🙠_____ _____ _____ _____ _____ _____ _____ _____ _____ _____

10) As soon as our mayor is elected, he held a meeting with his assistants.
🙠_____ _____ _____ _____ _____ _____ _____ _____ _____ _____

🙠🙠🙠 My Homework 🙠🙠🙠

➢ **_Exercise Seventeen_**
♣ Correct the mistake in each of the following sentences.

1) This photograph was take by my mother.
🙠_____ _____ _____ _____ _____ _____ _____ _____ _____ _____

2) The poor woman was give a lot of money by her neighbours.
🙠_____ _____ _____ _____ _____ _____ _____ _____ _____ _____

3) The retired clerk was award some gifts.
🙠_____ _____ _____ _____ _____ _____ _____ _____ _____ _____

4) The football court is always maintain before each game.
🙠_____ _____ _____ _____ _____ _____ _____ _____ _____ _____

5) This play was write by William Shakespeare.
🙠_____ _____ _____ _____ _____ _____ _____ _____ _____ _____

6) When will the new bridge be build?
🙠_____ _____ _____ _____ _____ _____ _____ _____ _____ _____

7) The telephone was invent by Alexander Graham Bell.
🙠_____ _____ _____ _____ _____ _____ _____ _____ _____ _____

8) Alan was offer a new job as a marketing manager.
🙠_____ _____ _____ _____ _____ _____ _____ _____ _____ _____

9) The new machine was being test when the supervisor came.
🙠_____ _____ _____ _____ _____ _____ _____ _____ _____ _____

10) My bank account was freeze because I didn't update my data.
🙠_____ _____ _____ _____ _____ _____ _____ _____ _____ _____

🙠🙠🙠 My Homework 🙠🙠🙠

➤ Exercise Eighteen
✦ Correct the mistake in each of the following sentences.

1) Coffee is make in Brazil and Yemen.
   ✎ _____

2) Stephen's arm was break in a car accident.
   ✎ _____

3) My grandmother has to be taken to hospital last night.
   ✎ _____

4) The plan was approve by our manager.
   ✎ _____

5) Donald got depress after he received his exam result.
   ✎ _____

6) The traffic rules must be obey by all people?
   ✎ _____

7) Be careful! The floor is be swept at the moment.
   ✎ _____

8) The cows are taken to the farm by Mark an hour ago.
   ✎ _____

9) The beach can be see from our veranda.
   ✎ _____

10) Dictionaries can't being taken outside the library.
    ✎ _____

🙰🙰🙰 My Homework 🙵🙵🙵

➤ Exercise Nineteen
✦ Correct the mistake in each of the following sentences.

1) My car is being washed when I arrived at the service station.
   ✎ _____

2) Smoking isn't allow in this area.
   ✎ _____

3) The applications are approved by the manager yesterday.
   ✎ _____

4) These apple trees were plant by my grandparents.
   ✎ _____

5) The plants in our garden are water every other day.
   ✎ _____

6) Will this parcel be sending tomorrow?
   ✎ _____

7) Some players weren't tell the plan of the match.
➢ _____

8) The kitchen ought to being cleaned daily.
➢ _____

9) Our house is surround by many tall trees.
➢ _____

10) The guests' lunch should been served on time.
➢ _____

❧❧❧ My Homework ❧❧❧

➢ **Exercise Twenty**
✦ Correct the mistake in each of the following sentences.

1) The high achievers are honour every semester.
➢ _____

2) The news was reading in an excellent accent.
➢ _____

3) These shirts should be wash now.
➢ _____

4) These electric wires has to be changed.
➢ _____

5) Shakespeare's sonnets were publish more than four centuries ago.
➢ _____

6) Will this road being completed before June?
➢ _____

7) The children were deceive by the clown's tricks.
➢ _____

8) My appointment with the dentist have to be cancel as I am very busy.
➢ _____

9) The floods couldn't control by the government.
➢ _____

10) Thousands of trees were burns down by the conflagration.
➢ _____

❧❧❧ My Homework ❧❧❧

SECTION 19 — Conditionals — If & Unless

If

Zero Conditional

| If | Present Tense | , | Present Tense |

OR

| Present Tense | if | Present Tense |

Examples:
- *If* you *heat* water, it *boils*.
- Water *evaporates if* you *boil* it.

First Conditional

| If | Present Tense | , | Future Tense |

OR

| Future Tense | if | Present Tense |

Examples:
- *If* you *hurry up*, you *will catch* the train.
- I *will buy* a new laptop *if* I *have* enough money.
- *If* it *rains* a lot, *I'm going to stay* at home.
- The referee *is going to cancel* the match *if* it *continues* snowing.

Second Conditional

| If | Past Tense | , | would / could / might | base form |

OR

| would + Base form / could + Base form / might + Base form | if | Past Tense |

Examples:
- *If* I *left* my homework at home, my teacher *would be* angry.
- My parents *would be* pleased *if* I *achieved* excellent success.

Third Conditional

If	Past Perfect	,	would have + Past Participle
		,	could have + Past Participle
		,	might have + Past Participle

OR

would + have + Past Participle	if	Past Perfect
could + have + Past Participle		
might + have + Past Participle		

OR

Had	1st Subject	Past Participle	,	would + Past
			,	could + Past Participle
			,	might + Past

✤ **Examples:**
✤ *If* I *had* enough time, I *would have finished the* task on time.
✤ John *would have succeeded if* he *had studied* well.
✤ *Had* Dale *been* careful, he *wouldn't have had* that serious accident.

Unless

First Conditional

Unless	Present Tense	,	Future Tense

OR

Future Tense	unless	Present Tense

✤ **Examples:**
✤ *If* you *don't drive safely*, you *will have* an accident.
✓ *Unless* you *drive safely*, you *will have* an accident.

✤ *If* the sun *doesn't shine*, we *won't go* diving.
✓ *Unless* the sun *shines*, we *won't go* diving.

✤ Ann *will be* annoyed if she *doesn't go* swimming.
✓ Ann *will be* annoyed unless she *goes* swimming.

✤ Adam *will miss* the train if he *doesn't hurry*.
✓ Adam *will miss* the train *unless* he *hurries*.

❧❧❧ *My Homework* ❧❧❧

Second Conditional

Unless	Past Tense	, , ,	would could might	base form

OR

would + base form could + base form might + base form	unless	Past Tense

Examples:
- *If* the players ***didn't train*** hard, they ***would lose*** the game.
- ✓ Unless the players **trained** hard, they would lose the game.

- Our teacher ***would be*** delighted ***if*** we ***didn't fail*** the test.
- ✓ Our teacher ***would be*** delighted ***unless*** we ***failed*** the test.

- No one ***would achieve*** progress in that company if they ***weren't given*** support.
- ✓ No one ***would achieve*** progress in that company unless they ***were given*** support.

- I ***would behave*** in a better way ***if*** Jane ***didn't insult*** me.
- I ***would behave*** in a better way ***unless*** Jane ***insulted*** me.

Third Conditional

Unless	Past Perfect	, , ,	would + have + Past Participle could + have + Past Participle might + have + Past Participle

OR

would + have + Past Participle could + have + Past Participle might + have + Past Participle	unless	Past Perfect

Examples:
- *If* I ***hadn't got up*** early, I ***would have been*** late for the meeting.
- ✓ ***Unless*** I ***had got up*** early, I ***would have been*** late for the meeting.

- My manager ***would have blamed*** me ***if*** I ***hadn't emailed*** the report.
- ✓ My manager ***would have blamed*** me ***unless*** I ***had emailed*** the report.

My Homework

	(A)		(B)
1.	If we heat ice,	A.	you wouldn't attend the lecture.
2.	If Omar wins the final round,	B.	you could call the police.
3.	Unless you came early,	C.	if you exercise regularly.
4.	If Sara doesn't feel better,	D.	if the weather is fine.
5.	If you lost your wallet,	E.	I would have bought that expensive car.
6.	If it rains heavily,	F.	if you run a red light.
7.	We will go swimming	G.	it is melted.
8.	You will get a fine	H.	I'm going to take my umbrella.
9.	If I had had enough money,	I.	she will see the doctor.
10.	You will be fit	J.	he will be rewarded.

> ### Exercise One
> - Look at the table. Match the beginnings and endings of these phrases.
> - Follow the example.

> If we heat ice, it is melted.

2) _____

3) _____

4) _____

5) _____

6) _____

7) _____

8) _____

9) _____

10) _____

My Homework

➢ Exercise Two

✦ Choose the correct answer from a, b, c or d.

1) If you prepare a good plan, you _____ in a better way.

a	would perform	b	could perform
c	will perform	d	wouldn't perform

2) If the questions had been easy, I _____ them correctly.

a	will answer	b	would answer
c	would have answered	d	can answer

3) The manager would have postponed the meeting if some of the employees _____ absent.

a	had been	b	are
c	were	d	being

4) We _____ fishing if the waves weren't high.

a	will go	b	can go
c	may go	d	would go

5) Unless Lilly _____ George, he wouldn't have been angry.

a	insults	b	had insulted
c	insult	d	insulted

6) I may be confused unless you _____ it again.

a	explains	b	to explain
c	explaining	d	explain

7) Unless you _____ my offer, I won't pay you.

a	accept	b	accepting
c	accepts	d	accepted

8) Unless the technician _____ my computer, I won't be able to use it.

a	fixing	b	fixed
c	fixes	d	fix

9) If you win the next match, you _____ a special reward.

a	receive	b	received
c	would receive	d	will receive

10) If the traffic lights are red, you _____.

a	must have stopped	b	must stop
c	are stopping	d	stopping

11) If I knew the answer, I _____ hesitate.

a	won't	b	may not
c	wouldn't	d	mustn't

12) If I _____ you, I would accept his proposal.

a	am	b	was
c	were	d	have been

13) If I see the new boss, I _____ welcome him.

a	would	b	could
c	had to	d	am going to

14) If Jack _____ his work earlier, he would have gone out for a walk.

a	finished	b	has finished
c	had finished	d	finishes

15) If you had invited us to dinner, we _____ your invitation.

a	would accept	b	would have accept
c	will accept	d	would have accepted

16) If I see my parents, I _____ them all my news.

a	will tell	b	would tell
c	could tell	d	would have told

17) If Tuka were here, she _____ us.

a	will help	b	would have helped
c	would help	d	may help

18) If Oraby had passed his final exams, his teachers _____ him.

a	would praise	b	would have praised
c	will praise	d	might praise

19) I would have got this job if I _____ good computer skills.

a	had	b	have
c	had had	d	have had

20) I may see a lot of wild animals if I _____ to the forest.

a	went	b	will go
c	had gone	d	go

21) If Ali read the instructions, he _____ this machine.

a	would operate	b	would have operated
c	will operate	d	may operate

22) What _____ if you found a treasure in your garden?

a	will you do	b	may you do
c	would you do	d	can you do

23) If you had left your notebooks at home, your teacher _____ annoyed.

a	would be	b	would have been
c	could be	d	will be

24) I would feel thrilled if I _____ top in all my exams.

a	come	b	have come
c	came	d	had come

25) If I _____ a lion in the street, I would scream and run away.

a	see	b	have seen
c	had seen	d	saw

My Homework

> ## Exercise Three

✦ Choose the correct answer from a, b, c, or d.

1) If I had gone to London, I _____ my English friends there.

a	would meet	b	could meet
c	would have met	d	can meet

2) If we _____ a map, we wouldn't have got lost.

a	have brought	b	had brought
c	brought	d	bring

3) If Ahmad _____ about the job, he could have applied for it.

a	has heard	b	reads
c	had heard	d	read

4) Unless Jane _____ smoking, she would have had a heart attack.

a	had stopped	b	has stopped
c	stopped	d	stops

5) If the weather _____ better, we would have camped there.

a	was	b	had been
c	has been	d	is

6) Unless the bus driver had been cautious, he _____ that tree.

a	could hit	b	would have hit
c	would hit	d	would be hitting

7) If Sally _____ a temperature, she should see a doctor.

a	has	b	had
c	have	d	had had

8) Unless Franklin has to go to class today, he _____ swimming.

a	would go	b	could go
c	will go	d	would have gone

9) If Andrew _____ to Paris, he will visit a lot of museums there.

a	travel	b	travels
c	had travelled	d	travelled

10) Unless Boody had enough money, he _____ be able to buy that expensive car.

a	won't	b	may not
c	would	d	wouldn't

11) If Donald had got up early, he _____ missed his flight.

a	will have	b	wouldn't have
c	would have	d	may have

12) Had my teacher helped me, I _____.

a	would fail	b	wouldn't have failed
c	might fail	d	will fail

13) Unless my mother had woken me up early, I _____ the school bus.

a	might miss	b	may miss
c	would miss	d	would have missed

14) _____ you hurry, you won't catch the first period.

a	If	b	Without
c	Unless	d	Would

15) _____ Ola didn't write the report, the manager would blame her.

a	If	b	Without
c	Unless	d	Shouldn't

16) _____ it stops snowing, we won't be able to go on driving.

a	If	b	Without
c	Unless	d	Shouldn't

17) If I lost my mobile phone, my father _____ angry.

a	may be	b	would be
c	is going to be	d	would have been

18) Tim _____ wet if he walked in the rain.

a	would get	b	may get
c	will get	d	might get

19) If you _____ a minute, I will come with you.

a	waited	b	wait
c	had waited	d	were waiting

20) If my friends visited me at home, I _____ very happy.

a	can be	b	would have been
c	would be	d	have been

21) If this computer is infected by a virus, you _____ use it.

a	couldn't	b	can't
c	wouldn't	d	would

22) What _____ if you found a lot of money?

a	would you do	b	may you do
c	have you done	d	can you do

23) You will gain a lot of benefits if you _____ for this bank.

a	works	b	worked
c	work	d	had worked

24) If I knew my parents were coming, I _____ them at the airport.

a	welcome	b	will welcome
c	may welcome	d	would welcome

25) If the factory offered Abdul-Rahman the job, he _____ it.

a	took	b	will take
c	may take	d	would take

🌺🌺🌺 *My Homework* 🌺🌺🌺

> ### *Exercise Four*
> ✦ Correct mistake in each of the following sentences.
> ✦ Follow the example.
> ➢ If we cool water, it freeze.
> ✓ ***If* we *cool* water, it *freezes*.**

1) If Salah play well, the trainer won't substitute him.
   🌺_____

2) Unless Tuka come on time, she will miss the first lecture.
   🌺_____

3) If we have enough time, we would visit the Wax Museum.
   🌺_____

4) If Sam guide us, we wouldn't have been lost.
   🌺_____

5) If Nora study hard, she would have got better marks.
   ✍ ___ ___ ___ ___ ___ ___ ___ ___ ___ ___

6) If Jackie lend me her dictionary, I'll be grateful.
   ✍ ___ ___ ___ ___ ___ ___ ___ ___ ___ ___

7) If Marlin apologize, I would forgive her.
   ✍ ___ ___ ___ ___ ___ ___ ___ ___ ___ ___

8) If Dina run quickly, she would have won the race.
   ✍ ___ ___ ___ ___ ___ ___ ___ ___ ___ ___

9) If Ted write the report, the manager would have thanked him.
   ✍ ___ ___ ___ ___ ___ ___ ___ ___ ___ ___

10) Unless you put your money in a safe place, it would have been stolen.
    ✍ ___ ___ ___ ___ ___ ___ ___ ___ ___ ___
    ___ ___ ___ ___ ___ ___ ___ ___ ___ ___

11) Unless the weather be terrible, we will go hunting.
    ✍ ___ ___ ___ ___ ___ ___ ___ ___ ___ ___

12) If I have a two-week vacation, I would have flown to Madrid.
    ✍ ___ ___ ___ ___ ___ ___ ___ ___ ___ ___

13) Unless Harry book the tickets, we wouldn't have been able to fly to Toronto.
    ✍ ___ ___ ___ ___ ___ ___ ___ ___ ___ ___
    ___ ___ ___ ___ ___ ___ ___ ___ ___ ___

14) If my father take a nap, he will feel better.
    ✍ ___ ___ ___ ___ ___ ___ ___ ___ ___ ___

15) If the football players train hard, they would have won the championship.
    ✍ ___ ___ ___ ___ ___ ___ ___ ___ ___ ___
    ___ ___ ___ ___ ___ ___ ___ ___ ___ ___

16) Unless Saleh explain the rule, I wouldn't have understood it.
    ✍ ___ ___ ___ ___ ___ ___ ___ ___ ___ ___

17) Unless we study the problem well, we wouldn't have reached a solution.
    ✍ ___ ___ ___ ___ ___ ___ ___ ___ ___ ___

18) Unless you make this mistake, you would have got the full mark.
    ✍ ___ ___ ___ ___ ___ ___ ___ ___ ___ ___

19) If you hadn't fastened the seat belt, you hit the windshield.
    ✍ ___ ___ ___ ___ ___ ___ ___ ___ ___ ___

20) Unless I review well, I won't be able to answer correctly.
    ✍ ___ ___ ___ ___ ___ ___ ___ ___ ___ ___

✍✍✍ My Homework ✍✍✍

Exercise Five
- Correct mistake in each of the following sentences.
1) Unless I be exhausted, I would have helped you.
   _____
2) If Keith be tired, he wouldn't have stopped working.
   _____
3) Unless I had studied hard, I know the answer.
   _____
4) If I be your teacher, I would teach you perfectly.
   _____
5) If I have enough money, I lend you some.
   _____
6) If I had brought my camera, I take some lovely pictures.
   _____
7) The teacher be angry if you forgot your home assignment.
   _____
8) If the students had been given significant advice, they make such silly mistakes.
   _____
9) We get affluent harvest if we had used modern farming methods.
   _____
10) The morning lecture cancel tomorrow if the professor is absent.
    _____

❀❀❀ My Homework ❀❀❀

Exercise Six
- Correct mistake in each of the following sentences.
1) I attend your wedding ceremony if you had invited me.
   _____
2) If Michael win the car rally, he will get a lot of prizes.
   _____
3) If Neil eat so much junk food, he would have suffered from stomach troubles.
   _____
   _____
4) Unless it stop raining, we won't go sightseeing.
   _____
5) If they lose the final game, they would have been blamed.
   _____

6) Diana be for class if her school bus doesn't come on time.
   ✎_____

7) If I be you, I would agree on his suggestion.
   ✎_____

8) If my teacher praise my work, I will be pleased.
   ✎_____

9) If the accident take place at night, we wouldn't have been able to rescue the injured.
   ✎_____
   _____

10) If Carter follow the law, he wouldn't have been arrested.
    ✎_____

🙢🙢🙢 *My Homework* 🙠🙠🙠

➢ **Exercise Seven**
  ✚ Rearrange the given words to form correct sentences.
  ➢ / come / teacher / angry / time / be / The / if / won't / you / on /
  ✓ The teacher won't be angry if you come on time.

1) / weather / nice / If / a / walk / will / have / we / is / the /
   ✎_____

2) / time / swimming / will / Karl / go / has / enough / If / he /
   ✎_____

3) / store / disk / have / can't / You / you / extra / space / any / additional / data / unless
   ✎_____
   _____

4) / if / had / vacation / you / you / Where / go / would / a /
   ✎_____

5) / you / If / would / I / change / career / were / my /
   ✎_____

6) / saved / money/ Dan / he / travel / Madrid / If / a lot of / would / to /
   ✎_____

7) / had / her/ have / the / Unless / best / she / done / Sarah / failed / would / test /
   ✎_____
   _____

8) / home / if / had / have / early / they / caught / parents / the / would / been / now / My / by / bus /

9) / marriage / were / you/ I / his / I / would / accept / proposal / for / If /

10) / a / the / package / gets / will / job / she / Tuka / salary / generous / take / if /

🌸🌸🌸 My Homework 🌸🌸🌸

➢ **Exercise Eight**
✦ Rearrange the given words to form correct sentences.
1) / next / I/ results / I / call / once / will / you / If / get / week / exam / the / at /

2) / parents / concerned / return / late / Your / if / will / you / home / be /

3) / don't / train / won't / the / I / I / morning / If / catch / hurry /

4) / bad / is/ will / weather / on / Unless / the / we / go / beach / Saturday / to / the / very /

5) / gangsters / had/ the / the / called / I / I / If / would / seen / have / police /

6) / succeeded / would/ Unless / you / you / your / done / had / have / not / best /

7) / have / lost / number / you / I / your / telephone / called / If / hadn't / I / would /

8) / Saleh / exercises / thirty / day / would / his / for / better / If / health / be / minutes / a /

9) / listened / advice/ sick / would / become/ my / not / If / have / had / to / doctor's / I / I /

   ✎ ____ ____ ____ ____ ____ ____ ____ ____ ____ ____
   ____ ____ ____ ____ ____ ____ ____ ____ ____

10) / waves / been/ the / would / have/ sunk / not / high / had / Unless / the / ship / very /

   ✎ ____ ____ ____ ____ ____ ____ ____ ____ ____ ____
   ____ ____ ____ ____ ____ ____ ____ ____ ____

≽≽≽ *My Homework* ≼≼≼

> ## Exercise Nine
> ✢ Rewrite these sentences using 'If'. Follow the example.
> ➢ We will go hiking tomorrow.
> ➢ We will enjoy our time.
> ✓ **If** we **go** hiking tomorrow, we **will enjoy** our time.

1) We will go to Aswan next winter.
➢ We will visit the Island of the Plants.
   ✎ ____ ____ ____ ____ ____ ____ ____ ____ ____ ____

2) Mr. Lee will start a new business.
➢ He will earn a lot of money.
   ✎ ____ ____ ____ ____ ____ ____ ____ ____ ____ ____

3) Noah will get ready for the final exam.
➢ He will achieve a high score.
   ✎ ____ ____ ____ ____ ____ ____ ____ ____ ____ ____

4) The next course will start in June.
➢ Mark will join it.
   ✎ ____ ____ ____ ____ ____ ____ ____ ____ ____ ____

5) My parents will travel to Dubai.
➢ They will stay in a five-star hotel.
   ✎ ____ ____ ____ ____ ____ ____ ____ ____ ____ ____

6) The meeting will be at seven thirty.
➢ We won't be able to watch the match.
   ✎ ____ ____ ____ ____ ____ ____ ____ ____ ____ ____

7) Leila will go shopping.
➢ She will buy a lot of dresses.
   ✎ ____ ____ ____ ____ ____ ____ ____ ____ ____ ____

8) Jane will graduate next July.
➢ She will apply for a full-time job.
   ✎ ____ ____ ____ ____ ____ ____ ____ ____ ____ ____

9) Mary and her family will go to the zoo.
> They will see a lot of animals and birds there.
🖋 _____

10) Greg will treat his mother kindly.
> She won't be angry.
🖋 _____

My Homework

> *Exercise Ten*
    ✚ Rewrite these sentences using (If). Follow the example.
    > Peter doesn't have to walk to his office because he has a car.
    ✓ If Peter **didn't have** a car, he **would walk** to his office.

1) Edward isn't ready for the test because he doesn't attend classes.
🖋 _____

2) Ann doesn't meet tourists because she doesn't speak foreign languages.
🖋 _____

3) Alice doesn't work in a bank because he is poor at figures.
🖋 _____

4) Salama doesn't answer well because he doesn't study.
🖋 _____

5) My parents are disappointed because I often neglect my homework.
🖋 _____

6) Paul scores many goals because he trains hard.
🖋 _____

7) Our teacher doesn't give ample time to practise speaking in class, so our communications skills are weak.
🖋 _____

8) Keith arrives late because he doesn't hurry up.
🖋 _____

9) I can't help you because I don't have time.
🖋 _____

10) Cats can't fly because they don't have wings.
🖋 _____

11) I can't help you because I am not a doctor.
🖋 _____

12) Alex is not fit because he doesn't exercise regularly.
🖋 _____

13) Amy can't buy this dress because she doesn't have enough money.
🖋 _____

14) Blake can't take pictures because he doesn't have a camera.
🖎____ ____ ____ ____ ____ ____ ____ ____ ____

15) Austin takes this medicine because he has a headache.
🖎____ ____ ____ ____ ____ ____ ____ ____ ____

16) Alison doesn't go out for a walk because he has a lot of work.
🖎____ ____ ____ ____ ____ ____ ____ ____ ____

17) Charles doesn't get up early because he goes to bed late.
🖎____ ____ ____ ____ ____ ____ ____ ____ ____

18) Salem feels better because he takes his medicines on time.
🖎____ ____ ____ ____ ____ ____ ____ ____ ____

19) Sue doesn't invite her aunts for lunch because she attends a night class.
🖎____ ____ ____ ____ ____ ____ ____ ____ ____

20) Dane was jailed because he committed a severe crime.
🖎____ ____ ____ ____ ____ ____ ____ ____ ____

🙢🙢🙢 My Homework 🙠🙠🙠

➢ *Exercise Eleven*

✚ Rewrite these sentences using (If). Follow the example.

➢ Brian had an accident because he drove recklessly.

✓ **If** Brian **hadn't driven** recklessly, he **would not have had** an accident.

1) Morgan didn't leave early because he had a lot of work to do.
🖎____ ____ ____ ____ ____ ____ ____ ____ ____

2) I was late for my flight because there was a traffic jam.
🖎____ ____ ____ ____ ____ ____ ____ ____ ____

3) The robbers didn't attack the bank because the policemen were alert.
🖎____ ____ ____ ____ ____ ____ ____ ____ ____

4) I didn't understand her words because she spoke in a very low voice.
🖎____ ____ ____ ____ ____ ____ ____ ____ ____

5) Mark didn't drive to work because his car broke down.
🖎____ ____ ____ ____ ____ ____ ____ ____ ____

6) My sister won the race because she trained very hard.
🖎____ ____ ____ ____ ____ ____ ____ ____ ____

7) The boxer won the final round because he played well.
🖎____ ____ ____ ____ ____ ____ ____ ____ ____

8) We didn't go on driving because it rained heavily.
🖎____ ____ ____ ____ ____ ____ ____ ____ ____

9) I took a taxi because my car got punctured.
🖎____ ____ ____ ____ ____ ____ ____ ____ ____

10) Fagin was angry because Oliver didn't carry out his orders.
🖎____ ____ ____ ____ ____ ____ ____ ____ ____

11) Oliver got depressed because Fagin treated him unkindly.
✎ _____ _____ _____ _____ _____ _____ _____ _____

12) We didn't go diving because the waves were very high.
✎ _____ _____ _____ _____ _____ _____ _____ _____

13) Ibrahim didn't buy a new car because he lost his money.
✎ _____ _____ _____ _____ _____ _____ _____ _____

14) Olivia felt excited because she passed the final test.
✎ _____ _____ _____ _____ _____ _____ _____ _____

15) Ava didn't go on holiday because she was ill.
✎ _____ _____ _____ _____ _____ _____ _____ _____

16) Sheryl was in trouble because she was careless.
✎ _____ _____ _____ _____ _____ _____ _____ _____

17) Scott lost his way because he didn't follow the instructions.
✎ _____ _____ _____ _____ _____ _____ _____ _____

18) Tammy's mobile phone was broken because she wasn't careful.
✎ _____ _____ _____ _____ _____ _____ _____ _____

19) Roy wasn't taken to hospital because he wasn't seriously injured.
✎ _____ _____ _____ _____ _____ _____ _____ _____

20) Suzy didn't feel better because she didn't take her medicine on time.
✎ _____ _____ _____ _____ _____ _____ _____ _____

❧❧❧ My Homework ❧❧

> ### *Exercise Twelve*
  ✤ Rewrite these sentences using (Unless).
  ✤ Follow the example.

1) We won't buy any goods today if they aren't cheaper than yesterday.
   ✎ _____ _____ _____ _____ _____ _____ _____ _____

2) My brothers would have started a business investment if they hadn't lost their money in the stock market.
   ✎ _____ _____ _____ _____ _____ _____ _____ _____

3) If you don't invite Adam to the party, he will be upset.
   ✎ _____ _____ _____ _____ _____ _____ _____ _____

4) You won't win the game if you don't train regularly.
   ✎ _____ _____ _____ _____ _____ _____ _____ _____

5) If Sondos doesn't wear a coat, she will feel cold.
   ✎ _____ _____ _____ _____ _____ _____ _____ _____

6) Your father will be angry if you don't pass the test.
   ✎ _____ _____ _____ _____ _____ _____ _____ _____

7) Mary will get fat if she doesn't stop eating.
   _____

8) If you don't leave now, you will miss the train.
   _____

9) I won't get the job if I don't accept the terms of the contract.
   _____

10) If you don't do your best, you won't achieve your goals.
    _____

11) Sophia won't be late if she hurries up.
    _____

12) The children will hurt themselves if they aren't careful.
    _____

13) Taylor will not cash the check if she doesn't go to the bank.
    _____

14) The plants won't grow well if you don't water them regularly.
    _____

15) The president will be blamed if he doesn't find solutions to the environmental problems.
    _____

16) My mother will be angry if I don't make my bed.
    _____

17) Nolan won't come to the meeting if he is busy.
    _____

18) My grandfather will feel tired if he doesn't sleep well.
    _____

19) My grandmother will be nervous if we don't clean the house.
    _____

20) The teacher will be annoyed if we don't come to class on time.
    _____

My Homework

> ## Exercise Thirteen
> - Rewrite these sentences using (Unless).
> - Follow the example.
> - You **would do** your work **if** you **didn't waste** your time.
> ✓ You would do your work well unless you wasted your time.

1) If Omar wasn't stuck in traffic, he would catch his flight.
   _____

2) The teacher would blame us if we didn't do the exercises correctly.
   _____

3) The wheat wouldn't grow well if you didn't irrigate it.
   ✎_____

4) If you didn't go to the stadium, you wouldn't meet the players.
   ✎_____

5) The conference would be cancelled if the ministers didn't come.
   ✎_____

6) You wouldn't understand the lesson if you missed your class.
   ✎_____

7) We would miss the school excursion if you didn't get up early.
   ✎_____

8) The doctor wouldn't help you if you didn't pay him.
   ✎_____

9) If you didn't fix the laptop, you wouldn't log on the Internet.
   ✎_____

10) If Jack didn't forget the appointment, he would be there on time.
    ✎_____

11) Phillip wouldn't sail round the world if he didn't have enough money.
    ✎_____

12) If you didn't correct your mistakes, you would lose the game.
    ✎_____

13) If Robert and I didn't come to the meeting, the boss would be angry.
    ✎_____

14) If the driver didn't buckle up, he would be in danger.
    ✎_____

15) If you didn't show him the way, he would be lost.
    ✎_____

16) The robbers wouldn't be arrested if the policemen didn't chase them.
    ✎_____

17) These machines wouldn't live longer if you didn't maintain them regularly.
    ✎_____

18) The car battery would die if you didn't charge it well.
    ✎_____

19) The conference would be postponed if the invitees didn't come on time.
    ✎_____

20) The plane wouldn't take off if the wings weren't fixed.
    ✎_____

❦❦❦ My Homework ❧❧❧

Exercise Fourteen

- Rewrite these sentences using (Unless).
- Follow the example.
  - The boxer wouldn't have won if he hadn't deceived his rival.
  - ✓ The boxer **wouldn't have won unless he had deceived** his rival.

1) The baby wouldn't have cried if his mother hadn't left him alone.

2) We would have completed our trip if it hadn't rained heavily.

3) They wouldn't have gone fishing if the waves had been high.

4) Helen wouldn't have been promoted if she hadn't exerted strenuous efforts.

5) The bank wouldn't have been robbed if the guards had been watchful.

6) We would have left the cinema if the movie hadn't been interesting.

7) The driver would have hit the tree if it hadn't been attentive.

8) The players would have lost the game if they hadn't followed their trainer's plan.

9) The policeman would have shot the robbers if they hadn't surrendered.

10) I would have married Kathy if her parents hadn't opposed.

11) If the two students hadn't insulted each other, the school principal wouldn't have punished them.

12) If Leila hadn't gone to the United States, she wouldn't have met her husband.

13) If the teacher hadn't felt so tired this morning, he wouldn't have postponed the lecture.
✎ _____ _____ _____ _____ _____ _____ _____ _____ _____ _____
_____ _____ _____ _____ _____ _____ _____ _____ _____

14) I wouldn't have been able to buy this car if you hadn't lent me that money.
✎ _____ _____ _____ _____ _____ _____ _____ _____ _____ _____

15) If she hadn't remembered my birthday, I would have been upset.
✎ _____ _____ _____ _____ _____ _____ _____ _____ _____ _____

16) If Neil hadn't attended the concert, he wouldn't have met his friends there.
✎ _____ _____ _____ _____ _____ _____ _____ _____ _____ _____
_____ _____ _____ _____ _____ _____ _____ _____ _____

17) If the weather hadn't been worse, Fadi would have spent his vacation in Lebanon.
✎ _____ _____ _____ _____ _____ _____ _____ _____ _____ _____
_____ _____ _____ _____ _____ _____ _____ _____ _____

18) If you hadn't told me about the concert, I wouldn't have gone.
✎ _____ _____ _____ _____ _____ _____ _____ _____ _____ _____

19) Pam wouldn't have got a good mark in the test if she hadn't learned the new words.
✎ _____ _____ _____ _____ _____ _____ _____ _____ _____ _____
_____ _____ _____ _____ _____ _____ _____ _____ _____

20) You don't have to call me if you don't have a problem.
✎ _____ _____ _____ _____ _____ _____ _____ _____ _____ _____
_____ _____ _____ _____ _____ _____ _____ _____ _____ .

21) Kim doesn't watch TV if there isn't a football game.
✎ _____ _____ _____ _____ _____ _____ _____ _____ _____ _____
_____ _____ _____ _____ _____ _____ _____ _____ _____

22) If William doesn't apologize to his teacher, she won't accept him in her class.
✎ _____ _____ _____ _____ _____ _____ _____ _____ _____ _____
_____ _____ _____ _____ _____ _____ _____ _____ _____

23) Our plan won't succeed if we don't work together.
✎ _____ _____ _____ _____ _____ _____ _____ _____ _____

24) Adam can't start his new project if he doesn't get enough fund.
✎ _____ _____ _____ _____ _____ _____ _____ _____ _____

25) Your car engine will break down if you don't change its oil.
✎ _____ _____ _____ _____ _____ _____ _____ _____ _____

✿✿✿ My Homework ✿✿✿

SECTION 20 — **Wish Clauses**

Expressing wishes about the present and the future

We use the simple past to express a wish in the *present* or the *future*.

Subject	wish / wishes	Simple Tense
		could + inf.
		were

✦ **Examples:**
✦ I **wish** I **had** a lot of money.
✦ I **wish** I **could answer** all the questions in this test.
✓ I **wish** I **were** on the beach.

Expressing regrets about the past

We use the **past perfect** to express a regret about a **past** situation.

Subject	wish / wishes	Past Perfect

✦ **Examples:**
✦ I **wish** my team **had won** yesterday's match.
✦ Andy **wishes** her parents **had visited** her last week.

Expressing Complaints

We use **would + infinitive** to express a complaint.

I	wish	Subject	would	infinitive

✦ **Example:**
✦ I **wish** you would arrive on time every day.

Exercise One

- Use the given information to complete the sentences.
- Follow the example.
- I have a terrible backache.
- ✓ I wish I didn't have a terrible backache.

1) I don't speak Japanese.
   _____

2) I can't fly a plane.
   _____

3) Sally doesn't have a digital camera.
   _____

4) Daniel lives alone.
   _____

5) It isn't Monday.
   _____

6) My parents aren't here.
   _____

7) Mary has a lot of problems at work.
   _____

8) Lara doesn't work in an international company.
   _____

9) Marlin isn't a dentist.
   _____

10) I am not on the farm.
    _____

11) I didn't go Chicago last summer.
    _____

12) I didn't attend the annual meeting of the firm.
    _____

13) Jack didn't finish the project on time.
    _____

14) Layan didn't earn a lot of money last year.
    _____

15) I had a lot of family troubles.
    _____

16) I didn't read this interesting book.
    _____

17) Helen didn't come to the party.
    _____

18) Elisa arrived late.
    _____

19) The train didn't reach its destination on time.
✎ ____ ____ ____ ____ ____ ____ ____ ____ ____

20) The final match was boring.
✎ ____ ____ ____ ____ ____ ____ ____ ____ ____

✿✿✿ My Homework ✿✿✿

> ### *Exercise Two*
➕ Choose the correct answer from a, b, c, or d.

1) I wish I _____ a police officer.

a	am	b	have been
c	was	d	were

2) William wishes he _____ a modern car.

a	owns	b	had owned
c	has owned	d	owned

3) I wish I _____ all my money on gambling last night.

a	didn't spend	b	haven't spent
c	wasn't spending	d	hadn't spent

4) Ronald wishes he _____ a pilot.

a	was	b	is
c	were	d	have been

5) I wish I _____ low marks in yesterday's quiz.

a	did get	b	hadn't got
c	haven't got	d	wasn't getting

6) Sandra wishes she _____ married ten years ago.

a	has got	b	got
c	gets	d	had got

7) I wish I _____ drive a truck.

a	can	b	am able to
c	may	d	could

8) Edwin wishes he _____ the driving test.

a	did	b	does
c	doing	d	do

9) My parents wish they _____ in the country.

a	live	b	are living
c	have lived	d	lived

10) The driver wishes that he _____ his seat belt before the accident.

a	fasten	b	had fastened
c	has fastened	d	fastens

11) I wish it _____ last night.

a	didn't snow	b	hasn't snowed
c	wasn't snowing	d	hadn't snowed

12) My feet hurt me a lot. I wish I _____ a lot yesterday.

a	didn't walk	b	haven't walked
c	hadn't walked	d	wasn't walking

13) I feel pain in my eyes. I wish I _____ late last night.

a	hadn't stayed up	b	hasn't stayed up
c	didn't stay up	d	wasn't staying up

14) My parents are angry. They wish I _____ that expensive car.

a	hasn't bought	b	hadn't bought
c	didn't buy	d	wasn't buying

15) I wish you _____ my opinion concerning this matter.

a	understand	b	understood
c	are understanding	d	have understood

16) I wish I _____ my old car and buy a new one.

a	can sell	b	will sell
c	may sell	d	could sell

17) I wish I _____ a speaking course in the British Council.

a	had	b	have had
c	am having	d	to have

18) I wish I _____ my room last night.

a	cleaned	b	had cleaned
c	have cleaned	d	was leaned

19) I wish we _____ go swimming today.

a	will	b	should
c	could	d	may

20) I wish you _____ speak to your parents like that.

a	won't	b	can't
c	should	d	wouldn't

21) I miss my brothers and sisters. I wish they _____ here now.

a	am	b	was
c	were	d	have been

22) I wish you _____ so well-mannered to your fiancée. She's a really lovely girl.

a	am	b	was
c	were	d	have been

23) I wish I _____ more time for a vacation in Hawaii.

a	have	b	have had
c	had	d	having

24) I wish I _____ him all my secrets. Everyone knows them now.

a	hadn't told	b	had told
c	haven't told	d	don't tell

25) I wish I _____ that car. Its spare parts are very expensive

a	haven't bought	b	don't buy
c	can't buy	d	hadn't bought

My Homework

Exercise Three

- Add comments to the following sentences using I wish.
- Follow the example.
- You don't have a modern car.
- ✓ I wish I had a modern car.

1) You don't speak Japanese.
   ✎ _____

2) You can't do your home assignment alone.
   ✎ _____

3) You have eaten a lot of junk food and now feel stomach troubles.
   ✎ _____

4) You forgot to buy some food stuff for your family.
   ✎ _____

5) You don't have enough money to make a tour around Europe.
   ✎ _____

6) You live in a small apartment.
   ✎ _____

7) Your computer skills are very weak.
   ✎ _____

8) Your classmate is a very lazy student.
   ✎ _____

9) You didn't pass your final test.
   ✎ _____

10) You didn't catch your flight to Hamburg.
    ✎ _____

My Homework

SECTION 21 — Connecting Ideas

1- Coordinating Conjunctions

And – But – Yet – So – Or – Nor – For

Either...or... / Neither...nor...

1. And

AND is used to connect words or parts of sentences.
It shows additional information.

AND is used to connect two subjects doing the same action.

| 1ˢᵗ Subject | and | 2ⁿᵈ Subject | Verb |

+ **Example:**
+ *Mike* work**s** in a bank.
+ *Mathew* work**s** in a bank.
✓ *Mike* **and** *Mathew* work in a bank.

AND is used to connect two verbs done by the same subject.

| Subject | 1st Verb | and | 2nd Verb |

+ **Example:**
+ Jane *peeled* the orange.
+ She *ate* it.
✓ Jane *peeled* the orange **and** *ate* it.

AND is used to connect two objects of the same verb.

| Subject | Verb | 1ˢᵗ Object | and | 2ⁿᵈ Object |

✤ Example:
- Keith bought *a digital camera*.
- Keith bought *a mobile phone*.
- ✓ Keith bought *a digital camera* **and** *a mobile phone*.

AND is used to connect two adjectives that describe the same noun.

| Subject | Verb | 1st Adjective | and | 2nd Adjective |

✤ Example:
- Alice's car is **modern**.
- Alice's car is **powerful**.
- ✓ Alice's car is modern **and** powerful.

AND is used to connect two adverbs that describe the same verb.

| Subject | Verb | 1ˢᵗ Adverb | and | 2ⁿᵈ Adverb |

✤ Example:
- Ahmad speaks English **perfectly**.
- Ahmad speaks English **fluently**.
- ✓ Ahmad speaks English perfectly **and** fluently.

My Homework

2. Both . . . and

BOTH . . . AND is used to emphasize that something is true of two people, things, situations, etc.

BOTH . . . AND means 'this and that'.

| Both | 1st Subject | and | 2nd Subject | Verb |

- **Example:**
- *Jeannette* lives in Cordova.
- *Sally* lives in Cordova.
- ✓ **Both** Jeannette **and** Sally live in Cordova.

| 1st Subject | and | 2nd Subject | both | Verb |

- **Example:**
- Ali is in the computer lab.
- Mazin is in the computer lab.
- ✓ Ali and Mazin are both in the computer lab.

| Both | Verb |

- **Examples:**
- My brothers didn't go to school yesterday. Both were ill.
- The two boxers couldn't complete the final round. Both got exhausted.

| Subject | Verb | both | 1st Object | And | 2nd Object |

- **Example:**
- Clark studied physics in high school.
- Clark studied chemistry in high school.
- ✓ Clark studied **_both_** physics **_and_** chemistry in high school.

My Homework

3. But

BUT is used for introducing an idea that contrasts with or is different from what has just been said.

| Subject | Verb | , but | Subject | Verb |

+ **Examples:**
+ Emily has a new dress.
+ Lilly doesn't have a new dress.
✓ Emily has a new dress, **but** Lilly doesn't.

+ The test was difficult.
+ Jane could answer it.
✓ The test was difficult, **but** Jane could answer it.

3. Yet

YET is less common in spoken English. It is used to introduce a statement that is surprising.

| Subject | Verb | , yet | Subject | Verb |

+ **Example:**
+ This man doesn't speak English.
+ He seems to understand what we say.
+ This man doesn't speak English, **yet** he seems to understand what we say.

5. Or

OR is used to introduce another possibility.

✤ **Examples:**
- Is it a man?
- Is it a woman?
- ✓ Is it a man or a woman?
- That man may be Canadian.
- That man may be British.
- That man may be American.
- ✓ That man may be Canadian, British, or American.

OR is used in negative sentences when we mention two or more things.

✤ **Examples:**
- Jane can't dive.
- Jane can't swim.
- ✓ Jane can't or swim.

❧❧❧ *My Homework* ❦❦❦

6. Nor

NOR joins two negative sentences.

✤ **Example:**
- The streets are not narrow.
- The streets are not overcrowded.
- ✓ The streets are not narrow, *nor* are they overcrowded.

❧❧❧ *My Homework* ❦❦❦

7. For

FOR is used to introduce the reason for something mentioned in the previous statement.

✤ **Example:**
- We paid attention to our teacher.
- He was explaining new rules.
- ✓ We paid attention to our teacher for he was explaining new rules.

❧❧❧ *My Homework* ❦❦❦

8. So

SO is used to give the meaning of "as a result" or "therefore".

Reason	, so	Result

Subject	Verb	, so	Subject	Verb

Examples:
- The players trained very hard.
- The players won the match easily.
- ✓ The players *trained* very hard, *so* they *won* the match easily.

- The school is trying to implement modern teaching methods.
- The school is giving its teachers a lot of training.
- ✓ The school *is trying* to implement modern teaching methods, *so* it *is giving* its teachers a lot of training.

My Homework

9. Either...or

EITHER...OR is used to mean the first one or the second one.

Either	1st Subject	or	2nd Subject	Verb

Example:
- Either Mr Sherif or Mr Mustafa will represent the company.

Either	1st Subject	or	2nd Subject	Singular Verb

Example:
- Either Sarah or Jasmine does this task.

Either	1st Subject	1st verb	or	2nd Subject	2nd verb

Example:
- Either you submit your homework or you'll be marked absent.

Subject	Either	1st verb	or	2nd verb

Example:
> Tim either fixes the machine himself or sends another technician to fix it.

| Subject | Verb | 1st Object | or | 2nd Object |

Example:
> I am going to order either apple juice or ice cream.

10. Neither . . . nor

NEITHER . . . NOR is used to mean not the first one and not the second one.

| Neither | 1st Subject | nor | 2nd Subject | Verb |

Examples:
> Mr Sherif will not represent the company.
> Mr Mustafa will not represent the company
> ✓ **Neither** Mr Sherif **nor** Mr Mustafa will represent the company.

| Neither | 1st Subject | nor | 2nd Subject | Singular Verb |

Example:
> Kevin doesn't smoke.
> Albert doesn't smoke.
> ✓ **Neither** Kevin **nor** Albert **smokes**.

| Subject | Neither | 1st verb | nor | 2nd verb |

Example:
> Alan doesn't neglect his work.
> Alan doesn't make mistakes.
> ✓ Alan neither neglects his work nor makes mistakes.

| Subject | verb | Neither | 1st Object | 2nd Object |

Example:
> Jessie doesn't study German. Jessie doesn't study Chinese.
> ✓ Jessie studies neither German nor Chinese.

Exercise One
Choose the correct answer from a, b, c, or d.

1) Our teacher entered the classroom _____ started the new lesson.

a	but	b	or
c	and	d	so

2) My sister wanted to buy some dresses, _____ she went downtown.

a	for	b	so
c	yet	d	or

3) This month, my parents have been to Cairo _____ Madrid.

a	but	b	nor
c	so	d	and

4) I can speak French, _____ my brother can't.

a	but	b	or
c	and	d	so

5) My father read the contract _____ agreed to sign it.

a	but	b	or
c	and	d	so

6) We wanted to go swimming, _____ Mark refused.

a	and	b	so
c	or	d	but

7) Mary went to the meeting _____ explained her marketing plan.

a	and	b	so
c	or	d	but

8) Abdou can ride a horse, _____ Jack can't.

a	so	b	but
c	nor	d	and

9) Lara wants to achieve good results, _____ she works day and night.

a	for	b	but
c	and	d	so

10) Wearing seat belts is important _____ they save your life.

a	but	b	for
c	or	d	nor

11) Shall we have a swim _____ play computer games?

a	for	b	but
c	nor	d	or

12) It was stormy, _____ the pilot refused to take off.

a	yet	b	but
c	or	d	so

13) Jane had an accident, _____ she is in hospital.

a	for	b	but
c	or	d	so

14) We will have lunch now _____ then we will go to the farm.

a	or	b	nor
c	but	d	and

15) You can take the blue pants _____ the black ones.

a	or	b	but
c	nor	d	so

16) Shall we watch a movie _____ go rowing?

a	but	b	or
c	for	d	nor

17) The boss arrived late, _____ we couldn't hold the meeting.

a	but	b	for
c	so	d	nor

18) The mechanic stopped working _____ he got exhausted.

a	but	b	for
c	or	d	nor

19) We didn't follow the map, _____ we got lost.

a	but	b	so
c	or	d	nor

20) Adam can't dive, _____ can he swim.

a	or	b	nor
c	but	d	for

My Homework

> ## Exercise Two
> ✦ Choose the correct answer from a, b, c, or d.

1) My laptop doesn't work properly, _____ I am taking it to the repair shop.

a	but	b	for
c	so	d	nor

2) Nabila didn't solve the problem, _____ did she ask for help.

a	or	b	and
c	nor	d	but

3) Abdou solved the math problem correctly, _____ the teacher rewarded him.

a	so	b	for
c	but	d	nor

4) I tried to fix the car myself, _____ I couldn't.

a	but	b	for
c	or	d	and

5) You can travel to the city by bus _____ by train?

a	but	b	for
c	or	d	nor

6) This book is interesting, _____ I am going to read it once more.

a	so	b	for
c	or	d	nor

7) The play was boring, _____ we left the theatre.

a	so	b	and
c	nor	d	for

8) We can't go on working _____ it is severely cold.

a	so	b	for
c	or	d	nor

9) The baby was hungry, _____ he cried a lot.

a	so	b	because
c	or	d	nor

10) I left my wallet at home, _____ I borrowed some money from my dad.

a	but	b	nor
c	so	d	or

11) I don't like boxing _____ wrestling.

a	or	b	for
c	but	d	nor

12) We were thirsty, _____ we drank a lot of water.

a	for	b	or
c	but	d	so

13) I bought a pen, a pencil _____ an eraser.

a	for	b	so
c	yet	d	and

14) Sarah hasn't got any money, _____ she can't go shopping.

a	so	b	for
c	but	d	yet

15) The boys got extremely wet, _____ they didn't have umbrellas.

a	for	b	and
c	yet	d	so

16) We can go fishing, _____ we can have a walk.

a	or	b	but
c	so	d	for

17) I don't eat fish, _____ beef.

a	for	b	and
c	or	d	yet

18) My mother works many hours, _____ she is always tired.

a	or	b	but
c	so	d	for

19) This shop sells cell phones, digital cameras, _____ many other smart devices.

a	and	b	or
c	yet	d	so

20) Lilly doesn't like fish _____ grilled meat.

a	nor	b	so
c	or	d	yet

➤ Exercise Three
✦ Choose the correct answer from a, b, c, or d.

1) My grandfather's pickup truck is very old, _____ it is reliable.

a	yet	b	and
c	because	d	for

2) The players didn't play well, _____ they were defeated.

a	but	b	for
c	yet	d	so

3) Davis likes boating, _____ he doesn't like scuba diving.

a	so	b	and
c	or	d	but

4) I rarely log on the Internet, _____ so does my sister.

a	or	b	and
c	so	d	nor

5) The manager held a meeting with his staff _____ then he reviewed some important reports.

a	but	b	nor
c	and	d	or

6) Saleh can't speak Japanese _____ can he speak Chinese.

a	nor	b	but
c	or	d	for

7) Abdul-Rahman is smart _____ active.

a	but	b	so
c	and	d	for

8) Alan had a serious car accident, _____ he had to be taken to hospital.

a	for	b	so
c	nor	d	or

9) My camera was broken, _____ I bought another one.

a	or	b	yet
c	so	d	nor

10) My parents gave me a lovely birthday present, _____ I was very happy.

a	so	b	or
c	yet	d	nor

11) _____ Jane nor Alice speaks Arabic.

a	Either	b	Both
c	But	d	Neither

12) Mother: What are you going to study tonight?
✓ Leila: I am going to study _____ history or geography.

a	so	b	either
c	neither	d	both

13) Neither Adam _____ Malik will take part in the final game.

a	or	b	and
c	nor	d	but

14) Our teacher can't find either his dictionary _____ his pens.

a	nor	b	and
c	but	d	or

15) The police set Albert free. He was _____ suspected nor guilty.

a	neither	b	either
c	so	d	both

16) Both my parents _____ my aunts donate a lot of money to charity.

a	nor	b	or
c	so	d	and

17) The new shoes didn't fit me well, _____ I returned them to the shoe shop.

a	but	b	yet
c	so	d	for

18) Someone stole my digital camera, _____ I called the police.

a	but	b	or
c	so	d	nor

19) My sister should take an Arabic course, _____ she doesn't have enough time.

a	but	b	so
c	and	d	nor

20) The plane landed on time _____ all the passengers left it safely.

a	but	b	yet
c	and	d	nor

🌿🌿🌿 My Homework 🌿🌿🌿

> ## Exercise Four

➕ Choose the correct answer from a, b, c, or d.

1) By the end of the season the players were exhausted, _____ excited about winning two championships.

a	but	b	because
c	so	d	for

2) I invited Jason to the party, _____ he apologized.

a	but	b	because
c	so	d	for

3) Peter changed his clothes _____ went to bed.

a	but	b	yet
c	and	d	for

4) My sister won't go swimming, _____ my elder brother might.

a	but	b	or
c	and	d	nor

5) Kim couldn't spell the new word correctly, _____ could Yuhan.

a	but	b	or
c	and	d	nor

6) Gareth: Is Sam taller _____ shorter than you?
   ✓ Harry: He is as tall as me.

a	so	b	or
c	and	d	nor

7) The waves are very high today, _____ the ferry won't be able to sail.

a	but	b	or
c	so	d	nor

8) Both Rehab and Asmaà always _____ their homework on time.

a	but	b	or
c	and	d	nor

9) Taro didn't travel by plane, _____ did Hanson.

a	but	b	neither
c	and	d	nor

10) We didn't expect our team to win the final game, _____ it did.

a	but	b	or
c	and	d	so

11) David used to live in Dublin, _____ now he lives in London.

a	so	b	or
c	and	d	but

12) Jamal doesn't like wrestling, _____ does Osama.

a	but	b	or
c	and	d	nor

13) My grandparents live alone, _____ I visit them regularly.

a	but	b	or
c	so	d	nor

14) Both David and Louis _____ a lot of junk food.

a	eats	b	eat
c	eaten	d	eating

15) Neither George nor Amin _____ tennis well.

a	play	b	are playing
c	playing	d	plays

16) Neither my sister nor her classmates _____ their work.

a	neglects	b	are neglecting
c	neglect	d	to neglect

17) Malik drives safely, but Daniel _____.

a	didn't	b	don't
c	couldn't	d	doesn't

18) Both my sister and my mother _____ online shopping.

a	loving	b	loves
c	love	d	to love

19) Boxing or wrestling. I don't like _____ of them.

a	neither	b	both
c	either	d	not only

20) Martin neglected his lessons. He failed _____ his history test and his geography test.

a	either	b	neither
c	not only	d	both

✎✎✎ My Homework ✎✎✎

> ### Exercise Five

➕ Choose the correct answer from a, b, c, or d.

1) _____ Jane _____ Jessie attended the meeting. They were absent.

a	Both ____ and	b	Neither ____ nor
c	Either ____ or	d	Not only ____ but also

2) It was a serious accident, but _____ the driver _____ the passengers got hurt.

a	both ____ and	b	neither ____ nor
c	either ____ or	d	not only ____ but also

3) Next semester, I will study _____ music _____ art. I have already finished them.

a	both ____ and	b	neither ____ nor
c	either ____ or	d	not only ____ but also

4) We have _____ tea _____ coffee. Please go and buy some.

a	both ____ and	b	neither ____ nor
c	either ____ or	d	not only ____ but also

5) The teacher has only one extra seat in his class. He can add _____ Don _____ Tim to the class list.

a	both ____ and	b	neither ____ nor
c	either ____ or	d	not only ____ but also

6) I can't buy any of these two cars. _____ are very expensive.

a	Both	b	Neither
c	Either	d	Not only

7) _____ you come on time _____ stay out of the class.

a	Both ____ and	b	Neither ____ nor
c	Either ____ or	d	Not only ____ but also

8) Our teacher thanked _____ Mahmoud _____ Lamya for their hard work. They were pleased with his encouraging feedback.

a	both ____ and	b	neither ____ nor
c	either ____ or	d	not only ____ but as well

9) I met _____ Sandy _____ Sarah in the park. We spent nice time together.

a	both ____ and	b	neither ____ nor
c	either ____ or	d	not only ____ but also

10) _____ the USA _____ Saudi Arabia produce a lot of oil.

a	Both _____ with	b	Nether _____ nor
c	Either _____ or	d	Not only _____ but as well

11) Both Carter and David _____ tennis to football.

a	prefers	b	to prefer
c	preferring	d	prefer

12) Neither Mark nor his sister _____ diving.

a	to like	b	likes
c	like	d	liking

13) Neither Sebastian nor his brothers _____ diving.

a	going	b	goes
c	go	d	to go

14) _____ Jasmine _____ her mother is a nurse. They are dentists.

a	Both _____ and	b	Nether _____ nor
c	Either _____ or	d	Not only _____ but also

15) _____ my aunts _____ my uncles are fond of reading English novels. They love French ones.

a	Both _____ and	b	Neither _____ nor
c	Either _____ or	d	Not only _____ but as well

16) Ahmad is _____ polite _____ well-mannered. That's why everyone likes him.

a	both _____ and	b	neither _____ nor
c	either _____ or	d	and _____ neither

17) Salem can't find _____ his smartphone _____ his new camera.

a	both _____ and	b	neither _____ nor
c	either _____ or	d	not only _____ but also

18) All customers can pay for their purchases _____ in cash _____ by credit card. The two options are available.

a	both _____ with	b	neither _____ nor
c	either _____ or	d	not only _____ but as well

19) My parents can _____ rent an apartment _____ stay in five-star hotel. They have two options.

a	both _____ and	b	neither _____ nor
c	either _____ or	d	not only _____ but also

20) My family and I are planning to visit _____ Budapest _____ Istanbul next July. We haven't decided which one yet.

a	both _____ and	b	neither _____ nor
c	either _____ or	d	not only _____ but also

🌺🌺🌺 My Homework 🌺🌺🌺

2- Subordinating Conjunctions

| After | Subject | Present Simple | , | Subject | Imperative |

➕ **Examples:**
- After you finish eating, wash your hands.
- Submit the homework after you finish it.

| After | Subject | Present Simple | , | Subject | Present Simple |

➕ **Examples:**
- After I get up, I take a shower.
- After Alfred arrives at his office, he checks his email.

| After | Subject | Present Simple | , | Subject | Future Simple |

➕ **Examples:**
- After it stops raining, we will have a walk.
- After the mechanic fixes the car, he will check it.

| After | Subject | Past Simple | , | Subject | Past Simple |

➕ **Examples:**
- After I apologized to my teacher, he let me in.
- After my mother finished cooking, she welcomed her guests.

| After | Subject | Past Simple | , | Subject | Past Perfect |

➕ **Examples:**
- After Kim had harvested the wheat, he stored it.
- After I had eaten my lunch, my friends arrived.

Before

| Before | Subject | Present Simple | , | Subject | Imperative (Base form) |

✦ Examples:
- Review the reports before you leave the office.
- Before you buy a new dress, try it on.

| Before | Subject | Present Simple | , | Subject | Present Simple |

✦ Examples:
- Before football players play, they warm up well.
- Before Tom goes to bed, he reads a short story.

| Before | Subject | Present Simple | , | Subject | Future Simple |

✦ Examples:
- Before my sister starts the fall semester, she will have a short leave.
- Before I wear my new shirt, I will iron it.

| Before | Subject | Past Simple | , | Subject | Past Simple |

✦ Examples:
- Before the doctor wrote the prescription, he checked the patient well.
- Before Austin retired, his company rewarded him.

| Past Perfect | Subject | Before | , | Subject | Past Simple |

✦ Examples:
- The police had arrested the thief before he stole the wallet.
- Before the plane took off, the passengers had fastened their safety belts.

🙰🙰🙰 My Homework 🙰🙰🙰

383

Until and Till

UNTIL means up to the point in time or the event mentioned.

TILL and UNTIL have the same meaning.

| Let's | Base form | until | Present Simple |

| Let's | Base form | till | Present Simple |

Example:
➤ Let's wait until the doctor comes.

| Imperative | until | Present Simple |

| Imperative | till | Present Simple |

Examples:
➤ Sit down here until the teacher arrives.
➤ Don't move until the barber finishes.

| Present Simple | until | Present Simple |

| Present Simple | till | Present Simple |

Examples:
➤ We usually run until our bodies sweat.
➤ My father goes on working until he feels exhausted.

| Future Simple | until | Present Simple |

| Future Simple | till | Present Simple |

Examples:
➤ I won't have my lunch until my parents return home.
➤ The plane won't take off until the co-pilot comes.

| Past Simple | until | Past Simple |

| Past Simple | till | Past Simple |

+ Examples:
- Sally didn't leave until she finished her assignment.
- The students continued studying until the bell rang.

| Past Perfect | until | Past Simple |
| Past Perfect | till | Past Simple |

+ Example:
- We hadn't realized Anas was innocent until he defended himself.

| Once | Subject | Present Simple | , | Subject | Imperative |

+ Examples:
- Once you arrive at the office, call me.
- Once you see an accident, don't hesitate to help.

| Once | Subject | Present Simple | , | Subject | Present Simple |

+ Examples:
- Once my colleagues arrive, we have our breakfast together.
- Once the match finishes, all the fans leave the stadium.

| Once | Subject | Present Simple | , | Subject | Future Simple |

+ Example:
- Once I complete the assignment, I will submit it.

| Once | Subject | Past Simple | , | Subject | Past Simple |

Example:
➢ Once I got the money, I started building my new house.

Once	Subject	Past Simple	,	Subject	Past Perfect

Example:
➢ The plumber started fixing the leak once he had been paid.

As soon as

AS SOON AS means **once, when:**

As soon as	Subject	Present Simple	,	Subject	Imperative (Base form)

Examples:
➢ As soon as the water boils, put the raw meat into the pot.
➢ As soon as you find a solution to this problem, tell me.

As soon as	Subject	Present Simple	,	Subject	Present Simple

Examples:
➢ As soon as our supervisor arrives, we start the meeting.
➢ Neil has a shower as soon as he gets home.

As soon as	Subject	Present Simple	,	Subject	Future Simple

Example:
➢ As soon as we reach a decision, we will send you an email.

As soon as	Subject	Past Simple	,	Subject	Past Simple

➕ Example:
- As soon as I received Dan's email, I forwarded it to my manager.

As soon as	Subject	Past Perfect	,	Subject	Past Simple

➕ Examples:
- As soon as the technician had checked the tires, we resumed the trip.
- As soon as my father had come home, my sisters set the table for lunch.

If	Subject	Present Simple	,	Subject	Future Simple

➕ Example:
- If my teacher supports me, I will be very happy.

Unless	Subject	Present Simple	,	Subject	Future Simple

➕ Example
- Unless you apologize to Salma, she won't come to the party.

My Homework

➢ *Exercise Six*

✦ Choose the correct answer from a, b, c, or d.

1) Sam likes to walk along the city park when the sun _____.

a	rise	b	will rise
c	rises	d	risen

2) I _____ my parents my exam results as soon as I go home.

a	had told	b	told
c	should have told	d	will tell

3) I can't leave the test room until the students _____.

a	finished	b	finishes
c	will finish	d	finish

4) When you find a mistake, _____ it yourself.

a	corrects	b	correct
c	will correct	d	corrected

5) Don't visit me until I _____ you.

a	will call	b	calling
c	call	d	called

6) As soon as the Metro left the station, it _____.

a	breaks down	b	break down
c	broken down	d	broke down

7) You won't lose weight until you _____ exercise.

a	will take	b	took
c	take	d	takes

8) As soon as the goalkeeper's arm was broken, the referee _____ the game.

a	stopping	b	stop
c	stopped	d	will stop

9) Tuka will get her diploma when she _____ twenty-four.

a	will turn	b	turn
c	turned	d	turns

10) As soon as Alan gets up in the morning, he _____ his breakfast.

a	eats	b	had eaten
c	eat	d	ate

11) Before my mother _____ to bed, she washed up.

a	goes	b	go
c	went	d	has gone

12) I have to submit my homework before the clock _____ twelve.

a	will strike	b	would strike
c	strikes	d	strike

13) I want to have my breakfast _____ I go to the farm. I'm hungry.

a	before	b	till
c	until	d	during

14) When my daughter _____, I will reward her.

a	will succeed	b	succeeds
c	succeed	d	is going to succeed

15) Passengers always buckle up before the plane _____.

a	will take off	b	is going to take off
c	take off	d	takes off

16) After my father _____, he will do a tour of Spain on foot.

a	is going to retire	b	retires
c	retire	d	retired

17) As soon as the robbers saw the policemen, they _____.

a	run away	b	have run away
c	ran away	d	runs away

18) When the fox _____ the chickens, it chased them.

a	sees	b	see
c	has seen	d	saw

19) I will meet my friends as soon as I _____ this task.

a	will finish	b	finished
c	finishes	d	finish

20) The factory _____ until we get new raw materials.

a	closed down	b	will close down
c	had closed down	d	close down

My Homework

> ### *Exercise Seventeen*

Choose the correct answer from a, b, c, or d.

1) Before Ahmad installed the new software, he _____ his laptop for viruses.

a	will scan	b	scanned
c	is going to scan	d	has scanned

2) Once the sun rises, the farmers _____ the wheat seeds.

a	sows	b	will sow
c	had sown	d	were sowing

3) Once I meet my old teachers, I _____ them deeply for their tremendous efforts.

a	would thank	b	thanks
c	will thank	d	thanked

4) As soon as the plan is finished, we _____ the new project.

a	started	b	starts
c	had started	d	are going to start

5) As soon as I accessed my account, I _____ a lot of emails.

a	find	b	found
c	will find	d	may find

6) My family stayed on the beach until the sun _____.

a	sets	b	will set
c	has set	d	set

7) When I visited Hollywood, I _____ many famous movie stars.

a	see	b	saw
c	sees	d	have seen

8) You _____ the work location until you finish your task.

a	will leave	b	can't leave
c	leave	d	have left

9) After his first book was published, Saleh _____ writing a comic play.

a	will start	b	has started
c	started	d	start

10) As soon as the bus left the town, I _____ asleep.

a	will fall	b	fall
c	falls	d	fell

11) After Batool finished her high school, she _____ a scholarship to study at Oxford.

a	will win	b	wins
c	has won	d	won

12) My kids were hungry. They didn't leave _____ they had their lunch.

a	while	b	as
c	when	d	until

13) When the rain stops, we _____ more apples.

A	picked	b	had picked
C	are going to pick	d	picks

14) After Mr Wail became the factory manager, the profits _____ by 15 per cent.

A	will grow	b	grows
C	grew	d	has grown

15) Jane didn't feel well _____ she had taken her cough medicine. Now, she can breathe normally.

A	after	b	while
C	until	d	as

16) The policeman didn't let me go _____ I showed him my driver's license.

a	until	b	as
c	when	d	by the time

17) By the time the bank manager arrived at his office, he _____ many customers waiting for him.

a	will find	b	found
c	has found	d	finds

18) By the time my wife reached the station, the train _____.

a	is going to leave	b	has left
c	leaves	d	had left

19) When my grandfather got to the farm, he _____ that a lot of hay was submerged with water.

a	will find	b	has found
c	found	d	finds

20) Once you _____ to your office, call me.

a	had come	b	will come
c	came	d	come

🌸🌸🌸 My Homework 🌸🌸🌸

➢ **Exercise Eight**

↓ Choose the correct answer from a, b, c, or d.

1) When Malik saw the tiger, he _____.

a	drove away	b	has driven away
c	drive away	d	drives away

2) Most employees _____ when they reach the age of sixty.

a	retires	b	retire
c	retired	d	had retired

3) The bank clerk asked me to wait until he _____ the data of my bank account.

a	check	b	checked
c	is checking	d	checks

4) As soon as I upgraded the software of my computer, I _____ the company's portal.

a	accesses	b	access
c	am accessing	d	accessed

5) The driver _____ a bus as soon as he made a swerve to the right.

a	hit	b	will hit
c	hits	d	has hit

6) My sister won't take this job until she _____ married.

a	get	b	got
c	gets	d	getting

7) As soon Oliver inherited property worth over three million American dollars, he _____ a large house on the river.

a	will buy	b	bought
c	has bought	d	buys

8) Salman will achieve a lot of progress when he _____ his new college.

a	will join	b	is joining
c	joined	d	joins

9) Pierre left Canada after _____ his diploma in international law.

a	got	b	gets
c	getting	d	had got

10) Sebastian _____ to start his own farming business as soon as he gets a loan from the local bank.

a	will intend	b	is intending
c	intended	d	intends

11) Ahmad developed a new remote control system before he _____.

a	graduated	b	graduates
c	will graduate	d	graduate

12) Nicolas read the article very well before _____ it to the editor of the magazine.

a	giving	b	had given
c	gave	d	gives

13) Ali and his wife decided to visit Luxor after _____ Cordova.

a	leaving	b	left
c	leaves	d	had left

14) Once you fill in the application form, _____ it to the secretary.

a	forwards	b	forwarded
c	will forward	d	forward

15) Mr Mark applied the new teaching methods as soon as he _____ them.

a	learning	b	learnt
c	learns	d	learns

16) When it starts to rain, _____ your own raincoat and open your umbrella.

a	wear	b	wears
c	will wear	d	wore

17) The technician won't fix the machine _____ he is paid. He wants his money first.

a	after	b	as
c	until	d	while

18) The engine _____ until it is lubricated.

a	couldn't work	b	won't work
c	didn't work	d	hadn't worked

19) After _____ his old bike, Boody pumped its tires.

a	oiled	b	could oil
c	oiling	d	had oiled

20) The factory workers refuse to go on working _____ they are paid extra profits.

a	until	b	when
c	as	d	while

My Homework

➢ Exercise Four
✦ Choose the correct answer from a, b, c, or d.

1) The football fans erupted when their team _____ the game.

a	will win	b	wins
c	winning	d	won

2) After _____ the conference room, many TV reporters gathered around the UN Secretary.

a	had left	b	leave
c	leaving	d	left

3) When I checked Jane's car, I _____ a leak in the gas pipe.

a	discovered	b	will discover
c	discovers	d	discover

4) Lara gave a loud scream as soon as she _____ a big spider in the garden.

a	will see	b	sees
c	has seen	d	saw

5) As soon as the criminal was arrested by the police, they _____ him into prison.

a	threw	b	throws
c	will throw	d	have thrown

6) As soon as the new king was crowned, he _____ new taxes.

a	puts	b	will put
c	put	d	has put

7) As soon as Arnold called the police, they _____ at once.

a	came	b	will come
c	have come	d	come

8) When you feel heel pain, _____ your doctor immediately.

a	will consult	b	consulted
c	consult	d	consults

9) As soon as Martin got his salary, he _____ all his debts.

a	pays off	b	pays off
c	has paid off	d	paid off

10) We had a light meal before _____ the journey.

a	starting	b	started
c	starts	d	start

11) As soon as I meet my teacher, I _____ to her.

a	could apologize	b	will apologize
c	had to apologize	d	apologized

12) I won't forgive you until you _____ me the truth.

a	will tell	b	tells
c	told	d	tell

13) I always switch off the light before _____ to bed.

a	go	b	going
c	will go	d	went

393

14) My mother usually advises me to clean up _____ I make a mess.

a	until	b	while
c	after	d	before

15) Before Ann _____ our lunch, she often asks what we would like to eat.

a	will cook	b	cook
c	cooking	d	cooks

16) After _____ a shower, I dry my body.

a	taking	b	will take
c	had taken	d	takes

17) After _____ the new software, Abdul-Rahman restarted his laptop.

a	installed	b	installs
c	installing	d	had installed

18) As soon as Ahmad _____ smoking, his health got better.

a	quits	b	quitting
c	has quit	d	had quit

19) When Tuqa visits England, she _____ to stay in the countryside.

a	prefers	b	preferring
c	preferred	d	had preferred

20) Our teacher of English assigned a different task to each of the students before _____ the classroom.

a	leaves	b	will leave
c	left	d	leaving

🙢🙢🙢 *My Homework* 🙣🙣🙣

> **Exercise Five**

✤ Choose the correct answer from a, b, c, or d.

1) When you meet Lara, _____ her that I want to talk with her.

a	tells	b	told
c	tell	d	will tell

2) _____ the mugger, as soon as you see him.

a	Will arrest	b	Arrest
c	Arrest	d	Arrests

3) Our teacher entered as soon as we _____ for the lesson.

a	get ready	b	have got ready
c	gets ready	d	got ready

4) We _____ a long vacation after we finish the summer semester.

a	will have	b	had had
c	had	d	could have had

5) As soon as the mechanic _____, he checked the oil level.

a	come	b	comes
c	has come	d	came

6) Before you submit your homework, _____ them well.

a	reviews	b	review
c	will review	d	reviewing

7) After _____ my kids to school, I started cleaning their rooms.

a	sent	b	had sent
c	send	d	sending

8) Hesham and Saleh will resume their trip to the mountains as soon as the snow _____.

a	will stop	b	stop
c	stopped	d	stops

9) After my father finished working on the farm, he _____ like a rock.

a	sleep	b	sleeping
c	slept	d	to sleep

10) After _____ his first book, Ahmad retired from teaching.

a	publishes	b	had published
c	published	d	publishing

11) My son came out of the sea after a large fish _____ his knee.

a	scratched	b	scratches
c	scratching	d	scratch

12) The country's exports increased as soon as the government _____ its economic systems.

a	change	b	had changed
c	changes	d	changing

13) After I bought my mother some eggs, she _____ a delicious cake.

a	made	b	makes
c	Make	d	will make

14) I didn't answer any math problem until my teacher _____ the rules for me.

a	simplified	b	simplifying
c	simplifies	d	simplify

15) After _____ the new grammar lesson, our teacher our progress.

a	finished	b	had finished
c	finishes	d	finishing

16) When our aunt visited us, she _____ us a delicious cake.

a	made	b	has made
c	will make	d	makes

17) Mark promised to pay me back after _____ his salary.

a	gets	b	got
c	getting	d	will get

18) He was forced to resign because the company _____ heavy losses.

a	suffered	b	will suffered
c	suffers	d	can suffer

19) The doctors had the opportunity to save the old lady before _____ .

a	died	b	dies
c	dying	d	will die

20) By the time we reached the farm, our grandfather _____ the wheat.

a	had irrigated	b	will irrigate
c	irrigates	d	has irrigated

My Homework

> ### Exercise Six
Choose the correct answer from a, b, c, or d.

1) If Julia doesn't call me, I _____ for her.

a	couldn't wait	b	won't wait
c	didn't wait	d	haven't waited

2) We will be late unless you _____ .

a	had hurried	b	hurries
c	hurried	d	hurry

3) If Watson _____ early, he will arrive at the farm on time.

a	leaves	b	will leave
c	won't leave	d	left

4) Unless we arrive at the airport in an hour, we _____ check in.

a	couldn't	b	can't
c	didn't	d	hadn't

5) _____ you interact with your teacher actually, you won't understand.

a	If	b	When
c	Unless	d	While

6) You won't be able to operate this device unless you _____ its instructions manual.

a	reads	b	was reading
c	had read	d	read

7) You'll be able to recover soon if you _____ these pills on time.

a	will take	b	takes
c	took	d	take

8) The final wrestling round _____ if the Swedish wrestler is seriously injured.

a	has been cancelled	b	will be cancelled
c	will cancel	d	would be cancelled

9) _____ Helen stops drinking, her baby will be born deformed.

a	If	b	While
c	When	d	Unless

10) The bride and the bridegroom won't start their wedding ceremony _____ all their invitees arrive. They are still waiting.

a	unless	b	while
c	if	d	when

11) The woman will calm down when she _____ her kids.

a	will see	b	saw
c	see	d	sees

12) I won't give him the money until he _____ me politely.

a	asks	b	will ask
c	asked	d	ask

13) After I had reviewed the plans, I _____ them.

a	will approve	b	approved
c	approve	d	approves

14) The company's income won't _____ until we exert strenuous efforts.

a	double	b	doubled
c	will double	d	has doubled

15) The thief proved that he was innocent before _____ him.

a	will release	b	released
c	would release	d	releasing

16) Neil usually _____ the Internet before he goes to bed.

a	surfs	b	surf
c	will surf	d	surfed

17) Remember to switch the lights off before you _____.

a	sleeps	b	sleeping
c	sleep	d	slept

18) When we saw the fog, we _____ not to go on driving.

a	decides	b	decided
c	decide	d	have decided

19) My parents will move to a new district as soon they _____.

a	will retire	b	had retired
c	would retire	d	retire

20) Salma _____ her kids from school as soon she finished cooking.

a	brought	b	will bring
c	may bring	d	bring

21) _____ your bed before you leave the room.

a	Will make	b	Makes
c	Make	d	Made

22) If you _____ the subway, you will arrive faster.

a	had taken	b	took
c	takes	d	take

23) As soon as you arrive at the seaport, _____ me.

a	told	b	telling
c	tells	d	tell

24) When I meet my friends, I _____ them to dinner.

a	will invite	b	have invited
c	invited	d	invites

25) My supervisor will be pleased if I _____ this task on time.

a	had finished	b	finishes
c	Finish	d	finished

🙶🙶🙶 My Homework 🙷🙷🙷

CONTRAST

Although

ALTHOUGH is used for introducing a statement that makes the main statement in a sentence seem surprising.

+ **Examples:**
+ The exam was difficult.
+ I could answer it correctly.
✓ **Although** the exam **was** difficult, I **could answer** it correctly.

OR

✓ I **could answer** the exam correctly, **although** it **was** difficult.

+ Leila was tired.
+ She stayed up to watch the late night film on television.

✓ **Although** Leila **was** tired, she **stayed** up to watch the late night film.

OR

✓ Leila **stayed up** to watch the late night film **although** she **was** tired.

ALTHOUGH is used for introducing a statement that modifies the main statement.

+ There **will be** heavy snow in many parts of Canada tonight.
+ It **is** doubtful to reach the southwest until morning.

✓ There **will be** heavy snow in many parts of Canada tonight **although** it is doubtful to reach the southwest until morning.

My Homework

> *THOUGH* is less formal than *ALTHOUGH*. *EVEN* can be used with *THOUGH* for emphasis, but not with *ALTHOUGH*.

✦ Examples:
- Sue didn't want to go to the party. She knew her friends would be there.
- ✓ Sue didn't want to go to the party **although** she knew her friends would be there.

OR

- ✓ Sue didn't want to go to the party **even though** she knew her friends would be there.

> *THOUGH*, but not *ALTHOUGH* can be used at the end of a sentence.

- ✓ Sue knew that all her friends would be there. She didn't want to go, **though**.

My Homework

In spite of = Despite

> *IN SPITE OF* is used to show that something happened or is true although something else might have happened to prevent it.

In spite of	Noun		Subject	Past Simple
	-ing			

OR

Despite	Noun	,	Subject	Past Simple
	-ing			

✦ Examples:
- **In spite of** her excellent **skills,** Sally is still unemployed.
- **In spite of facing** a lot of difficulties in her new job, Monica managed to achieve noticeable success.

However – Nevertheless

However

However is used in order to add an idea or fact that is surprising or seems very different from what you have just said.

Example:

- I explained the issue in detail.
- Ola still didn't understand.
- ✓ I explained the issue in detail. ***However***, Ola still didn't understand.

Nevertheless

Nevertheless (in spite of what has just been mentioned)

Example:
- Paul said he didn't want to take this course.
- He may change his mind.

✓ Paul said he didn't want to take this course. ***Nevertheless***, he may change his mind.

In contrast – On the other hand

In contrast

In contrast is used to introduce different points or ideas, etc., especially when they are opposites.

Example:
- Girls like buying clothes and cosmetics. Boys prefer computer games.
- ✓ Girls like buying clothes and cosmetics. ***In contrast***, boys prefer computer games.

On the other hand

ON THE OTHER HAND is used to introduce different points or ideas, etc., especially when they are opposites.

✦ Example:

✦ Lucy loves reading romantic stories.
✦ Samuel prefers stories about science fiction.

✓ Lucy loves reading romantic stories. **On the other hand,** Samuel prefers stories about science fiction.

My Homework

 **Because** — BECAUSE is used to give reasons.

| Result | because | Reason |

| Subject | Verb | because | Subject | Verb |

✤ Examples:
- The coach was happy.
- His team won the final game.
- ✓ The coach **was** happy **because** his team **won** the final game.

As — AS is used to state the reason for something.

| Result | for | Reason |

| Subject | Verb | for | Subject | Verb |

✤ Examples:
- You may need some help **as** you are new.
- I borrowed some money from my friend **as** I left my wallet at home.

 **For** — FOR means BECAUSE. It is used formally in writing more than speaking.

| Result | for | Reason |

| Subject | Verb | for | Subject | Verb |

✤ Example:
- The ship was lost.
- The sailors didn't follow the navigation systems.
- ✓ The ship was lost **for** the sailors didn't follow the navigation systems.

Therefore – Consequently – As a result – for this (that) reason

Therefore

THEREFORE IS used to mention another person or thing after something else.
We use 'therefore' in order to introduce the logical result of something that has just been mentioned.
'Consequently, as a result, for this reason, and for that reason are used for the same purpose.

Reason		Therefore,	Result	
Subject	Verb.	Therefore,	Subject	Verb

Examples:
- My daughter is only sixteen. **Therefore,** she is not eligible to vote.
- The front tire of my car got punctured. **Therefore,** I had to replace it.

Reason		Consequently,	Result	
Subject	Verb.	Consequently,	Subject	Verb

Examples:
- The runner didn't train hard. **Consequently,** he couldn't win the race.
- Helen had a lot of mistakes in her home assignment. **Consequently,** her teacher asked her to redo it from start.

Reason		as a result,	Result	
Subject	verb	as a result,	Subject	verb

Examples:
- Many children eat junk food. **As a result,** they put on weight.
- These students do their best in class. **As a result,** their teachers are pleased with them.

	Reason	For this (that) reason	Result	
Subject	verb	For this (that) reason	Subject	verb

Examples:
- The boat was too small to accommodate that large number of refugees. **For that reason,** it sank into the sea.

 My Homework

3- Linking words across sentences

In addition – Furthermore – Besides – Moreover

They all have the same meaning.

In addition

IN ADDITION is used to mention another person or thing after something else.

Subject	Verb.	In addition,	Subject	Verb

Examples:
- Last night, it was windy. **In addition,** it was raining heavily.
- Yesterday, my uncle harvested a lot of wheat. **In addition,** he planted ten palm trees.

OR

Subject	Verb.	Furthermore,	Subject	Verb

Examples:
- Football is a popular sport. **Furthermore,** it is exciting.
- This computer is old. **Furthermore,** it is slow.

OR

Subject	Verb.	Moreover,	Subject	Verb

Examples:
- This new car is powerful. **Moreover,** it is well-equipped.
- My basketball team has the best players. **Moreover,** their coach is clever.

OR

Subject	Verb.	Besides,	Subject	Verb

Examples:
- The voice of the singer is fantastic. **Besides,** the music is great.

As well as

AS WELL AS is used to mean in addition to something or somebody.

Subject	Verb	1st Object	as well as	2nd Object

Examples:
- Mark is learning Arabic. He is learning Chinese.
- ✓ Mark is learning Arabic **as well as** Chinese.

My Homework

Not only . . . but also

We use not only but also to emphasize that something else is also true.

Subject	not only	1st Verb	but also	2nd Verb

Examples:
- Angela does her best in class. She revises her lessons at home.
- ✓ Angela **not only** does her best in class **but also** revises her lessons at home.

| Not only | helping Verb | subject | Verb | but also | 2nd verb |

✦ Examples:
- Anderson writes poetry. He draws portraits.
- ✓ **Not only** does Anderson write poetry **but** he **also** draws portraits.
- The farmer harvested the wheat. He irrigated some other crops.
- ✓ **Not only** did the farmer harvest the wheat **but** he **also** irrigated some other crops.

Not only ... but as well

| Subject | not only | 1st Verb | but | 2nd Verb | as well |

✦ Examples:
- Basim played perfectly.
- Basim scored three goals.
- ✓ Basim **not only** played perfectly**, but** he scored three goals **as well.**

So that / Such that

So ... that

SO THAT means with the purpose that; in order that.

| Subject | Present tense | so that | will / can / may + base form |

| Subject | Past tense | so that | would / could + base form |

✦ Examples:
- The students do their best **so that** they **will get** high scores.
- The bus driver is driving carefully **so that** he **won't have** an accident.
- I revise my lessons regularly **so that** I **can get** answers easily.

- Gina wore dark glasses **so that** she **would protect** her eyes.
- Mark hurried up **so that** he **wouldn't miss** the morning train.
- Donald's parents helped him **so that** he **could start** a new business.

Such ... that

SUCH THAT means with the purpose that, in order that.

Subject	Present tense	such	Noun + adj.	that	will + base form

Subject	Past tense	such	Noun + adj.	that	would + base form

✦ Examples:
- It is **such** an easy exercise **that** I **can answer** it easily.
- It is **such** a difficult problem **that** I **can't solve** it.
- They are **such** hard-working students **that** their teachers always praise them.

- It was **such** a hot day **that** we **went** swimming.
- It was **such** a long distance **that** I **couldn't go on** driving.
- They were **such** active players **that** they scored many points.

My Homework

> ### Exercise One
✦ Choose the correct answer from a, b, c, or d.

1) _____ the swimmer did his best, he couldn't win.

a	Although	b	But
c	Or	d	So

2) Keith didn't go to school _____ he was sick.

a	because	b	or
c	although	d	but

3) Sarah cleaned the kitchen. _____, she cooked a nice meal for her family.

a	Moreover	b	Nevertheless
c	However	d	Although

4) _____ his old age, my grandfather is still an active farmer.

a	Due to	b	Although
c	In spite of	d	Because

5) _____ an aunt in London, Billy has two aunts who live in Cordoba.

a	Since	b	Even though
c	Yet	d	In addition to

6) We went on driving _____ it was raining heavily.

a	so	b	although
c	or	d	nor

7) _____ music, Fred has a lot of other hobbies.

a	Besides	b	But
c	However	d	Although

8) I went to the bank _____ I wanted to open a new account.

a	so that	b	but
c	and	d	because

9) _____ getting up early, Dennis missed the school bus.

a	Because of	b	Moreover
c	But	d	Despite

10) The mechanic fixed the fuel leak. _____, he checked the oil level.

a	Because of	b	Besides
c	But	d	For

11) Saleh spent his summer vacation in Dubai _____ it cost a fortune.

a	because	b	although
c	since	d	therefore

12) The streets of the old city are muddy and slippery _____ it had rained for a long time.

a	although	b	but
c	or	d	because

13) Tom has a new house in London. _____, he has a villa in the country.

a	Because	b	Although
c	In addition	d	Since

14) _____ I warned Jack not to swim in this deep area, he went there.

a	However	b	Because
c	Although	d	As

15) Mr Watson grew corn this season. _____, he raised a lot of cattle.

a	For	b	Besides
c	Since	d	Although

16) My teacher blamed me _____ I neglected my homework.

a	because	b	however
c	although	d	so

17) Anas is a good swimmer. _____, he can dive well.

a	Although	b	In addition
c	Because	d	Since

18) _____ Abdul-Rahman being qualified for the job, the interviewer refused his application.

a	In spite of	b	Furthermore
c	Moreover	d	Because of

19) Carl's point of view was still vague _____ he explained it many times.

a	nevertheless	b	however
c	because of	d	although

20) The old man walked for five kilometres. _____, he did much exercise.

a	However	b	Furthermore
c	Although	d	Nevertheless

༄༅ My Homework ༄༅

> ## Exercise Two

↓ Choose the correct answer from a, b, c, or d.

1) I will lend you the money you've asked for _____ you promised to return it back when you get your salary.

a	as soon as	b	as long as
c	yet	d	despite

2) Carlos travelled to Mexico City _____ he wanted to see his parents.

a	because	b	but
c	because of	d	however

3) Mike read the instructions manual well, _____ he managed to operate the machine.

a	but	b	so
c	although	d	because

4) Dan may not be able to solve the math problem _____ he ignores the rules.

a	yet	b	due to
c	so	d	as

5) Raul trusts his friends _____ they don't lie to him.

a	for	b	in addition
c	nevertheless	d	even though

6) The manager didn't approve the plan _____ it needed to be reviewed.

a	however	b	although
c	since	d	besides

7) Millions of tourists visit Luxor yearly _____ it is the world's largest open-air museum.

a	yet	b	because
c	so	d	in spite of

8) We are going to send you another smartphone _____ the one you bought is out of order.

a	even though	b	but
c	however	d	as long as

9) Ahmad doesn't speak Chinese, _____ he faced a lot of troubles when visited China.

a	because of	b	but
c	because	d	so

10) Leo moved to Tokyo _____ he got a job there.

a	despite	b	due to
c	as	d	even though

11) The bus driver stopped suddenly. _____, I was about to hit the seat in front of me.

a	As	b	Even though
c	Despite	d	Therefore

12) We couldn't reach our destination on time _____ it was foggy.

a	yet	b	for
c	so	d	in spite of

13) Our secretary sent us an urgent email _____ we had to attend an important meeting.

a	so	b	yet
c	although	d	since

14) Lewis didn't get ready for the competition very well. _____, he couldn't win it.

a	Despite	b	However
c	In spite of	d	As a result

15) _____ Max isn't keen on sport, he went to the stadium with his friends.

a	But	b	Since
c	However	d	Although

16) You can't talk to my father _____ he is asleep.

a	because of	b	as
c	although	d	but

17) _____ you have enough time, could you help me review these articles?

a	Although	b	As soon as
c	As well as	d	As long as

18) The country suffers from an economic crisis _____ its production rate decreased.

a	for	b	furthermore
c	although	d	moreover

19) _____ my vacation starts tomorrow, I have prepared a good plan for camping in the mountains.

a	So	b	Moreover
c	Since	d	Furthermore

20) I don't mind working for extra hours _____ you pay me.

a	however	b	because of
c	but	d	as long as

✏✏✏ My Homework ✏✏✏

➢ **Exercise Three**

✤ Choose the correct answer from a, b, c, or d.

1) Our teacher explained the new grammar lesson clearly. _____, we worked out a lot of exercises.

a	However	b	Despite
c	Furthermore	d	Due to

2) My parents went shopping. _____, I have to take care of my little brother.

a	Nevertheless	b	Since
c	Although	d	As a result

3) My elder sister cleaned the house. _____, she cooked us a delicious meal.

a	However	b	Moreover
c	In spite of	d	Because of

4) Roy didn't attend yesterday's meeting. _____, he didn't know about the new projects.

a	Yet	b	As
c	In spite of	d	Consequently

5) The final test was too difficult for me to answer. _____, I asked for thirty extra minutes.

a	Because	b	Therefore
c	Moreover	d	Even though

6) My new house is large. _____, it is surrounded by a beautiful garden.

a	Furthermore	b	Though
c	Because of	d	In contrast

7) Our teachers helped us a lot. _____, we always remember them with much gratitude.

a	For this reason	b	Nevertheless
c	But	d	As long as

8) Donald formatted the infected laptop. _____, he installed an antivirus program on it.

a	Even though	b	Yet
c	Moreover	d	Because of

9) This cell phone is very expensive. _____, I won't buy it.

a	Therefore	b	Due to
c	Since	d	Besides

10) This machine can work around the clock. _____, its spare parts are cheap and available.

a	Despite	b	However
c	But	d	Furthermore

11) It was severely cold. _____, I put on a heavy coat.

a	Therefore	b	Yet
c	Although	d	As long as

12) Pollution causes serious health problems for us. _____, it affects the life of other living things.

a	Moreover	b	Due to
c	Although	d	So

13) Brian likes swimming in the early morning. _____, he enjoys jogging on the beach in the afternoon.

a	But	b	In spite of
c	Although	d	Moreover

14) James arrived at the airport forty minutes late. _____, he couldn't catch his flight to Frankfurt.

a	Even though	b	However
c	Due to	d	As a result

15) My car battery is dead. _____, I have to replace it at once.

a	Despite	b	As
c	However	d	Consequently

16) The snow piled up in front of our house. _____, we called the local authorities for help.

a	For this reason	b	Because
c	But	d	Because of

17) I can't move this rock alone _____ it is extremely heavy.

a	so	b	although
c	but	d	because

18) My old car has a lot of mechanical problems. _____, I plan to buy a modern one.

a	However	b	Yet
c	Therefore	d	Because

19) Juan's visit to China lasted for two months. _____, he visited many places there.

a	But	b	Because of
c	As a result	d	As

20) Ralph went to the dental clinic _____ he was suffering from a bad toothache.

a	so	b	because
c	but	d	although

✿✿✿ My Homework ✿✿✿

➤ **Exercise Four**

✦ Choose the correct answer from a, b, c or d.

1) Jane is a talented poet _____ being a short story writer.

a	but	b	as long as
c	in addition	d	as well as

2) Adam booked a ticket three days ago _____ he wanted to go to the game.

a	but	b	so
c	because	d	although

3) Carlos often makes grammar mistakes. _____, he has to join a remedial class.

a	Yet	b	Despite
c	For this reason	d	Moreover

4) My father felt a lot of pain in his back _____ he exerted strenuous efforts on the farm.

a	since	b	consequently
c	so	d	but

5) Addiction is a bad habit because it damages man's health. _____, it costs a lot of money.

a	Because of	b	Furthermore
c	Although	d	In spite of

6) This shop sells smartphones _____ laptops.

a	but	b	as long as
c	in addition	d	as well as

7) Omar _____ passed the final test _____ he got a high score.

a	so ___ that	b	not only ___ but also
c	such ___ that	d	either ___ or

8) Not only Jane but also Ali _____ English very well.

a	speak	b	speaking
c	speaks	d	to speak

9) Not only smoking but also addiction _____ dangerous for us.

a	are	b	were
c	to be	d	is

10) Not only _____ I enjoy swimming, but I am interested in diving as well.

a	did	b	does
c	to do	d	do

11) Not only _____ Martin pass the final test, but he got high marks as well.

a	did	b	does
c	to do	d	do

12) Not only did Karin attend my wedding party but also _____ me a lovely present.

a	gives	b	giving
c	gave	d	has given

13) Not only _____ all night but also there was a bad storm.

a	it was snowing	b	it snowed
c	is it snowing	d	was it snowing

14) The police officer not only arrested the thug but _____ him to the police station as well.

a	took	b	has taken
c	takes	d	to take

15) _____ did the manager rewarded Allan, _____ gave him a promotion.

a	Both ___ and	b	Not only ___ but also
c	Either ___ or	d	Neither ___ nor

16) _____ are my parents going to Egypt for a couple of weeks, _____ Tunisia for ten days.

a	Both ___ and	b	Not only ___ but also
c	Either ___ or	d	Neither ___ nor

17) This smartphone is not only cheap but also _____ a lot of applications.

a	does it have	b	having
c	has	d	had

18) I will take _____ fish _____ meat for lunch. I can't eat both of them.

a	both ___ and	b	not only ___ but also
c	either ___ or	d	neither ___ nor

19) _____ my father _____ my mother decided to spend the weekend in Dubai. They have already booked two tickets.

a	Both ___ and	b	Not only ___ but also well
c	Either ___ or	d	Neither ___ nor

20) Neither my uncle nor my aunt _____ interested in scuba diving.

a	are	b	have been
c	is	d	were

My Homework

➢ *Exercise Five*
✦ Correct the mistake in each of the following sentences.
1) Tim was in a hurry because he took a taxi.
✎ _____
2) Rachel behaved politely in spite of the man insulted her.
✎ _____
3) My mobile phone didn't work so its battery was dead.
✎ _____
4) I painted my old car, and it still looks dull.
✎ _____
5) Jane swam for a long distance, but she got tired.
✎ _____

6) My grandfather is retired, and my grandmother is either.
✎ _____
7) Although being exhausted, Pamela went on working in her garden.
✎ _____
8) I speak neither Japanese or Chinese. I'm going to learn them later.
✎ _____
9) You can reach your destination neither by bus or by train. You have two options.
✎ _____
10) I always have a glass of juice during breakfast, and neither does Sue.
✎ _____

🙢🙢🙢 *My Homework* 🙠🙠🙠

➢ *Exercise Six*
✦ Correct the mistake in each of the following sentences.
1) I dialled the number many times, so no one answered.
✎ _____
2) Emma's parents had a car accident, but she was sad.
✎ _____
3) Lee has a lot of friends, but he is a friendly man.
✎ _____
4) Eric goes climbing every weekend although he is fond of climbing.
✎ _____
5) Dale moved to a larger house so he has a large family.
✎ _____
6) It was raining heavily, however I put up my umbrella.
✎ _____

7) Jana runs a large IT company so he has a lot of experience.
➢ ____ ____ ____ ____ ____ ____ ____ ____ ____ ____

8) Kevin couldn't get the job so he was physically weak.
➢ ____ ____ ____ ____ ____ ____ ____ ____ ____ ____

9) The teacher gave the weak students remedial classes because they passed the final test.
➢ ____ ____ ____ ____ ____ ____ ____ ____ ____ ____

10) I ran into one of my old friends downtown moreover I was very excited.
➢ ____ ____ ____ ____ ____ ____ ____ ____ ____ ____

༄༄༄ My Homework ༄༄༄

➢ **Exercise Seven:**
↳ Correct the mistake in each of the following sentences.

1) Nelson was late for the meeting although the manager blamed him.
➢ ____ ____ ____ ____ ____ ____ ____ ____ ____ ____

2) Adam went hunting on the weekend, although he didn't catch any animals.
➢ ____ ____ ____ ____ ____ ____ ____ ____ ____ ____

3) The weather was fine, but we stayed in the park for a long time.
➢ ____ ____ ____ ____ ____ ____ ____ ____ ____ ____

4) We didn't go diving, so the waves were extremely high.
➢ ____ ____ ____ ____ ____ ____ ____ ____ ____ ____

5) Saad's luggage was too heavy because he couldn't carry it alone.
➢ ____ ____ ____ ____ ____ ____ ____ ____ ____ ____

6) My father rented a car so his car was being fixed.
➢ ____ ____ ____ ____ ____ ____ ____ ____ ____ ____

7) Daniel's paragraph was very good, therefore the teacher didn't like it.
➢ ____ ____ ____ ____ ____ ____ ____ ____ ____ ____

8) Rahaf and her brother were disappointed because their team won the semi-final match.
➢ ____ ____ ____ ____ ____ ____ ____ ____ ____ ____

9) The boy is smiling because the joke.
➢ ____ ____ ____ ____ ____ ____ ____ ____ ____ ____

10) We will be there on time therefore there is a metro every four minutes.
➢ ____ ____ ____ ____ ____ ____ ____ ____ ____ ____

🌸 My Homework 🌸

➢ **Exercise Eight**

✚ Correct the mistake in each of the following sentences.

1) John is smart as soon as ambitious.
   ✎ _____

2) We love our teachers so they are helpful and supportive.
   ✎ _____

3) The supervisor blamed the workmen although they left the location early.
   ✎ _____

4) The helicopter couldn't take off because a mechanical problem.
   ✎ _____

5) In spite of it was windy, we didn't stop driving.
   ✎ _____

6) Mr Holman is pleased because of his farm produces a lot of apples.
   ✎ _____

7) The hypermarket was full of customers because I couldn't buy all that I needed.
   ✎ _____

8) I went to the clothes shop to change the shirt because of it was too tight for me.
   ✎ _____

9) The truck driver was imprisoned although he caused a terrible accident.
   ✎ _____

10) The school bus broke down because we arrived at our school late.
    ✎ _____

🌸 My Homework 🌸

➢ **Exercise Nine**

✚ Correct the mistake in each of the following sentences.

1) Nirvana sold her jewellery therefore she wanted money.
   ✎ _____

2) There are many high achievers in this class because of they had good teachers.
   ✎ _____

3) I cannot speak Greek and I can speak Spanish.
   ✎ _____

4) Both Muhammad and Jack plays chess very well.
   ✎ _____ _____ _____ _____ _____ _____ _____ _____ _____ _____

5) Many fans liked Totti but Raul as talented footballers.
   ✎ _____ _____ _____ _____ _____ _____ _____ _____ _____ _____

6) The street cleaners got tired because of they were muddy and slippery.
   ✎ _____ _____ _____ _____ _____ _____ _____ _____ _____ _____

7) Jeannette was fined because speeding.
   ✎ _____ _____ _____ _____ _____ _____ _____ _____ _____ _____

8) In addition growing many crops, Lee has a lot of cattle on his farm.
   ✎ _____ _____ _____ _____ _____ _____ _____ _____ _____ _____

9) I have a lot of homework to do. In addition to, I don't like hunting.
   ✎ _____ _____ _____ _____ _____ _____ _____ _____ _____ _____

10) The mechanic managed to fix the car despite it is very old.
    ✎ _____ _____ _____ _____ _____ _____ _____ _____ _____ _____

≈≈≈ My Homework ≈≈≈

SECTION 22

Reported Speech

REPORTED SPEECH is also referred to as indirect speech. It is used to talk about the past. Consequently, the verbs have to be in the past.

Verb Change

Direct Speech	Indirect (Reported) Speech
Simple Present	Simple Past
play – plays	*played*
Present Continuous	Past Continuous
am / is / are playing	*was / were / playing*
Present Perfect	Past Perfect
have – has played	*had played*
Present Perfect Continuous	Past Perfect Continuous
have – has been playing	*had been playing*
Simple Past	Past Perfect
played	*had played*
Future	Conditional
will – shall play	*would play*
Future Continuous	Conditional Continuous
will – shall be playing	*would be playing*
Conditional	Conditional
would play	*would play*

Expressions of Time and Place

Direct Speech	Indirect (Reported) Speech
today	that day
tonight	that night
yesterday	the day before
the day before	two days before
tomorrow	the next day
the day after tomorrow	in two days' time
next week	the following week
last week	the previous week
a year ago	a year before
three days ago	three days earlier
now	then
here	there

Pronouns and Adjectives

Direct Speech	Indirect (Reported) Speech
I	*he – she*
me	*him – her*
my	*his – her*
mine	*his – hers*
we	*they*
us	*them*
our	*their*
ours	*theirs*
this	*that*
these	*those*

Reporting Statements

When we change the statement into reported speech, we change the verb *said to* into *told* or *informed*.

Example:

➢ Thomas said to us, 'My sister got a scholarship in Harvard University last year.'

✓ Thomas told us that his sister had got a scholarship in Harvard University the year before.

➢ **Exercise One**

✦ Change the direct speech into reported speech.

1) 'I call my grandparents every day.'
✓ Layan told Salma _____

2) Ahmad said to me, 'I phoned my aunt last night.'
🕮 _____

3) Tuka said to us, 'I will help this patient as far as I can.'
🕮 _____

4) Batool said to her mother, 'My new dress is very expensive.'
🕮 _____

5) Abdul-Rahman said, 'I have to finish my assignment as soon as I can.'
🕮 _____

6) Jane said to her friends, 'I am going to get married next week.'
🕮 _____

7) Henry said to his parents, 'I can meet my friends tomorrow.'
🕮 _____

8) Neil said to his father, 'I am planning to buy a farm in the country.'
🕮 _____

9) George said, 'I always keep my mobile phone charged.'
🕮 _____

10) Anas said to me, 'My doctor advised me to give up smoking.'
🕮 _____

🎀🎀🎀 **My Homework** 🎀🎀🎀

➢ **Exercise Two**

✦ Change the direct speech into reported speech.

1) Lee said to his colleagues, 'I am going to fly to China next month.'
🕮 _____

2) Adrian said to the tourists, 'I can't speak Chinese.'
➢ _____

3) The manager said to his employees, 'The company will expand its projects next summer.'
➢ _____

4) Jack said to me, 'What time is the game?'
➢ _____

5) The teacher said to his students, 'I am sorry, but I can't explain the new lesson today.'
➢ _____

6) Donald said to his boss, 'I have just received an important email.'
➢ _____

7) The professor said to Sally, 'Your research paper has to be submitted on time.'
➢ _____

8) Leila said to me, 'I am able to work out this complicated problem.'
➢ _____

9) Max said to us, 'My parents are going to visit Madrid soon.'
➢ _____

10) Ola said to me, 'I spent a lovely vacation with my family in Alexandria.'
➢ _____

🙚🙚🙚 *My Homework* 🙘🙘🙘

➢ *Exercise Three*
✢ Change the direct speech into reported speech.
1) Mark said to us, 'I don't like baseball.'
➢ _____
2) Mary said to me, 'I have been studying all night.'
➢ _____

3) Albert said to us, 'The conference will be postponed till tomorrow.'
✎ ____ ____ ____ ____ ____ ____ ____ ____ ____ ____
____ ____ ____ ____ ____ ____ ____ ____

4) John said to his friends, 'The food in this restaurant is very delicious.'
✎ ____ ____ ____ ____ ____ ____ ____ ____ ____ ____
____ ____ ____ ____ ____ ____ ____ ____

5) Dr. Karma said, 'Shakespeare's plays were translated into several languages.'
✎ ____ ____ ____ ____ ____ ____ ____ ____ ____ ____
____ ____ ____ ____ ____ ____ ____ ____

6) Ann said to her parents, 'I won a scholarship in a British university.'
✎ ____ ____ ____ ____ ____ ____ ____ ____ ____ ____
____ ____ ____ ____ ____ ____ ____ ____

7) Johan said to us, 'I studied pharmacy in a Chinese university.'
✎ ____ ____ ____ ____ ____ ____ ____ ____ ____ ____
____ ____ ____ ____ ____ ____ ____ ____

8) Nada said to me, 'I will bring you a lovely birthday present.'
✎ ____ ____ ____ ____ ____ ____ ____ ____ ____ ____
____ ____ ____ ____ ____ ____ ____ ____

9) Ted said to us, 'I taught English in Korea last year.'
✎ ____ ____ ____ ____ ____ ____ ____ ____ ____ ____

10) Our teacher said to us, 'Winter is very cold in Russia.'
✎ ____ ____ ____ ____ ____ ____ ____ ____ ____ ____
____ ____ ____ ____ ____ ____ ____ ____

✿✿✿ My Homework ✿✿✿

➢ **Exercise Four**

✦ Change the direct speech into reported speech.

1) Martina said to her mother, 'I have a dentist's appointment at 6:15 p.m.'
✎ ____ ____ ____ ____ ____ ____ ____ ____ ____ ____
____ ____ ____ ____ ____ ____ ____ ____

2) Mido said to us, 'My team will train hard for the final game.'
✎ ____ ____ ____ ____ ____ ____ ____ ____ ____ ____
____ ____ ____ ____ ____ ____ ____ ____

3) Kevin said, 'I'm reading a wonderful novel by Jane Austen.'
✎ ____ ____ ____ ____ ____ ____ ____ ____ ____ ____
____ ____ ____ ____ ____ ____ ____ ____

4) Arnold said, 'My daughter is going to graduate next year.'
✎ ____ ____ ____ ____ ____ ____ ____ ____ ____ ____
____ ____ ____ ____ ____ ____ ____ ____

5) The driver said to the policeman, 'I fasten my seat belt while driving.'
→ _____

6) Lisa said to her pals, 'The teacher praised my work and appreciated it.'
→ _____

7) Lama said, 'The policeman was angry because I ran the red light.'
→ _____

8) Marwa said, 'I will finish my task in a few minutes.'
→ _____

9) Keith said to her friends, 'I admire my grandparents.'
→ _____

10) Ronald said to his friends, 'Mary doesn't have any travel plans.'
→ _____

🕮🕮🕮 My Homework 🕮🕮🕮

➢ **Exercise Five**
↳ Change the direct speech into reported speech.

1) William said to us, 'I haven't been to Rome before.'
→ _____

2) Edmond said to me, 'I have been working on this plan for three days.'
→ _____

3) Hoor said to her sisters, 'I will arrive before sunset.'
→ _____

4) Paul said to us, 'I was jogging in the park when I saw Yara.'
→ _____

5) Heidi said to Nehal, 'My parents are spending their annual vacation in Aswan.'
→ _____

6) Wilson said to me, 'I didn't attend the meeting yesterday.'
→ _____

7) Lama said to Walid, 'My aunts will move to a new house next week.'
➢ _____

8) Malik said to Omar, 'I was watching a movie when you called me.'
➢ _____

9) Sandra said, 'I have never gone diving.'
➢ _____

10) Joseph and Leon said to me, 'We are going to discuss the problem with our parents tonight.'
➢ _____

❀❀❀ My Homework ❀❀❀

➢ **Exercise Six**
+ Change the direct speech into reported speech.
1) Oscar said to Alexander, 'I can fix my laptop myself.'
➢ _____

2) Henry said to his uncle, 'I want you to help me work out this math problem.'
➢ _____

3) Freddie said to Samuel, 'My classmates passed the final test because they did their best.'
➢ _____

4) Arthur said to us, 'The meeting was postponed until further notice.'
➢ _____

5) Adam said, 'My car broke down on the road to the city.'
➢ _____

6) Michael said, 'My father retired two years ago.'
➢ _____

7) Stanley said to his teammates, 'We have to win this championship to please our fans.'
➢ _____

8) Harley said to his family, 'I will go fishing with my friends tomorrow.'
🙠 ____ ____ ____ ____ ____ ____ ____ ____ ____ ____
____ ____ ____ ____ ____ ____ ____ ____ ____

9) Alex said, 'I have already read the reports.'
🙠 ____ ____ ____ ____ ____ ____ ____ ____ ____ ____

10) Elliot said, 'I wrote a lot of poems about nature.'
🙠 ____ ____ ____ ____ ____ ____ ____ ____ ____ ____

🙠🙠🙠 My Homework 🙢🙢🙢

➢ Exercise Seven

✢ Change the direct speech into reported speech.

1) Mary said, 'I am going to have my supper with my family.'
🙠 ____ ____ ____ ____ ____ ____ ____ ____ ____ ____
____ ____ ____ ____ ____ ____ ____ ____ ____

2) Batool said to Tuka, 'The professor appreciated my research paper a lot.'
🙠 ____ ____ ____ ____ ____ ____ ____ ____ ____ ____
____ ____ ____ ____ ____ ____ ____ ____ ____

3) Jessica said, 'We will have our graduation party next Thursday.'
🙠 ____ ____ ____ ____ ____ ____ ____ ____ ____ ____
____ ____ ____ ____ ____ ____ ____ ____ ____

4) Nora said to us, 'I had a walk in the park last night.'
🙠 ____ ____ ____ ____ ____ ____ ____ ____ ____ ____
____ ____ ____ ____ ____ ____ ____ ____ ____

5) Teresa said, 'My husband is going to get a new job.'
🙠 ____ ____ ____ ____ ____ ____ ____ ____ ____ ____
____ ____ ____ ____ ____ ____ ____ ____ ____

6) Sofia said to me, 'I won't travel to Rome next summer.'
🙠 ____ ____ ____ ____ ____ ____ ____ ____ ____ ____
____ ____ ____ ____ ____ ____ ____ ____ ____

7) Ibrahim said to us, 'My brother won the school prize for drawing yesterday.'
🙠 ____ ____ ____ ____ ____ ____ ____ ____ ____ ____
____ ____ ____ ____ ____ ____ ____ ____ ____

8) Yunus said to Dina, 'You are invited to attend my sister's birthday party.'
🙠 ____ ____ ____ ____ ____ ____ ____ ____ ____ ____
____ ____ ____ ____ ____ ____ ____ ____ ____

9) Jasmine said to Rehab, 'My parents left to Madrid last week.'
🙠 ____ ____ ____ ____ ____ ____ ____ ____ ____ ____
____ ____ ____ ____ ____ ____ ____ ____ ____

10) Rose and Anna said to us, 'We are going to spend the weekend in the country.'
✍ _____ _____ _____ _____ _____ _____ _____ _____
_____ _____ _____ _____ _____ _____ _____ _____

🌸🌸🌸 *My Homework* 🌸🌸🌸

➢ **_Exercise Eight_**
✦ Change the direct speech into reported speech.
1) Julia said to Hend, 'I will inform our manager about the new deal.'
✍ _____ _____ _____ _____ _____ _____ _____ _____

2) Abdul-Rahman said to Ahmad, 'I will take my car to maintenance tomorrow.'
✍ _____ _____ _____ _____ _____ _____ _____ _____
_____ _____ _____ _____ _____ _____ _____ _____

3) Oraby said to me, 'My family helped me reach my goals.'
✍ _____ _____ _____ _____ _____ _____ _____ _____

4) Mai said to her kids, 'You might start doing your homework now.'
✍ _____ _____ _____ _____ _____ _____ _____ _____
_____ _____ _____ _____ _____ _____ _____ _____

5) Lexi said to her classmates, 'The exam results are going to be sent by email soon.'
✍ _____ _____ _____ _____ _____ _____ _____ _____
_____ _____ _____ _____ _____ _____ _____ _____

6) The teacher said to Olivia, 'Your math skills improved a lot.'
✍ _____ _____ _____ _____ _____ _____ _____ _____
_____ _____ _____ _____ _____ _____ _____ _____

7) Jacob said to his friends, 'I'm staying in a five-star hotel.'
✍ _____ _____ _____ _____ _____ _____ _____ _____

Darcy said to his sisters, 'We might have a lot of work on the farm tomorrow.'
✍ _____ _____ _____ _____ _____ _____ _____ _____
_____ _____ _____ _____ _____ _____ _____ _____

8) Oliver said, 'I worked in this workshop two years ago.'
✍ _____ _____ _____ _____ _____ _____ _____ _____

Basant said to Ayah, 'I will go skiing with my family on the weekend.'
✍ _____ _____ _____ _____ _____ _____ _____ _____
_____ _____ _____ _____ _____ _____ _____ _____

🌸🌸🌸 *My Homework* 🌸🌸🌸

➤ Exercise Nine

✦ Change the direct speech into reported speech.

1) Rawan said to Mennah, 'My parents gave me a lot of presents on the occasion of my birthday.'
   ✎ _____
   _____

2) Emad said to Amr, 'I will take you to the beach tomorrow morning.'
   ✎ _____
   _____

3) Jude said to her classmates, 'Our teacher looks tired today.'
   ✎ _____
   _____

4) Tom said to Alice, 'I take my kids to school every morning.'
   ✎ _____
   _____

5) Linda said to me, 'My sister didn't visit New York last week.'
   ✎ _____
   _____

6) Carol said to Angela, 'I won't go to the jungle alone.'
   ✎ _____
   _____

7) Wesam said to Samah, 'I make delicious dinner for my family every day.'
   ✎ _____
   _____

8) The dentist said to Ahmad, 'I will pull out your wisdom tooth.'
   ✎ _____
   _____

9) The taxi driver said me, 'I am sorry I am busy now.'
   ✎ _____
   _____

10) Julie and Jana said to us, 'We swam for three hours yesterday.'
    ✎ _____
    _____

My Homework

➢ **_Exercise Ten_**

✦ Change the direct speech into reported speech.

1) Muhammad said to Nada, 'I bought you some pretty flowers.'
 ✐ ____ ____ ____ ____ ____ ____ ____ ____ ____ ____
 ____ ____ ____ ____

2) Rita said to us, 'This geometry exercise is very difficult.'
 ✐ ____ ____ ____ ____ ____ ____ ____ ____ ____ ____
 ____ ____ ____ ____

3) Osama said to Basel, 'Your ideas about the project are important.'
 ✐ ____ ____ ____ ____ ____ ____ ____ ____ ____ ____
 ____ ____ ____ ____

4) Robin said to me, 'I am fond of listening to classical music.'
 ✐ ____ ____ ____ ____ ____ ____ ____ ____ ____ ____
 ____ ____ ____ ____

5) Ali said to his friends, 'I like driving classic cars.'
 ✐ ____ ____ ____ ____ ____ ____ ____ ____ ____ ____
 ____ ____ ____ ____

6) Ellen said, 'My mother doesn't have time to visit the Louvre.'
 ✐ ____ ____ ____ ____ ____ ____ ____ ____ ____ ____
 ____ ____ ____ ____

7) Yousra said to Samar, 'I will join the school basketball team.'
 ✐ ____ ____ ____ ____ ____ ____ ____ ____ ____ ____
 ____ ____ ____ ____

8) Willie said to Gina, 'I am preparing our lunch now.'
 ✐ ____ ____ ____ ____ ____ ____ ____ ____ ____ ____
 ____ ____ ____ ____

9) Zeyad said to Saleh, 'I met my new teacher yesterday morning.'
 ✐ ____ ____ ____ ____ ____ ____ ____ ____ ____ ____
 ____ ____ ____ ____

10) Anas said to Marwa, 'I was on the farm with my father.'
 ✐ ____ ____ ____ ____ ____ ____ ____ ____ ____ ____
 ____ ____ ____ ____

✎✎✎ *My Homework* ✎✎✎

Reporting yes-no Questions

When we change the yes-no questions into reported speech, we change the verb said as follows.

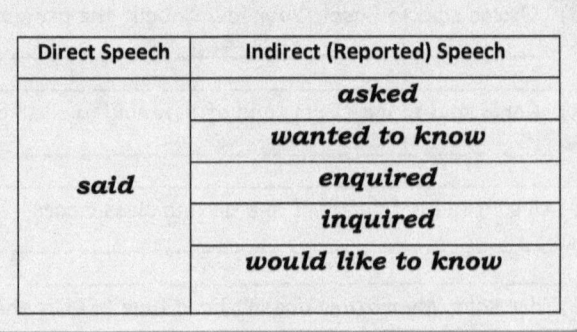

Direct Speech	Indirect (Reported) Speech
said	*asked*
	wanted to know
	enquired
	inquired
	would like to know

When we change the yes-no questions into reported speech, we join the two sentences using 'if' or 'whether'. We may also use 'whether or not'.

+ **Example:**

➤ Isabel said to me, 'Did the teacher give new homework?'
✓ Isabel asked me if the teacher had given new homework.

➤ *Exercise Eleven*
+ Change the direct speech into reported speech.
1) 'Is your new teacher from Canada?'
🖎 Maha asked me *if* ____ ____ ____ ____ ____ ____ ____ ____
____ ____ ____ ____ ____ ____ ____ ____ ____

2) 'Are these computers upgraded?'
🖎 My manager asked me ____ ____ ____ ____ ____ ____ ____ __
____ ____ ____ ____ ____ ____ ____ ____

3) 'Was the wedding party magnificent?'
- Lilly asked me _____

4) 'Were you on the farm?'
- My father asked me _____

5) 'Do you live alone?'
- My teacher asked me _____

6) 'Does your sister study dentistry?'
- I asked Abdou _____

7) 'Did your family sell the old house?'
- I asked Basim _____

8) 'Have you received their response?'
- The secretary asked me _____

9) 'Has Elena got a raise in her salary?'
- I asked Lobna _____

10) 'Will you fly to Dublin next Monday?'
- Sue asked me _____

✎✎✎ My Homework ✎✎✎

➢ **Exercise Twelve**
✤ Change the direct speech into reported speech.

1) 'Can you fix this laptop for me?'
- I asked Michael _____

2) 'Would you bring me some fruit juice, please?'
- I asked the waiter _____

3) 'Could you help me change the battery of my car, please?'
- I asked the electrician _____

433

4) 'Am I mistaken, sir?'
🖎 I asked my teacher ___ ___ ___ ___ ___ ___ ___ ___
___ ___ ___ ___ ___ ___ ___ ___ ___ ___ ___ -

5) 'Are you staying in a five-star hotel?'
🖎 I asked my friends ___ ___ ___ ___ ___ ___ ___
___ ___ ___ ___ ___ ___ ___ ___ ___ ___ ___ -

6) 'Is it raining heavily outside?'
🖎 My parents asked me ___ ___ ___ ___ ___ ___ ___ ___
___ ___ ___ ___ ___ ___ ___ ___ ___ ___ ___ -

7) 'Were you driving fast when you hit the rock?'
🖎 The police officer asked me ___ ___ ___ ___ ___ ___ ___
___ ___ ___ ___ ___ ___ ___ ___ ___ ___ -

8) 'Was Lina cooking when the fire broke out?'
🖎 The fireman asked me ___ ___ ___ ___ ___ ___ ___ ___
___ ___ ___ ___ ___ ___ ___ ___ ___ ___ ___

9) 'Did you take the six-o'clock train to the city?'
🖎 My grandfather asked me ___ ___ ___ ___ ___ ___ ___
___ ___ ___ ___ ___ ___ ___ ___ ___ ___ ___ -

10) 'Would you mind lending me your camera?'
🖎 Hala asked me ___ ___ ___ ___ ___ ___ ___ ___
___ ___ ___ ___ ___ ___ ___ ___ ___ ___ ___

🖎🖎🖎 *My Homework* 🖎🖎🖎

➢ **_Exercise Thirteen_**
✦ Change the direct speech into reported speech.
1) Sandy said to me, 'Do you walk to school?'
🖎 ___ ___ ___ ___ ___ ___ ___ ___ ___ ___
___ ___ ___ ___ ___ ___ ___ ___ ___ ___

2) Taqwa said to Lolo, 'Did you buy a new house last year?'
🖎 ___ ___ ___ ___ ___ ___ ___ ___ ___ ___
___ ___ ___ ___ ___ ___ ___ ___ ___ ___

3) Hans said to his wife, 'Have you finished cooking yet?'
🖎 ___ ___ ___ ___ ___ ___ ___ ___ ___ ___
___ ___ ___ ___ ___ ___ ___ ___ ___ ___

4) Caroline said to me, 'Is this book about the Nile?'
🖎 ___ ___ ___ ___ ___ ___ ___ ___ ___ ___
___ ___ ___ ___ ___ ___ ___ ___ ___ ___

5) Paul said to Omar, 'Can you help me work out this algebra exercise?'
   ✍ _____
   _____

6) Gerard said Samuel, 'Do you need to exchange your currency for American dollars?'
   ✍ _____
   _____

7) The policeman said to me, 'Did you see the shoplifter?'
   ✍ _____
   _____

8) Nadine said to her sister, 'Will you do the dishes for your mother?'
   ✍ _____
   _____

9) Celia said to Tim, 'Have you written a reply to the manager's email?'
   ✍ _____
   _____

10) My mother said to us, 'Are you enjoying yourselves?'
    ✍ _____
    _____

✿✿✿ My Homework ✿✿✿

➢ **Exercise Fourteen**

✤ Change the direct speech into reported speech.

1) My manager said to me, 'Can you check these files, please?'
   ✍ _____
   _____

2) Ronald said to his family, 'Are we going to travel by ship?'
   ✍ _____
   _____

3) Dan said to me, 'Did you lend your brother the money he asked for?'
   ✍ _____
   _____

4) My grandmother said to me, 'Do you know who broke my glasses?'
   ✍ _____
   _____

5) Our teacher said to us, 'Did you start your review for the final exam?'
➤ _____

6) The security man said to me, 'Does your uncle live alone?'
➤ _____

7) Yomna said to Rami, 'Will we fly to Cairo in November?'
➤ _____

8) Youssef said to his father, 'Can you explain this dream for me?'
➤ _____

9) The librarian said to me, 'Did you borrow these books last month?'
➤ _____

10) I said to the pharmacist, 'Can I take this medicine three times a day?'
➤ _____

My Homework

Reporting Wh- Questions

When we change the *wh-questions* into reported speech, we change the verb *said* as follows:

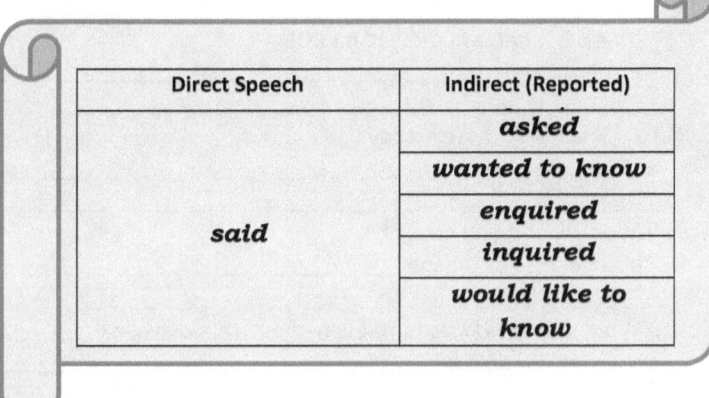

Direct Speech	Indirect (Reported)
said	*asked*
	wanted to know
	enquired
	inquired
	would like to know

When we change the wh-questions into reported speech, we join the two sentences using the same question word.

✦ **Example:**

➢ Abdullah said to me, 'Why did the train arrive late?'
✓ Abdullah asked me why the train had arrived late.

➢ *Exercise Fifteen*
✦ Change the direct speech into reported speech.

1) 'Where is my mobile phone?'
🔖 My sister asked me ____ ____ ____ ____ ____ ____ ____ ____ ____ ____ ____ ____ ____ ____ ____ ____ ____ ____

2) 'What time are you going to leave?'
🔖 Martin asked me ____ ____ ____ ____ ____ ____ ____ ____ ____ ____ ____ ____ ____ ____ ____ ____ ____ ____

3) 'When are you leaving to Barcelona?'
🔖 My coach asked me ____ ____ ____ ____ ____ ____ ____ ____ ____ ____ ____ ____ ____ ____ ____ ____ ____

4) 'How can I solve this problem?'
🙠 Dan asked his teacher ___ ___ ___ ___ ___ ___ ___ ___
___ ___ ___ ___ ___ ___ ___ ___ ___ ___

5) 'Why did you behave this way?'
🙠 The teacher asked Liza ___ ___ ___ ___ ___ ___ ___
___ ___ ___ ___ ___ ___ ___ ___ ___

6) 'Who will stay with me?'
🙠 My grandmother asked me ___ ___ ___ ___ ___ ___ ___ _
___ ___ ___ ___ ___ ___ ___ ___ ___

7) 'How many students did you meet?'
🙠 Mr Alan asked me ___ ___ ___ ___ ___ ___ ___ ___ __
___ ___ ___ ___ ___ ___ ___ ___ ___

8) 'How much do I have to pay?'
🙠 I asked the cashier ___ ___ ___ ___ ___ ___ ___ ___ _
___ ___ ___ ___ ___ ___ ___ ___ ___

9) 'Which car did you choose?'
🙠 The salesman asked me ___ ___ ___ ___ ___ ___ ___
___ ___ ___ ___ ___ ___ ___ ___ ___

10) 'What did the doctors tell you about this disease?'
🙠 My sister asked me ___ ___ ___ ___ ___ ___ ___ ___ _
___ ___ ___ ___ ___ ___ ___ ___ ___

🙠🙠🙠 My Homework 🙠🙠🙠

> ### Exercise Sixteen
✤ Change the direct speech into reported speech.
1) 'When are you going to get married?'
🙠 Alan asked me ___ ___ ___ ___ ___ ___ ___ ___
___ ___ ___ ___ ___ ___ ___ ___ ___ ___

2) 'Why are you late?'
🙠 My teacher asked me ___ ___ ___ ___ ___ ___ ___ ___
___ ___ ___ ___ ___ ___ ___ ___ ___ ___

3) 'How much is this smartphone?'
🙠 I asked the salesman ___ ___ ___ ___ ___ ___ ___ ___
___ ___ ___ ___ ___ ___ ___ ___ ___ ___

4) 'Who is our new math teacher?'
🙠 I asked my classmates ___ ___ ___ ___ ___ ___ ___
___ ___ ___ ___ ___ ___ ___ ___ ___

5) 'Who do you go hiking with?'
🙠 My parents asked me ___ ___ ___ ___ ___ ___ ___ ___
___ ___ ___ ___ ___ ___ ___ ___ ___

6) 'How many tourists did you meet downtown?'
➢ My supervisor asked me ___ ___ ___ ___ ___ ___ ___ ___ ___ ___ ___ ___ ___ ___ ___

7) 'How do you usually spend your free time?'
➢ George asked me ___ ___ ___ ___ ___ ___ ___ ___ ___ ___ ___ ___ ___ ___ ___

8) 'Who was that active football player?'
➢ My coach asked me ___ ___ ___ ___ ___ ___ ___ ___ ___ ___ ___ ___ ___

9) 'How was your flight?'
➢ The pilot asked me ___ ___ ___ ___ ___ ___ ___ ___ ___ ___ ___ ___

10) 'How often do you visit your uncles?'
➢ My grandparents asked me ___ ___ ___ ___ ___ ___ ___ ___ ___ ___ ___ ___

➢ My Homework

➢ **_Exercise Seventeen_**
✦ Change the direct speech into reported speech.
1) 'What are you going to cook for lunch?'
➢ I asked my wife ___ ___ ___ ___ ___ ___ ___ ___ ___ ___ ___ ___ ___ ___ ___ ___

2) 'What time do you usually get up in the morning, Amira?'
➢ I asked Alan ___ ___ ___ ___ ___ ___ ___ ___ ___ ___ ___ ___ ___ ___ ___

3) 'Why didn't you catch the 6:30 train to Manila?'
➢ My uncle asked me ___ ___ ___ ___ ___ ___ ___ ___ ___ ___ ___ ___ ___ ___ ___

4) 'How far is the nearest bank from here?'
➢ The tourist asked me ___ ___ ___ ___ ___ ___ ___ ___ ___ ___ ___ ___ ___

5) 'Who did Maha go to London with?'
➢ I asked Mr Taha ___ ___ ___ ___ ___ ___ ___ ___ ___ ___ ___ ___ ___

6) 'How long will your parents stay in Paris?'
➢ I asked Osama ___ ___ ___ ___ ___ ___ ___ ___ ___ ___ ___ ___ ___

7) 'When can I meet you for dinner?'
➢ I asked Helen ___ ___ ___ ___ ___ ___ ___ ___ ___ ___ ___ ___ ___

8) 'When did you see your friend Saleh?'
🙢 I asked my son _____ _____ _____ _____ _____ _____ _____ _____ _____ _____ _____ _____ _____ _____ _____ _____

9) 'What will you bring your mother as a birthday present?'
🙢 I asked Abdou _____ _____ _____ _____ _____ _____ _____ _____ _____ _____ _____ _____ _____ _____ _____ _____

10) 'Why did you leave your books at home?'
🙢 My teacher wanted to know _____ _____ _____ _____ _____ _____ _____ _____ _____ _____ _____ _____ _____ _____

🙢🙢🙢 *My Homework* 🙠🙠🙠

➢ *Exercise Eighteen*
✦ Change the direct speech into reported speech.

1) 'Where did you spend your previous summer vacation?'
🙢 I asked Tony and Jack _____ _____ _____ _____ _____ _____ _____ _____ _____ _____ _____ _____ _____ _____ _____ _____

2) 'How much does this iPad cost?'
🙢 I asked the saleswoman _____ _____ _____ _____ _____ _____ _____ _____ _____ _____ _____ _____ _____ _____ _____

3) 'What have you been doing?'
🙢 My mother asked me _____ _____ _____ _____ _____ _____ _____ _____ _____ _____ _____ _____ _____ _____ _____

4) 'Whom did you call last night?'
🙢 The police officer asked John _____ _____ _____ _____ _____ _____ _____ _____ _____ _____ _____ _____ _____ _____

5) 'How are you?'
🙢 My new teacher asked me _____ _____ _____ _____ _____ _____ _____ _____ _____ _____ _____ _____ _____ _____

6) 'How long have you been working for this bank?'
🙢 The interviewer asked Manal _____ _____ _____ _____ _____ _____ _____ _____ _____ _____ _____ _____ _____ _____

7) 'How shall I inform my manager about this loss?'
🙢 Greg would like to know _____ _____ _____ _____ _____ _____ _____ _____ _____ _____ _____ _____ _____ _____

8) 'How many runners are going to share in the final race?'
🙢 The trainer wanted to know _____ _____ _____ _____ _____ _____ _____ _____ _____ _____ _____ _____ _____ _____

9) 'Whose cell phone is missing?'
➢ The teacher asked us ____ ____ ____ ____ ____ ____ ____ ____ ____ ____ ____ ____ ____ ____ ____ ____ ____

10) 'Who are some of your favourite writers?'
➢ My teacher asked me ____ ____ ____ ____ ____ ____ ____ ____ ____ ____ ____ ____ ____ ____ ____ ____

➢➢➢ *My Homework* ➢➢➢

Reporting Imperatives

When we change the *imperative* into reported speech, we join the two sentences using *to* for affirmative imperative, and *'not to'* for negative.

Direct Speech	Indirect (Reported) Speech
said to	*asked*
	ordered
	warned
	begged
	commanded
	urged
	requested
	instructed
	reminded
	wanted
	told
	forbade
	told
	advised
	proposed
	desired
	suggested
	required

Direct Speech	Indirect (Reported) Speech
Said to	*recommended*
	wished
	insisted
	whispered

Examples:
- My father said to me, 'Wash your hands before eating.'
- My father told me **to** wash my hands before eating.

- My grandfather said to me, 'Don't waste your time.'
- My grandfather advised me **not to** waste my time.

Exercise Nineteen
Change the direct speech into reported speech.

1) 'Do your homework before you start watching TV?'
- My sister advised me _____ _____ _____ _____ _____ _____ _____ _____ _____ _____ _____ _____ _____ _____ _____ _____

2) 'Don't make noise in class.'
- The teacher ordered his schoolboys _____ _____ _____ _____ _____ _____ _____ _____ _____ _____ _____ _____ _____

3) 'Don't switch off the computer before you finish your test.'
- The supervisor asked the students _____ _____ _____ _____ _____ _____ _____ _____ _____ _____ _____ _____

4) 'Quit smoking as soon as you can.'
- The doctor advised my grandfather _____ _____ _____ _____ _____ _____ _____ _____ _____ _____ _____

5) 'Make your bed before you leave to school.'
- My mother told me _____ _____ _____ _____ _____ _____ _____ _____ _____ _____ _____

6) 'Don't use my cell phone, please.'
- My classmate asked me _____ _____ _____ _____ _____ _____ _____ _____ _____ _____ _____

7) 'Respect your teachers and help your classmates.'
- My uncle told me _____ _____ _____ _____ _____ _____ _____ _____ _____ _____ _____ _____

8) 'Warm up in order to share in the match.'
→ The coach asked his player _____
_____

9) 'Get ready to start the race.'
→ The trainer urged me _____
_____

10) 'Set your alarm before you sleep.'
→ My grandmother reminded me _____
_____

≈≈≈ My Homework ≈≈≈

> ## Exercise Twenty
↓ Change the direct speech into reported speech.

1) 'Water these roses every morning.'
→ My brother told me _____
_____

2) 'Don't drive fast on highways.'
→ The police officer warned me _____
_____

3) 'Brush your teeth twice a day.'
→ The dentist advised my brother _____
_____

4) 'Don't come to your class late.'
→ The principal urged the students _____
_____

5) 'Don't waste your time playing computer games.'
→ My parents warned me _____
_____

6) 'Review all your lessons well before the final exam.'
→ Our teachers advised us _____
_____

7) 'Put your cell phone on silent mode during the lecture.'
→ The professor asked us _____
_____

8) 'Study well in order to achieve excellent results.'
→ My friends desired me _____
_____

9) 'Could you please be quiet?'
→ My neighbour asked me _____
_____

10) 'Don't buy an old car.'
➢ My grandparents advised me ____ ____ ____ ____ ____ ____ ____ ____ ____ ____ ____ ____ ____ ____

🐚🐚🐚 My Homework 🐚🐚🐚

> ### *Exercise Twenty One*
✤ Find the mistake in each of the following sentences and correct it.

1) Saleh said that she has visited the Philippines the week before.
➢ _____

2) My teacher wanted to know why some of my classmates are making noise in class.
➢ _____

3) Ernest told that he had never been to Korea.
➢ _____

4) My sisters told me that they are buying some new clothes when I called them.
➢ _____

5) Martin wanted to know if I will visit him the following week.
➢ _____

6) The students said that he had never caused any troubles in class.
➢ _____

7) The doctor said that he has done his best to save woman's life.
➢ _____

8) The mechanic told me that my car need a lot of spare parts.
➢ _____

9) The manager told me that he was working on a new project now.
➢ _____

10) The audience wanted to know when the new performance will start.
➢ _____

🐚🐚🐚 My Homework 🐚🐚🐚

➢ Exercise Twenty Two

✦ Find the mistake in each of the following sentences and correct it.

1) The pharmacist asked me if I have taken that medicine the day before.
☙ _____

2) The player told his coach that he can't take part in the final match.
☙ _____

3) Mr Saleh told me that he will issue a new book next year.
☙ _____

4) My mother told that she had a dentist's appointment at 7:45 p.m.
☙ _____

5) My uncle said that he has bought a new family van the week before.
☙ _____

6) My supervisor asked me when did I maintain the fax machine.
☙ _____

7) The doctor would like to know whether I will take the pills or not.
☙ _____

8) Ayah tells Nour that she didn't like watching action movie.
☙ _____

9) Jodie told her manager that she won't be late for the meeting.
☙ _____

10) Jimmie said that he works as a math teacher from 1990 to 1999.
☙ _____

☙☙☙ *My Homework* ☙☙☙

➢ *Exercise Twenty Three*

✦ Find the mistake in each of the following sentences and correct it.

1) The doctor advised me drink as much water as possible.
   ➢ _____
   _____

2) Omar told that me he is waiting for the bus when it started to snow.
   ➢ _____
   _____

3) Jean asked me help her write a reply to her manager's email.
   ➢ _____
   _____

4) Salem said that he won't go to the party the next day.
   ➢ _____
   _____

5) Pierre advised his sister not walk alone in the jungle.
   ➢ _____
   _____

6) The man informed the police officers that his car has been stolen the day before.
   ➢ _____
   _____

7) The nurse advised the patient take his medicine on time.
   ➢ _____
   _____

8) Ernie told me that his family will move to another city the following month.
   ➢ _____
   _____

9) The secretary said that she hadn't receive the emails yet.
   ➢ _____
   _____

10) The optician told me that my eyes have to be checked carefully.
    ➢ _____
    _____

My Homework

➢ *Exercise Twenty Four*

✦ Find the mistake in each of the following sentences and correct it.

1) The security man asked me show him my ID.
   ✎ _____

2) The referee warned the football player don't play in a tough way again.
   ✎ _____

3) The carpenter told the landlord that the broken window can't be repaired.
   ✎ _____

4) The students asked their teacher explain the difficult grammar rules once more.
   ✎ _____

5) My aunt said that she should pay the bills that day.
   ✎ _____

6) My neighbour asked me if I am leaving to another apartment.
   ✎ _____

7) Mark wanted to know where did Martin go the day before.
   ✎ _____

8) Rahaf urged her classmates to double their efforts before the end-of-term tests.
   ✎ _____

9) Mamdouh told Maggie that her essay is perfect.
   ✎ _____

10) Sohair asked her daughters to did the washing-up later.
    ✎ _____

❦❦❦ My Homework ❦❦❦

> ## *Exercise Twenty Five*
Find the mistake in each of the following sentences and correct it.
1) Dan's parents asked him why he wants to become a civil engineer.
   _____

2) Andrew asked his friend not reveal his secret to anybody.
   _____

3) Leila wanted to know if my family will accept her wedding invitation.
   _____

4) Ahmad would like to know how long will it take to finish the website.
   _____

5) The interviewer asked me if I have designed websites for American companies before.
   _____

6) The teacher told Walid that he should hand his homework in on time.
   _____

7) My manager told me that I can reach him at that number at nine thirty.
   _____

8) The tour guide told us that he will guide us through the old town.
   _____

9) My father wanted me meet my uncle at the airport.
   _____

10) The thief begged us do not take him to the police station.
    _____

My Homework

➤ *Exercise Twenty Six*

Find the mistake in each of the following sentences and correct it.

1) The pilot said that the plane will reach its destination in two hours.
   _____

2) The flight attendant wanted to know what kind of meal we prefer.
   _____

3) The soccer player said that he scores fifteen goals the year before.
   _____

4) Emad told me that he has already invited his neighbours to the party.
   _____

5) Adel wanted to know how much the new house costs.
   _____

6) My friend asked me how far is our new farm from the city.
   _____

7) The boys begged their parents to letting them visit their grandparents in the country.
   _____

8) Khalid advised his son to been careful while driving on highways.
   _____

9) Santos said that he can't fix the laptop himself.
   _____

10) Sandra urged her sisters don't be lazy in class.
    _____

My Homework

Comparatives and Superlatives

The Comparative with Adjectives and Adverbs

AN ADJECTIVE **is** a word that qualifies a noun.

AN ATTRIBUTIVE ADJECTIVE **precedes** a noun.

Example:

- a new car
- Jerica bought a **new** car.
- an old villa
- We found the car **near** an old villa.
- large farms
- There are many **large** farms near the city.

AN ADVERB is a word that adds more information to a verb.

Examples:

- Ahmad is a careful driver.   (An adjective + a noun)
- ✓ The adjective describes the noun 'driver'.

- Ahmad drives carefully.   (A verb + an adverb)
- ✓ The adverb describes the verb 'drives'.

- This is a quick train.
- ✓ This train runs quickly.

My Homework

The order of Adjectives

> When we use multiple **ADJECTIVES** to describe **A NOUN**, they are used in a serial order before they modify.

1- Articles, Qualifiers, or Other Noun Markers

a
an
the
some
many
Albert's

2- What we think, opinion

smart	attractive	lovely	true	delicious	pleasing	striking

3- Size

giant	tiny	slight	fat	enormous

4- Age

old	new	young

5- Shape

round	square	slim	curved	fat

6- Color / Aspect

green	white	blue	red	yellow

7- Nationality

American	English	Canadian	Australian	Irish	Egyptian	Saudi

8- Religion

Muslim	Catholic	Protestant	Jewish

9- Material			
wooden	*woollen*	*plastic*	*steel*

10- Purpose			
conference room	*press conference*	*living room*	*scratch paper*

11- The noun									
engineer	*girl*	*desk*	*man*	*office*	*book*	*woman*	*car*	*bus*	*computer*

✦ Examples:
➢ Lilly bought a new white silk dress for her sister.
➢ My grandfather keeps his money in an old red wooden box.

My Homework

Regular Adverb Forms | **Irregular Adverb Forms**

We add *-ly* to the normal **ADJECTIVE** to change it into an

Adjective	Adverb
quick	quick*ly*
terrib*e*	terrib*ly*
useful	useful*ly*
easy	easi*ly*

Adjective	Adverb
fast	fast
hard	hard
late	late
early	early
daily	daily
good	well
enough	enough
logic	logically
basic	basically
long	long
low	low
deep	deep / deeply
near	near / nearly
far	far
high	high / highly

✤ Examples:

➢ Mahmoud is a **good** typist. [Adjective]
✓ Mahmoud types **well**. [Adverb]

➢ We took an **early** train to Tokyo. [Adjective]
✓ This train leaves for the suburbs very **early**. [Adverb]

Note:

Adjectives like *fatherly, friendly* can't be used as adverbs. Instead, we say, '*in a fatherly way*'.

- ➢ My teacher gave me **fatherly** advice to work harder. [Adjective]
- ✓ My teacher treats us **in a fatherly way**. [Adverb]

- ➢ Mr. Sam is a friendly person. [Adjective]
- ✓ Mr. Sam behaves **in a friendly way**. [Adverb]

Note:

> The adverb form of *good* is *well*.

- ➢ Suzan is a good cook. [Adjective]
- ✓ Suzan cooks well. [Adverb]

My Homework

Present and Past Participles as Adjectives

Present Participle; the *-ing* Form

In the present participle, the *noun* performs the action.

an exciting game	a thrilling movie
a surprising visit	an exhausting mission

Past Participle Form

In the past participle, the *noun* receives the action.

excited fans	amused spectators
surprised teachers	scared children

✚ Examples:
- ➢ My grandmother used to tell us amusing stories.
- ➢ Adam's kids were terrified when they saw the lion on the stage.

Forming Comparative Adverbs

One-Syllable Adverbs

Adjective	Comparative
fast	faster
hard	harder
late	later
well	better
high	higher
highly	more highly

Two-Syllable Adverbs

Adjective	Comparative
slowly	more slowly
quickly	more quickly
carefully	more carefully
carelessly	more carelessly
badly	worse

We use –er with some two-syllable adjectives. Others can take –er or more.

Adjective	Adjective + er	more + Adjective
friendly	friendlier	more friendly
handsome	handsomer	more handsome

We use more with some one-syllable adjectives.

Adjective	Comparative	Adjective	Comparative
right	more right	wrong	more wrong
real	more real	ill	more ill

> *Less* is the opposite of *more*.

+ **Example:**

➢ London is **more** crowded **than** Belfast.
✓ Belfast is **less** crowded **than** London.

Irregular Comparative Forms

Adjective	Comparative	Adjective	Comparative
good	better	bad	worse
little	less	much	more
far	farther	far	further

Forming Superlative Adjectives

One-Syllable Adverbs

Adjective	Superlative
fast	*the* fast**est**
hard	*the* hard**est**
late	*the* late**st**
well	*the* best

Two-Syllable Adverbs

Adjective	Superlative
slowly	*the* most slowly
quickly	*the* most quickly
gently	*the* most gently
badly	*the* worst

Forming Superlative Adverbs

One-Syllable Adverbs

Adjective	Comparative
fast	*the* fast*est*
hard	*the* hard*est*
late	*the* late*st*
well	*the* best

Two-Syllable Adverbs

Adjective	Comparative
slowly	*the* most slowly
quickly	*the* most quickly
gently	*the* most gently
badly	*the* worst

We use *-est* with some two-syllable adjectives. Others can take *-est* or *most*.

Adjective	Adjective + *-est*	*most* + Adjective
friendly	*the* friendl*iest*	*the most* friendly
handsome	*the* handsome*st*	*the most* handsome
slowly	*the* slow*est*	*the most* slowly

We use *more* with some one-syllable adjectives.

Adjective	Superlative	Adjective	Superlative
right	*the most* right	wrong	*the most* wrong
real	*the most* real	ill	*the most* ill

The least is the opposite of *the most*.

✤ **Examples:**
➢ London is **the most crowded** city in England.
➢ We have to look for **the least expensive** hotel in the city.

Irregular Superlative Forms

Adjective	Superlative	Adjective	Superlative
good	the best	bad	the worst
little	the least	much	the most
far	the farthest	far	the furthest

Example:
- Omar behaves the most **politely** of all.

My Homework

The *as . . . as* construction

Subject	verb	as	adjective	as	noun/pronoun

1st Subj.	1st verb	as	adjective	as	2nd subj.	2nd verb

Example:
- Maria is **as** beautiful **as** her elder sister.
- Chris is **as** modest **as** his grandfather is.

Subject	verb	as	adverb	as	noun/pronoun

Examples:
- Claudia always drives **as** safely **as** her father.
- Michael behaves **as** politely **as** his grandfather does.

My Homework

➢ Exercise One
Write the comparative and superlative forms of these adjectives.

	ADJECTIVE	COMPARATIVE	SUPERLATIVE
1	small		
2	large		
3	easy		
4	hot		
5	snowy		
6	fantastic		
7	real		
8	early		
9	late		
10	dangerous		
11	high		
12	thin		
13	wide		
14	deep		
15	bad		

🌺🌺🌺 *My Homework* 🌺🌺🌺

➢ Exercise Two
Write the comparative and superlative forms of these adjectives.

	ADJECTIVE	COMPARATIVE	SUPERLATIVE
1	far		
2	good		
3	cheap		
4	heavy		
5	right		
6	expensive		
7	big		
8	quiet		
9	wet		
10	exciting		
11	quick		
12	wrong		
13	popular		
14	common		
15	ill		

🌺🌺🌺 *My Homework* 🌺🌺🌺

➢ **Exercise Three**
✦ Write the base form of the comparative adjectives and adverbs.

1	prettier	
2	sadder	
3	more honestly	
4	less fascinating	
5	shorter	
6	more truthful	
7	more exciting	
8	more happily	
9	hungrily	
10	speedily	
11	brightly	
12	intensely	
13	more wonderful	
14	wetter	
15	drizzlier	

❧❧❧ *My Homework* ☙☙☙

➢ **Exercise Four**
✦ Write the base form of the superlative adjectives and adverbs.

1	the rainiest	
2	the most important	
3	the most reasonably	
4	the best	
5	the solidest	
6	the stiffest	
7	the coolest	
8	the hottest	
9	the driest	
10	the wettest	
11	the worst	
12	the furthest	
13	the most independent	
14	the largest	
15	the fattest	

❧❧❧ *My Homework* ☙☙☙

➢ **Exercise Five**
✦ Write the base form of the superlative adjectives and adverbs.

1	the happiest	
2	the latest	
3	the most showery	
4	the least lenient	

5	the softest	
6	the hardest	
7	the coolest	
8	the busiest	
9	the thirstiest	
10	the mistiest	
11	the drizzliest	
12	the wildest	
13	the hastiest	
14	the most primitively	
15	the most originally	

> ## Exercise Six
✦ Fill the gaps with an adjective derived from the given base form.
✦ Follow the example.

➢ We enjoyed an _____ comic play last night.   (excite)
✓ We enjoyed an <u>exciting</u> comic play last night.

1. Some students got _____ when they saw the exam paper.   (confuse)

2. We received _____ news about my sister's success.   (amaze)

3. The police could find the _____ car near the post office.   (steal)

4. The thief crept into the villa through a _____ window.   (break)

5. The child was _____ when he saw the wild dog.   (horrify)

6. Sarah was _____ when she saw the math test.   (puzzle)

7. Atif was _____ when he found his precious watch.   (delight)

8. Amin was _____ because he managed to solve the problem.   (relieve)

9. We got _____ news concerning our exam results.   (break)

10. I have read _____ article about Christopher Columbus.   (thrill)

11. This old house has a _____ design.   (please)

12. The exam result of my daughter is _____.   (satisfy)

13. Adam thinks that teaching is not a very _____ career.   (reward)

14. Hatem looked _____ when I told him the news.   (surprise)

15. The captain of the soccer team behaved in an _____ way.   (astonish)

16. Ann didn't understand the _____ Algebra problem. Therefore, she asked for her father's help. (puzzle)
17. My parents looked _____ because my brother was late. (worry)
18. This factory uses highly _____ equipment to produce cars. (advance)
19. I was _____ when I saw my fiancée for the first time. (fascinate)
20. Hafez could draw a very _____ portrait for his daughter. (charm)

🌿🌿🌿 *My Homework* 🍃🍃🍃

> ## *Exercise Seven*
✦ Find the mistake in each of the following sentences and correct it.
✦ Follow the example.
> Our manager moved to a big new office.
✓ Our manager moved to a new big office.

1) I need a wooden square small desk.
🌿 _____
2) My grandmother used to read English yellow old books.
🌿 _____
3) The old man was wearing a woollen red bad coat.
🌿 _____
4) There is a green giant old tree in front of our school.
🌿 _____
5) My family moved to a white, new, beautiful house.
🌿 _____
6) In the past, people used to live in small wooden simple cottages.
🌿 _____
7) My brother bought some wooden black attractive chairs.
🌿 _____
8) There are green many tall trees in the park.
🌿 _____
9) I met some Egyptian young polite tourists in the Wax Museum.
🌿 _____
10) When I visited China, I brought Chinese attractive many souvenirs.
🌿 _____

11) We watched a long American exciting movie last night.
   ➤ ___ ___ ___ ___ ___ ___ ___ ___ ___ ___

12) Tim parked his car in a closed large well-designed parking lot.
   ➤ ___ ___ ___ ___ ___ ___ ___ ___ ___ ___

13) Saud had a long tiring flight to South Africa.
   ➤ ___ ___ ___ ___ ___ ___ ___ ___ ___ ___

14) Abdul-Aziz likes German old-fashioned classic cars.
   ➤ ___ ___ ___ ___ ___ ___ ___ ___ ___ ___

15) We enjoyed a Japanese homemade nice meal yesterday.
   ➤ ___ ___ ___ ___ ___ ___ ___ ___ ___ ___

🌸🌸🌸 My Homework 🌸🌸🌸

➤ **_Exercise Eight_**
✦ Use an adverb instead of the adjective in these sentences.
✦ Follow the example.
  ➤ Abdul-Aziz is a quick runner.
  ✓ Abdul-Aziz runs quickly.

1) Salma is a polite young woman.
   ➤ Salma behaves ___ ___ ___ ___ ___ ___ ___

2) Dina is a good singer.
   ➤ ___ ___ ___ ___ ___ ___ ___ ___ ___ ___

3) Jane Austen is a fantastic writer.
   ➤ ___ ___ ___ ___ ___ ___ ___ ___ ___ ___

4) Saleh is a creative teacher.
   ➤ ___ ___ ___ ___ ___ ___ ___ ___ ___ ___

5) Our new manager is a perfect project planner.
   ➤ ___ ___ ___ ___ ___ ___ ___ ___ ___ ___

6) This is a slow bus.
   ➤ ___ ___ ___ ___ ___ ___ ___ ___ ___ ___

7) Salah is a skilful football player.
   ➤ ___ ___ ___ ___ ___ ___ ___ ___ ___ ___

8) Paul is a lazy student.
   ➤ ___ ___ ___ ___ ___ ___ ___ ___ ___ ___

9) Emad is a reckless truck driver.
   ➤ ___ ___ ___ ___ ___ ___ ___ ___ ___ ___

10) The little child gave a loud cry.
   ➤ ___ ___ ___ ___ ___ ___ ___ ___ ___ ___

11) This old man is hard worker.
✎ _____

12) Hessah is a fast reader.
✎ _____

13) Michael is a heavy smoker.
✎ _____

14) Dan's behaviour is strange.
✎ _____

15) Hala is an expert musician.
✎ _____

🌿🌿🌿 My Homework 🍃🍃🍃

> ### *Exercise Nine*
✤ Find the mistake in each of the following sentences and correct it.
✤ Follow the example.
> Martin speaks most clearly than Paul.
✓ Martin speaks <u>more</u> clearly than Paul.

1) My mobile phone doesn't work proper.
✎ _____

2) Our mother always wakes up earliest than us all.
✎ _____

3) My elder sister is a very better swimmer.
✎ _____

4) There is large garden around our house.
✎ _____

5) This is the more wonderful football stadium I have ever seen.
✎ _____

6) The streets of my village are always a clean.
✎ _____

7) I usually run more rapid than my friends.
✎ _____

8) Salwa is the tall student in our class.
✎ _____

9) Ibrahim's stomach pains him terrible.
✎ _____

10) My father can speak Chinese fluent.
✎ _____

11) Fahad is rich than his brother.
➢ ___ ___ ___ ___ ___ ___ ___ ___ ___ ___

12) Noran is the good student in our school.
➢ ___ ___ ___ ___ ___ ___ ___ ___ ___ ___

13) Merhan is the intellectual girl among her friends.
➢ ___ ___ ___ ___ ___ ___ ___ ___ ___ ___

14) Abdou always thinks logical.
➢ ___ ___ ___ ___ ___ ___ ___ ___ ___ ___

15) My grandfather is very old, but he still works a hard.
➢ ___ ___ ___ ___ ___ ___ ___ ___ ___ ___

🕮🕮🕮 *My Homework* 🕮🕮🕮

➢ *Exercise Ten*
✦ Find the mistake in each of the following sentences and correct it.
✦ Follow the example.

1) The little child was walking steady.
➢ ___ ___ ___ ___ ___ ___ ___ ___ ___ ___

2) Zeyad drives more reckless than Eyad.
➢ ___ ___ ___ ___ ___ ___ ___ ___ ___ ___

3) It's a bad habit to eat quick.
➢ ___ ___ ___ ___ ___ ___ ___ ___ ___ ___

4) Ahmad's work is getting good all the time.
➢ ___ ___ ___ ___ ___ ___ ___ ___ ___ ___

5) The new version of this car is powerful than the old one.
➢ ___ ___ ___ ___ ___ ___ ___ ___ ___ ___

6) It's always an awful to walk in the forest at night.
➢ ___ ___ ___ ___ ___ ___ ___ ___ ___ ___

7) I'm sorry. I'm a bit later.
➢ ___ ___ ___ ___ ___ ___ ___ ___ ___ ___

8) The River Nile is long than the Tigris.
➢ ___ ___ ___ ___ ___ ___ ___ ___ ___ ___

9) The Strait of Dover is the narrow part of the English Channel.
➢ ___ ___ ___ ___ ___ ___ ___ ___ ___ ___

10) Silk is soft than cotton.
➢ ___ ___ ___ ___ ___ ___ ___ ___ ___ ___

11) The Great Pyramid of Giza is the old of the Seven Wonders of the Ancient World.
➢ ___ ___ ___ ___ ___ ___ ___ ___ ___ ___

12) If you follow the map, you can reach your destination a fast.
🖎 _____ _____ _____ _____ _____ _____ _____ _____ _____ _____

13) As soon as the plane took off, it flew highly.
🖎 _____ _____ _____ _____ _____ _____ _____ _____ _____ _____

14) My teachers always advise me not to drive a fast.
🖎 _____ _____ _____ _____ _____ _____ _____ _____ _____ _____

15) Our teacher seemed nervously because some students came to class late.
🖎 _____ _____ _____ _____ _____ _____ _____ _____ _____ _____

🖎🖎🖎 *My Homework* 🖎🖎🖎

➢ *Exercise Eleven*

✤ Choose the correct answer from a, b, c, or d.

1) Bahrain is _____ Arab country.

a	lovely	b	a lovely
c	lovelier	d	loveliest

2) This is the _____ grammar test I have ever had.

a	easier	b	easy
c	easiest	d	an easy

3) London is one of the _____ cities in Europe.

a	more wonderful	b	most wonderful
c	a wonderful	d	wonderful

4) Some students think that it is _____ to learn Chinese.

a	most difficult	b	a difficult
c	difficult	d	more difficult

5) The teacher said that Graham is _____ than Ted.

a	lazier	b	laziest
c	lazy	d	a lazy

6) Justine is _____ student.

a	intelligent	b	more intelligent
c	an intelligent	d	most intelligent

7) It is always _____ in Kuwait in the summer.

a	hot	b	hotter
c	a hot	d	hottest

8) The students had a _____ discussion about their trip to the country.

a	longest	b	a long
c	longer	d	long

9) We gave Dolly a _____ present on her birthday.

a	nicer	b	nice
c	nicest	d	a nice

10) Last night, we had _____ time at my sister's birthday party.

a	a great	b	great
c	greater	d	greatest

11) Lara and her family had _____ meal outdoors.

a	more delicious	b	most delicious
c	a delicious	d	delicious

12) The Dead Sea is the _____ lake in the world.

a	deeper	b	a deep
c	deep	d	deepest

13) Tuka is the _____ pharmacist among her colleagues.

a	less hard-working	b	more hard-working
c	most hard-working	d	hard-working

14) Mount Everest is the world's _____ mountain peak.

a	high	b	highest
c	higher	d	a high

15) Mohamed Salah is one of the _____ soccer players.

a	most famous	b	more famous
c	famous	d	a famous

16) This is one of the _____ winters we have ever had.

a	a cold	b	cold
c	colder	d	coldest

17) My brother is _____ runner.

a	faster	b	a fast
c	fast	d	fastest

18) My sister is the _____ student in her school.

a	cleverest	b	clever
c	cleverer	d	a clever

19) The teacher refused to accept new students in his _____ classroom.

a	a crowded	b	crowded
c	crowdedly	d	more crowded

20) Romantic poems are _____ than any other ones.

a	more enjoyable	b	an enjoyable
c	enjoyable	d	most enjoyable

✎✎✎ My Homework ✐✐✐

➢ *Exercise Twelve*

✦ Choose the correct answer from a, b, c, or d.

1) China is the _____ country in the world.

a	most populated	b	populated
c	more populated	d	a populated

2) Football is one of the _____ sports.

a	more popular	b	a popular
c	popular	d	most popular

3) This is the _____ joke I have ever heard.

a	silly	b	sillier
c	silliest	d	a silly

4) Ted writes _____ than Erin.

a	nicely	b	more nicely
c	most nicely	d	nice

5) My father bought me _____ iPad last week.

a	modern	b	more modern
c	a modern	d	most modern

6) Abdul-Rahman's bike isn't very fast. He wants _____ one.

a	fastest	b	a fast
c	fast	d	a faster

7) Charles Dickens is the _____ English novelist.

a	greatly	b	greater
c	great	d	greatest

8) Yesterday, I read _____ article about the Olympic Games.

a	most important	b	important
c	an important	d	more important

9) Andrew: How is your father?
   Eliza: He is much _____ now.

a	better	b	good
c	a good	d	best

10) I think that Jackson is the _____ in our school basketball team.

a	badly	b	bad
c	worse	d	worst

11) My younger sister's hair is golden and _____.

a	curliest	b	curlier
c	a curly	d	curly

12) This is the _____ Algebra test I have ever had.

a	easier	b	easiest
c	an easy	d	easy

13) My brother likes fresh fruit juice _____ than tea.

a	better	b	best
c	a good	d	good

14) William Shakespeare is the _____ English playwright.

a	more famous	b	famous
c	famous	d	most famous

15) I have already read _____ book about the atom.

a	useful	b	most useful
c	a useful	d	more useful

16) My digital watch is _____ than your alarm clock.

a	more accurate	b	most accurate
c	accurate	d	an accurate

17) Our teacher of English always speaks in _____ way.

a	educated	b	more educated
c	an educated	d	most educated

18) The trainer was _____ because his team won the final game.

a	delighted	b	more delighted
c	a delighted	d	most delighted

19) Some fans left the stadium because the match was _____.

a	a boring	b	most boring
c	more boring	d	boring

20) My brothers were so _____ when they passed their test.

a	more excited	b	an excited
c	excited	d	most excited

❧❧❧ My Homework ❧❧❧

> ### Exercise Thirteen
✦ Choose the correct answer from a, b, c, or d.

1) The sun is _____ star.

a	useful	b	usefully
c	more useful	d	a useful

2) Gold is _____ metal.

a	precious	b	more precious
c	most precious	d	a precious

3) The student's answer to the teacher's question sounded _____.

a	correctly	b	a correct
c	correctness	d	correct

4) This is _____ a great idea.

a	sure	b	a sure
c	surely	d	sureness

5) My sister always dresses _____.

a	a beautiful	b	beautifully
c	beautiful	d	beauty

6) Students have to talk to their teacher _____.

a	polite	b	politeness
c	a polite	d	politely

7) My sister is fond of reading _____ stories.

a	strangely	b	a strange
c	strange	d	stranger

8) The player looked at the referee _____.

a	angry	b	anger
c	angrily	d	an angry

9) I pay a _____ visit to my grandparents on their farm.

a	regularly	b	regularity
c	regular	d	a regular

10) _____ driving helps motorists avoid accidents.

a	Safely	b	Safety
c	A safe	d	Safe

11) Your family and mine are _____ related.

a	close	b	a close
c	a closely	d	closely

12) Our teacher of French speaks French _____.

a	well	b	a good
c	good	d	best

13) Our new neighbour is a _____ person.

a	friend	b	friends
c	friendly	d	friends'

14) Samar and Lina are twins. They are both _____.

a	a gorgeous	b	most gorgeous
c	gorgeous	d	more gorgeous

15) Ann's twin girls are Lama and Lara. Lama is as _____ as Lara.

a	beautifully	b	a beautiful
c	beautiful	d	beautify

16) My elder sister is the _____ cook I have ever known.

a	most amazing	b	more amazing
c	amazing	d	amazingly

17) Majid is so smart that he can answer this difficult test _____.

a	easy	b	an easy
c	easily	d	easiest

18) This is the _____ exam I have ever taken.

a	easy	b	an easy
c	easily	d	easiest

19) You have to send this email as _____ as possible.

a	quick	b	quicker
c	quick	d	quickly

20) My grandfather always advises me to work _____.

a	a hard	b	hardly
c	hardest	d	hard

🙶🙶🙶 *My Homework* 🙷🙷🙷

> *Exercise Fourteen*

↳ Look at this table about five students and choose the correct answer from a, b, c, or d.

	Age	Weight	Height	Grade
Linda	21	76	165	95
Salma	23	82	167	75
Sue	24	80	170	95
Ghada	21	79	170	97
Jana	19	82	175	93

1) Jana is the _____ student.

a	taller	b	as tall as
c	tallest	d	tall

2) Salma is as _____ as Jana.

a	heavier	b	heavy
c	a heavy	d	heaviest

3) Linda is the _____ student.

a	short	b	shorter
c	a short	d	shortest

4) Ghada has the _____ grade in the final exam.

a	good	b	better
c	best	d	as good as

5) Sue is as _____ as Ghada.

a	a tall	b	taller
c	tallest	d	tall

6) Jana is the _____ student.

a	heavier	b	heavy
c	a heavy	d	heaviest

7) Salma's grade isn't _____ Ghada's.

a	good	b	better
c	best	d	as good as

8) Ghada is as _____ Linda.

a	old	b	heavy
c	tall	d	good

9) Sue is the _____ student.

a	oldest	b	youngest
c	tallest	d	heaviest

10) Salma is _____ than Ghada.

a	taller	b	better
c	lighter	d	older

11) Jana is the _____ student.

a	youngest	b	tallest
c	oldest	d	shortest

✺✺✺ *My Homework* ✺✺✺

SECTION 24 — *Punctuation*

> **PUNCTUATION is** *the marks we use in writing that divide sentences and phrases.*

Example:

- did collins buy a new apartment in new jersey last april
- Did Collins buy a new apartment in New Jersey last April?

Capitalization is the use of capital letters in writing.

We use a capital letter in the following cases:

For the first word in a sentence	He wrote a letter to his father.
For the first word in a question	Does she like music?
For the subject pronoun *I*	Sue and I will go to the party.
For the names of people	Batool and Tuka flew to Iowa.
For the names of continents	Asia and Africa are large continents.
For the names of countries	Oman and Kuwait export oil.
For the names of cities	Paris is a lovely city.
For the names of towns	Tala is a small Egyptian town.
For the names of villages	Kom El-Sheikh Ebaid is a small beautiful village near Tanta, Egypt.
For the names of oceans	Morocco overlooks the Atlantic Ocean.
For the names of seas	The Adriatic Sea contains 1,300 islands.

For the names of rivers	The Tigris flows from the mountains of Turkey through Iraq.
For the names of canals	The Panama Canal connects the Atlantic Ocean with the Pacific Ocean.
For the names of islands	Crete is a famous Greek island.
For the names of peninsula	The Arabian Peninsula is located northeast of Africa.
For the names of gulfs	The Gulf of Mexico formed nearly 300 million years ago.
For the names of lakes	Many tourists visit Lake Como in Italy.
For the names of mountains	The Alps extend from France to Slovenia.
For the names of deserts	The Sahara Desert is located in Africa.
For the names of monuments	The Sphinx is an ancient statue in Giza.
For the names of landmarks	The Statue of Liberty is visited by more than three million people a year.
For the titles of rulers	King Fahad (Saudi Arabia) Queen Anne (the UK) President Sadat (Egypt) Sultan Qaboos (Oman) Sheikh Jaber (Kuwait) Prince William (the UK) Princess Diana (the UK) Emperor Akihito (Japan) Empress Michiko (Japan)

For the job titles	Dr Abdul-Rahman
For the initials of someone's name	T. S. Eliot
For the days of the week	Monday
For the days of the year	January
For the names of holidays and special celebrations	Christmas Eid-al-Fitr All Saints' Day Ramadan Good Friday
For the names of newspapers, and magazines.	My father reads the *Times* every day. *Focus* is a German weekly magazine.
For the titles of books	*Oliver Twist*
For the titles of films	*Independence Day*
For the titles of plays	*Antony and Cleopatra*
For nationalities	American / British / Egyptian
For languages	English / French / Arabic / Chinese

My Homework

THE FULL STOP (PERIOD) *is used at the end of a sentence.*

+ **Example:**

> ➢ My family may leave to toronto next friday
> ✓ My family may leave to Toronto next Friday.

THE FULL STOP (PERIOD) *is used in abbreviations.*

+ **Example:**

> ➢ eg = for example
> ✓ e.g. = for example

THE COMMA *is used*

to separate items in a list.	i bought a camera a watch a shirt and a hat
	I bought a camera, a watch, a shirt and a hat.
to add extra information to a sentence.	mr saleh ibrahim our new teacher of english helped us a lot in this course
	Mr Saleh Ibrahim, our new teacher of English, helped us a lot in this course.
to indicate natural pauses.	when i finish this course i will apply for a job in a private school
	When I finish this course, I will apply for a job in a private school.
to separate names and persons.	are you leaving to the city harrison
	Are you leaving to the city, Harrison?

THE SEMICOLON is used

to join two closely related sentences into one longer sentence.	the computer was invented as a result it started to be used in all fields
	The computer was invented years ago; as a result, it started to be used in all fields.

THE COLON is used

before a list introduced by a complete sentence.	i sent the wedding invitations to many people my relatives, my neighbours my friends and my colleagues at work
	I sent the wedding invitations to many people: my relatives, my neighbours, my friends, and my colleagues at work.
before a quotation.	my father said to me i have already bought a new house for you
	My father said to me: 'I have already bought a new house for you.'
to separate hours from minutes.	we are going to leave at 9 45 a.m.
	We are going to leave at 9:45 a.m.
between the name of a character and the words they speak	teacher why are you late

edwin i missed the school bus |
| | Teacher: Why are you late?

Edwin: I missed the school bus. |

THE QUESTION MARK is used

at the end of yes/no questions.	malik did alan come on time
	nour yes he did
	Malik: Did Alan come on time?
	Nour: Yes, he did.
at the end of wh- questions.	mother who called when i was at work
	nada your friend elisa
	Mother: Who called when I was at work?
	Nada: Your friend Elisa.

THE APOSTROPHE is used

to show who something or someone belongs to.	i saw ahmad s daughter
	I saw Ahmad's daughter.
	this is dan s laptop
	This is Dan's laptop.
to show that one or more letters are missing in a contraction	i ve finished my task sir
	I've finished my task sir.
	she s my sister
	She's my sister.
	they re in the gym
	They're in the gym.

before the letter 's' to show the plural of a letter or number.	there are five 5's in 25
	There are five 5's in 25.
	there are four e s in referee
	There are four e's in 'referee'.

THE EXCLAMATION MARK (POINT) is used

at the end of a sentence to show a strong feeling or emotion such as surprise, sympathy or fear.	what a pity you failed to pass the test
	What a pity you failed to pass the test!
to give strong orders.	don t touch that electric wire
	Don't touch that electric wire!
after interjections.	Hello
	Hello!
	watch out
	Watch out!

THE QUOTATION MARKS are

placed around a word or sentence to say that is what somebody wrote or said.	samuel said may i borrow your dictionary for three days ali
	Samuel said, 'May I borrow your dictionary for three days, Ali?'

My Homework

➢ **_Exercise One_**
✦ Punctuate the following sentences and rewrite them correctly.
✦ Follow the example.
  ➢ my friend taro comes from japan
  ✓ My friend Taro comes from Japan.

1) sam christian lives in toronto ontario canada
🗞 ___ ___ ___ ___ ___ ___ ___ ___ ___ ___

2) istanbul is a famous turkish city
🗞 ___ ___ ___ ___ ___ ___ ___ ___ ___ ___

3) does harry study italian or spanish
🗞 ___ ___ ___ ___ ___ ___ ___ ___ ___ ___

4) is the plane going to take off at 11 30
🗞 ___ ___ ___ ___ ___ ___ ___ ___ ___ ___

5) arnold said to me can you fix my mobile phone
🗞 ___ ___ ___ ___ ___ ___ ___ ___ ___ ___

6) when hend gets home she s going to cook
🗞 ___ ___ ___ ___ ___ ___ ___ ___ ___ ___

7) yes i would like to visit hanover and berlin
🗞 ___ ___ ___ ___ ___ ___ ___ ___ ___ ___

8) dahab is a fantastic resort on the red sea
🗞 ___ ___ ___ ___ ___ ___ ___ ___ ___ ___

9) antonio and annie started a new catering business in rome
🗞 ___ ___ ___ ___ ___ ___ ___ ___ ___ ___

10) my friend said to me we really should be leaving now
🗞 ___ ___ ___ ___ ___ ___ ___ ___ ___ ___

🗞🗞🗞 *My Homework* 🗞🗞🗞

➢ **_Exercise Two_**
✦ Punctuate the following sentences and rewrite them correctly.

1) mr ibrahim is fond of french poetry
🗞 ___ ___ ___ ___ ___ ___ ___ ___ ___ ___

2) george bernard shaw is a famous irish dramatist
🗞 ___ ___ ___ ___ ___ ___ ___ ___ ___ ___

3) bahrain is a beautiful kingdom on the arabian gulf
🗞 ___ ___ ___ ___ ___ ___ ___ ___ ___ ___

4) did marawan take his English test last monday
🗞 ___ ___ ___ ___ ___ ___ ___ ___ ___ ___

5) yomna and her family have moved to new orleans recently
✍ _____

6) yesterday was sunday november 19
✍ _____

7) the nile is a major river in north-eastern africa
✍ _____

8) no i didn t break my mother s vase
✍ _____

9) well you can call again tomorrow morning to see if miss sarah is in
✍ _____

10) tomorrow sunday we will spend some time on the beach
✍ _____

My Homework

> **Exercise Three**

➕ Punctuate the following sentences and rewrite them correctly.

1) charles dickens wrote a famous novel called great expectations
✍ _____

2) hassan spent his vacation in tunisia and algeria last year
✍ _____

3) my little sister has large bright blue eyes
✍ _____

4) boxing day is an official holiday in britain
✍ _____

5) salma lived in liverpool as a child
✍ _____

6) a lot of people immigrate to the united states yearly
✍ _____

7) after batool finished her english test she left the online test room
✍ _____

8) while stewart was driving he felt tired
✍ _____

9) i like japanese cars but ahmad prefers german ones
✍ _____

10) dover castle is the largest in england

My Homework

➤ **Exercise Four**
✦ Punctuate the following sentences and rewrite them correctly.

1) last night we watched an american movie called the wax museum

2) in 2013 marseille served as the european capital of culture

3) rawan please answer the phone

4) mennah said to us my father runs a charity for the poor

5) michael and jane got married in march

6) the mona lisa was painted between 1503 and 1506

7) will david and paul arrive at 9 45

8) is brad going to fly to nebraska tomorrow

9) adam and mike are meeting in omaha next friday

10) sir george everest was a welsh surveyor and geographer

My Homework

➤ **Exercise Five**
✦ Punctuate the following sentences and rewrite them correctly.

1) the girl s father was glad because she passed the french test

2) i can't see smith he must be absent

3) where will majid and ramon spend the easter

4) it s exciting to study chinese this year
🖎 ____ ____ ____ ____ ____ ____ ____ ____ ____ ____

5) dr ibrahim will see ten patients on monday
🖎 ____ ____ ____ ____ ____ ____ ____ ____ ____ ____

6) edgar and neil used to live in rio de janeiro
🖎 ____ ____ ____ ____ ____ ____ ____ ____ ____ ____

7) real madrid and barcelona are going to meet again in march
🖎 ____ ____ ____ ____ ____ ____ ____ ____ ____ ____

8) no lara yelled do it again
🖎 ____ ____ ____ ____ ____ ____ ____ ____ ____ ____

9) i have a small white french car
🖎 ____ ____ ____ ____ ____ ____ ____ ____ ____ ____

10) mr nelson who is a math teacher will visit us on monday
🖎 ____ ____ ____ ____ ____ ____ ____ ____ ____ ____

🖎🖎🖎 My Homework 🖎🖎🖎

➢ **Exercise Six**

✤ Find the mistake in each of the following sentences. Each sentence contains one mistake.

1) The students books were left in the library.
🖎 ____ ____ ____ ____ ____ ____ ____ ____ ____ ____

2) Our new teacher way of teaching is useful to us.
🖎 ____ ____ ____ ____ ____ ____ ____ ____ ____ ____

3) the ten o'clock bus leaves on time.
🖎 ____ ____ ____ ____ ____ ____ ____ ____ ____ ____

4) Would you like another cup of tea, sir
🖎 ____ ____ ____ ____ ____ ____ ____ ____ ____ ____

5) The teacher corrected twenty one quiz sheets.
🖎 ____ ____ ____ ____ ____ ____ ____ ____ ____ ____

6) This is my friend Samuel Johns, M D.
🖎 ____ ____ ____ ____ ____ ____ ____ ____ ____ ____

7) They had jam, cheese eggs and brown bread for breakfast.
🖎 ____ ____ ____ ____ ____ ____ ____ ____ ____ ____

8) Yes I speak Japanese very well.
🖎 ____ ____ ____ ____ ____ ____ ____ ____ ____ ____

9) After Dan let his friends in he shut the door.
🖎 ____ ____ ____ ____ ____ ____ ____ ____ ____ ____

10) If you come late your parents will get angry.
✎ _____

🌿🌿🌿 My Homework 🌿🌿🌿

➢ **_Exercise Seven_**
✚ Find the mistake in each of the following sentences. Each sentence contains one mistake.

1) Brian, who is my son won a school prize yesterday.
✎ _____

2) Fatin is going to buy a pencil sharpener a red pen, and an eraser.
✎ _____

3) My father, by the way is very worried about you.
✎ _____

4) Have a nice trip sir.
✎ _____

5) Daniel said, 'I will be late.
✎ _____

6) This camera is mine not Alfred's.
✎ _____

7) I asked kenneth to come and take his notebooks.
✎ _____

8) My parents are in the garden drinking their mid morning coffee.
✎ _____

9) No I don't like spicy food.
✎ _____

10) *Antony and cleopatra* is a tragedy by William Shakespeare.
✎ _____

🌿🌿🌿 My Homework 🌿🌿🌿

➢ **_Exercise Eight_**
✚ Find the mistake in each of the following sentences. Each sentence contains one mistake.

1) Ayman's sister won't be there but his brother might.
✎ _____

2) Im so happy to meet you today.
✎ _____

3) Tyson house will be painted tomorrow.
✎ _____

4) I may visit my family in Toronto next saturday.
✎ _____

5) My brother promised to visit me in april.
✎ _____

6) Saleh Al-Shalaby the Egyptian author wrote a new book last year.
✎ _____

7) Mary is wearing a nice T shirt today.
✎ _____

8) The London Cairo flight was enjoyable.
✎ _____

9) Tuka replied 'I will send you my feedback soon.'
✎ _____

10) Miss Batool's plan included developing our listening, speaking reading, and writing skills.
✎ _____

My Homework

> ## Exercise Nine
✦ Find the mistake in each of the following sentences. Each sentence contains one mistake.

1) This new restaurant serves cheap wonderful meals.
✎ _____

2) Lets watch an action movie together.
✎ _____

3) The supervisor was happy because the workshop was well organized.
✎ _____

4) Somebody glasses were left in the computer lab yesterday.
✎ _____

5) Mr Saleh has a two year-old grandson.
✎ _____

6) Sarah has only one thing on her mind marriage.
✎ _____

7) Charles Dickens is a world renowned novelist.
✎ _____

8) We thanked the soccer referee for his perfect self control.
➢ _____ _____ _____ _____ _____ _____ _____ _____ _____ _____

9) 'Are we on time' Leila asked.
➢ _____ _____ _____ _____ _____ _____ _____ _____ _____ _____

10) The Shaftesbury avenue is a major street in West End of London.
➢ _____ _____ _____ _____ _____ _____ _____ _____ _____ _____

🙢🙢🙢 *My Homework* 🙠🙠🙠

> ## *Exercise Ten*

✦ Find the mistake in each of the following sentences. Each sentence contains one mistake.

1) The national Air and Space Museum develops new exhibits on the history of aviation.
➢ _____ _____ _____ _____ _____ _____ _____ _____ _____ _____

2) *A Passage to India* is a famous English novel by E. M Forster.
➢ _____ _____ _____ _____ _____ _____ _____ _____ _____ _____

3) When we were in France, we visited calais.
➢ _____ _____ _____ _____ _____ _____ _____ _____ _____ _____

4) We didn't understand why our teacher was angry
➢ _____ _____ _____ _____ _____ _____ _____ _____ _____ _____

5) My friend had to go to hospital as he had a severe backache
➢ _____ _____ _____ _____ _____ _____ _____ _____ _____ _____

6) Being sick Margret couldn't go to school.
➢ _____ _____ _____ _____ _____ _____ _____ _____ _____ _____

7) Alice do your homework before going to bed.
➢ _____ _____ _____ _____ _____ _____ _____ _____ _____ _____

8) I read *Gullivers Travels* many times.
➢ _____ _____ _____ _____ _____ _____ _____ _____ _____ _____

9) we spent the night in a student's hostel near the city.
➢ _____ _____ _____ _____ _____ _____ _____ _____ _____ _____

10) My family enjoyed their stay in Indonesia last july.
➢ _____ _____ _____ _____ _____ _____ _____ _____ _____ _____

🙢🙢🙢 *My Homework* 🙠🙠🙠

Relative Pronouns

A *relative pronoun* marks a relative clause. It has the same referent in the main clause of a sentence that the relative modifies.

✦ Example:
- ➢ The police arrested <u>the shoplifter</u>. <u>He</u> stole Linda's mobile phone.
- ✓ The police arrested the shoplifter <u>who</u> stole Linda's mobile phone.

Who is used for people. It may replace the subject.

✦ Example:
- ➢ We met the new teacher. <u>She</u> lives next door to the school.
- ✓ We met the new teacher <u>who</u> lives next door to the school.

Whom is used for people. It may replace the object.

✦ Example:
- ➢ We visited the Chinese student. The university honoured him last week.
- ✓ We visited the Chinese student <u>whom</u> the university honoured last week.

Which is used for the things we mean. It may replace the subject.

✦ Example:
- ➢ Mike shot the wolf. It attacked his sheep last night.
- ✓ Mike shot the wolf <u>which</u> killed his sheep last night.

> *Which* is used for the things we mean. It may replace the object.

+ **Example:**

➢ Leila bought a new car. It is very expensive.
  ✓ The car <u>which</u> Leila bought is very expensive.

> *That* can be used instead of *who* or *which*.

+ **Examples:**

➢ The police arrested <u>the shoplifter</u>. <u>He</u> stole Linda's mobile phone.
  ✓ The police arrested the shoplifter <u>that</u> stole Linda's mobile phone.

➢ We met the new teacher. <u>She</u> lives next door to the school.
  ✓ We met the new teacher <u>that</u> lives next door to the school.

➢ We visited the Chinese student. The university honoured him last week.
  ✓ We visited the Chinese student <u>that</u> the university honoured last week.

➢ Mike shot the wolf. It attacked his sheep last night.
  ✓ Mike shot the wolf <u>that</u> killed his sheep last night.

➢ Leila bought a new car. It is very expensive.
  ✓ The car <u>that</u> Leila bought is very expensive.

> We can drop *whom* or *which* when they replace an object.

+ **Examples:**

  ✓ We visited the Chinese student <u>whom</u> the university honoured last week.
   =
  ✓ We visited the Chinese student the university honoured last week.

  ✓ The car <u>which</u> Leila bought is very expensive.
   =
  ✓ The car Leila bought is very expensive.

> *Whose* is used to say which person or thing the speaker means. It replaces *my*, *his*, *her*, *their*, etc.

✤ **Examples:**
➢ I am your new neighbour. <u>My</u> car was stolen an hour ago.
   I am your new neighbour <u>whose</u> car was stolen an hour ago.

➢ This is our new English teacher. <u>Her</u> skills are perfect.
   This is our new English teacher <u>whose</u> skills are perfect.

| Using other relative pronouns |

> *When* must be preceded by the word *time* or by the name of a period of time such as *day*, *month*, or *year*.

✤ **Example:**
➢ Ramadan is the ninth <u>month</u> of the Muslim year. Muslims do not eat or drink between dawn and sunset <u>in Ramadan</u>.
   Ramadan is the ninth month of the Muslim year <u>when</u> Muslims do not eat or drink between dawn and sunset.

> *Where* must be preceded by the word *place* or by the name of a kind of place such as *house*, *village*, or *town*.

✤ **Example:**
➢ I always visit the <u>village</u>. I was born and brought up <u>there</u>.
   I always visit the village <u>where</u> I was born and brought up.

My Homework

Using relative pronouns with prepositions

o *Study these examples:*
➢ The apartment <u>where</u> we stayed was well-furnished.
=
The apartment <u>in which</u> we stayed was well-furnished.
=
The apartment <u>which</u> we stayed <u>in</u> was well-furnished.

➢ The day <u>when</u> we met was wonderful.
=
✓ The day on which we met was wonderful.
=
✓ The day which we met on was wonderful.

❧❧❧ *My Homework* ❧❧❧

➢ **Exercise One**
✦ Rewrite these sentences using the correct relative clause.
✦ Follow the example.

✦ **Example:**
➢ We went to the National Museum. We met some Mexican tourists there.
✓ We went to the National Museum <u>where</u> we met some Mexican tourists.

1) I called my neighbour. His house was broken into last night.
❧ _____

2) Dubai is a busy city. You can meet thousands of tourists in Dubai.
❧ _____

3) I thanked the mechanic. He fixed my car very well.
❧ _____

4) This is the tourist. I met him in the music festival.
❧ _____

5) This is the farm. My uncle bought it last month.
❧ _____

6) I can't forget those days. We were so glad then.
❧ _____

7) I forgot to send the email. I wrote it two hours ago.
❧ _____

8) Did you thank the taxi driver? He took you to the airport in the early morning.
➢ ____ ____ ____ ____ ____ ____ ____ ____ ____ ____

9) I saw the children in the park. They were playing hide-and-seek there.
➢ ____ ____ ____ ____ ____ ____ ____ ____ ____ ____

10) We visited our aunt. She lives in Lincoln.
➢ ____ ____ ____ ____ ____ ____ ____ ____ ____ ____

➢➢➢ My Homework ➢➢➢

> ## *Exercise Two*
- Rewrite these sentences using the correct relative clause.

1) We talked to the police officer. He arrested the burglar.
➢ ____ ____ ____ ____ ____ ____ ____ ____ ____ ____

2) I saw an old man on the farm. He was feeding the hens.
➢ ____ ____ ____ ____ ____ ____ ____ ____ ____ ____

3) A bee is an insect. This bee gives us pure honey.
➢ ____ ____ ____ ____ ____ ____ ____ ____ ____ ____

4) My grandparents own a large farm. They grow a lot of vegetables there.
➢ ____ ____ ____ ____ ____ ____ ____ ____ ____ ____

5) Most students live in dormitories. They eat, sleep, and study there.
➢ ____ ____ ____ ____ ____ ____ ____ ____ ____ ____

6) The subway is always crowded. I take it to my office every day.
➢ ____ ____ ____ ____ ____ ____ ____ ____ ____ ____

7) Helena is the capital city of Montana. It was established in 1864.
➢ ____ ____ ____ ____ ____ ____ ____ ____ ____ ____

8) Celina cooked a meal yesterday. It was delicious.
➢ ____ ____ ____ ____ ____ ____ ____ ____ ____ ____

9) The Atlantic is a huge ocean. Several species of fish live there.
➢ ____ ____ ____ ____ ____ ____ ____ ____ ____ ____

10) Our neighbours are sociable and friendly. We invited them to dinner.
➢ ____ ____ ____ ____ ____ ____ ____ ____ ____ ____

➢➢➢ My Homework ➢➢➢

> ## *Exercise Three*
- Rewrite these sentences using the correct relative clause.

1) I visited the school. I received my elementary education there.
➢ ____ ____ ____ ____ ____ ____ ____ ____ ____ ____

2) I met a woman. The woman was a pharmacist.
➤ _____

3) These are the farmers. Their camels were lost in the desert.
➤ _____

4) These are the farmers. They found their lost camels.
➤ _____

5) These are the camels. They were lost in the desert.
➤ _____

6) This is the desert. The farmers' camels were lost there.
➤ _____

7) I broke the vase. My grandmother bought it fifty years ago.
➤ _____

8) I bought a house with a double garage. I keep my two cars there.
➤ _____

9) These are the rabbits. My brother hunted them yesterday.
➤ _____

10) My sisters went to the park. They enjoyed their time there.
➤ _____

✤✤✤ My Homework ✤✤✤

➤ *Exercise Four*
✦ Rewrite these sentences using the correct relative clause.

1) My father bought a car yesterday. It is dark blue.
➤ _____

2) Many tourists visit Luxor yearly. They see one third of the world's monuments there.
➤ _____

3) The oil company is in Dhahran. Saleh works in it.
➤ _____

4) The movie was boring. Ann went to it last night.
➤ _____

5) This is the homework. My teacher asked me to redo it.
➤ _____

6) Our teacher will reward the high achievers. They exerted strenuous efforts.
➤ _____

7) The child threw the tennis ball into the garden. It disappeared there.
✎ ____ ____ ____ ____ ____ ____ ____ ____ ____ ____

8) Salma goes to a medical school in London. She studies medicine there.
✎ ____ ____ ____ ____ ____ ____ ____ ____ ____ ____

9) Abdul-Rahman found an online recruitment website. He submitted his résumé on it.
✎ ____ ____ ____ ____ ____ ____ ____ ____ ____ ____

10) The principal counselled the reluctant students. They usually make troubles in class.
✎ ____ ____ ____ ____ ____ ____ ____ ____ ____ ____

❧❧❧ *My Homework* ❧❧❧

➢ **Exercise Five**

✦ Rewrite these sentences using the correct relative clause.

1) We moved to a new campus. It has a lot of facilities.
✎ ____ ____ ____ ____ ____ ____ ____ ____ ____ ____

2) Saleh has two daughters. They are pharmacists.
✎ ____ ____ ____ ____ ____ ____ ____ ____ ____ ____

3) Eyad goes to an international school. He studies biology and physics there.
✎ ____ ____ ____ ____ ____ ____ ____ ____ ____ ____

4) Neil lost his father's wallet. It contained his visa cards.
✎ ____ ____ ____ ____ ____ ____ ____ ____ ____ ____

5) This is the policeman. He saved the old woman.
✎ ____ ____ ____ ____ ____ ____ ____ ____ ____ ____

6) This is the lawyer. His car was damaged.
✎ ____ ____ ____ ____ ____ ____ ____ ____ ____ ____

7) Adam went to a dental clinic. The dentist checked his teeth there.
✎ ____ ____ ____ ____ ____ ____ ____ ____ ____ ____

8) The mechanic checked my old car. He said that it couldn't be fixed.
✎ ____ ____ ____ ____ ____ ____ ____ ____ ____ ____

9) The runner won a gold medal. He belongs to my family.
✎ ____ ____ ____ ____ ____ ____ ____ ____ ____ ____

10) Joseph told us about the concert. He went to it last Saturday.
✎ ____ ____ ____ ____ ____ ____ ____ ____ ____ ____

❧❧❧ *My Homework* ❧❧❧

Exercise Six

Choose the correct answer from a, b, c, or d.

1) Andrew bought an old van _____ needs repairs.

A	who	b	when
C	when	d	that

2) We entered the house _____ door is painted blue.

A	what	b	where
C	which	d	whose

3) We met the mayor _____ was elected a week ago.

A	where	b	who
C	whose	d	when

4) My parents asked me _____ broke the window of my room.

A	that	b	who
C	whose	d	when

5) This is the garden in _____ my parents like to have their lunch.

A	that	b	what
C	where	d	which

6) The school honoured the teachers _____ results were high.

A	that	b	who
C	whose	d	when

7) This is the umbrella _____ protects me in rainy weather.

A	that	b	who
C	whose	d	when

8) The soccer coach thanked the player _____ scored three goals.

A	what	b	who
C	where	d	when

9) I went to the bank _____ I could update my account.

A	what	b	who
C	where	d	when

10) This is the month _____ we have a family reunion.

A	what	b	who
C	where	d	when

11) My manager encourages the employees _____ work hard.

A	what	b	who
C	where	d	when

12) We travelled to Madrid _____ we spent a nice vacation.

A	what	b	who
C	where	d	when

13) These are the glasses _____ I bought last night.

A	that	b	who
C	where	d	when

14) I found the headscarf _____ my sister was looking for.

A	what	b	whose
C	which	d	who

15) It was a beautiful day _____ I met my old friends.

A	when	b	whose
C	which	d	who

16) This is the student about _____ I told you.

A	who	b	whose
C	which	d	whom

17) She's the woman _____ brought up her kids well.

A	who	b	whose
C	which	d	whom

18) This is not the bread _____ we asked for.

A	when	b	who
C	where	d	that

19) My mother went to mall _____ is near our house.

A	when	b	which
C	where	d	what

20) Michael found the handbag _____ belongs to me.

A	when	b	whose
C	that	d	what

🌸🌸🌸 *My Homework* 🌸🌸🌸

➤ *Exercise Seven*

➕ Choose the correct answer from a, b, c, or d.

1) This is the engineer _____ designed my new villa.

A	who	b	when
C	whom	d	whose

2) I called the lawyer _____ office is next to the court.

A	who	b	whom
C	when	d	whose

3) We couldn't meet the employee _____ you told us about.

A	where	b	whom
C	when	d	whose

4) Majid engaged the young woman _____ I told him about last week.

A	that	b	which
C	whose	d	when

5) We visited the museum _____ contains a lot of wonderful statues.

A	where	b	what
C	when	d	which

6) Do you know the company _____ Alan works for?

A	where	b	who
C	whose	d	which

7) This is boat _____ is going to take us to the other side of the river.

A	what	b	whose
C	that	d	where

8) I thanked the pharmacist _____ gave me the right medicine.

A	what	b	who
C	where	d	when

9) This is the pharmacy _____ my sisters work.

A	what	b	who
C	where	d	when

10) I'm reading about the city _____ Marwa comes from.

A	what	b	who
C	where	d	when

11) Always remember the classmates _____ studied with you one day.

A	what	b	that
C	where	d	when

12) Aida went to Cordoba University _____ she studies literature.

A	what	b	who
C	where	d	when

13) Dina and Yara are the famous doctors _____ I told you about.

A	what	b	whom
C	where	d	when

14) We phoned the woman _____ mobile phone was lost.

A	who	b	whose
C	which	d	whom

15) The policemen questioned the woman _____ car was lost.

A	when	b	whose
C	which	d	who

16) We live in the old house _____ was built sixty years ago.

A	who	b	whose
C	which	d	whom

17) The carpenter wanted to fix the bench _____ Malik was sitting on.

A	where	b	whose
C	which	d	who

18) Zainab didn't like the dress _____ I bought for her.

A	when	b	who
C	where	d	that

19) My grandmother told us an amusing story _____ happened years ago.

A	when	b	which
C	where	d	what

20) We are going to sell the house _____ we live.

A	that	b	which
C	where	d	what

🕮🕮🕮 *My Homework* 🖋🖋🖋

> ### *Exercise Eight*
Find the mistake in each of the following sentences and correct it.

1) They young men who team lost the final game were frustrated.
   ✎ ____ ____ ____ ____ ____ ____ ____ ____ ____

2) The tie whose I bought for Alan appealed to him.
   ✎ ____ ____ ____ ____ ____ ____ ____ ____ ____

3) The mobile phone whom you gave me is very good.
   ✎ ____ ____ ____ ____ ____ ____ ____ ____ ____

4) The meeting room when we will meet in is next to the library.
   ✎ ____ ____ ____ ____ ____ ____ ____ ____ ____

5) The house where my parents sold was very old.
   ✎ ____ ____ ____ ____ ____ ____ ____ ____ ____

6) The race where my horse won was very difficult.
   ✎ ____ ____ ____ ____ ____ ____ ____ ____ ____

7) George Bernard Shaw is the English dramatist which wrote the famous comedy *Arms and the Man*.
   ✎ ____ ____ ____ ____ ____ ____ ____ ____ ____
   ____ ____ ____ ____ ____ ____ ____ ____ ____

8) The kites where the children flew looked beautiful.
   ✎ ____ ____ ____ ____ ____ ____ ____ ____ ____

9) I couldn't find the dictionary whose I borrowed from you.
   ✎ ____ ____ ____ ____ ____ ____ ____ ____ ____

10) The driver which truck broke down called his brother for help.
    ✎ ____ ____ ____ ____ ____ ____ ____ ____ ____

🌸🌸🌸 *My Homework* 🌸🌸🌸

> ### *Exercise Nine*
Find the mistake in each of the following sentences and correct it.

1) I forgot the tickets where I bought for the party.
   ✎ ____ ____ ____ ____ ____ ____ ____ ____ ____

2) This is the café which I met my friends.
   ✎ ____ ____ ____ ____ ____ ____ ____ ____ ____

3) This is the gold ring whose I bought for my sister.
   ✎ ____ ____ ____ ____ ____ ____ ____ ____ ____

4) I don't remember the place when we last met.
   ✎ ____ ____ ____ ____ ____ ____ ____ ____ ____

5) Sam sent me copies of the new books whom he wrote.
   ✎ ____ ____ ____ ____ ____ ____ ____ ____ ____

6) I painted the garage when I keep my car.
☙ _____ _____ _____ _____ _____ _____ _____ _____ _____

7) My brother liked the new suit whose I bought for my wedding party.
☙ _____ _____ _____ _____ _____ _____ _____ _____ _____

8) We thanked Dr Ibrahim whose works at a famous hospital in Middlesbrough.
☙ _____ _____ _____ _____ _____ _____ _____ _____ _____

9) Salma's parents didn't like the dress where she bought.
☙ _____ _____ _____ _____ _____ _____ _____ _____ _____

10) My mother didn't find the money who she lost in the park.
☙ _____ _____ _____ _____ _____ _____ _____ _____ _____

My Homework

➤ **Exercise Ten**
✦ Find the mistakes in the following sentences and correct them.

1) I'm going to write to my friend where he lives in Manchester.
☙ _____ _____ _____ _____ _____ _____ _____ _____ _____

2) The camera when I bought yesterday is digital.
☙ _____ _____ _____ _____ _____ _____ _____ _____ _____

3) This is our neighbour whom sons are polite.
☙ _____ _____ _____ _____ _____ _____ _____ _____ _____

4) We attended a meeting where lasted for two hours.
☙ _____ _____ _____ _____ _____ _____ _____ _____ _____

5) I took my family to the beach on where we spent a lovely time.
☙ _____ _____ _____ _____ _____ _____ _____ _____ _____

6) This is the student whom teachers always praise.
☙ _____ _____ _____ _____ _____ _____ _____ _____ _____

7) Mohamed Salah thanked Kahraba where assisted in making his goals.
☙ _____ _____ _____ _____ _____ _____ _____ _____ _____

8) This is the stadium where was built last summer.
☙ _____ _____ _____ _____ _____ _____ _____ _____ _____

9) We are going to visit Luxor, where is called the world's greatest open-air museum.
☙ _____ _____ _____ _____ _____ _____ _____ _____ _____

10) These are the sentences when I could study today.
☙ _____ _____ _____ _____ _____ _____ _____ _____ _____

My Homework

Appendix number 01

Section One Answers

✓ **Exercise One (Page: 01)**

| 1 | a | 2 | a | 3 | a | 4 | a | 5 | an | 6 | a | 7 | a | 8 | a | 9 | an | 10 | a |

✓ **Exercise Two (Page: 02)**

| 1 | a | 2 | an | 3 | a | 4 | an | 5 | a | 6 | a | 7 | a | 8 | an | 9 | a | 10 | an |

✓ **Exercise Three (Page: 03)**

| 1 | an | 2 | an | 3 | a | 4 | a | 5 | a | 6 | an | 7 | an | 8 | a | 9 | a | 10 | an |

✓ **Exercise Four (Page: 04)**

| 1 | a | 2 | a | 3 | an | 4 | an | 5 | a | 6 | an | 7 | a | 8 | a | 9 | a | 10 | a |

✓ **Exercise Five (Page: 05)**

| 1 | some | 2 | some | 3 | a | 4 | some | 5 | a | 6 | a | 7 | an | 8 | a | 9 | an | 10 | some |

✓ **Exercise Six (Page: 06)**

| 1 | a / some | 2 | a / a | 3 | a / some | 4 | a / a | 5 | a / a | 6 | a / some | 7 | some / a |

✓ **Exercise Seven (Page: 10)**

| 1 | the | 2 | a | 3 | a | 4 | the | 5 | the | 6 | the | 7 | the | 8 | the | 9 | the | 10 | an |

✓ **Exercise Eight (Page: 11)**

| 1 | the / the | 2 | a / the | 3 | an / the | 4 | an / a / the | 5 | a / an | 6 | a / an | 7 | a / the |

✓ **Exercise Nine (Page: 12)**

| 1 | d | 2 | a | 3 | b | 4 | b | 5 | d | 6 | d | 7 | b | 8 | b | 9 | d | 10 | c |

✓ **Exercise Ten (Page: 14)**

| 1 | d | 2 | d | 3 | d | 4 | c | 5 | d | 6 | a | 7 | d | 8 | d | 9 | d | 10 | b |

✓ **Exercise Eleven (Page: 16)**

| 1 | d | 2 | d | 3 | a | 4 | d | 5 | d | 6 | a | 7 | d | 8 | d | 9 | d | 10 | d |

✓ **Exercise Twelve (Page: 17-18)**

| 1 | | 2 | | 3 | | 4 | | 5 | | 6 | d | 7 | b | 8 | d | 9 | d | 10 | c |

✓ **Exercise Thirteen (Page: 19-21)**

| 1 | d | 2 | d | 3 | b | 4 | d | 5 | d | 6 | d | 7 | d | 8 | c | 9 | c | 10 | d |

✓ **Exercise Fourteen (Page: 21-22)**

1. Ramy is a farmer.	2. Suzanna has a new dress.
3. Margret and Madonna are friends.	4. My brother is a good driver.
5. I have two ears.	6. They got a new computer.

✓ **Exercise Fifteen (Page: 24-25)**

| 1 | a | 2 | b | 3 | b | 4 | c | 5 | c | 6 | b | 7 | b | 8 | c | 9 | a | 10 | d |

✓ **Exercise Sixteen (Page: 26-27)**

| 1 | everywhere | 2 | everyone | 3 | no one | 4 | Someone | 5 | anybody | 6 | Someone |
| 7 | something | 8 | anything | 9 | | somewhere | 10 | Someone |

Section Two Answers

✓ **Exercise One (Page: 31)**

| 1 | boys | 2 | try | 3 | families | 4 | wife | 5 | mile | 6 | box |
| 7 | doors | 8 | ox | 9 | mice | 10 | woman |

✓ **Exercise Two (Page: 32)**

| 1 | Foxes are animals. | 2 | Flies are insects. | 3 | Cars are vehicles. | 4 | Geese are birds. |

✓ **Exercise Three (Page: 32-33)**

| 1 | France and Germany are European countries. | 2 | Jane and Lina are teachers. |

499

✓ **Exercise Four (Page:33-35)**

| 1 | c | 2 | d | 3 | b | 4 | d | 5 | b | 6 | a | 7 | d | 8 | d | 9 | b | 10 | d |

✓ **Exercise Five (Page:35-36)**

| 1 | chicken | 2 | men | 3 | women | 4 | people | 5 | glasses | 6 | faxes | 7 | letters |

Section Three Answers

✓ **Exercise One (Page:37)**

| 1 | He | 2 | She | 3 | I | 4 | She | 5 | He | 6 | It | 7 | It | 8 | He | 9 | She | 10 | He |

✓ **Exercise Two (Page:38)**

| 1 | You | 2 | She | 3 | He | 4 | It | 5 | She | 6 | He | 7 | It | 8 | It | 9 | She | 10 | You |

✓ **Exercise Three (Page:39)**

| 1 | It | 2 | It | 3 | It | 4 | She | 5 | He | 6 | It | 7 | You | 8 | She | 9 | It | 10 | It |

✓ **Exercise Four (Page:39)**

| 1 | He | 2 | She | 3 | It | 4 | It | 5 | They | 6 | They | 7 | They | 8 | It | 9 | They | 10 | She |

✓ **Exercise Five (Page:40)**

| 1 | c | 2 | b | 3 | b | 4 | d | 5 | d | 6 | a | 7 | d | 8 | c | 9 | d | 10 | d |

✓ **Exercise Six (Page:42)**

| 1 | d | 2 | d | 3 | b | 4 | a | 5 | c | 6 | a | 7 | c | 8 | a | 9 | c | 10 | d |

✓ **Exercise Seven (Page:44)**

| 1 | a | 2 | c | 3 | b | 4 | b | 5 | d | 6 | b | 7 | a | 8 | c | 9 | b | 10 | a |

✓ **Exercise Eight (Page:46)**

| 1 | b | 2 | c | 3 | c | 4 | b | 5 | c | 6 | b | 7 | b | 8 | a | 9 | c | 10 | b |

✓ **Exercise Nine (Page:48)**

| 1 | a | 2 | c | 3 | d | 4 | c | 5 | a | 6 | a | 7 | c | 8 | c | 9 | c | 10 | d |

✓ **Exercise Ten (Page:49-51)**

| 1 | a | 2 | c | 3 | d | 4 | c | 5 | c | 6 | c | 7 | c | 8 | b | 9 | d | 10 | b |

✓ **Exercise Eleven (Page:52)**

| 1 | d | 2 | a | 3 | d | 4 | a | 5 | c | 6 | a | 7 | c | 8 | d | 9 | b |

✓ **Exercise Twelve (Page:53)**

| 1 | my | 2 | your | 3 | him | 4 | He | 5 | mine | 6 | She | 7 | his | 8 | I | 9 | They | 10 | m |

✓ **Exercise Thirteen (Page:54)**

| 1 | It's | 2 | Its | 3 | It | 4 | It | 5 | It's | 6 | It | 7 | It | 8 | It | 9 | It's | 10 | Its |

✓ **Exercise Fourteen (Page:55)**

| 1 | those | 2 | this | 3 | this | 4 | that | 5 | this |

✓ **Exercise Fifteen (Page:56)**

| 1 | d | 2 | a | 3 | b | 4 | d | 5 | d | 6 | b | 7 | d | 8 | a | 9 | b | 10 | b |

✓ **Exercise Sixteen (Page:57)**

| 1 | These are my brothers. | 2 | Those are tall trees. | 3 | These men are English. |

✓ **Exercise Seventeen (Page:58)**

| 1 | These | 2 | That | 3 | Those | 4 | this | 5 | patient |

Section Four Answers

✓ **Exercise One (Page:65)**

| 1 | a | 2 | c | 3 | c | 4 | d | 5 | a | 6 | d | 7 | a | 8 | c | 9 | b | 10 | b |

✓ **Exercise Two (Page:67)**

| 1 | c | 2 | a | 3 | b | 4 | c | 5 | a | 6 | b | 7 | b | 8 | a | 9 | d | 10 | c |

✓ **Exercise Three (Page:68)**

| 1 | b | 2 | a | 3 | b | 4 | b | 5 | a | 6 | d | 7 | b | 8 | a | 9 | d | 10 | a |

✓ **Exercise Four (Page:70)**

| 1 | d | 2 | c | 3 | a | 4 | b | 5 | a | 6 | a | 7 | c | 8 | b | 9 | c | 10 | a |

✓ **Exercise Five (Page:71)**

| 1 | in | 2 | on | 3 | on | 4 | from | 5 | on | 6 | at | 7 | on | 8 | on | 9 | in | 10 | to |

✓ **Exercise Six (Page:75)**

| 1 | in | 2 | at | 3 | in | 4 | in | 5 | in | 6 | in | 7 | in | 8 | at | 9 | at | 10 | at |

✓ **Exercise Seven (Page:76)**

| 1 | in | 2 | in | 3 | on | 4 | for | 5 | from | 6 | in | 7 | ago | 8 | at | 9 | a | 10 | at |

✓ **Exercise Eight (Page:78)**

| 1 | until | 2 | for | 3 | by | 4 | on | 5 | on | 6 | to | 7 | in | 8 | in | 9 | in | 10 | After |

✓ **Exercise Nine (Page:80)**

| 1 | in | 2 | on | 3 | On | 4 | in | 5 | in | 6 | on | 7 | to | 8 | on | 9 | by | 10 | at |

Section Five Answers

✓ **Exercise One (Page:82)**

| 1 | am | 2 | is | 3 | am | 4 | is | 5 | are | 6 | are | 7 | are | 8 | is | 9 | are | 10 | is |

✓ **Exercise Two (Page:83)**

| 1 | am | 2 | is | 3 | are | 4 | is | 5 | is | 6 | are | 7 | are | 8 | is | 9 | are | 10 | is |

✓ **Exercise Three (Page:83)**

| 1 | are | 2 | is | 3 | is | 4 | am | 5 | is | 6 | are | 7 | is | 8 | are | 9 | are | 10 | is |

✓ **Exercise Eight (Page:89)**

| 1 | Are the students late? | 2 | Am I mistaken? | 3 | Are the farmers on the farm? |

✓ **Exercise Ten (Page: 95)**

| 1 | c | 2 | a | 3 | d | 4 | c | 5 | a | 6 | a | 7 | d | 8 | b | 9 | a | 10 | b |

✓ **Exercise Twelve (Page:97)**

| 1 | Julia was absent yesterday too. | 2 | The teachers were in their offices yesterday … . |

✓ **Exercise Fourteen (Page:100)**

| 1 | There is | 2 | There are | 3 | There are | 4 | There are | 5 | There is | 3 | There are |

✓ **Exercise Nineteen (Page:105)**

| 1 | have | 2 | have | 3 | has | 4 | has | 5 | has | 6 | have | 7 | have | 8 | has | 9 | has | 10 | has |

✓ **Exercise Twenty-four (Page:110)**

| 1 | do | 2 | don't | 3 | does | 4 | don't | 5 | does |

Section Six Answers

✓ **Exercise One (Page:113)**

| 1 | a | 2 | b | 3 | d | 4 | a | 5 | d | 6 | b | 7 | a | 8 | a | 9 | d | 10 | d |

✓ **Exercise Two (Page:114)**

| 1 | doesn't work | 2 | doesn't hurry | 3 | doesn't rely | 4 | doesn't fly | 5 | doesn't come |

✓ **Exercise Four (Page:117)**

| 1 | We watch football matches every week. | 2 | I usually meet my friends at the weekend. |

✓ **Exercise Seven (Page:120)**

| 1 | doesn't work | 2 | doesn't help | 3 | walks | 4 | visits | 5 | corrects | 6 | speak |

501

✓ Exercise Eight (Page:121)

| 1 | Yusuf visits his friends weekly. | 2 | Hagar usually listens to music at night. |

✓ Exercise Ten (Page:125)

| 1 | a | 2 | d | 3 | a | 4 | a | 5 | c | 6 | b | 7 | b | 8 | b | 9 | a | 10 | c |

✓ Exercise Eleven (Page:128)

| 1 | What do they study? | 2 | Whom does Omar want to meet? |

✓ Exercise Thirteen (Page:130)

| 1 | Suzan and Olfat are always punctual. | 2 | I sometimes visit my grandparents on Saturday. |

Section Eight Answers

✓ Exercise One (Page:140)

| 1 | c | 2 | a | 3 | c | 4 | b | 5 | d | 6 | d | 7 | a | 8 | d | 9 | c | 10 | a |

✓ Exercise Seven (Page:150)

| 1 | My mother is making me a cup of tea. | 2 | The boys are hiking in the mountains. |

✓ Exercise Eight (Page:152)

| 2 | The boy is playing a game. | 2 | The girl is reading a story. | 2 | The man is drinking coffee. |

✓ Exercise Twelve (Page:157)

| 1 | No, she isn't watching a match on TV. She is helping her mother in the kitchen. |

✓ Exercise Thirteen (Page:158)

| 1 | takes | 2 | arrives | 3 | is coming | 4 | use | 5 | is raining | 6 | is walking | 7 | walks |

✓ Exercise Fifteen (Page:163)

| 1 | has | 2 | is browsing | 3 | cost | 4 | is knocking | 5 | are crossing | 6 | is reading | 7 | is jogging |

Section Nine Answers

✓ Exercise One (Page:167)

| 1 | I was sleeping. | 2 | Grey and Ellie were having a nice meal. |

✓ Exercise Five (Page:172)

| 1 | I was reading short stories. | 2 | He was flying a kite. | 3 | She was chatting with her friend... |

✓ Exercise Seven (Page:175)

| 1 | c | 2 | d | 3 | b | 4 | d | 5 | d | 6 | d | 7 | b | 8 | a | 9 | d | 10 | c |

✓ Exercise Eleven (Page:179)

| 1 | I was going to the park when you met.... | 2 | I was talking to my father when you entered. |

Section Ten Answers

✓ Exercise Three (Page:186)

| 1 | I have been here for three days. | 2 | I haven't met Martin since we were in London. |

✓ Exercise Seven (Page:194)

| 1 | a | 2 | d | 3 | c | 4 | a | 5 | d | 6 | d | 7 | c | 8 | d | 9 | c | 10 | a |

✓ Exercise Nine (Page:196)

| 1 | met | 2 | just | 3 | gone | 4 | drunk | 5 | hasn't yet | 6 | ever | 7 | yet | 8 | for | 9 | since | 10 | yet |

Section Eleven Answers

✓ Exercise Three (Page:203)

| 1 | has been jogging | 2 | has been working | 3 | has been smoking | 4 | has been running |

Section Twelve Answers

✓ **Exercise One (Page:205)**

| 1 | d | 2 | a | 3 | d | 4 | c | 5 | d | 6 | c | 7 | d | 8 | b | 9 | c | 10 | a |

✓ **Exercise Two (Page:210)**

| 1 | We bought some food yesterday. | 2 | My uncle went to his farm yesterday. |

✓ **Exercise Seven (Page:213)**

| 1 | didn't drink | 2 | didn't help | 3 | didn't phone | 4 | didn't train | 5 | didn't weep |

✓ **Exercise nine (Page:216)**

| 1 | d | 2 | c | 3 | d | 4 | a | 5 | c | 6 | b | 7 | a | 8 | d | 9 | a | 10 | c |

✓ **Exercise Ten (Page:217)**

| 1 | ago | 2 | past | 3 | last | 4 | Yesterday | 5 | last | 6 | past | 7 | yesterday | 8 | ago | 9 | last |

✓ **Exercise Thirteen (Page:223)**

| 1 | What did Lewis win? | 2 | Why did Liza cry? | 3 | When did they arrive? |

✓ **Exercise Fourteen (Page:224)**

| 1 | No, the train didn't arrive on time. It arrived late. | 2 | No, I didn't study English. I studied math. |

✓ **Exercise Seventeen (Page:227)**

| 1 | grew | 2 | gave | 3 | took | 4 | spent | 5 | flew | 6 | read | 7 | taught | 8 | bought | 9 | sold |

✓ **Exercise Nineteen (Page:230)**

| 1 | b | 2 | c | 3 | b | 4 | d | 5 | c | 6 | d | 7 | b | 8 | d | 9 | b | 10 | c |

Section Thirteen Answers

✓ **Exercise One (Page:238)**

| 1 | had celebrated | 2 | had eaten | 3 | had stolen | 4 | joined | 5 | had cooked |

✓ **Exercise Four (Page:242)**

| 1 | After Saleh had finished his task, he rested for some time. |

✓ **Exercise Six (Page:247)**

| 1 | c | 2 | b | 3 | a | 4 | d | 5 | a | 6 | d | 7 | c | 8 | a | 9 | a | 10 | d |

Section Fourteen Answers

✓ **Exercise One (Page:250)**

| 1 | My parents were exhausted because they had been jogging for a long time. |

Section Fifteen Answers

✓ **Exercise Three (Page:261)**

| 1 | a | 2 | d | 3 | d | 4 | a | 5 | d | 6 | b | 7 | c | 8 | c | 9 | b | 10 | d |

✓ **Exercise Five (Page:264)**

| 1 | Samar isn't going to be on time tomorrow. |

✓ **Exercise Nine (Page:269)**

| 1 | We will study math this term. | 2 | Batool and Tuka will visit their aunt this weekend. |

Section Sixteen Answers

✓ **Exercise One (Page:291)**

| 1 | b | 2 | b | 3 | a | 4 | c | 5 | a | 6 | b | 7 | a | 8 | b | 9 | d | 10 | c |

✓ **Exercise Four (Page:296)**

| 1 | a | 2 | d | 3 | d | 4 | b | 5 | b | 6 | c | 7 | c | 8 | c | 9 | b | 10 | b |

Section Seventeen Answers

✓ **Exercise One (Page:303)**

| 1 | Wash your car daily please. | 2 | Don't drink too much black coffee. |

Section Eighteen Answers

✓ **Exercise One (Page:319)**

| 1 | The Internet is surfed by.. | 2 | These classes are taught by… | 3 | A lot of wheat is grown… |

✓ **Exercise Six (Page:324)**

| 1 | be | 2 | be | 3 | been | 4 | being | 5 | being | 6 | been | 7 | been | 8 | being | 9 | been | 10 | be |

✓ **Exercise Twelve (Page:332)**

| 1 | given | 2 | produced | 3 | to be removed | 4 | sold | 5 | to be installed | 5 | must be demolished |

✓ **Exercise Fifteen (Page:336)**

| 1 | The farmers are going to till the field. | 2 | The dentist pulled out my bad teeth. |

Section Nineteen Answers

✓ **Exercise One (Page:346)**

| 1 | c | 2 | c | 3 | a | 4 | d | 5 | b | 6 | d | 7 | a | 8 | c | 9 | d | 10 | b |

✓ **Exercise Four (Page:349)**

| 1 | plays | 2 | comes | 3 | had | 4 | had guided | 5 | had studied | 6 | lends | 7 | apologized |

✓ **Exercise Seven (Page:354)**

| 1 | If we go to Aswan next winter, we will visit the Island of the Plants. |

✓ **Exercise Twelve (Page:360)**

| 1 | The baby wouldn't have cried unless his mother had left him alone. |

Section Twenty Answers

✓ **Exercise One (Page:363)**

| 1 | I wish I spoke Japanese. | 2 | I wish I could fly a plane. | 3 | Sally wished she had a digital…. |

✓ **Exercise Two (Page:365)**

| 1 | d | 2 | d | 3 | b | 4 | c | 5 | b | 6 | d | 7 | d | 8 | a | 9 | c | 10 | b |

Section Twenty-one Answers

✓ **Exercise One (Page:374)**

| 1 | c | 2 | b | 3 | d | 4 | a | 5 | c | 6 | d | 7 | a | 8 | b | 9 | d | 10 | b |

✓ **Exercise Four (Page:378)**

| 1 | a | 2 | a | 3 | c | 4 | a | 5 | d | 6 | b | 7 | c | 8 | c | 9 | b | 10 | a |

✓ **Exercise Six (Page:388)**

| 1 | c | 2 | d | 3 | d | 4 | b | 5 | c | 6 | d | 7 | c | 8 | b | 9 | d | 10 | a |

✓ **Exercise Eleven (Page:396)**

| 1 | b | 2 | d | 3 | a | 4 | b | 5 | c | 6 | d | 7 | d | 8 | b | 9 | d | 10 | a |

✓ **Exercise Twelve (Page:408)**

| 1 | a | 2 | a | 3 | a | 4 | c | 5 | d | 6 | b | 7 | a | 8 | d | 9 | d | 10 | b |

✓ **Exercise Sixteen (Page: 415)**

| 1 | Tim was in a hurry, so... | 2 | Rachel behaved politely although the man insulted her. |

Section Twenty-Two Answers

✓ **Exercise One (Page:422)**

| 1 | Layan told Salma that she called her grandparents every day. |
| 2 | Ahmad told me that he had phoned his aunt the night before. |

✓ **Exercise Six (Page:426)**

| 1 | Oscar told Alexander that he could fix his computer himself. |
| 2 | Henry told his uncle that he wanted him to help him work out that problem. |

✓ **Exercise Nine (Page:429)**

| 1 | Rawan told Mennah that her parents had given her a lot of presents on the occasion... |
| 2 | Emad told Amr that he would take him to the beach the next day morning. |

✓ **Exercise Eleven (Page:431)**

| 1 | Maha asked me if my new teacher was from Canada. |
| 2 | My manager asked me if those computers were upgraded. |

✓ **Exercise Fifteen (Page:436)**

| 1 | My sister asked me where her mobile phone was. |
| 2 | Martin asked me what time I was going to leave. |

✓ **Exercise Nineteen (Page:442)**

| 1 | My sister advised me to do my homework before watching TV. |
| 2 | The teacher ordered the schoolboys not to make noise in class. |

✓ **Exercise Twenty-one (Page:444)**

| 1 | had visited | 2 | were making | 3 | said | 4 | were buying | 5 | would visit | 6 | they had never |

✓ **Exercise Twenty-six (Page:449)**

| 1 | would reach | 2 | preferred | 3 | had scored | 4 | had | 5 | had cost |

Section Twenty-Three Answers

✓ **Exercise Six (Page:461)**

| 1 | confused | 2 | amazing | 3 | stolen | 4 | broken | 5 | horrified | 6 | puzzled | 7 | delighted |

✓ **Exercise Eight (Page:463)**

| 1 | Salma behaves politely. | 2 | Dina sings well. | 3 | Jane Austin writes fantastically. |

✓ **Exercise Ten (Page:465)**

| 1 | steadily | 2 | recklessly | 3 | quickly | 4 | well | 5 | enough | 6 | awful | 7 | late | 8 | longer |

✓ **Exercise Thirteen (Page:469)**

| 1 | d | 2 | d | 3 | d | 4 | c | 5 | b | 6 | d | 7 | c | 8 | c | 9 | d | 10 | d |

Section Twenty-Four Answers

✓ **Exercise Two (Page:479)**

1	Mr. Ibrahim is fond of French.......	2	George Bernard Shaw is a famous Irish dramatist.
3	Bahrain is a beautiful kingdom on the Arabian Gulf.
4	Did Marawan take his English test last Monday?
5	Youmna and her family have moved to New Orleans recently.

✓ **Exercise Eight (Page:483)**

1	Ayman's sister won't be there, but his brother might.		
2	I'm so happy to meet you today.	3	Tyson's house will be painted tomorrow.

✓ **Exercise Nine (Page:484)**

1	This new restaurant serves cheap, wonderful meals.
2	Let's watch an action movie together.
3	The supervisor was happy because the workshop was well-organized.

Section Twenty-Five Answers

✓ **Exercise One (Page:489)**

1	I called my neighbor whose house was broken into last night.
2	Dubai is a busy city where you can meet thousands of tourists.
3	I thanked the mechanic who (that) fixed my car very well.

✓ **Exercise Six (Page:493)**

1	d	2	d	3	b	4	b	5	d	6	c	7	a	8	b	9	c	10	d

✓ **Exercise Eight (Page:496)**

1	whose	2	which/that	3	which/that	4	where	5	which/that	6	which/that

Appendix number 02
Irregular Verbs

No-change Verbs

The verbs that have the same spelling in its three forms.

Infinitive	Past Tense	Past Participle	Meaning
bet	bet	bet	
broadcast	broadcast	broadcast	
burst	burst	burst	
bust	bust	bust	
cast	cast	cast	
cost	cost	cost	
cut	cut	cut	
fit	fit fitted	fit fitted	
forecast	forecast forecasted	forecast forecasted	
hit	hit	hit	
hurt	hurt	hurt	
input	input	input	
let	let	let	
miscast	miscast	miscast	
offset	offset	offset	
put	put	put	
quit	quit	quit	
read	read	read	
recast	recast	recast	
reset	reset	reset	
retrofit	retrofit retrofitted	retrofit retrofitted	
set	set	set	
shed	shed	shed	

shut	shut	shut	
slit	slit	slit	
spit	spit (*esp US*)	spit (*esp US*)	
split	split	split	
sublet	sublet	sublet	
spread	spread	spread	
thrust	thrust	thrust	
typecast	typecast	typecast	
typeset	typeset	typeset	
undercut	undercut	undercut	
upset	upset	upset	
wed	wed wedded	wed wedded	
wet	wet wetted	wet wetted	

One-change Verbs

The verbs that have the same spelling in the past tense and the past participle.

Infinitive	Past Tense	Past Participle	Meaning
bend	bent	bent	
bind	bound	bound	
bleed	bled	bled	
breed	bred	bred	
bring	brought	brought	
build	built	built	
burn	burnt burned	burnt burned	
catch	caught	caught	
cling	clung	clung	
creep	crept	crept	

deal	dealt	dealt	
dig	dug	dug	
dive	dived dove (*US*)	dived	
dream	dream dreamed	dream dreamed	
feed	fed	fed	
feel	felt	felt	
fight	fought	fought	
find	found	found	
flee	fled	fled	
fling	flung	flung	
get	got	got gotten	
grind	ground	ground	
hang	hung hanged	hung hanged	
hear	heard	heard	
hold	held	held	
keep	kept	kept	
kneel	knelt kneeled (*esp US*)	knelt kneeled (*esp US*)	
lay	laid	laid	
lead	led	led	
lean	leant leaned	leant leaned	
leap	leapt leaped	leapt leaped	
learn	learnt learned	learnt learned	
leave	left	left	
lend	lent	lent	

light	lit lighted	lit lighted	
lose	lost	lost	
make	made	made	
mean	meant	meant	
meet	met	met	
misunderstand	misunderstood	misunderstood	
mow	mowed	mown mowed	
pay	paid		
plead	pleaded	pleaded pled	
prove	proved	proved proven	
say	said	said	
seek	sought	sought	
sell	sold	sold	
send	sent	sent	
sew	sewed	sewed sewn	
shine	shone	shone	
shoe	shod	shod	
shoot	shot	shot	
show	showed	showed shown	
shrink	shrunk shrank	shrunk	
sit	sat	sat	
sleep	slept	slept	
slide	slid	slid	
sling	slung	slung	

smell	smelt	smelt	
	smelled	smelled	
sow	sowed	sowed	
		sown	
speed	sped	sped	
	speeded	speeded	
spell	spelt	spelt	
	spelled	spelled	
spin	spun	spun	
spoil	spoilt	spoilt	
	spoiled	spoiled	
stand	stood	stood	
stick	stuck	stuck	
sting	stung	stung	
stink	stank	stunk	
	stunk		
strike	struck	struck	
string	strung	strung	
sweep	swept	swept	
swell	swelled	swelled	
		swollen	
swing	swung	swung	
teach	taught	taught	
tell	told	told	
think	thought	thought	
weave	wove	woven	
	weaved	weaved	
weep	wept	wept	
win	won	won	
wind	wound	wound	
wring	wrung	wrung	

One-change Verbs

The verbs that have the same spelling in the Infinitive and the past tense. The past participle has a different form.

Infinitive	Past Tense	Past Participle	Meaning
beat	beat	beaten	
bid	bid	bidden	

Two-change Verbs

The verbs that have three different forms.

Infinitive	Past Tense	Past Participle	Meaning
arise	arose	arisen	
awake	awoke	awoken	
bear	bore	born	
became	became	become	
begin	began	begun	
bite	bit	bitten	
blow	blew	blown	
break	broke	broken	
choose	chose	chosen	
come	came	come	
draw	drew	drawn	
drink	drank	drunk	
drive	drove	driven	
eat	ate	eaten	
fall	fell	fallen	
fly	flew	flown	
freeze	froze	frozen	
give	gave	given	
go	went	gone	
grow	grew	grown	

hide	hid	hidden	
know	knew	known	
lie	lay	lain	
mistake	mistook	mistaken	
overcome	overcame	overcome	
ride	rode	ridden	
ring	rang	rung	
rise	rose	risen	
saw	sawed	sawn	
see	saw	seen	
shake	shook	shaken	
sing	sang	sung	
sink	sank	sunk	
speak	spoke	spoken	
spring	sprang	sprung	
steal	stole	stolen	
stride	strode	stridden	
strive	strove	striven	
swear	swore	sworn	
swim	swam	swum	
take	took	taken	
tear	tore	torn	
throw	threw	thrown	
tread	trod	trodden	
wake	woke	woken	
wear	wore	worn	
write	wrote	written	

Feedback

Your feedback enriches me.

Saleh@alshalaby.com

my-homework.info

www.ingramcontent.com/pod-product-compliance
Lightning Source LLC
Chambersburg PA
CBHW030258080526
44584CB00012B/358